AF734951

Process Management and Burnout Prevention

"This is an extremely interesting and novel approach to burnout, exploring the link between business process management and burnout. This is a must-read for those interested in both process management and burnout. And the links between both."

—Sir Cary L. Cooper, *CBE, Professor of Organizational Psychology & Health, Alliance Manchester Business School, University of Manchester, England, President of the Chartered Institute of Personnel and Development, President of the Institute of Welfare, Co-Chair of the National Forum for Health and Wellbeing at Work*

"In an era when AI and emerging technologies are reshaping work environments, this book presents a groundbreaking, human-centric approach to process management, vital for enhancing employee engagement and mental well-being. Its fusion of empathetic strategies with practical insights offers a transformative perspective on workplace efficiency and burnout prevention, making it essential reading for leaders and HR professionals in creating sustainable, healthy organizational cultures."

—Ganna Pogrebna, *Professor of Behavioral Analytics and Data Science at the University of Sydney, Australia, and Lead of the Behavioural Data Science strand at the Alan Turing Institute, London, England. Executive Director of the Artificial Intelligence and Cyber Futures Institute at Charles Sturt University, Australia*

"Blending rigorous academic research with real-world insights, this book is a must-read for anyone seeking to navigate the complexities of work efficiency and psychological well-being."

—Kurt Matzler, *Professor of Strategic Management, University of Innsbruck, Austria, and Director of the Executive MBA programme at the Management Center Innsbruck, Austria. Author of* The High Performance Mindset: Race Across America, *listed in Forbes Ten Best Business Books of 2023*

"Many of us are working very hard to make the world a better place, sometimes so hard that we risk falling into the state of burnout. Burnout may have various causes, but it most often results from how we organise our work and perceive our job demands. This book gives us guidance on avoiding burnout, with a touch of fun and magic on the side!"

—Petra Molthan-Hill, *Professor of Sustainable Management and Education for Sustainable Development at Nottingham Business School, England. Co-Chair of the UN Principles of Responsible Management (PRME) Working Group on Climate Change & the Environment*

"If we want to maintain a strong and healthy workforce, we need to change the way we work. This also means that we face the enormous challenge of training and developing employees and managers towards a people-centred working environment. The authors show us the way forward."

—Nils Stieglitz, *President and CEO of the Frankfurt School of Finance & Management. Professor for Strategic Management, Frankfurt a.M., Germany*

Yevgen Bogodistov · Jürgen Moormann

Process Management and Burnout Prevention

A Human-Centred Approach to Reducing Work-Related Stress

palgrave
macmillan

Yevgen Bogodistov
Management Center Innsbruck
Innsbruck, Austria

Jürgen Moormann
Frankfurt School of Finance & Management
Frankfurt a.M.
Germany

ISBN 978-3-031-56614-1 ISBN 978-3-031-56615-8 (eBook)
https://doi.org/10.1007/978-3-031-56615-8

© The Editor(s) (if applicable) and The Author(s), under exclusive license to Springer Nature Switzerland AG 2024

This work is subject to copyright. All rights are solely and exclusively licensed by the Publisher, whether the whole or part of the material is concerned, specifically the rights of translation, reprinting, reuse of illustrations, recitation, broadcasting, reproduction on microfilms or in any other physical way, and transmission or information storage and retrieval, electronic adaptation, computer software, or by similar or dissimilar methodology now known or hereafter developed.
The use of general descriptive names, registered names, trademarks, service marks, etc. in this publication does not imply, even in the absence of a specific statement, that such names are exempt from the relevant protective laws and regulations and therefore free for general use.
The publisher, the authors and the editors are safe to assume that the advice and information in this book are believed to be true and accurate at the date of publication. Neither the publisher nor the authors or the editors give a warranty, expressed or implied, with respect to the material contained herein or for any errors or omissions that may have been made. The publisher remains neutral with regard to jurisdictional claims in published maps and institutional affiliations.

Cover illustration: erhui1979/Getty

This Palgrave Macmillan imprint is published by the registered company Springer Nature Switzerland AG
The registered company address is: Gewerbestrasse 11, 6330 Cham, Switzerland

Paper in this product is recyclable.

Foreword

As the Vice President People & Organisation at the sporting goods company PUMA, I face many challenges ranging from individual to organisational issues that I have to respond to. We organised the work at PUMA in a very human-centred manner. On the one hand, this increases the commitment of individual employees, but on the other hand, it leads to very intensive work by the HR team. We are constantly looking for new ways to further improve our HR processes as there is no limit to perfection.

While looking for fresh approaches to organising work, we cooperate with several research institutions, such as the Management Center Innsbruck, known as MCI: The Entrepreneurial School. During one of my visits to Innsbruck, I was introduced to Yevgen and, later, to his colleague (and now co-author of this book) Jürgen. I must say, I was overwhelmed and at the same time inspired by the way they see human-centred work in a company. They talked about the synergy effect between (as we know it as less human-centred) process management and (as we know it as less process-oriented) HR management. Their idea was somehow simple but new—they argued for the necessity to organise work differently and, hence, avoid psychological strain in firms. Moreover, both argued not only that the strain will be prevented but engagement can be enhanced.

I travel a lot and I meet many people (be they employees, or middle and top managers) from for-profit and non-profit organisations around the world. I have found that burnout is one of the issues that is becoming more and more pressing. In the European Union, the European Agency for Safety and

Health at Work has launched a "Healthy Workplaces 2023–2025" campaign, and I know why: the new technologies that were originally intended to improve working life have created new causes of stress, constant distractions, and the "monkey mind"—a state in which employees jump back and forth between many tasks, trying to maintain a high level of effectiveness combined with constant availability. Employees have less time for themselves, forget the importance of sports, and fall into a state of complete exhaustion. While we at PUMA are succeeding in terms of employee wellbeing, I see other companies suffering from—let's face it—outdated methods of work organisation. In these times, Yevgen and Jürgen's concept seems to be an urgent call for a rethink in process management.

As you read this book, you may find that you have encountered similar problems. It doesn't matter if your background is in HR (like me) or organizing business processes, their thoughts could be very helpful to you. As Yevgen and Jürgen talked about the way they treat processes and their respective employees, it struck me how differently organisations would look and function if they implemented just 10 per cent of their suggestions. I believe that we wouldn't have to deal with problems like workplace burnout—they simply wouldn't happen!

This book is a great work by authors who not only have profound experience in research but also in practice in the two fields of process management and business psychology. Jürgen is not only a well-known professor of process management, he also advises large financial companies on how their processes can be improved or completely redesigned. Yevgen is a known professor in the field of business psychology and x-HR director who knows all the intricacies of working with employees and managers. Together, they have not only written a practical book on human-centred process management. They have created a comprehensive book that combines current research with simple practical suggestions. I think this book is exactly what all companies urgently need!

However, the book also states that human-centred process management is not an easy task. As both authors write (and I agree with them), people are "autopoietic" actors. They evolve and adapt their behaviour to each new step the company takes. Fortunately, the book delivers several suggestions in this regard. I especially like the detailed description of Design Thinking and how to apply it to the needs of employees. Equipped with this (and many other) tool(s), you will be ready to rethink your organisation and avoid psychological problems. Happy and satisfied employees are the best indicator of your company's success. At PUMA, we know that!

I am grateful for the opportunity to write these words for this book. I am pleased to have contributed to this work by sharing my thoughts and ideas. Now I hope you will enjoy this text and learn something new for your organisation, be it a non-profit or for-profit. Good luck on the journey that begins on the very next page!

Dietmar Knoess
Vice President People
and Organisation
PUMA SE
Herzogenaurach, Germany

Preface

“Work hard, be kind, and amazing things will happen”, said US-American talk-show host, writer, and producer Conan O’Brien and *we disagree*. First, working hard and being kind may go at odds with each other as you will learn on the pages of our book. Second, if you work hard and be kind the opposite can happen—you might end up in a state of burnout. Here, we say “might” and not “will”, because there is indeed a way to be efficient, effective, remain kind, and achieve the most amazing thing—you will enjoy your work. It sounds like a utopia while, if you look around, our working life runs with an accelerating speed into a dystopia—a working realm that is undesirable and frightening. Look around and talk to your colleagues. How many of them have a vision of a happy working society?

Society appears to be split into two big groups—those who stick to the past talking about “how good things used to be”, even though the 1980s will never come back, and those who live in the far future romanticising what we need, even though they have no clue about how to get there. This makes the book market either rather conservative, emphasising “business as usual” or very romantic, calling for more “mindfulness meditation, well-being, and positive psychology”. Unfortunately, both streams lack a connection to reality. Of course, reality is subjective as we make sense of what we see, and our vision (of Yevgen and Jürgen) is also our subjective perception of the situation that deviates from the groups mentioned. If you also have this feeling of common sense being squeezed between yesterday and tomorrow, this book might be for you.

We are passionate researchers and, coincidentally, we both used to work for some time in the real world. We conducted plenty of studies in the fields of process management and business psychology. While Jürgen has a much longer process management history, Yevgen is a bit more into business psychology. During our cooperation, we conducted studies out of academic curiosity (and for fun). Once we performed a study because we could not agree on whether emotions play a role in process design (by the way, they do; we tested it). Such discussions led us to an interesting thought—what if process management is ready to come to the next stage of its evolution? Our experience and knowledge of business psychology enabled us to rethink process management and offer the next evolutionary step—human-centred process management. We found a way to apply and update our traditional tools and let them curate the occupational disease of the century—burnout.

If you, like us, want to understand how to update your tools and skills to be able to address psychological issues at work—this book is for you. You will learn about the aspect of work that process management has largely ignored hitherto. We build a bridge to some psychological (yet, commensurable) theories that finally allow us to address psychological issues in a systematic way. And there is not much to be relearned—most of the tools will be familiar to you from your process management, quality management, or Lean Six Sigma training courses. We'll just show you a small tweak to make your firm become really effective and efficient. We say "really" because most firms are not. What we learn about efficiency and effectiveness today lacks the understanding of psychological job demands and resources. The classical battle for increased performance is often at odds with the exhaustion of personnel, don't you think?

We have to state that this book is *not* for you if:

- You only rely on the old way of working. "Work hard, be kind, and the magic will happen…"— It won't!
- You believe in (magic) solutions that are simple and will curate a complex problem. "Try mindfulness meditation and your work will become better forever!"—It won't!
- You are already in a state of burnout. We can help prevent this state, but if you are in the state, you won't be able to objectively evaluate your situation.

This book is a result of fun from our research, practical work, and great discussions. It is positive and, let's be honest, we are not psychologists who consult patients in oak-panelled rooms. We don't write about how terrible burnout is, nor do we write about the magic of spiritual practices to cope with the state of mental and emotional exhaustion. We focus on how not to get there. And, believe us, it is a lot of fun to make your firm remain efficient and effective while making your employees and managers happier. Ultimately, it is a game. This book will help you know the rules of the game.

When we started writing the book we thought about how great it would be to have illustrations to grasp the attention of readers. Indeed, we remember visual information better than letters and words. For instance, in our mind, we transfer words into images that we associate with networks of learned concepts. Thus, having pictures would be great. There was only one issue with pictures—none of us could draw in a convincing way. Looking for a professional artist was beyond the scope of our endeavour. Luckily, a friend of ours drew our attention to a new technology (at the time of writing) namely, the AI-based tool for creating illustrations based on text prompts called Dall-E from OpenAI. We tried it out and after some training, we produced illustrations of the desired quality. Don't get us wrong—for most pictures, we made several trials and made lots of modifications. Yet, we don't want to mislead you about using AI for this purpose. By the way, *not a single sentence of this book was written by ChatGPT* or similar software—which you will probably notice from our German-Ukrainian English.

Enjoy and make notes. Write between the lines. Reflect. Play with your own ideas and work situations. Scribble on the margins of the book. Make this book look heavily used. Yeah, and don't show your notes to others—everyone must form his or her own opinion about human-centred process management. Feel free to disagree. Disagree, criticise, and test it. And send us your (success) stories—we are eager to include them in the new edition of the book if we decide to produce one. Express your emotions: fear, anger, or joy. These are the reflections and emotions that will make you learn and remember!

Innsbruck, Austria — Yevgen Bogodistov
Frankfurt a.M., Germany — Jürgen Moormann

Acknowledgements

This book is not just a result of our work—many of our family members, friends, and colleagues made this project appear. We cannot mention all of them by name. This especially relates to our family members who tolerated our long hours spent at work and at home to write "just a few lines". Yet, some of our friends and colleagues we want to mention by name as without them this book would not have been possible.

Ganna Pogrebna, a rockstar in the field of behavioural economics, cybersecurity, and AI, inspired us to start this book project. "You need to write a book about your research. Most people don't read your academic papers and they need to know what you have achieved", she said. Ganna planted the first seed of this project and with this book you can read the result. Thank you, Ganna.

Daniel Beimborn, our colleague and a passionate researcher, helped us concretise the topic of the book. He helped us shape the scope so that it is neither too broad nor too narrow. Daniel also helped us define the final audience and emphasised the need for a book for practitioners (as opposed to another book for theorists). We thank you.

Oleksandr Siryi is a friend of Yevgen, who helped polish the thoughts, provided us with ideas concerning illustrations, and helped us with some of the graphical issues. He is a multi-talented person who immediately understood the potential of our endeavour and supported us enormously. We are grateful to have Oleksandr as our friend and supporter.

Andreas Altman, the rector of the MCI: The Entrepreneurial School, supported us from the beginning. He saw the potential of our cooperation in research and joint writing. He not only found the topic appealing but he also helped us promote our ideas and draw attention to the topic of our research. He is a great person and we are proud to have him close to us.

Dietmar Knoess, Global Head of HR of Puma, is the leader who read our book in its early version and recognised how much it can change the business world. Dietmar is known for his employee-centric view and emphasises the "be yourself" value of Puma. This value, in particular, shows how important it is to develop organisational processes around people instead of "fitting notes into music". We have a great respect for him.

Also we would like to thank our students who elaborated with us on our ideas, shared their experience with us, and gave a broad spectrum of feedback for our homework. This includes students from our classes at the MCI ("Project, Process, and Quality Management" and "Business Psychology") and the Frankfurt School of Finance & Management ("Business Engineering" and "Process Management") who applied different tools from this book and/or even developed ideas on early burnout identification. As young individuals with less restrictions and path dependencies, they provided us with novel ideas and insights! We thank you all very much.

Moreover, we would like to mention several consultants from UMS Consulting GmbH & Co. KG, a consultancy agency in Frankfurt a.M. Special thanks go to our long-time cooperation partners, namely Stephan Lunau, Olin Roenpage, Thomas Reble, as well as Dr Dietrich Alexander Herberg (now freelance executive consultant). Several UMS senior experts showed us what is really demanded by firms. For this, we thank Jacek Korzewski, Emanuele Strada, and Kenneth Chan. Now, we return the favour with our tools that can expand your repertoire! Thank you very much for all the inspiration!

Finally, we would like to thank David Gilmour and Pink Floyd. Even if David doesn't know it, his music was the most listened to by both of us while writing this book! We wonder if artists like David Gilmour know how many scientific discoveries were made and academic papers written while listening to lines like "On the turning away …". Thank you, David! Thank you, Pink Floyd!

As mentioned, our thanks also go to all those we have not mentioned by name—because there are many. They have all contributed to the publication of this book. Any mistakes are, of course, our own.

Contents

1 Introduction 1
- 1.1 Why Does One Need This Book? 1
- 1.2 How to Read This Book 5
- References 7

2 (A Very Short) History of Process Management 9
- 2.1 As a Take-off 10
- 2.2 Sī vīs pācem, parā bellum 12
  - 2.2.1 From a Tribe at a Camp Fire to an Army 12
  - 2.2.2 Universal Soldiers 15
- 2.3 Traditional Workflow Management 18
  - 2.3.1 An Engineer at the Right Place 18
  - 2.3.2 Action-Oriented Data Processing 20
  - 2.3.3 Process Management: Riding the Ground Swell of Firms' Rethinking 22
  - 2.3.4 Process Improvement and Innovation 24
  - 2.3.5 Digitisation, Digitalisation, and Digital Transformation 26
  - 2.3.6 From Process Mining to AI-Driven Automation 29
- 2.4 Human-Centred Process Management 30
- References 33

3 (A Very Short) Introduction to Burnout 35
3.1 What Is Burnout? 36
3.2 Why Does Burnout Appear? 38
3.3 Job Demands 40
3.4 Job Resources 42
3.5 Perception of Resources 46
3.6 State and Trait 50
3.7 Resource Conversion 54
3.7.1 Quantitative Approach to Job Demands and Job Resources 55
3.7.2 Qualitative Approach to Job Demands and Job Resources 63
3.8 Sustainability at Work 64
References 65

4 Identifying Burnout Using Process Management Inventory 67
4.1 Let's Make It Worse! 67
4.2 Individual vs Process Management? 71
4.3 Following the Process 73
4.4 Visual Process Management 75
4.4.1 Take a Smile—Give a Smile! 77
4.4.2 Creative Students' Ideas 77
4.5 Tarot Cards: What About a Little Magic? 80
4.5.1 The Devil Is in the Details 80
4.5.2 Writer's Block 83
4.5.3 Why Does It Work? 84
4.5.4 What Is the Problem with the Method? 85
4.6 The Hero with a Thousand Faces 86
4.6.1 Chronological Approach 87
4.6.2 Current Situation 89
4.7 Thematic Apperception Test 89
4.8 Don't Promise when Happy, Don't Decide When Angry 92
4.9 The Root Cause 95
4.10 Why Not Simply Use the Existing Tools? 97
4.11 Can Burnout Appear All of a Sudden? 98
References 101

5 Burnout Prevention Using Process Management Tools 105
5.1 Finding the Bottleneck 105
5.2 Make a Magic Tetrahedron from a Magic Triangle 108
5.3 Teach with a Case 110

5.4 Eight Wastes and Lean Management 113
5.5 How to Eliminate the Eight Wastes? 119
5.6 Analysis of Process Design and Its Complexity 121
5.6.1 Analysis of Process Variations 121
5.6.2 Analysis of Media Discontinuities 122
5.6.3 Analysis of Process Interruptions 123
5.6.4 Analysis of Interfaces 123
5.7 Analysis of Process Design Concerning Psychological Issues 124
5.7.1 Analysis of Process Variations 124
5.7.2 Analysis of Media Discontinuities 124
5.7.3 Analysis of Process Interruptions 125
5.7.4 Analysis of Interfaces 125
5.8 Optimisation at What Cost? 126
5.9 Process Improvement and Burnout 129
5.9.1 Start with the Process 130
5.9.2 Think About the Nature of Change 131
5.9.3 Time Horizon 133
5.9.4 Plan the Investment of Your Time and Efforts 134
5.9.5 Who to Start with? 136
5.9.6 Scope of Change 136
5.9.7 Risks and Uncertainty 137
5.9.8 Make It Stats-Driven! 138
5.9.9 Where Is the End? 139
5.10 Process Innovation and Burnout 140
5.10.1 Start with the Problem 141
5.10.2 Changing Organisational Culture 142
5.10.3 (How Much) Time for a Big Change? 143
5.10.4 Time and Efforts 145
5.10.5 But You Have Support … Don't You? 147
5.10.6 Process Innovation Is Usually Cross-Functional 148
5.10.7 No Pain—No Glory 150
5.10.8 Driven by Information Systems 150
5.10.9 Big Bang 151
5.11 Burnout and Process Improvement/Process Innovation 152
5.11.1 Burnout Accompanying Process Changes 152
5.11.2 Burnout Prevention as a Part of Process Changes 154
5.11.3 Changing Your Processes to Prevent Burnout 155
5.11.4 Path Dependence 162
References 165

6 Let's Practise and Make It Tangible 169
6.1 Design Thinking for Vision Development 169
6.1.1 Main Stages in a Design Thinking Seminar 170
6.1.2 Preparation of the Seminar 171
6.1.3 First Phase: Beginning with Empathy 175
6.1.4 Second Phase: Defining the Pain Points 178
6.1.5 Third Phase: Ideate 180
6.1.6 Fourth Phase: Let's Prototype It 183
6.1.7 Fifth Phase: Testing the Prototype 185
6.1.8 Repeat … 187
6.2 Design Thinking for Burnout Prevention 187
6.3 House of Cards … Sorry, House of Quality 189
6.3.1 Structure: Why Is It Called a "House"? 190
6.3.2 Room 1: What Do They Want? 190
6.3.3 Room 2: Characteristics and Measures 193
6.3.4 Room 3: Relationships or How to Best Achieve Meet Our Customers' Needs 197
6.3.5 Room 4: Whom Do You Compete with? 199
6.3.6 Room 5: Our Capabilities or Who Takes Care of What? 201
6.3.7 Room 6 (Basement): What Should We Start with? 202
6.3.8 Roof: Correlations of "Hows" 207
6.3.9 Drilling Down and Moving Forward 208
6.3.10 What to Do Next: Implementation 211
6.4 Network Diagram: Let's Look at the Critical-for-Burnout Path 214
6.4.1 Main Elements of a Network Diagram 215
6.4.2 Network Diagram for Psychological Issues 216
6.4.3 More Complex Notation of Psychological Resources in Process Management 219
6.4.4 Notation for Tracking of Burnout-Related Issues 222
6.5 Catapult Exercise: Learning Six Sigma and DMAIC 226
6.5.1 Building a Catapult and Setting the Target 227
6.5.2 Intended and Actual Mean 229
6.5.3 Upper and Lower Specification Limits 229
6.5.4 Distribution, Variance, and Standard Deviation 230
6.5.5 Calculating the Level of Sigma 232
6.6 DMA(G)IC 237
6.6.1 Define 237

6.6.2 Measure 238
6.6.3 Analyse 250
6.6.4 Improve 251
6.6.5 Control 252
6.6.6 DMA[G]IC? 253
6.7 What About Burnout? 254
6.7.1 Defining Burnout-Related Aspects 254
6.7.2 Measuring Social Systems 256
6.7.3 Analysis of Far Too Complex Relationships 261
6.7.4 Improving a Running Motor 263
6.7.5 Control: Quis Custodiet Ipsos Custodes? 264
6.8 What If You Redesign the Process? 266
References 270

7 Can a Firm Develop a Burnout Resilience Capability? 273
7.1 Being Capable, Being Able, Being Competent, Having Power, or Having Potential? 273
7.2 Understanding a Capability 276
7.2.1 Consequences of a Capability 276
7.2.2 Antecedents of a Capability 279
7.2.3 Structure of a Capability 283
7.2.4 Measuring a Capability 285
7.2.5 Making Conclusions 288
7.3 Burnout Resistance Capability 288
7.4 Burnout Resilience Capability? 290
7.5 Criticism of the Capability Approach 292
7.5.1 Do Firms Need Capabilities to Withstand Burnout and Similar Issues? 292
7.5.2 Is Positive Psychology Enough? 293
7.5.3 What If We Increase the Resource Base? 294
References 295

8 Epilogue 297
References 300

Appendix 301

References 305

About the Authors

Yevgen Bogodistov is a Professor of Project and Process Management at the MCI: The Entrepreneurial School. The Management Centre Innsbruck (MCI) is one of the highly-ranked business schools in Austria known for its combination of social and technical sciences and a strong focus on entrepreneurship. Yevgen is a passionate researcher and conducts his investigations at the intersection of Information Systems, Strategic Management, and Organisational Behaviour. Yevgen mostly performs fundamental research. But beyond that, he regularly publishes in professional journals for practitioners to enable a transfer of knowledge from the more abstract field of social sciences to the concrete business world.

Yevgen used to work at the European University Viadrina in Frankfurt (Oder), Neu-Ulm University of Applied Sciences, and the Frankfurt School of Finance & Management (all located in Germany). Before his academic career, Yevgen worked in a medium-sized firm in Ukraine, where he obtained positions of a leading economist, HR specialist, HR director, and, finally, a Chief Operating Officer. Later, Yevgen was active in politics as a project coordinator at the Konrad Adenauer Foundation in Kyiv, Ukraine. Yet, driven by his intellectual curiosity and his wish to contribute to the common good, Yevgen joined a doctoral programme on dynamic capabilities and relationships organised by the European University Viadrina Frankfurt (Oder) and the German Graduate School of Management & Law Heilbronn, where he received his Ph.D. degree (Dr. rer. pol.). He then met Jürgen in Frankfurt (Main) and joined Jürgen's ProcessLab—a research centre focused on process management and process innovation—where both developed a new view on human-centred process management.

Jürgen Moormann is a Professor of Bank and Process Management at the Frankfurt School of Finance & Management. The Frankfurt School is one of the leading business schools in Germany, with triple accreditation and an excellent international research record. Jürgen's teaching and research focuses on Strategy Development, Business Engineering, and Process Management, especially in the financial services industry. He is the author/editor of 13 books and has published around 300 articles in academic and practice-oriented journals. He has presented his research findings in numerous conference papers at national and international levels. Jürgen has been a Visiting Professor at the University of Colorado at Colorado Springs, USA, the University of New South Wales, Sydney, Australia, the Queensland University of Technology, Brisbane, Australia, and the University of Hong Kong, China. He is a member of several academic and practice-related advisory boards.

Before his academic career, Jürgen conducted an apprenticeship at Commerzbank AG, one of the largest banks in Germany, studied business administration at the Universities of Kiel, Germany, and Zurich, Switzerland, and completed a Ph.D. programme at the University of Kiel (Dr. sc. pol.). This time was followed by five years of consulting work in several German banks. In parallel, he worked as an external lecturer at the EBS University, Germany, and the University of Liechtenstein. Jürgen is a process management professional who has always believed that problems in companies rarely occur because of flowcharts with depicted processes, but rather because of the "human factor", which is far too often ignored in the IS-driven process world.

Abbreviations

AI	Artificial Intelligence
ANOVA	Analysis of Variance
ARIS	Architecture of Integrated Information Systems
BMC	Business Model Canvas
CBI	Copenhagen Burnout Inventory
CBV	Capability-Based View
CEO	Chief Executive Officer
CFO	Chief Financial Officer
COO	Chief Operating Officer
COPIS	Customers, Output, Process, Input, Suppliers
C_p	Process Potential
C_{PK}	Process Capability
C_{pL}	Process Potential for Lower Specification Limit
CPU	Central Processing Unit
C_{pU}	Process Potential for Upper Specification Limit
CTO	Chief Technology Officer
CTQ	Critical to Quality
CTQL	Critical to Quality of Life
DCE	Discrete Choice Experiment
DMADV	Define, Measure, Analyse, Design, Verify
DMAGIC	Define, Measure, Analyse, Generalise, Improve, Control
DMAIC	Define, Measure, Analyse, Improve, Control
DNA	Deoxyribonucleic Acid
DPMO	Defects Per Million Opportunities
EI	Emotional Intelligence

ERP	Enterprise Resource Planning
EU	European Union
EUR	Euro
FAQ	Frequent Asked Questions
GDPR	General Data Protection Regulation
HoQ	House of Quality
HR	Human Resources
ID	Identification
IS	Information Systems
ISO	International Organisation for Standardisation
IT	Information Technology
JD-R	Job Demands and Resources
KPI	Key Performance Indicator
LSL	Lower Specification Limit
MBI	Maslach Burnout Inventory
PIN	Personal Identification Number
QFD	Quality Function Deployment
R&D	Research and Development
RAM	Random-Access Memory
RBV	Resource-Based View
r_d	Resource Depletion
r_r	Resource Replenishment
SAM	Self-Assessment Manikin
SDG	Sustainable Development Goal(s)
SIPOC	Suppliers, Inputs, Process, Outputs, Customers
TAT	Thematic Apperception Test
TIM WOODS	Transport, Inventory, Movement, Waiting, Overproduction, Overprocessing, Defects, Skills
TQM	Total Quality Management
UML	Unified Modeling Language
USL	Upper Specification Limit

List of Figures

Fig. 1.1	Structure of this book	6
Fig. 3.1	Example of a typical DCE decision situation	59
Fig. 3.2	Alternative DCE example with the focus on job demands and job resources	61
Fig. 3.3	Depiction of a possible drop/growth in the utility for job resources	62
Fig. 4.1	Visual board for working tools	75
Fig. 4.2	Capturing emotions in a company's lift	76
Fig. 4.3	Example of a simple data collection on emotional climate	78
Fig. 4.4	Motivation indicator	79
Fig. 4.5	Tarot deck for issue discovery	82
Fig. 4.6	Examples of tarot cards	83
Fig. 4.7	The Hero's Journey, one of the interpretations	86
Fig. 4.8	Our Campbell cards, drawn by Veselina Ivanova: the "Ordinary (Students') World" (left), the "Supreme Ordeal" (middle), and the "Helpers" (right, first version of the deck)	87
Fig. 4.9	"Master of the Two Worlds"	88
Fig. 4.10	Gender issue in data analysis	91
Fig. 4.11	Pictures with different levels of abstraction	92
Fig. 5.1	Self-Assessment Manikin applied in our research	132
Fig. 5.2	Effort-impact analysis	134
Fig. 5.3	Levels of change and their degree of business transformation	146
Fig. 5.4	Interplay between process innovation and process improvement	152
Fig. 5.5	Transformation model by Kotter	156

Fig. 6.1 BMC for strategy development 173
Fig. 6.2 Needs and pains graph 174
Fig. 6.3 Structure of the House of Quality 191
Fig. 6.4 Needs of (internal) customers, Room 1, House of Quality 194
Fig. 6.5 Characteristics and measures, Room 2, House of Quality 196
Fig. 6.6 Positioning of Room 1 and Room 2 in the House of Quality 196
Fig. 6.7 Relationships, Room 3, House of Quality 198
Fig. 6.8 Competitors, Room 4, House of Quality 200
Fig. 6.9 Legend for symbols used for the relationships and analysis of competitors 200
Fig. 6.10 Distribution of necessary organisational capabilities among departments, Room 5, House of Quality 203
Fig. 6.11 Rooms 1 to 5, House of Quality 203
Fig. 6.12 Prioritisation of actions, Room 6, House of Quality 206
Fig. 6.13 Overview of the House of Quality, Rooms 1–6 206
Fig. 6.14 Example of a correlation of characteristics or measures, Roof, House of Quality 208
Fig. 6.15 Overview of the final House of Quality 209
Fig. 6.16 Practical example of the House of Quality 213
Fig. 6.17 Structure of a simple network diagram 215
Fig. 6.18 Network diagram for resource depletion, if replenishment is ignored 216
Fig. 6.19 Network diagram with depletion and replenishment of psychological (and physiological) resources 217
Fig. 6.20 Basic figures of a process flow notation 220
Fig. 6.21 Exemplary process of brewing tea 220
Fig. 6.22 Cross-functional tea brewing 222
Fig. 6.23 Additional symbols used in flowcharts 222
Fig. 6.24 Set of symbols indicating psychological and physiological job demands and resources 223
Fig. 6.25 Set of symbols for the gradation of job demands and resources 224
Fig. 6.26 Simple process including an indication of job demands and resources 225
Fig. 6.27 Results of a catapult exercise including a superimposed curve 231
Fig. 6.28 Results of a catapult exercise with manipulated data; 20 cm are deduced from each of the previously noted hits 234
Fig. 6.29 Sample shots for the analysis phase 241
Fig. 6.30 MS Excel regression settings 242
Fig. 6.31 Regression results 243
Fig. 6.32 Calculating an additional variable to check for non-linearity 244
Fig. 6.33 Results including the squared independent variable 245
Fig. 6.34 Data prepared for the ANOVA 246
Fig. 6.35 Running the ANOVA using MS Excel 246
Fig. 6.36 Results of the ANOVA in MS Excel 247

Fig. 6.37 Introducing dummies 248
Fig. 6.38 Calculation with dummy variables 249
Fig. 6.39 Repetitive calculation with a different variable skipped 250

List of Tables

Table 3.1	Sample items for your survey	56
Table 5.1	Characteristics related to process improvement	129
Table 5.2	Process observation form	131
Table 5.3	Characteristics related to process innovation	141
Table 6.1	Conversion of process potential into the level of sigma and defects	237
Table 6.2	Simplified scheme for statistical test selection	240
Table A1	Evaluation sheet for consequences with regard to burnout resistance capability	302
Table A2	Evaluation sheet for antecedents of the burnout resistance capability	303

1 Introduction

Abstract In this chapter, we share with you our motivation for the book. First of all, we outline the latest developments in the field of process management and discuss whether it will disappear as a field of research (spoiler alert: it will not!). Next, we describe some observed issues with process management in firms. It seems that the field of study became way too technical leaving its most important element—the human—unnoticed. Finally, we explain the logic behind this book and its structure.

1.1 Why Does One Need This Book?

This book is the result of many years of research, academic thought, and observations from practice. Nowadays, we think that everyone is familiar with the concept of business processes and how to manage these processes. Going back even further, process management—in a rudimentary form—is several thousand years old, we argue. At the same time, we all have the feeling that the current state of process management is not what we would like it to be. While many scholars and practitioners search for new technologies that will shape the future of business processes and their management, such as big data, artificial intelligence, cloud computing, and others, we would like to focus on a different aspect—the human being who is still not being seen as the core of a process but who actually is the core of a process. It is not about the customer, though. No, we don't want to underestimate the role of the customer—a customer has been and still is the Alpha and Omega of

© The Author(s), under exclusive license to Springer Nature Switzerland AG 2024

Y. Bogodistov and J. Moormann, *Process Management and Burnout Prevention*,
https://doi.org/10.1007/978-3-031-56615-8_1

a process-oriented organisation. Yet, our business world is "broken" if our process view neglects the human—employees and managers, isn't it?

Although the history of processes and their management accounts for thousands of years, the last hundred years massively changed the way we perceive this world. It was Frederick W. Taylor who introduced the scientific approach to organisations and who initiated a revolution in the manner business is performed. In his endeavour, he tried to split any work into the smallest chunks. On the one hand, he created the process as a series of activities brought in concordance in order to produce the final product. On the other hand, such an approach generated highly specialised spheres of operations that with time accumulated into what we call silos, i.e. employees thought about what was important for their operations and not about the bigger picture. Thus, managers caught in the world of Taylor thought about their set of operations as "kingdoms" that would rather see other kingdoms as intruders than elements of the same process landscape.

Moreover, Taylor's approach implied a big (societal) conflict that is reaching its culmination now. Burnout, boreout, disengagement, absenteeism, and other related symptoms quickly spread "diseases" across society. This is a sign for us that we should do something about it. This wave of psychological problems with organisational processes is not new and started rising shortly after the principles of work execution by Taylor dominated the business landscape. Have you asked yourself why the demand for motivational theories started growing in the 1950s? Wasn't it the time when business met the first negative consequences of the massive implementation of Taylor's approach?

If you look at the current state of our society, you will notice that plenty of things are "broken". For instance, all economic systems (be it communist, socialist, capitalist, or any other system) have one goal in common—growth! Growth implies increasing resource demands. The latter implies both higher resource consumption and higher waste generation. The whole world runs into global deterioration by constantly "improving" production, cutting down palm forests, and polluting the sea with plastic and other waste. Wouldn't you say that the ideas by of Taylor who taught us how to foster production accelerated this doomsday scenario drastically?

When we talk about doomsday, whatever form it might have, we immediately think of the sustainability discussion that has been and is a big issue in the economy and society worldwide in the last decade. Particularly in Western countries, sustainability has become a part of our lives as in almost each of our classes we deliberately include the topic of sustainability. And do you know what is the issue with sustainability? First, we don't know what it is. We have 17 Sustainable Development Goals presented by the United Nations (UN) but they are rather vague and even misleading (Hickel 2019). As specialists in the field of process management, we know what "Garbage In, Garbage Out" (GIGO) means. May it be due to the necessity of the UN to compromise the interests of hundreds of national and international actors, it doesn't make the organisation of work much better. Second, as you have seen from the previous paragraph, growth implies resource consumption. For now, we cannot offer working models that do not imply growth. The recent developments in the field of circular economy are a promising approach but it is not clear whether researchers will manage to find a solution before it is too late. Finally, desirability for sustainability is the biggest issue. We all would like to live in a cleaner and healthier world, but are we ready to get rid of some habits such as driving cars, flying by plane, or buying unnecessary goods and services? With this constant contradiction between what is good and what we want, we keep living in a state of cognitive dissonance. Consequently, we either close our eyes on what is happening or we start legitimising ourselves. Both are perfect coping mechanisms for cognitive dissonance as it is way too stressful to live in a conflict with oneself. By the way, we have a similar coping mechanism for coping with burnout—we distance ourselves from other people and work, we start behaving cynically, and lose the feeling of respect with regard to others and, consequently, self. By "we", we mean the average worker born without free WiFi in the maternity ward.

At the same time the new generation, i.e. those who start their working lives in these years, becomes suspicious with regard to the traditional values of our society. Young people want to be different, they want to have more time for themselves, and they want to have more opportunities for realising themselves and achieving the maxim postulated by John Lennon when he said:

> When I was 5 years old, my mother always told me that happiness was the key to life. When I went to school, they asked me what I wanted to be when I grew up. I wrote down 'happy'. They told me I didn't understand the assignment, and I told them they didn't understand life.[1]

[1] There is a debate about whether John Lennon said this phrase (O'Gorman 2020). You can read more about the discussion here: https://www.radiox.co.uk/artists/beatles/did-john-lennon-say-ringo-wasnt-even-best-drummer/.

New generations are looking for happiness. However, we design the jobs as we have learned and as we are used to designing them. Thus, most of the jobs they would like to have are hardly concordant with the modern business management approach. With our vision of how organisations should work, we scare the young idealists. And what if the feelings of young people are not a matter of fashion (which according to movements such as Fridays for Future may indeed be the case)? Then the business life they will experience will ruin their dreams. It is just a question of time. Soon we will see a huge drop in happiness and a huge increase in burnout and depression. And, again, this seems to be the consequence of how we organise our work. By the way, have you thought that, in the end, you have spent a good third of your adult life at work?

Now, we would like to ask you a question: Will the new developments in the field of artificial intelligence, big data, process mining, or cloud computing ease the situation? Will these technologies motivate people to create value for all members of our society? Will a perfect analysis of human behaviour lead to new products and services that will make people happier? As you can imagine, we doubt it. Similar to Taylor, these new technologies will speed up this development that is actually moving us to the abyss. Do we need to accelerate?

We do not argue that the current process management is a completely wrong approach. On the contrary, we argue that it is process management that will help our society overcome difficult times. We just need to change the right set screws to bring about a fundamental rethink in our business world and get people to change their thinking.

And yes, this book is the result of several years of research in the field of process management and burnout. Do you know that burnout is not an illness but a work-related issue? There are no drugs against burnout. But as it is a consequence of the wrong organisation of work we can fight against it by organising our work in a human-centred way. And which field of study is responsible for the organisation of work? Yes, of course, it is the field of business process management!

In this book, we added two aspects to business process management. First, we extended the resources a process designer has to consider when developing or improving a process. In the next two chapters of the book, we show how important it is to add psychological and physiological resources of individuals to the management of a process. However, as these two new types of resources belong to the broader category of "resources", we can apply the established logic of modern process management. Second, we decided to use improvement tools from process management to emphasise the usage of psychological and physiological resources in the current process management practice.

In this book, we try to find answers to the following questions: Why and how does suboptimal process design lead to burnout? What can we do with this suboptimality? Can we develop processes that help prevent burnout and other related issues? Which tools from the process management toolbox can we apply to treat psychological issues of employees and managers in times of constantly growing work demands and pace of learning?

1.2 How to Read This Book

In Chapter 2, we introduce very briefly the history of process management to share our view on the discipline and to help those readers who are lateral entrants (e.g. psychologists or human resources specialists) understand the basics of process management. Chapter 3 aims, on the contrary, at process management practitioners. Here we introduce the concept of burnout and psychological resources. Knowing these resources helps understand why some processes that are "optimally" designed (from a process management perspective) are not as optimal as one might think and can cause psychological problems. In Chapter 4, we look at what would a good process manager do if she or he discovers a suboptimality (or "waste", "muda", or "constraint"). She or he would immediately try to eliminate this sub-optimality. In this book, we offer a range of ideas about how to identify work aspects that are accompanied by psychological issues (Chapter 4), how to prevent burnout (Chapter 5), and how to include accountability for psychological and physiological resources in the existing process improvement tools (Chapter 6). Finally, we try to give an answer to the question of whether an organisation can develop a capability for burnout resistance and burnout resilience. Figure 1.1 provides an overview of the chapters and their relationships to each other.

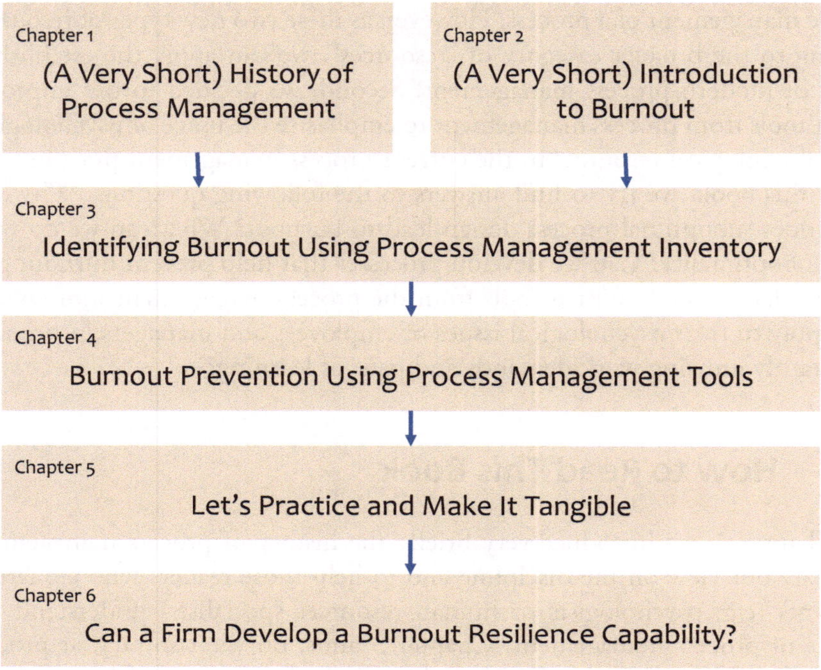

Fig. 1.1 Structure of this book

The main idea of this book is to provide you with both theory and practical tools to address organisational issues. Therefore, we use plenty of examples and stories from our life. Examples of Yevgen are indicated by:

and the examples of Jürgen are indicated by:

This book is a compilation of our experiences, observations, and analysis of academic sources. It is not perfect but, as we hope, interesting for you. We cannot solve the above-mentioned problems such as global warming, air pollution, and the disappearance of the meaning of work. But what if a small change in focus—becoming human-centred—may alter not only the way we organise work but also the way people perceive themselves and perceive their environment? Will this shift make our world a bit better? Hopefully. But if we want to be sure, we must try it out.

References

Hickel, Jason. 2019. The contradiction of the sustainable development goals: Growth versus ecology on a finite planet. *Sustainable Development* 27: 873–884. Wiley.

O'Gorman, Martin. 2020. The truth behind John Lennon's "happy" quote. *Radio X*.

2

(A Very Short) History of Process Management

Abstract This chapter is about business process management. For those who come with a different background, we provide the basic information that one needs to know how to approach business processes. We deliver a brief overview of the history of process management, using analogies and brief stories. This is not the way process management is presented in academic textbooks, but we assume that the readers of this chapter need to capture the "essence" of process management and not all the details of its development. We show how process management has evolved from solving resource problems in primitive societies through military science to what we propose as the next step in the evolution—human-centred process management.

© The Author(s), under exclusive license to Springer Nature Switzerland AG 2024
Y. Bogodistov and J. Moormann, *Process Management and Burnout Prevention*, https://doi.org/10.1007/978-3-031-56615-8_2

2.1 As a Take-off

The current state of process management is quite ambiguous. Why? Each time I teach process management, I jump between traditional concepts and new technologies. On the one hand, process management is a fascinating field of study—it has an inspiring history, it introduces structure into our work—the things we all perform but only a few people manage to perfectly align and orchestrate,—and it delivers a range of tools that help make your (business) life better. On the other hand, being a part of the Information Systems (IS) domain, process management feels like a "poor sister" in the big family of IS-related fields of study. One could split students into two groups: those who like business informatics and those who like management. But which of them is the target audience of process management? Business informatics specialists often hold process management for "soft science", while managers hold process management for "pure informatics". Our target group is, actually, a small group of people who are able to work on the interface of both fields of study. And, do you want to know the secret? This interface is exciting and, if you develop competence in this field, you will enjoy plenty of well-paid work opportunities. Moreover, this work might make you happy, if you implement knowledge from this book.

Yevgen Bogodistov

Being an expert in process management is not a question of learning, although learning is important. Process management is more a question of philosophy, mindset, and the way you communicate with the rest of the business world. All the specialists in the field of process management that both Yevgen and I work with have extensive knowledge from training, textbooks, and of course from their experience. But that is not enough. It's not just knowledge and experience that makes a process management expert. It's about so much more.

I teach process management on a regular basis. As a result, my students have acquired (at least basic) knowledge of process management. For some of them, process management remained a discipline of drawing boxes and arrows, IT-based of course. Others, however, realised how exciting and pervasive the design of a company's processes can be. This can be seen in my elective "Business Engineering: Creating Powerful Organisations". It all starts with looking at a company's or business unit's strategy. Based on this, the students develop the process architecture. Similar to the architecture of a building, the architecture of the company defines everything that is relevant and specific to the company (which can also be a start-up). The students learn to design the processes taking into account new technologies, sales concepts, the company's context, etc. This is where students discover that process management is not only the foundation for all activities which happen in a company. They also learn that designing excellent processes requires strategic thinking, creativity, and openness to innovation. I firmly believe (and most process management scholars would agree) that this is the only way to create an operational competitive advantage for companies. Students (as well as employees and managers) who understand the scope and importance of process design in its broadest sense will become happy students/employees/managers. I believe that the potential of process management is far from exhausted and that we can and must do more with it.

Jürgen Moormann

If we want to better utilise the potential that process management offers us, we need to overcome some psychological barriers of our students. First, they have a certain distrust of the field of business administration. Every day more students come into class searching for an alternative for their future. They search for self, they search for harmony, and they search for a better world where more is about happiness than about money earning. This is usually more pronounced for students studying disciplines other than business administration.

Second, actually resulting from the first, more and more students focus on human behaviour. All courses related to business communication, business psychology or intercultural relations are encountered with great hope. At the same time, courses such as research methods, project management, or process management are met with a certain degree of distance. Of course, it is only our observation and there are many students who love maths, statistics and programming. Yet, an average student seems to need a relatedness to human beings and not to numbers. They dislike being treated as a cog in a machine and instead desire a workplace at a socially responsible company with an individualistic approach to employees (Alonso-Almeida and Llach 2019). Many feel uncomfortable with treating individuals as if they were variables in a set of equations. Unfortunately, process management treats people as a resource in a set of equations in resource planning. Process management with its history and principles is at the core of business administration. Yet, we have something to offer to our students as well as to the readers of this book.

With this book, we want to show that organising, viewed from a human-centred perspective, is not only a relevant but fascinating field for shaping companies. First, this book is rooted in process management, i.e. if process management is your profession, you will feel well reading through our theories and stories. Second, we just put things a little bit upside down! We show how process management can be applied to treat problems caused by process management itself. We also show how to make process management really human-centred. We emphasise that not only a firm's customer is a human. Our employees and managers matter too—they are our internal customers. Have you noticed that on a regular process map, human resources are treated as if they all possess nearly the same qualities? But this is not the case, we argue. Interested? If you want to know more, we need to start with a brief look at history. Since it is not the dry theory that makes you "feel" process management, process management can be told through many (hi)stories that may make the field a bit more "alive". Let's start!

2.2 Sī vīs pācem, parā bellum

2.2.1 From a Tribe at a Camp Fire to an Army

When scholars talk about the history of process management, they usually start with Taylor and his approach to work organisation. It is a good way to go, indeed. Yet, we think one should start with primitive tribes some thousands of years ago. At that time, people had to stick to each other in order to survive. The life of the whole tribe was dependent on each individual's efforts. Everyone tried to do the best she or he could and had time for it. Those, who knew how to hunt, went hunting; those, who could fight, were protecting the tribe; and those, who could cook, took care of the meals. Yet, the distribution of roles (or the division of labour) was not strict. First, many could be good in different areas, e.g. hunting and fighting. Second, the small size of the tribe combined with the environmental threats forced people to be generalists.

While analysing different models of relationships, anthropologist Alan Fiske argued that there are four basic models of relationships. One of these models, "communal sharing" as Fiske (1991) calls it, describes the relationships mentioned above. In terms of process management, we see that each member of the tribe had to be ready to jump in if something happened and hunters had to guard and the guardians had to cook if it was necessary for survival. The more general skills one possessed, the more universal and beneficial she or he was for the tribe. Haslam and Fiske (1999, 242) wrote: "Members of an in-group are treated as equivalent elements of a bounded set; consequently individual distinctiveness is ignored."

There are a few things that we as human beings retained over all the years of human evolution. One of the most prominent aspects of a human being is her or his desire for war. We fight, we conquer, and we dominate: be it in school, on the battlefield, or on the market—we need to fight. Competition has always been a congruent part of our lives and it dictates how we dress, how we work, and how we relax. War, we argue, became the beginning of the functional specialisation, division of labour, and, consequently, process management.

In their early history, humans noticed that they had to fight. Even though many didn't want to, they had to in the event they were attacked. And there was always someone to attack. If you don't want to die and/or lose all you possess, you need to prepare for war. As the Latin aphorism says: "Sī vīs pācem, parā bellum", i.e. "if you want peace, prepare for war". This constant danger of war or the desire to conquer made people think about the effectiveness of their armies: how can we win? Yet, the resources were scarce. Therefore, humans had to think about efficiency too: how can we win with the given (limited) resources?

Wars waged by dictators teach us about effectiveness without efficiency—covering battlefields with bodies of almost unarmed soldiers appeared to be a very effective strategy by Stalin and his generals. Of course, we speak about effectiveness without efficiency. One could argue that manpower was the only "given" and almost unlimited resource. Yet, it is rather a consequence of dictatorship than a clever allocation of resources, we argue. Moreover, if one looks at the soldiers as human beings and not just numbers, one would understand that any war needs to be run efficiently.[1]

Thousands of years of wars taught people about how to be more efficient: the army has to be trained, organised, and specialised. Each unit has its functions, dictated by weaknesses and threats. For instance, have you ever thought about the strengths and weaknesses of the cavalry? The strength is obvious—if cavalry rides fast, it is an almost unstoppable power for land units. Cavalry wipes away the infantry and destroys the order of the enemy. But what about the weakness of the cavalry? First, it needs time and space to achieve the needed speed—if the cavalry is slow or stands still, it represents a perfect target for any land unit. A horseman is unmaneuverable and can be attacked by several weapons such as a sword, spear, or sling. Second, the horses run out of power very fast after riding with the speed necessary to wipe out the enemy infantry. We are not specialists to give precise numbers, but let's assume that one needs 800 metres to accelerate to the necessary (maximum) speed. After about 2,000 metres, horses run out of power, slow down, have to turn, etc. If for some reason your cavalry did not achieve its goals, the horseman will hardly survive.

Now imagine that you are one of the generals. You have to decide how your army will be formed, e.g. will you need more horsemen or infantry (remember the scarcity of resources)? Each time you would have to think about the possible enemy: are these the Barbarians with less cavalry but stronger archers or Persians with great cavalry and weak infantry?[2] One would have to think about the battle as a kind of resource match. One would need to have a perfect understanding of resources in order to be able to act in a dynamic environment with the highest degree of efficiency. Moreover, the army requires a lot of support processes: the troops have to be supplied with food, ammunition, clothes in accordance with the season, etc. And, believe us, all these processes were organised to the best of the technological opportunities of that time.

What we find in business is largely inherited from the military (Talbot 2003). By the way, have you ever thought about the success of one of the

[1] Avoiding war is the best solution, of course. Unfortunately, in this world, you are not always asked whether you would like to participate in war. Your country might be simply attacked overnight. In this event, efficiency and effectiveness are the crucial aspects that will help you win.

[2] We are not military historics and use countries and types of weaponry just for example.

first biggest international corporations—the East Indian Company? We don't want to draw your attention to the fact that they (legally) owned an army. We want to draw your attention to the fact that they were an army. With ranks, hierarchies, functions, units, a clear specialisation (e.g. spices, cotton, tea, opium), and very aggressive with regard to their competitors. Indeed, they had their own fleet, their own army with soldiers and artillery, and were even regularly cooperating with soldiers and officers from the British army. Their success shaped the business landscape for almost 300 years: other firms copied hierarchy, functions, roles, ranks, and other aspects. We don't know whether competition is also an inherited feature from the military or a natural part of our evolution, but we know that "the war in business", i.e. the competition on the market, is constantly increasing. While a war between two countries is usually about a big shift in all aspects of life and may even lead to the complete extermination of one or the other nation, in business we usually have way too many armies on the same battlefield—your market. Therefore, if one wants to win, she or he has to be very good or even the best one. If one fails, her or his company disappears from the market landscape.

2.2.2 Universal Soldiers

Many countries tried to find a universal recipe for success. In the case of the military, countries have always struggled to develop a universal soldier—a person who is able to conduct different functions and each to a perfect extent. Such a soldier would, for example, be a good stormtrooper, a perfect defender, a tank operator, and a helicopter or plane pilot. We see it in movies, such as the main protagonist played by Bruce Willis in "Die Hard" or the Jedi Knights in Star Wars—they can do everything. In real life, however, we meet an obstacle called "resource allocation". We do not speak about the availability of helicopters or machine guns. The biggest obstacle are the physical and cognitive capacities of individuals.

Being a warrior means being good at something or, put differently, being better than the enemy. If the enemy shoots better, we will most likely not survive a fight. If they build better fortifications, we might not succeed in our attack. If their artillery is better trained, we won't even be able to approach their positions. Being better in all functions than units that spent months and years on training is hardly feasible. And being "slightly worse" means losing the fight.

Consequently, one has to focus and dedicate all time to a specific function. Additional functions are learned in parallel if time is available. Being good at everything is very unlikely. In the best-case scenario, we can prepare some generalists, such as infantry that can both attack, defend, or even build simple fortifications. As a result, armies try to prepare specialised units and put them together in the event of trouble. A good army is not an army of generalists but an army of specialists who can be allocated to units of mixed functions in order to encounter new challenges. Depending on the (expected) challenge, different compositions of units will be needed.

Interestingly, while firms learned structures and planning from the military, the military took a different development. On the one hand, the US Army War College introduced the term "VUCA" (an acronym for the volatile, uncertain, complex, and ambiguous environment) that dominates the business now (Baran and Woznyj 2020). On the other hand, in a peaceful time, the military is excluded from the competition because there is only one Ministry of Defense in a country (Grant and Jordan 2015). This absence of competition might make the military rigid. In warfare, this changes dramatically. In this case, the enemy becomes the radical form of a competitor and winning the competition means surviving. The more often armies are involved in warfare, the more VUCA-ready they are. The fewer armies fight, the more outdated they become. By contrast, the business world with its competition evolved faster than rigid armies. Be it due to the intense development of the business or due to path dependency of military services, the business has developed away from the army and evolved at such a pace that the military struggles to catch up with for-profit organisations. And the quantum leap in business happened when Henry Ford and Alfred P. Sloan implemented the ideas of division of labour introduced by Adam Smith and perfected by Frederick W. Taylor.

A Short Exercise

Imagine (or try it in real life) that you play a game against a colleague. You have 60 soldiers whom you can train as cavalry, swordsmen, or pikemen. Cavalry beats swordsmen, swordsmen beat pikemen, and pikemen beat cavalry. Who would you invest in? As you see the game becomes a game of luck as paper-scissors-stone. Fortunately, you can compose troops, e.g. train 40 cavalrymen, 10 pikemen, and 10 swordsmen. Will this additional complexity increase your chance to win? Not at all—it will just make the planning harder. What if we add one more additional variable—terrain: e.g. swamp, field, and forest? Cavalry reveals its potential in the field but is impaired in the swamp. Pikemen are not bad in the forest, very good in the field, and very bad in a swamp. Swordsmen are good in the forest, not bad in the swamp, and not bad in the field.

Each time you add the next degree of complexity, you add a degree of uncertainty. Yet, the game remains a game of luck as you don't know what the other player is going to do with her or his troops. There is a reason why we don't believe that war is a game of luck. First, in contrast to the paper-scissors-stone game, we have some information ranging from gossip to espionage. Consequently, we can plan the appropriate troops for each battle. Second, we try to estimate the behaviour of the enemy—knowing the country, its history, and previous behaviour we may prepare better for an expected move. Third, we can try to provoke a battle in the appropriate terrain: we call this war stratagem.

Now think of your business. There are many firms with similar resources. And competition is not different from the battlefield. If the world was so simple as in strategic management books, then firms would win immediately after knowing their differentiation and cost advantage. But real life is a complex game with too many variables, including not only product-related variables (such as quality of the product) but also image, operational excellence, available sales network, and even the creation of new market opportunities. How is it different from predicting your enemy's moves, deploying your troops, or provoking the enemy to fight on the terrain that best suits your current troop type?

2.3 Traditional Workflow Management

2.3.1 An Engineer at the Right Place

Frederick Winslow Taylor (1856–1915) was an engineer who changed business forever. He liked to observe, think, and measure. With his engineering-driven thinking, he came up with the idea to specialise. Although we know that the military services knew it to some extent, they did not approach the issue with such a high degree of reflection, organisation, and willingness to measure. In his approach, he stood on the shoulders of the great thinker and philosopher Adam Smith. Looking at the work of generalists, e.g. mechanics, who composed the car in small teams starting from scratch and ending up with the running final product, Taylor proposed to split this complex workflow into simple chunks. Finding a good generalist is not easy and they cost a lot. It is not because they can do *everything*, by no means. It is because you need a unique combination of skills and knowledge. The more unique the combination, the harder it is to find a person who combines all these abilities. Moreover, if something happens to this person, no one can substitute for her or him. The solution by Taylor was genius and terrible at the same time: on the one hand, he split the task into a set of activities that could be addressed easily. It was a real leap forward. Yet, on the other hand, he went too far with his simplification. For instance, some employees were responsible for only screwing down nuts of the same type.

Taylor discovered something important: If you split the job into smaller and simpler tasks, you can

1. assign these tasks to less qualified employees. This made production much cheaper. However, one had to invest in their training as well as supervision.
2. control all the activities within a workflow of, for example, car manufacturing.

The approach of Taylor followed these four principles (Taylor 1911; Pruijt 1997):

1. All rule-of-thumb work methods should be replaced with methods based on the scientific study of the tasks. I.e. it is not only about knowing

the basic functions and relying on tacit knowledge, it is about a precise description, measurement, and control of all activities within a task.
2. Select, train, and develop employees in accordance with the focal task and underlying activities. Taylor was against letting employees train themselves.
3. In order to control the quality of the performed task, one had to provide workers with a detailed description of the task and supervise them. The focus was set on simple discrete tasks.
4. Management takes an important role in planning the work. Workers follow the instructions of the manager.

Taylor's approach had interesting consequences: First, as he continued developing his approach to organising blue-collar work, he also found that one needed control mechanisms to monitor those who were in charge of control. You can develop this idea ad infinitum, or, put differently, the bureaucratisation of business starts growing with the increase of process complexity.

Second, in order to produce the final product, all tasks had to be synchronised. Being late for only one seemingly unimportant task could slow down the whole production process. The whole firm became a well-tacted organism where each position on the production line was dependent on the previous position.

Third, the quality was jeopardised by less qualified personnel. Even the simplest tasks can have unexpected results that require intervention. Yet, the main idea of Taylor was to simplify the processes in order to make them cheaper, faster, and less dependent on skilled and, thus, expensive and rare workers. Finally, if a new situation occurred, the worker whose capabilities were limited to "screwing down the same nut" was not able to cope with it.

Fourth, a lack of relation to the final results reduced the responsibility and involvement of employees. Not only did the employees lack the bigger picture (the final car), but they were (almost) not accountable for their errors. How can you be accountable for something you have no idea about?

Fifth, nowadays we try to increase the value added for our customers. In the case of Taylorism though, everyone was obsessed with the universality and simplicity of the process. This resulted in low added value per worker. While the number of workers kept growing, the added value remained the same, and the relationships remained less than trusting (Pruijt 1997). Trust is, of course, important for the final product quality as the motivation in this type of relationship remains very low (Ryan and Deci 2000).

Sixth, individual specialisation resulted in the institutionalisation of larger functions within the firm—known as departments. All previously named issues combined lead to the silo-thinking where each employee and each department takes care, first of all, of themselves and then of the rest of the firm. The customer does not even appear in this approach.

Albeit with certain negative manifestations, the idea of Taylor made a revolution in business. Complex products, such as Ford's cars, became cheap and quickly produced (even though the quality was not always perfect). Most of the weaknesses were addressed in the later stages of the evolution of workflow management, for instance with the introduction of the automation.

2.3.2 Action-Oriented Data Processing

There were two main results that emerged in the next phase of the traditional workflow history. First, the negative consequences of Taylorism became more obvious. The number of organisations that wanted to organise their processes in accordance with the principles of Taylor was rapidly growing. Firms competed by using the same mechanism—scientific management. They pretty soon reached the limits of workflow management in Taylor's meaning. In addition, firms evolved rapidly and discovered that from a certain point in time, Taylor's simplification goes at odds with professionalism, individual and organisational competencies, and, in the long run, loss of competitive advantage.

Second, new technologies appeared. These technologies allowed for better activities' planning, resource allocation, organisation of communication, etc. Theoretically, the new technologies would allow tracking the workflows, monitoring their outcomes, and proposing analysis-based improvements. Finally, if the activities are well described and well organised, we can automate some activities. As soon as a worker logs in with his/her employee ID, we can trigger several events, e.g. save the working time data (timestamp) for salary calculation.

Why was this a new phase in the history of workflow management? Think of the siloed nature of the firm's internal work culture as a consequence of Taylor's paradigm. The new institutional theory explains this phenomenon very well—each function becomes reflected in a department that is not only an organisational unit but also an institution with a set of formal and informal rules. Employees from such functions become oriented towards their internal efficiency metrics (e.g. the number of product parts produced within an hour or the number of defects). Each task that crosses an imaginary line between departments (e.g. a manufactured product delivered to the sales department) has to cross a border between two "kingdoms". As the interests of departments differ, internal tensions might appear ("Why does manufacturing send us more products as we manage to sell?!").

Action-oriented data processing reduced these tensions as no one could be attributed the feeling of guilt. It is not the manufacturing employees who trigger certain actions by the sales department but a (depersonalised) process, action, or activity. Crossing borders between organisational functions (i.e. departments) became easier and encountered less resistance.

Consequently, one could

1. reduce operations time, i.e. save time and effort on waiting to activate certain processes or activities.
2. reduce paper flow, because even the simplest solutions based on primitive technology would help activate programmes directly or inform workers with a blinking lamp or a message.
3. plan resources better. The more you strive towards action-oriented data processing, the more detailed you have to describe the processes. The better you know the workflows and the resources assigned, the higher the level of efficiency that you can achieve. Finally, you learn to plan all activities and allocate resources.

Yet, this phase introduced something Henry Ford criticised his customers for. He said that if he had asked his customers about their wishes, they would have wished for faster horses. Let's be honest, action-oriented data processing was a great advancement, but actually, it was a "faster horse" when compared to the initial form of workflow management introduced by Taylor. Thanks to action-oriented data processing, activities at the lower level were seamlessly linked, so that the workflow ran smoothly and the intervention of managers became largely unnecessary. In this way, the workflow started to become separated from the organisational hierarchy. As a result of looking at the work as a set of events and triggered activities, the concept of workflow management gained popularity. Yet, only in the next phase, we saw a complete rethinking of the process and the real appearance of process management. We started modelling the workflow in a way that could be translated into the programming code, i.e. get reflected in the software. As a result, ERP (enterprise resource planning) systems appeared on the market, reflecting a distant storm causing a ground swell.

2.3.3 Process Management: Riding the Ground Swell of Firms' Rethinking

Do you want to hear something interesting? In academia, process management belongs to the domain of Information Systems (IS)! Why IS? Theoretically, there are domains of operations research, organisational behaviour, or organisational theory. Why IS then? The answer can be found between the previous workflow history and the current phase of process management.

With the advancement of IT, action-oriented data processing came to a new level—one had not only to think about the activities, their triggers, and, in turn, activities they trigger but also about how to automate the workflow. The better the description of the workflow and the higher the calculation capacities of computers, the deeper the level of possible automation. It was not only about hardware. The software was necessary to, first, program the events and the activities and, second, to bring all activities to one complex programme system. Such a system was called an ERP system. Workflow management was a meta-level that was necessary to translate real-life activities into a set of commands that could be replicated in a computer. Have you noticed that UML (Unified Modeling Language) works for both experts in the field of process management and programmers? Now you know why.

As a result of this translation of activities into programmes, we noticed that:

1. Processes are not dependent on the hierarchies. Indeed, hierarchies were made up at a certain point in time to reflect the functions and allow for management and control. Yet, as technology advanced the role of controllers 'controlling the other controllers and so on' diminished. The question "Quis Custodiet Ipsos Custodes" (i.e. who controls the controllers; Latin: "Who will guard the guards themselves?") has been mostly answered.
2. Processes, if well understood, help improve work, increase efficiency, avoid defects, and introduce transparency. By the way, our research showed that the transparency of the processes reduced communication issues and, in turn, reduced the level of burnout (Bogodistov et al. 2020).
3. The best results can be achieved if we focus on the main goal of the process—to deliver the desired product or service to the customer. Before, a product was a result of planning but not of the vision of each department which thought about its own problems. A process view helps us understand the redundancy of many aspects of a traditional firm's life.

This new understanding was groundbreaking: all the (thousands of) years before, we have been thinking that a hierarchy is the only way to achieve desired results. Moreover, the competition was growing while organisations became more and more bureaucratic as a heritage of Taylor's paradigm. Suddenly it became obvious that the paradigm by Taylor was correct only under the condition of information asymmetry (we were not able to know about all the details of a complex process), motivational problems (if people did not want to perform certain tasks), or control mechanisms (e.g. supervising the supervising supervisors of an employee). The new technological advancements allowed processes to be transparent and well-running, people to be motivated to perform even more complex tasks, and a few managers to have a perfect overview of all activities of their firm. Finally, workflows became processes—a flat organisation of work that could be oriented towards the final recipient—the customer—and not towards the interests of siloed departments.

Process management scholars started thinking about new forms of organisations where the hierarchies (i.e. departments) were absent or subordinated to the process (Schmelzer and Sesselmann 2020). What if firms only need top management to set strategic goals and process owners, i.e. those who are responsible for a process starting at a customer (i.e. a customer's desire) and ending at a customer (i.e. the delivered product or service)? Theoretically, such an approach would reduce information asymmetry and bring the quality of products and services to a new level. Moreover, some firms tried to introduce something close to the notion of a holacracy (Laloux 2014)—a form of organisation where there are no departments with their heads and attached bureaucracies but projects with changing roles. One might be an owner of a specific process for a certain period of time. At the same time, you might be a data analyst in another process. Holacracy was more about project management but you got the idea, didn't you?

Unfortunately, organisational forms without departments did not become dominant or even popular. However, we observe mixed models that merge hierarchies and process-oriented structures. Most firms retain a functional structure but try to be process-oriented and blur the borders between departments. For instance, the same person may get instructions from several managers—the department leader and the owner of the process in which this subordinated person is involved. We observe a variety of forms each trying to generate a different combination of classical structures and hierarchy-avoiding process orientation. It seems that a pure process-oriented organisation is not feasible (at the moment) and a fully hierarchical organisation with a strict functional separation is not effective. The quest for a perfect solution is a life-long quest for each organisation as it should fit both the external (market) and internal (personnel) needs. Moreover, as the market is in flux and as each person is constantly evolving in her or his thoughts, the structure will also remain in flux.

2.3.4 Process Improvement and Innovation

Process management was initially meant to find weaknesses in the way of work and organise the work better. The initial idea by Taylor was to describe with a high degree of precision each operation within a workflow. Still based on Taylor's thinking, the aim was to describe with a high degree of precision each operation within a workflow. This is needed also today for several reasons (e.g. transparency, manageability, or regulatory purposes). Yet, there was another stream of thinking coming up—quality management. While business process management was more about the analysis, organisation, and improvement of the process itself, quality management focused on the quality of the final product from the customer's perspective.

In the beginning, quality management was more about control over the execution of well-described simple tasks (and over those who control their execution). Later, a profound understanding of processes combined with pressure from competitors made quality management become a constant search for better ways (i.e. process improvement) or even novel ways (process innovation) to conduct day-to-day activities. The increasing competition has led to a plethora of product variants in all industries. For instance, if you think of SUVs, they are offered in all shapes and forms by almost all car manufacturers. The differentiation between products diminishes as competing SUV models offer only slightly different designs, slightly different interiors, and slightly different arrangements of warning and display symbols. If a firm wants to succeed, it needs to continue providing its product, yet at a better price and without a loss of quality. Thus, firms have to focus on cost-cutting, processing time reduction, and quality assurance—the three core elements relating a process to the final product or service. Simplified said, if several firms work on similar products or services, those who manage to produce them faster, cheaper, or with a higher quality achieve a competitive advantage.

In their search for process improvement, firms applied numerous tools that grew into philosophies. For instance, Total Quality Management (TQM) was born in the 1980s. TQM led to an obsession with customer satisfaction, process orientation, and total employee involvement towards a common firm's goal.

Lean Production, which came to life a decade later, proposed the philosophy of "waste reduction", whereby under "waste" the protagonists understood any unnecessary process elements that do not add value for customers. Lean Production was complemented by Lean Management and the latter evolved into the broader understanding of Lean Thinking. The "Lean" concept was not only about the tools of waste elimination but about the way of thinking—i.e. your processes should not only be lean but also value-adding which included market-oriented organisational structures, industrialised processes, sourcing strategies, and new forms of managing lean organisations.

A slightly different approach can be found under Six Sigma proponents—a methodology focusing on defects and their elimination. Even though defects are broadly conceptualised in the methodology (from missing bolts to motivational problems), the idea was simple—find a way to measure the average number of defects and frequency of their appearance, find the standard deviation (i.e. "sigma") and try to reduce it while decreasing the average number of defects close to zero. This approach became popular about a decade after the introduction of Lean Management and pretty soon it encountered a huge limitation: the bigger perspective of business processes was lacking as well as customer centricity. For this reason, the two methodologies were merged into Lean Six Sigma as there were almost no incompatibilities.

By the way, if you buy any recent book on TQM, Kaizen, Lean Thinking, Six Sigma, or Lean Six Sigma, you will notice that the tools largely overlap. Even the philosophies approximate the common idea—improving processes in any available way in order to increase customer satisfaction and make a firm prosperous. In all methodologies we work with time, costs, and quality. It seems that we could propose a common approach to process improvement without any problems. The only problem is the silo-thinking of different schools and their desire to create a little kingdom (or a market segment) in order to earn money. As often the differentiation is lacking, these schools introduce confusing names (sometimes imported from other languages, e.g. Japanese) and introduce some unnecessary obstacles. They use marketing to whitewash the lack of differentiation. And, by the way, they succeed.

Process innovation is worth mentioning as it is a very different approach. In the case of process improvement, we talked about the three key elements of a process—time needed to produce the product or service, costs associated with its production, and the quality of the final result. You can imagine a triangle with the poles of time, cost, and quality—the so-called "magic triangle of workflow organisation" that we discuss in this book later—i.e. process improvement is about reaching a well-balanced solution stretched between the three poles. You can decide what you focus on, e.g. you can make something faster, but then you will have to sacrifice either costs, quality, or both. Thus, your processes are optimal if the only way to change one of the key elements goes at odds with the other two variables. If you can still reduce time without impacting costs and quality—there is room for further process improvement. If you have reached the limits of this triangle, process innovation is needed. Hence you need to develop a new process that will offer new potential with regard to time, costs, and quality. Creating a new process will change the initial limitations. Think of the process of opening a bank account in a bank branch. In the 1990s banks did all they could to improve this process. Yet, the Internet and digitalisation came and the banks happily introduced online banking. Opening an account online was a completely new process with different settings concerning the same final product (a bank account) and associated time, costs, and quality. Digitalisation changed process management drastically …

2.3.5 Digitisation, Digitalisation, and Digital Transformation

While 'organisation' was (and still is) thinking about the best way to organise a firm, technology kept evolving. While process management became a jewel of the IS field (many would doubt it but if you look at the salaries of process management personnel, you will understand what we mean) and the number of students focusing on business process management grew, technology has changed the landscape again. It was digitisation that opened doors to new opportunities for firms.

Some scholars, especially the German-speaking, promote the term "digitalisation" and stress that there is a huge difference: *digitisation* transfers physical objects into numbers, e.g. if you convert your vinyl to mp3 or if you scan a document and run an optical character recognition (OCR) procedure to extract text from a picture. *Digitalisation*, in contrast, is about a larger transformation tackling social and information systems. For instance, having all documents in a digital form and easily available may help change the whole interaction of ill persons with doctors and health insurance companies and, thus, change the perception of our culture. Some call this shift in social relationships due to digitalisation a *digital transformation* emphasising the groundbreaking change technology brings with it.

So, digitalisation made things look different. At the beginning of the 1990s, process management was more about planning a workflow. This could be done much better with digital tools than without them. Yet, digital tools, such as ARIS, were an accompanying instrument or sometimes even a goal of process management. For instance, if a firm wanted to create clarity and generate an overview on a workstation computer, it needed to describe the processes in order to be able to replicate them in its software. Enterprise resource planning, controlling, and efficient management were the main goals of such activities.

Nowadays, all aspects of our and firms' lives are going to be digitalised. We stop understanding why we need a printed and signed document if it can be sent immediately from the email postbox of the responsible person. Our meetings can largely be held online and the employees and managers use WhatsApp instead of going to the kitchen to make a cup of coffee and informally discuss something with colleagues. All of a sudden, we have found that the world is so digitalised that we can combine tasks that were not compatible before. For instance, employees from different firms from different countries can exchange any type of information in compatible formats (e.g. MP3, MP4, docx) and can use industry-standard interfaces (e.g. USB, HDMI, RJ45) to share their knowledge or connect to local area networks. Universal interfaces and universal file formats, as well as standardisation in technological terms, opened a new horizon for process management.

Again, process management had to catch up—we as scholars were not ready to cope with the new technological advancements. For instance, while managers existed for hundreds of years, "management" had not been proclaimed as discipline till Taylor. By the end of the 1980s, the obsession with quality (TQM, ISO 9000 and similar standards, quality circles, etc.) led to a search for a systemic approach and, thus, the advancement of process and operations management (Slack et al. 2004). Consequently, successful tools and methods were incorporated in academia and advanced our research and teaching practices.

Similarly, when practice introduces new technologies (which are often pushed forward by consulting companies), we lag behind with theories and mechanisms to use the enormous potential of digitalisation. Technologies like cloud computing and data analytics became popular and supported separate functions such as active customer management (Gadatsch 2020). In order to facilitate the integration of new technologies into business processes in both for-profit and non-profit organisations, countries such as Germany started offering grants and state support for research (universities) and development (start-ups) in the field of digitalisation. Ukraine has even set up a Ministry for Digital Transformation in 2019 to disseminate digitalisation throughout the public organisations in the country. All in all, we see that the necessity to organise work is not only driven by practice and academia but also receives support at national (initiatives, ministries) and international levels (international organisations).

Process management starts looking outdated. For now, everybody wants to have more "agility" instead of "classical" process management. Yet, agility is just a new (and, by the way, relatively small) development in the eyes of a tradition that goes back thousands of years to organise work. Agility is a good example for the renewal of the discipline thanks to technology that makes communication and exchanges much easier (MS Teams, Zoom etc.). This looks new, because until now we lacked the capacity to work in iterations while keeping in touch with customers and taking their wishes into account at every step of the respective process, e.g. by using "sprints", when developing new applications. In the past, the only way to reduce the complexity of the environment and get things done was to have a well-structured waterfall approach. If you doubt our correctness, think of an individual dressmaker only a few decades ago. Making a dress was a process that required constant interaction with a customer who had to reflect on the fabric selection, pattern, first design, tailoring, and so on. Doesn't it sound "agile" to you? However, if we do not think of an individual dressmaker but a large clothes producer, we will have to think of hundreds or thousands of employees involved in working for millions of customers of different sorts (wholesalers, clothing chains, and individual buyers to mention some) all over the world. Without internet webpages with contact forms, an opportunity to meet customers from any country online, or even the use of augmented reality to try a new dress, agility was hardly possible, even though we originally had this capacity.

Digitalisation created another opportunity for process management—a huge stream of data. Think of a simple security camera at a petrol station. It creates millions of bits of data per second. Each picture (and there are 3o pictures shown per second of a video with 30 fps, frames per second) can be used to understand the place, identify activities, range of products, customer preferences, etc. And this camera is not even meant for this type of information gathering. How much information could one get from a product management system of a large store? How much data will we receive if we combine both—data about the products bought and data from the security cameras in order to estimate customer behaviour? Yes, we talk about big data. Previously, processing such amounts of data was hardly possible. In the recent decade, we not only learned to process large, structured data sets (e.g. your SPSS© files containing data from surveys) but also big data coming from different sources in different formats. Now we learned how to do data mining and find relationships that were unthinkable hitherto.

2.3.6 From Process Mining to AI-Driven Automation

One of the interesting ways to use tons of data your firm is producing is to run process mining. The method has a very interesting thought in its background: Nowadays almost every activity leaves a digital trace. Think of the process of planning a meeting—you need to send emails to agree on the time, date, and location, you need to enter the planned data in the calendars of invited employees, and, finally, you receive an email with a notification that the invitation has been accepted. Doesn't matter what the precise content of the emails was, we got time stamps, the sender's and the recipient's address. Knowing this information, we may trace who is involved in the process, what the workflow is (sequence of actions), how often the process is executed, and so on. Have you ever thought about how complex the processes can be? On paper (i.e. process map known to most firms), the process may look simple. In practice, however, it may have many variations. Do you want to know how many? We used to have a guest at our research centre who talked about his bank experience with process mining. They took one of the processes and analysed the digital traces to understand its complexity. They discovered 188 variations of the process! Big data analysis allows you to see "how things are done here" and not how management assumes them to be done.

The potential of process management continues to grow. With the introduction of artificial intelligence (AI), we received new opportunities for process improvement and process innovation. AI can help us find the connections we were not aware of and would never be aware of due to the complexity and amount of data. Now AI can help us

1. Analyse text and digitalise all hitherto non-digitalised aspects of a firm's life.
2. Make a sophisticated resource planning that will process not only firm-level data but also data from each individual.
3. Automate plenty of activities that seemed complex before the AI era.

Is AI the new phase in the history of process management? At the moment, it is hard to predict. It might play a minor role such as the once-trendy concept of agility. However, AI has the potential to introduce a radical change to our understanding of how to deal with processes and how to manage them. If we utilise the above-mentioned potential towards AI-driven process improvement, automation and innovation, we may speak of the new phase in the history of process management. But there is something we know for sure about the next phase of process management—it will be about people.

2.4 Human-Centred Process Management

It is an interesting fact that process management seems to be in a decline phase: there are fewer academic papers published and there are only a few new theoretical advancements in the discipline. We can state that the discipline is at a crossroads. Yet, you don't have to worry: first, even if we assume that there will be no further developments of the concept (though that doesn't seem to be the case), it will take some dozens of years until process management will lose its popularity. Process management is way too strong and way too effective. It is a concept deeply rooted in practice and theory. Even if nothing significant will emerge, firms will continue to use it. Think of motivation—some theories are half a century old and still they are being successfully applied. Second, we already see some avenues for future process management:

1. For instance, a group of scholars started working on process science, i.e. the discipline might go towards organisational theory development (vom Brocke et al. 2021). These theories are of crucial importance for scholars in the field of management. We still lack an understanding of the precise mechanisms of interaction of people with each other and of people with a firm's resources (routines and capabilities). As in our example with process mining, many interactions are not captured by formal processes. Time stamps and other digital traces help us measure a part of "organising" a firm's work. But what about informal interactions and information flows that happen in a kitchen at the coffee machine? Or what about the formal interactions that will leave no traces such as business negotiations with a closed door (and turned-off devices)? We also know that a company can achieve the desired results through its capabilities, i.e. through routines that are consciously developed and used; but "[t]o understand challenges such as innovation, value creation, and safety across micro and macro levels of analysis, it is necessary to break theoretical entities such as routines and capabilities into their component elements" (Salvato and Rerup 2011, 469). Process management could contribute to this discussion, as this discipline looks very closely at the smallest components of a process—the activities. Process management has much to offer to organisational theorists.
2. During the past two decades, strategic management scholars have tried to develop a capability-based view of the firm. While Barney and followers developed a resource-based view (J. Barney 1991; J. B. Barney et al.

2011), emphasising the role of specific resources (valuable, rare, inimitable, and non-substitutable) for sustained competitive advantage, other scholars asked themselves whether all firms with such resources achieve a sustained competitive advantage and whether all firms without these resources lack the sustained competitive advantage. They emphasised the notion of organisational capabilities (or competencies, if you like)—abilities to get used of the resources and achieve outstanding results (Helfat and Peteraf 2003; Hoopes and Madsen 2008; Bogodistov and Wohlgemuth 2017; Bogodistov and Moormann 2019). What researchers found is that each capability is a routine (but not each routine is a capability—we will talk about this later in the book). Process management may go this avenue and propose solutions to understand routines better and, thus, help create organisational capabilities.

3. Finally, there is an aspect that process management was lacking all the time. We talk about human beings. IS scholars argue that processes represent a firm's DNA. Knowing this DNA, one can perfectly understand a firm. Moreover, as DNA is unique, processes are also unique for each firm. Even though they might have the same name (e.g. procurement process), the concrete form, included activities, involved resources etc. will differ between firms. Even though DNA is usually associated with human beings and human identity, in the event of process management it is not the case. Initially, Taylor did his best to exclude human nature from the equation of work. Think of the reason to simplify and define all tasks—it was and is about reducing the dependence on complex skills and human mistakes.

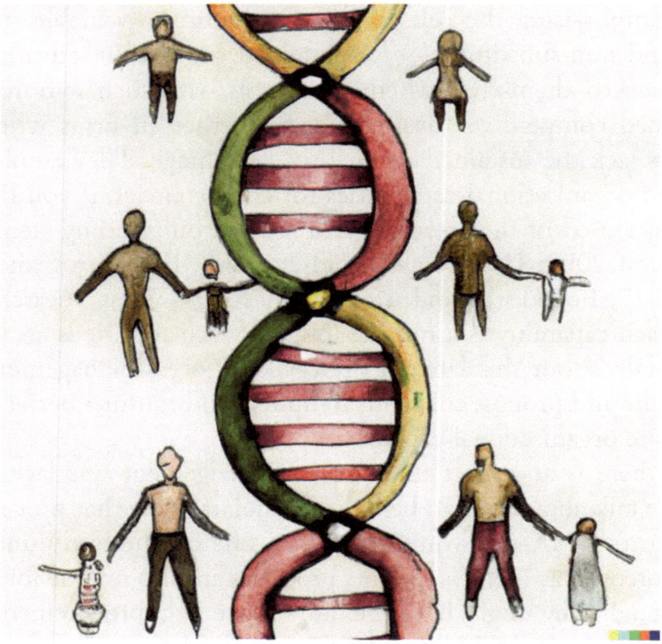

We don't know in which of the proposed directions process management is going to evolve. It may happen that all three directions will merge into a new form of process management 4.0. Why? Because there is no contradiction between these approaches and they all are highly demanded. For instance, routines are the patterns of interaction (both formal and informal) of employees with each other. Routines are at the heart of organisational capabilities. If one wants to know how to develop a capability, she or he has to understand organisational routines. Finally, employees are at the core of each activity within a routine or a capability.

In this book, however, we would like to stress the human-centred aspects of the development of process management. First, human-centricity is highly demanded and largely missing—work-related issues become the source of high losses, whereas human-centred firms manage to evoke intrinsic motivation and make employees walk the extra mile. There seems to be a large discrepancy between the process designed on paper and its actual implementation. Second, a human-centred approach is demanded by each individual, by companies and other organisations, and by society in general. The ISO 9001 norm emphasises the customer orientation of firms' processes. If we talk about internal processes, our employees and managers are our customers. And it is not about external pressure—ISO 9001 only formalises the for a long time observed issues of human centricity.

Before writing this book (and, actually during writing this book), we conducted plenty of research. We showed the effects of psychological factors on process management as well as of process management on how people feel. Our studies ranged from how emotions influence preferences concerning process design to how transparency of processes reduces the number of conflicts and, thus, reduces burnout. We also investigated how digitalisation is perceived through the lens of social costs. In this book, we are going to share with you our findings, our thoughts, and our experience from practice. We hope that the book will help you not only have a look at your processes with the eyes of your employees but also understand how to change processes to reduce exhaustion and strengthen well-being while retaining your efficiency and effectiveness. If you succeed, you will be able to develop an organisation of a new type—a human-centred firm that is so much more sensible with regard to employees that they feel at work as if they were at home, stick to their "alma mater", and enjoy hard work. "Hard" will change its meaning: have you ever thought that one describes a day as "hard" both after a long day of boring activities and an engaging activity requiring high levels of creativity? Such days are differently hard—in the first case, one wants to rest whereas in the second case, one wants to celebrate. In this book, we focus on how to design or improve your processes to have more of the "hard but happy" option. Enjoy! But first, we need to understand what are we fighting against and what is the consequence of not having human-centred processes. Therefore, in the next chapter, we talk about the burnout state.

References

Alonso-Almeida, María Del Mar, and Josep Llach. 2019. Socially responsible companies: Are they the best workplace for millennials? A cross-national analysis. *Corporate Social Responsibility and Environmental Management* 26: 238–247. Wiley.

Baran, Benjamin E., and Haley M. Woznyj. 2020. Managing VUCA: The human dynamics of agility. *Organizational Dynamics* 50: 100787.

Barney, Jay. 1991. Firm resources and sustained competitive advantage. *Journal of Management* 17: 99–120.

Barney, Jay B., David J. Ketchen, and Mike Wright. 2011. The future of resource-based theory: Revitalization or decline? *Journal of Management* 37: 1299–1315.

Bogodistov, Yevgen, and Jürgen Moormann. 2019. Theorizing on operational excellence: A capability-based approach. *Academy of Management Proceedings* 2019: 12174.

Bogodistov, Yevgen, Fynn Malte Reck, Jürgen Moormann, and Oleksandr P. Krupskyi. 2020. Wandel im Gesundheitswesen: Analyse der Auswirkungen auf Ärzte und Patienten am Beispiel der Ukraine. *Das Gesundheitswesen* 82: 236–241.

Bogodistov, Yevgen, and Veit Wohlgemuth. 2017. Enterprise risk management: A capability-based perspective. *Journal of Risk Finance* 18: 234–251.

Fiske, Alan Page. 1991. *Structures of social life: The four elementary forms of human relations: Communal sharing, authority ranking, equality matching, market pricing*. New York, NY: Free Press.

Gadatsch, Andreas. 2020. *Grundkurs Geschäftsprozess-Management: Analyse, Modellierung, Optimierung und Controlling von Prozessen*. Wiesbaden: Springer.

Grant, Robert M., and Judith Jordan. 2015. *Foundations of strategy*. Chichester, West Sussex: Wiley.

Haslam, Nick, and Alan Page Fiske. 1999. Relational models theory: A confirmatory factor analysis. *Personal Relationships* 6: 241–250. Wiley.

Helfat, Constance E., and Margaret A. Peteraf. 2003. The dynamic resource-based view: Capability lifecycles. *Strategic Management Journal* 24: 997–1010.

Hoopes, David G., and Tammy L. Madsen. 2008. A capability-based view of competitive heterogeneity. *Industrial and Corporate Change* 17: 393–426.

Laloux, Frederic. 2014. *Reinventing organizations*. Brussels: Nelson Parker.

Pruijt, Hans D. 1997. *Job design and technology: Taylorism vs anti-taylorisam*. London: Psychology Press.

Ryan, Richard M., and Edward L. Deci. 2000. Self-determination theory and the facilitation of intrinsic motivation, social development, and well-being. *American Psychologist* 55: 68–78.

Salvato, Carlo, and Claus Rerup. 2011. Beyond collective entities: Multilevel research on organizational routines and capabilities. *Journal of Management* 37: 468–490.

Schmelzer, Hermann J., and Wolfgang Sesselmann. 2020. *Geschäftsprozessmanagement in der Praxis: Kunden zufrieden stellen - Produktivität steigern - Wert erhöhen*. 9th, ext. ed. Munich: Hanser.

Slack, Nigel, Michael Lewis, and Hilary Bates. 2004. The two worlds of operations management research and practice: Can they meet, should they meet? *International Journal of Operations & Production Management* 24: 372–387.

Talbot, Philip A. 2003. Management organisational history—A military lesson? *Journal of European Industrial Training* 27: 330–340.

Taylor, Frederick W. 1911. *The principles of scientific management*. Norwood, MA: Plimpton Press.

vom Brocke, Jan, Wil van der Aalst, Thomas Grisold, Waldemar Kremser, Jan Mendling, Brian Pentland, Jan Recker, Maximilian Roeglinger, Michael Rosemann, and Barbara Weber. 2021. Process science: The interdisciplinary study of continuous change. SSRN Electronic Library.

3

(A Very Short) Introduction to Burnout

Abstract This chapter deals with the psychological underpinnings of burnout and other related phenomena. The main aim of this chapter is to give an overview of the psychological mechanisms for those who do not come from the field of business psychology. Using short stories and examples, we show how burnout appears and what are the main drivers for its appearance (or its prevention). This chapter equips you with the basic knowledge in the field of burnout and provides you with one of the core theories tackling burnout—the Job Demands-Resources model. The most interesting thing is that this theory is compatible (commensurable) with the theories of business process management, i.e. process managers can learn why and how process management tools can address burnout.

© The Author(s), under exclusive license to Springer Nature Switzerland AG 2024
Y. Bogodistov and J. Moormann, *Process Management and Burnout Prevention*,
https://doi.org/10.1007/978-3-031-56615-8_3

3.1 What Is Burnout?

The investigation of burnout started in the 1980s. Some researchers observed an interesting phenomenon in clinics: nurses and doctors had to engage in emotional interactions with patients. Suffering from several health issues, patients expressed emotions such as anger, fear, frustration, despair, embarrassment, etc. This chronic stress exhausted hospital personnel and caused several negative consequences such as a lack of willingness to engage in emotional interactions, cynicism in communication with patients and colleagues, as well as a feeling of low self-efficacy. Therefore, Maslach and Jackson (1981) proposed to focus on three dimensions of burnout:

1. Emotional exhaustion,
2. Personal accomplishment, and
3. Depersonalisation.

Thus, if we talk about burnout syndrome, we assume that the person experiences issues with regard to each of these dimensions. Consequently, based on the work by Maslach and followers, one of the definitions of burnout is …

> A psychological syndrome of emotional exhaustion, depersonalization, and reduced personal accomplishment that can occur among individuals who work with other people in some capacity. (Maslach et al. 1997, 192)

At the same time, there is criticism with regard to this definition. Maslach and her followers developed both a concept and a measurement tool—the Maslach Burnout Inventory (MBI). However, there is a certain circular argument in this approach: "Burnout is what the MBI measures, and the MBI measures what burnout is" (Kristensen et al. 2005, 193). Moreover, further factor analyses for the MBI revealed that the dimensions of one construct appear to represent three separate constructs. Instead of one scale indicating a person's burnout, the MBI Manual gives three separate scores (Maslach and Jackson 1981).

For this reason, Kristensen and colleagues proposed their own conceptualisation of burnout. Accordingly, burnout syndrome was related to mental and physical exhaustion whereas it was not the same as just fatigue or exhaustion. The scholars defined burnout as

> ... the degree of physical and psychological fatigue and exhaustion experienced by the person. (Kristensen et al. 2005, 197)

This definition became a part of the Copenhagen Burnout Inventory—a novel instrument that captures burnout in three other dimensions: personal burnout (i.e. how tired or exhausted the participant is), work-related burnout (i.e. how tired or exhausted the participant due to his/her work is), and client-related burnout (i.e. how tired or exhausted the participant due to his/her work with clients is). This approach allows for measuring both the general level of burnout and the burnout caused by "people work". This "people work" may relate to clients (or patients, or internal customers of your process) as well as to colleagues of your team. Any communication costs you energy. For preventing burnout, of course, it is important to know which element of your processes (clients, colleagues, or your personal issues transferred to work) causes the state of physical or psychological exhaustion. The inventors of the CBI made some interesting observations: the three dimensions of burnout as proposed by Maslach and followers might not be correct (Kristensen et al. 2005). First, "depersonalisation" has a different nature as compared to emotional exhaustion. While exhaustion is a state, depersonalisation is a "coping strategy", i.e. the way one responds to the exhaustion and increased emotional work demands. Consequently, depersonalisation should not be analysed as a part of the burnout construct. It should rather be analysed in relation to other coping strategies, e.g. emotion regulation such as emotional suppression or emotional reappraisal (Gross and John 2003). Second, the lack of self-efficacy (lack of feeling of personal accomplishment, lack of belief that one can impact a certain situation) is, according to Danish academics, a consequence of emotional exhaustion and a part of it. The latter has an interesting implication: First, if you see signs of low self-efficacy, it might not be the early sign of burnout but a late consequence of it! Second, you need to be aware of another problem with the burnout definition. The signs of burnout are hardly distinguishable from depression. The fact that burnout is poorly defined in terms of precise criteria, as well as the heterogeneity of depressive disorders (Bianchi et al. 2015), can complicate a manager's job. The approach we describe below might help with burnout prevention but not with depressive disorders. If a manager confuses depression with burnout, she or he might resort to process management whereas consultation with a therapist would be necessary. We would like to help with a simple approach: depression won't go away after you finish your work and go home. But burnout will. If you feel better on the weekend, on holidays, or after a change of environment, it is most likely burnout. Yet, in a deep state of burnout, there can be spillover effects into other areas of life (Hakanen and Schaufeli 2012). Research suggests that burnout can trigger depression (Armon et al. 2014) or that the relationship between burnout and depression develops in tandem (Ahola et al. 2014).

3.2 Why Does Burnout Appear?

One of the leading theories explaining the appearance of burnout is the Job Demands-Resources (JD-R) Model. In this model, scholars assume that each individual has his/her specific amount of resources. The scholars propose the notion of psychological and physiological resources that each individual possesses and spends during the day. Psychological resources are the things, activities, and objects which bring you energy. The same applies to physiological resources: a good sleep or a well-lit desk can bring you some energy as can doing sports activities.

At the same time, some things, activities, and objects may steal your energy. Some employers demand their employees express positive emotions when talking to clients. However, not all of us feel positive all the time, and showing feelings that we don't feel takes energy. Showing feelings that one does not feel is called "surface acting" (Lee et al. 2010). When this activity does not match one's actual state of mind, it consumes energy. Moreover, in some places, individuals have to deal with angry customers, they are pressed for time and experience stress, or they have to accomplish boring monotonous tasks. Such activities deplete the psychological resources of employees.

Not only the psychological resources can be depleted, but starting a day with a full amount of energy may end up in complete tiredness due to physical activities, noisy environment, insufficient light on the desk, etc. Physiological factors may drain energy as well as psychological factors.

Psychological and physiological demands can be attributed to any job: long working hours, the necessity to communicate, and the probability of conflicts are an inherent part of work in an office. For instance, a firm has a limited number of resources (be it pencils, time of managers, scarce office space, or access to the kitchen). To work, employees have to compete for these resources which may lead to conflicts. Communication with colleagues may be as emotionally demanding as communication with customers or suppliers. As a result, employees constantly deploy their resources and lose energy.

A firm may help employees, however. There are several ways to provide employees with energy. Social support, fast conflict resolutions, flexible working times, and appropriate equipment are examples of job resources that can outweigh job demands. The main idea of the Job Demands-Resources Model is that there is a balance of psychological and physiological job demands and resources. If an employee gives more of the resources than he/she gets, he/she starts losing energy and ends up in a state of emotional exhaustion. If this resource loss appears regularly, a burnout state occurs. By contrast, if one receives energy (support, acknowledgement, positive feedback, a day off, etc.) he/she may work more productively and even increase his/her motivation.

The JD-R Model may be enriched by the Resource Conservation Theory. According to the latter, individuals tend to accumulate psychological resources. If they see that the resources are not accumulated (e.g. due to an excessive depletion) or even vanish, they may deliberately or unconsciously avoid resource-depleting activities. For instance, if communication with colleagues costs energy and doesn't bring positive results, employees stop showing emotions and start behaving cynically. According to Kristensen and colleagues (2005), cynicism is the coping mechanism that individuals apply to cope with emotional exhaustion and may indicate burnout.

3.3 Job Demands

Every job has several requirements. These requirements can usually be found in the job description. However, burnout is caused not (only) by the formal requirements listed in the job description, but by those tasks that are seldom listed. For instance, in some professions, politeness and "service with a smile" are assumed and required even though not mentioned explicitly. The job of a professor requires that you are always polite and politically correct, compassionate, and empathetic (although, in our opinion, many professors do not conform to this implicit norm). Even more pronounced is the requirement for emotional labour in health care. Nurses, doctors, and other clinic personnel have to deal with emotion-laden clients who experience and express a whole range of emotions from fear of death and anger of being treated not in the desired way to happiness and relief due to positive results of medical analyses. Slightly less emphasised is the role of emotional labour in other industries. Shop assistants and waiters are assumed to smile, whereby the punishment for non-conformity appears immediately in the form of small tips or changing the minds of customers and leaving the shop or restaurant.

According to the Job Demands-Resources Model, those demands that have certain psychological and physiological costs may lead to high strain and, later, to burnout. In simple words, job demands are those things that steal your energy. In a more complex form,

> Job demands refer to those physical, psychological, social, or organisational aspects of the job that require sustained physical and/or psychological (cognitive and emotional) efforts or skills and are therefore associated with certain physiological and/or psychological costs. (Bakker and Demerouti 2007, 312)

The scholars also add social and organisational aspects to their definitions. Of course, one can expect that social, organisational, physiological, and psychological dimensions are highly correlated: bad time management in a firm (organisational dimension) will unavoidably drain an employee's energy be it due to conflicts with others (social), overload of psychological capacities (psychological), or overtime burden (physiological).

The following types of job demands can be found in the extant literature:

Psychological job demands:

- Work pressure,
- time pressure,
- emotional demands,

- role ambiguity,
- emotionally demanding interactions with peers, clients, patients, or management (emotional labour),
- conflict with others,
- job insecurity,
- emotional dissonance,
- organisational changes,
- etc.

Physiological job demands:

- Work overload,
- unfavourable physical conditions,
- shift work,
- physical workload,
- health risks (risk of getting infected, dangerous tasks).

As can be seen, physiological job demands are seldom addressed in the burnout literature. One of the reasons may be the fact that they are easier to understand and imagine than psychological job demands. A further reason may be their simplicity: it is obvious what a physically active job is (i.e. requiring physical activities and utilising muscle work). Nevertheless, scholars often forget about other physiological factors that make employees lose their energy, such as insufficient light, small working areas, old monitors, monotonous work, a too-cold or too-warm environment, and loss of electrolytes due to sweating, and noise. Indeed, there is some muscle work behind your eyes trying to focus on a small font of a printed document. We should not oversimplify the physiological job demands as they lead to similar strain as the psychological demands do.

Psychological job demands represent an even more interesting category. While physiological demands can often be easily handled (through brighter lighting or changing the monitor), psychological job demands are harder to cope with. For instance, the Relational Models Theory suggests that we use four elementary cognitive models of relationships that unite our attitudes towards morals, work distribution, exchange, motivation, decision-making, etc. (Fiske 1991; Haslam and Fiske 1999). Interestingly, we use all four models and switch between them depending on the counterpart or situation. In a dangerous situation, for example, we might switch to an authoritarian model, where we take orders and give instructions. This might speed up the response to the danger. After the crisis has ended, however, we can return to the relationship model we used before, e.g. partnership-like (so-called "Equality Matching") or family-like (so-called "Communal Sharing") relationships. However, we still do not know why people prefer specific models of relationships for certain people or situations and why conflicts under some conditions appear even in established relationships. Moreover, individuals learn—as soon as they understand that the conflict appeared due to a specific reason they might adapt their behaviour. Firms may change their organisational culture and emotional climate in order to cope with psychological issues. Again, employees will respond to the changes in a firm's internal policy and change their perception of the job demands. Psychological job demands are in constant flux even though the business process and the activities constituting this business process may remain constant.

3.4 Job Resources

Just as a firm can expect an investment of psychological and physiological resources from its employees, it can support employees with some psychological and physiological resources. There are many things that "deliver" positive energy to individuals. These things can be either of a psychological or physiological nature. In a simple way, we can define job resources as those things and events that bring positive energy. In more complex terms,

> Job resources refer to those physical, psychological, social, or organisational aspects of the job that are
>
> - functional in achieving work goals,
> - reducing job demands and the associated physiological and psychological costs, or
> - stimulating personal growth, learning, and development (Bakker and Demerouti 2007, 311).

It is interesting to notice that job resources are approached in a more differentiated way than job demands. Here are three options:

Indeed, it is hard to say how to "outweigh" the strain, resulting from conflicts. For this reason, first, firms may try to compensate for the loss of psychological resources through other things or events that may bring energy to employees and managers. Nevertheless, there are some psychological resources that directly address the loss of psychological resources. If one has conflicts with other team members, offering an alternative position of similar status in another team might help. Empowering might also help, but is rather unlikely. Anyway, if the task or situation that is draining energy can directly be "outweighed" by some psychological resources, one should go for this option.

How Conflicts Can Escalate Thanks to an Intervention

I made a rather contradictory observation: when I went through officer training, I was quite disappointed in the approach of "empowering". One of my peers (Cadet A) suffered the "law of grandfather", whereby he was hazed by another peer (Cadet B). Our arguments never helped—being at the same level of power does not give you the opportunity to command other peers. Then, however, an officer in the rank of a colonel intervened. The colonel gave the humiliating task of cleaning an armoured personnel vehicle (if you knew the nature of "dirt", you would understand how humiliating the task was). Cadet B had to do the job, while Cadet A was empowered to "control the process". Despite the colonel's expectations that a change in roles in humiliation would change the relationship between both, the next day the situation became even worse—Cadet B became even more aggressive. You can imagine what were the psychological costs of Cadet A during each day of officer training. After each day of training, he was completely exhausted. The luckiest day was when he graduated and never had to return to the place where any activity had such a high psychological cost (humiliation). If you think that it was just because of the nature of education (military traditions) then better think again. Bullying in the office, disrespect, or (gender) discrimination have the same effect on your employees and managers.

Second, as soon as an energy-draining situation is identified, a manager can try to reduce the demands. Unfortunately, often resource depletion is taken for granted (e.g. "Sales managers have to talk to clients, as it is their job!"). Managers think about work in terms of functionality and financial resources (or equipment) but rarely in terms of psychological resources and their finitude. If they understand that psychological resources are as important as financial ones, they may start reducing their demands. Even sales managers have administrative tasks to accomplish. Switching between different tasks in order to introduce breaks into emotionally demanding interactions may be one of the ways to reduce demands without negatively impacting organisational processes.

Third, one should not underestimate the role of individuality. We all are formed by our habits, knowledge, experience, and self-perception. We tell you a "secret": not only is the constellation of these aspects unique for every person, but it is also constantly evolving. Acknowledging the dynamic nature and the fact that the employees are "growing" is crucial. A boring task may drain your energy. Yet, as soon as one understands that this "boredom" is a necessary step for a further career, he or she will be happy to participate in this task in order to achieve more. Of course, not everyone has the ambition to grow, but everyone has her or his vision of self in the future. Allowing to go on this path of spiritual development is just as motivating as organisational ladder climbing by a careerist.

There Are Many Ways to Motivate People

When I worked in the field of HR, the most recent trend was to introduce a complex scheme of grading in order to motivate personnel. At this time, Ukrainian firms noticed that money is not the only motivator. Moreover, money may destroy motivation if too directly introduced (see the example with young football players below). Firms looked for different benefit options, which could individually be selected by each employee. This is one of the simple ways to let people indicate what brings them energy or where they are willing to invest their energy. Clever managers might use this tool to understand how to balance out job demands and job resources.

The job resources can directly support or compensate for some psychological and physiological job demands. If employees have to work overtime, allowing them to come to work later the next day is a direct replenishment of the resource. I.e. if one misses some hours of sleep, he or she can catch up on those hours. If instead of coming later, employees receive another resource, e.g. acknowledgement, an additional vacation day in winter, or similar, we talk about compensation for the resource instead of a replenishment (discussed further in this book).

We found the following psychological job resources in the academic literature:

Psychological job resources:

- Social support and supervisor support,

- performance feedback,
- autonomy,
- task significance and task identity,
- job control (which might reduce job demands),
- participation in an organisation's life and decision-making,
- job security,
- opportunities for further development,
- skill variety,
- etc.

With regard to physiological resources, the task was harder. These resources are often mentioned but seldom listed. Therefore we propose our own examples of physiological job resources.

Physiological job resources:

- Flexible working hours,
- work from home (at least before Covid pandemic),
- meditation classes at work, an opportunity to sleep at work,
- supporting employees (nurses, assistants),
- automation (RPA, robotic process automation),
- own office room,
- air conditioning, air heating (in cold times/regions),
- water filters and CO_2-machines in offices,
- cafeterias, internal kitchens,
- coffee machines and snack automats,
- fitness rooms or access to gym,
- female hygiene items in restrooms,
- showers in the office building,
- ear protection, hand protection gloves,
- social distancing opportunities (distance between tables and working places),
- internal transport (segways, bicycles),
- healthy food in cafeterias,
- eye control (regular oculist visit to the office),
- ergonomic chairs, tables (bar tables), screens with eye protection mode,
- etc.

3.5 Perception of Resources

Here we come to a very interesting aspect of the JD-R model: it is not really universally applicable to all individuals. The general argument is that there should be a balance between job demands and job resources. Yet, think about the following: we do enjoy working with statistics, testing different research models, working with factor analysis and the like. But many of our colleagues suffer only from the word "statistics". Consequently, the same task might be perceived differently and the energy may be depleted depending on the individual's perception of the task. This relates to psychological resources.

Concerning physiological resources the same approach is applicable, although not to the same extent. For instance, we may like dark rooms as they calm us down, whereas our colleagues turn on the lights right after the afternoon. Yet, even though we like dark rooms, we get tired if we have to read or write with poor lighting. The same applies to noise. Some people do not notice background noise, and others cannot focus on their tasks if their neighbour colleague talks by phone. Thus, although there are some individual differences and preferences, physiological job demands are usually straightforward if compared to psychological demands.

There are practical implications dictated by the perception issues. For instance, employees and managers can understand that job demands can be turned into job resources. The Self-Determination Theory of motivation by Ryan and Deci (2000) gives us some advice in this regard:

- *Relatedness:* A sense of relatedness plays a great role in perception. The same task without context may be found boring. Knowing the context, it might suddenly become interesting. Not only does the context matter but also the relation to certain persons is significant. If an individual knows that the task is important for someone who the individual knows and values, the boring task becomes important too. Imagine the power of words "It is important to me that you and not someone else perform the task!" Said by someone important to you, these words might evoke an influx of energy and willingness to perform.
- *Competence:* Those who feel competent feel relaxed and approach a task differently. If we succeed in convincing our students that they are capable of solving a complex problem and assure them that their work falls precisely within their area of competence, we can be fairly certain of a good or even very good result. For instance, each year we supervise Bachelor's and Master's theses. These theses are in a certain way standardised,

e.g. a student should find a research gap, address it with a proper method, and report her or his academic results. Yet, all students are different. Some are good in maths and statistics while others are good in theory; some are potential academics while others are potential practitioners; some adore creative tasks while others prefer well-structured execution. And we believe that the only way to write a good thesis and have fun is to address each student's competence. Consequently, during individual coaching, we emphasise each student's individual strengths. To some students, we say "It is a great opportunity to show everyone how good you can write about theory. And statistics are just a small part of the task. After you are done with theory, statistics are easily done!" To other students with the same task, we say "Here you can show how great you are in statistics. Find what the data says. Writing theory is simple after all the tests are done." To practitioners, we say "Wow, the idea is great and will definitely help several firms! Now, let's add a bit of academic approach to reassure that your great idea is needed (research gap) and holds for different firms under different conditions!" And yes, in the end, it is the same standardised Bachelor's or Master's thesis.

- *Autonomy:* Make your employees understand that they are in control of their work. Think of the following: Deadlines, threats, directives and the like destroy the feeling of autonomy. "If there is a deadline for everybody, then the result does not really depend on me and my level of engagement"—or, put in psychological terms, the locus of causality is external (deadline) and not internal (own engagement).

As a manager, you can apply this knowledge to turn job demands into job resources. As an employee, you can find a way to enjoy a task. As soon as you understand how to make each task "enjoyable", you will find a way to manage your (or your employees') job demands and job resources balance.

Gamification represents another way to cope with resource depletion. A manager can organise several seminars to teach employees, e.g. in cybersecurity. Attending such events takes time and energy, especially if these seminars are conducted in an online format. However, there are gamified applications available in the market. Employees may "play a game" where they learn the basics of cybersecurity and receive points and badges for their success. These badges can then be used in internal social networks or even be used for promotion within the company (Pogrebna and Skilton 2019). Employees might enjoy gamification solutions more than online seminars. Thus the job demand becomes a job resource (a fun task) or the job demand gets accompanied by a job resource (points and badges accompanying necessary learning activities).

How I Started Loving Statistics

*When I started my doctorate studies, I was pretty bad at statistics. I was afraid of it. I hated it. My last statistics course was a dozen years ago and, as you can assume, you need to be good at statistics if you want to succeed in your academic career. So I took two books: "Statistics for Dummies" by Deborah J. Rumsey (*2016*), and "Discovering statistics using SPSS" by Andy Field (*2018*). Later, I discovered a nice series of YouTube videos by James Gaskin (*2013*). At this moment, I already had the data from my first experiment. I applied what I learned from the books and the videos and came up with some results, which I needed to interpret. I kept searching for other tutorials. While reading books was boring (I did not have data and I did not know what kind of data I would have), the application of statistical tools to my research was fun. The more data I collected, the more eager I was to discover a way to make more out of it. I learned about structural equation modelling. I helped my colleague develop and run a model. After two weeks of trying, he invited me to join the project and take over the methodological part. I was surprised and flattered by this fact.*

Later, I joined a team of researchers at the Frankfurt School of Finance & Management. In my first week, I redeveloped a questionnaire, as I already knew all the issues we would have to deal with after the data was collected (yeah, I already collected a lot of experience at that time). As you can imagine, as soon as the data was collected I managed to develop (and run) a very interesting model. In only a few weeks, I was "the statistics man" and "the data cruncher". The more I was acknowledged for my skills, the more I wanted to learn about new tools, new methods, and new ways to collect and "crunch" data. Now I teach research methods as one of my classes and I do my best to show my students not only the formula, but the real-life problems which we can transfer into numbers, resolve, and then translate back into the language of practitioners. I do love statistics!

Unfortunately, there are also many ways to make things worse. Actually, "worse" means nothing but transforming job resources into job demands, or, put differently, turning fun things into energy-draining things. In a firm where I used to work, we had a tradition: All departments (and we were at that moment just a small enterprise with 35 employees) prepared something for the New Year firm's event. Some people wrote a funny sketch, some people prepared a genre scene, some wrote a song, etc. It was really enjoyable laughing at our problems and even the top management participated in this "floor show". And then after about two years, all the fun disappeared.

A person from our firm contacted all departments, asking them to send the planned activities in advance via email (to know which location to rent for the event). Moreover, all departments were assumed to prepare something. What we made for fun suddenly became obligatory. As you can imagine, the atmosphere became forced and more stressful. That is how our intrinsic motivation stopped being intrinsic.

3.6 State and Trait

There is no common understanding of why some people like the same tasks that others hate. Rephrasing George Orwell's 1984: "All *resources* are created equal but some are more equal than others." Moreover, one can enjoy a task and later start hating it. We have two important factors here: state and trait.

Simply explained, a state is temporary. It is the way you feel or behave for a certain (usually short) time span. Trait, by contrast, is a stable long-term characteristic of your personality. It is the way you are. If we talk about the changes concerning resource perception, it is most probably about the state of an individual. Perception can change due to the change in your state.

There is a story about a change in the perception of job resources. We cannot remember from where we know it and maybe we adapted it too much to our needs, but we would like to share it with you:

Young Football Players

It happened in a small village. Some kids found a nice place to play football: right behind the house of an old man. Let's call him Dr Smith. When they played they screamed for fun, howled when they were hit by the ball, and laughed when they won. Of course, it was too noisy for Dr Smith. He could have shouted at the kids and forced them to go away. Yet, he was wise: He knew that shouting would just provoke kids to come back the next day and be even noisier. So, he came to them and said: "Hey, kids! I enjoy your game so much that I would like to pay you! I will pay €1 for each game I can watch from my window!"

"That is great!"—so thought the kids. "We can not only play but also earn some pocket money!"

They came the next day, and the next one, and till the end of the week. They got tired but the incentive was too good—free ice cream for each game.

When they came the next week, Dr Smith came to them and said that he could pay only €0.50 this week, as he didn't have enough money. "Ok"—said the kids, but the game brought them less fun. They didn't want to play for only half of their salary. Every day this week, they came late, played lazy, and finished earlier.

Finally, Dr Smith told them that he could not pay anymore.

"So that's what you are up to!" said the kids, went away, and never came back.

We hope this story shows you how intrinsic motivation can be destroyed. As you noticed, what was fun (job resource, energy to play) became a disappointment (job resource, strain of playing).

In the event of a state, it is hard to estimate how the task will be perceived: as energy-draining or as energy-bringing. As a manager, you have to understand the state of your employees. Interestingly, you can rely on your intuition. Nature (evolution, to be more precise) gives us a strong ability to recognise the emotions and feelings of other people. Probably, you can anticipate the reaction concerning a certain task before you tell your employees.

If you don't know your team well enough to anticipate the reaction, you can start talking about the task and observe the reaction. We are sure you will notice whether they become happy, angry, or sad about the task. This should indicate whether you introduced a job demand or a job resource.

Another good option is to simply ask your employees what they like to do. You can also approach the issue not as a practitioner but as an academic and make a short survey about the perception of different aspects of work. In the next sections, we will talk about how to measure job demands and job resources. Anyway, as long as the issue is about the *state*, you can manage the balance between job demands and job resources.

Things become interesting in the event of a *trait*. Indeed, we are all unique and, consequently, we are unique in our resource perception. You probably know people who are introverted or extroverted. You can imagine that the requirement to be empathetic, and polite and to smile at clients all the time (also known as 'emotional labour') may be energy-draining for introverts. In our lives, we develop capabilities to communicate with others even though we might be introverted and enjoy the silence around us. On the one hand, this makes corporate life convenient: once you know the personal traits (characteristics), you can adjust the job requirements to reduce strain. For instance, if you know that someone is an extrovert, you can plan more communication activities for that employee or manager. Yet, on the other hand, we all learned to smile and be polite. How do you know that the employee or a manager is an extrovert and not an introvert who learned to communicate as if she or he enjoys it? For this reason, we can address the learned (rather than the felt) aspects of personality when adjusting job requirements. Addressing the traits (concealed by the learned behaviours) is not an easy task.

Concerning traits, you must not oversimplify. Introverts also need communication and attention. Moreover, an introvert may understand an introverted client or peer better than the extroverted one. For this reason, "playing on traits" is challenging and ethically questionable. Where is the line between an adjustment of job requirements and discrimination by psychological traits? This question cannot be easily answered within this section. Yet, we may give you a hint. Let your employees decide. Let them select what they want and what they enjoy. Your task as a manager is to offer a set of tasks to select from, to propose a number of options for how to conduct the tasks or to announce the expected outcomes. Let your employees choose the path to solving the task that they feel comfortable with. Let them decide how they want to approach the problem. And if there are tasks no one is comfortable with, let them toss a coin. The chance will decide who is going to decide.

And if there are tasks that are unpleasant for everyone, they can be taken in turns. Then it's sometimes one person's turn, sometimes the other's.

When thinking about your business processes, try to look at them through the lens of competencies and not skills. It is not about a specific training and university degree (although they also matter), but about competence, i.e. "being good at". You probably know some colleagues who have similar training but one is good at talking to clients and the other is good at working with data using MS Excel spreadsheets. The variety of tasks in your firm is huge, and each task might fit someone's competencies making her or him feel good while performing the task. In this book, we argue that your main goal as a process manager is not only to plan the processes and develop the list of tasks but also to match the individual preferences and competencies (stemming from your employees' and managers' states and traits) with different types of tasks. In this way, you may ensure that not only the "job is done" but also that your firm's emotional climate is positive. "Happy wife, happy life!" they say in the Philippines. This statement can be transferred to a firm, whereby "happy wife" corresponds to your employees and managers, and "happy life" reflects both the employees' and managers' well-being and your firm's performance.

Of course, if you have an opportunity to learn the states and traits of your employees, your life may become easier. There are plenty of tests which allow you to evaluate the "big five" personality traits (openness to experience, conscientiousness, extraversion, agreeableness, and neuroticism), emotional intelligence, motivation profile, and others. We don't recommend you test your employees as this may evoke a feeling of being observed or as a "probe into the most intimate aspects of an individual's life" (Creech 1966, 332), but we recommend you look into these tests. Go through the questions to understand what extraversion or emotional intelligence means. In their Big Five test, Open-Source Psychometrics Project[1] refers to the paper by Goldberg (1992). Here is an example of questions about extraversion: "I talk to a lot of different people at parties" or "I don't mind being the centre of attention" for extroversion. Consequently, observe the behaviour of employees and managers at your firm's events. Those who are proactive in talking to others and creating situations where they are in the spotlight are more likely to be extroverts than those who are "… quiet around strangers" and "stay in the background". Remember, spontaneous behaviour is a very good indicator of traits. Being equipped with this knowledge will help you understand what

---

[1] Open-Source Psychometrics Project, Big Five test: https://openpsychometrics.org/tests/IPIP-BFFM/.

people value, what they are good at, and what types of activities will fit them better. Consequently, you will be able to organise the processes much more efficiently and effectively.

3.7 Resource Conversion

In one of our ongoing research projects we are trying to formalise the JD-R model. We want to develop a formula to make process managers better understand employees and plan their work accordingly. During our work, we suddenly encountered a mathematical problem. Or, vice versa, maths made a weird prediction such as "Just add more job resources!". Would it work for you, if you had to work twice as hard and your manager would give twice as many compliments?

Sure, getting a compliment may help. A compliment acknowledges your work, it shows that your work and you matter. But is there a linear relationship, i.e. if you have to work four hours more, your superior should tell you four more compliments? No. Moreover, the second compliment might be not only unnecessary but also harmful. Acknowledgement may depreciate and become a mockery.

This brings us to the understanding of the complexity of job demands and resources. While the model suggests that the resources are accountable and that the calculation is assumed to be simple, in real life we need to outbalance apples by oranges. Moreover, each next orange has diminishing utility and, thus, has to be weighted in the calculation differently (i.e. we need a dynamic weighting of job demands and job resources). This complexity does not mean that the theory is useless. On the contrary, the complexity draws attention to the firm's internal issues and gives a hint about how to approach these issues.

Think of stress as a physiological response to the "demand, situation or circumstance that disrupts a person's equilibrium and initiates the stress response of increased autonomic arousal" (Lloyd et al. 2002, 256). How many of such demands, situations, and circumstances appear as a matter of a suboptimal work organisation? How often do the unresolved, even minor problems accumulate and lead to spontaneous conflicts? How often do process managers take into account the non-linear and self-reinforcing effects of the usage of psychological and physiological resources in teams (Sterman 2000)? How can we prevent burnout resulting from chronic stress and disbalance of job demands and job resources? One thing we know for sure is that systemic stress management and burnout prevention is a task of complexity which has not been known to process management hitherto.

3.7.1 Quantitative Approach to Job Demands and Job Resources

The best way to proceed is to survey your employees and managers—of course, if they don't mind being surveyed, and after you have explained the goal of the survey (to help find the best fitting activities without cutting salary). For this, we need to include two aspects in the survey. One aspect has been mentioned in the previous section: people perceive tasks differently and, therefore, may get energy from them or deplete their energy into them. The second aspect is the diminishing or growing utility. Yes, there might be some tasks which can deliver you more energy when repeated. Remember the story about loving statistics—the energy from something where you develop your competence could grow.

To organise your processes in a human-centred way, you can start with the process itself—something that you are already competent at. The first thing you need to do is to set up a list of activities within your process. When you finish the list of activities, rephrase it into a statement and create a rating scale below it. Use a scale ranging from "Costs me a lot of energy" to "Brings me a lot of energy" (Table 3.1 with some examples).

We suggest distributing the scale among your employees. Important: you cannot take the values and make an average. As job demands and resources are individual, having a "mean" is similar to measuring the mean body temperature in the hospital: the mean may lie at 36.6 °C, yet if dead bodies and patients with fever participated in the data collection, the conclusion might

Table 3.1 Sample items for your survey

Please evaluate the statements below:						
Performing calls with our clients						
Costs me a lot of energy	☐	☐	☐	☐	☐	Brings me a lot of energy
Performing calls with our partners						
Costs me a lot of energy	☐	☐	☐	☐	☐	Brings me a lot of energy
Entering data in our database						
Costs me a lot of energy	☐	☐	☐	☐	☐	Brings me a lot of energy[2]
			...			

be a bit "misleading". Looking at the standard deviation might help, but still, it would make much more sense to build clusters of employees who prefer the same type of tasks and events. It would be even better if you could approach each individual separately but in big firms this might be an organisational challenge.

The second thing you need to do is to understand the diminishing marginal utility, which refers to the phenomenon that each additional unit of gain leads to an ever-smaller increase in subjective value. Of course, the best way to know the marginal utility for sure is to conduct an experiment. As you might not be able to put your managers and employees in an experimental lab, you may try natural experiments. If you want to learn more about experimental research, you need to grab a nice book on quantitative research methods. For the purpose of this section, we offer you a short explanation: an experiment is about trying something out.

In an *experiment*, you change one or several conditions and see what happens. It is important that you change these conditions not for everyone but only for some people, let's say a half. The second half of the participants will retain the old conditions, i.e. nothing changes for them. For instance, we may show half of our team a motivating video on interesting work in the office and the other group a video on punishing some employees for wrongdoing by their supervisor. Then we compare the productivity of these two groups. If all other conditions are equal (we call it *ceteris paribus* or *c.p.*), we can assume that the observed effect has been caused by the video.

[2] We had a small debate here. Yevgen prefers 7-point Likert scales as they capture more of the variance in response. Jürgen prefers 5-point Likert scales as they are easier to use and capture sufficient variance for this task. We agreed on a 5-point Likert scale but you may use the larger scales depending on your analysis.

Consequently, with an experiment, we may check causality—the productivity changes after our intervention. This is what makes experiments so powerful. A simple correlational analysis does not show causation (correlation ≠ causation).

Yet, experiments have several disadvantages. For instance, we can change only a few conditions as each additional change makes the analysis more complex. Additionally, it is hard to control for confounding effects. If we go back to our example with the motivating video and the video on punishing employees for wrongdoing by their supervisor, how can we be 100% sure that the time of the day, weather, screen size, or other factors did not influence productivity in addition to or instead of the video? As you see, experiments might not be so easy to organise.

In a *natural experiment* (e.g. pandemic, heat wave), we do not manipulate anything—nature does it for us. Imagine a situation if half of the team moves to work from home (e.g. because they had contact with a Corona-infected employee), while the other half keeps working in the office as usual. If there is a difference in productivity, you may assume that it is caused by the (home-)office. You can apply this notion to any "natural" condition, e.g. one part of the team uses a different software or one part of the team gets rewarded for the perfectly closed negotiation. Important is that all other conditions remain the same (do all employees working from home use the same software?). Yet, the weakness of natural experiments is the number of confounding effects. In our example, we also have to control for effects on productivity caused by chores at home, kids, pets, the additional workload in the office due to missing employees, and so on.

And still, experiments are (one of) the most powerful methods to learn about the effects of your decisions or external events. It may happen that coincidentally (by "nature") some employees had to perform more of a specific task or that some employees received a reward, while others did not. This can be the starting point to observe how the reward or task-related strain impacted the employees' behaviour.

Unfortunately, natural experiments do not depend on you. While scientists have the opportunity to work with different populations (e.g. they can test their theories in different firms in different countries with data collected many years ago), you are probably limited by the data of your firm. Consequently, alternative methods such as surveys might be useful here.

The main strength of a *questionnaire* is that you can ask directly what you want. Why should you let half of the employees watch a video and then test their productivity if you can directly ask them whether motivation or punishment will lead to higher productivity? Probably you have already noticed the weakness of surveying your employees—who would ask for punishment for themselves and his/her team if they can ask for motivation? Social desirability (i.e. willingness to give answers commonly accepted by and expected from society), ordering bias (i.e. the order of questions might impact the answers given), confirmation bias (i.e. the propensity of the surveyor to focus on expected aspects of the investigated situation while ignoring other aspects), or many other biases may make the collected data based on questionnaires very weak.[3] Moreover, if you run a cross-sectional survey, you may find a correlation and not causation: you will not know whether A causes B or B causes A if you include questions measuring A and B in your survey.

Yet, the weaknesses of a method should not discourage you—you just need to learn to formulate questions correctly. There are books available about conducting surveys. Or you can simply search for existing questionnaires or hire a professional who helps you develop questions that address the desired construct in a non-biassing and unbiassed way. And if you need to prove causality to know that you are fighting the problem and not its symptoms, you can either perform several surveys to see whether A in t_0 impacts B in t_1 (however, this is not a perfect solution) or you can conduct a discrete choice experiment.

A *discrete choice experiment* (DCE) is a combination of a survey and an experiment, whereby a participant is asked to pick one of two options.[4] Each option contains several aspects of the object of interest, e.g. a work description. You can find a simplified example below (Fig. 3.1):

"Which of the two options would you prefer?

- Early shift, 3 coffee breaks, 1 h Task A, 2 h Task B, rest of the tasks as usual, in cooperation with department C; or
- Late shift, 2 coffee breaks, 2 h Task A, 1 h Task B, rest of the tasks as usual, in cooperation with department D?"

Then, you repeat the task for the same participant, but you change the aspects of work, e.g.:

[3] If you want to learn more about biases and how to avoid them, we recommend a book by our colleagues Ganna Pogrebna and Karen Renaud (Big Bad Bias Book, forthcoming).

[4] Actually, it can be any number of options. We work with a simple selection between two options while others use 4, 5, or even 7 options to select from. You can also add the option "None of the proposed options". If you want to know more about the method, feel free to visit Yevgen's YouTube DCE Playlist: https://www.youtube.com/playlist?list=PLrn-FTfgRQDQCtgZaENM2yT4FoWmEpUQk.

We are currently thinking about redesigning our processes. Examine the options below.

Which of the two options would you prefer?

Option 1	Option 2
Early shift	Late shift
3 coffee breaks	2 coffee breaks
1h task A, 2h task B	2h task A, 1h task B
In cooperation with department C	In cooperation with department D
☒	☐

Fig. 3.1 Example of a typical DCE decision situation

- Early shift, 1 coffee break, 2 h Task A, 2 h Task B, rest of the tasks as usual, in cooperation with department D; or
- Late shift, 3 coffee breaks, 2 h Task A, 1 h Task B, rest of the tasks as usual, in cooperation with department D?"

And again, e.g.:

- Early shift, 2 coffee breaks, 1 h Task A, 1 h Task B, rest of the tasks as usual, in cooperation with department C; or
- Late shift, 2 coffee breaks, 1 h Task A, 1 h Task B, rest of the tasks as usual, in cooperation with department D?"

The idea behind these tasks is to identify preferences of a participant regarding each aspect of work and, in addition, to test causality. With regard to the depth, the questions are close to those of a quantitative survey. Imagine that you would have asked participants about their preferences concerning tasks, shifts, cooperation with colleagues, etc. using a regular survey with statements and Likert scales. This would lead, first, to biassed responses (as everybody would indicate their preferences but not the readiness to trade them off against other work aspects) and, second, you may find many correlations but you will not know the causation. In our case, with regard to causality, the questions above are not like in a regular questionnaire. If you look at how the questions are formulated, you will notice that each time we ask to select between two opportunities, we introduce a manipulation as in a field experiment. If you show two options and ask a person to select one of them, you reveal the individual demands that are better addressed through one of the proposed options (Lancaster 1991). Obviously, if a person has preferences concerning one of the proposed options her or his expected utility is better addressed by some of the aspects entailed in this option (McFadden 1974). Put differently, if you are asked to select between two options, the one that you select entails something better than the second one. What you see in the two (or more) options impacts the decision you make, i.e. we have a specific type of experiment here. Besides causality, we see something very interesting here: the preference indicates which aspects of work are desired. This can be used as an indicator of low job demands or even some job resources that we associate with these aspects of work.

Moreover, if you survey your employees in this way, you can include several aspects related to your processes and investigate the impact of different aspects of your work on your employees' job demands and resources. By selecting between well-described options, you can understand what each employee or most employees value. The necessity to choose between two options puts a participant in a situation where she or he has to "give up" something in order to "get" something. This allows us to investigate the trade-off value of each aspect. If you add a scalable variable, e.g. price, time to invest, or expected quality of the result in some units, you will be able to calculate the "willingness-to-pay"[5] for each (!) tested aspect of work easily. If you look at the sample questions above, you will notice that we do have scalable variables—the number of coffee breaks and hours of work on a specific task. It is not a problem to calculate the value of an hour of Task A in hours of Task B. Let's assume that Task A is not a pleasant one, and Task B is a desired one. With a DCE we can calculate, how many hours of Task B should you offer to an employee or manager in order to make her or him perform an hour of Task A? We can even calculate the value in "coffee breaks"—how many coffee breaks should a firm offer to an employee or manager to make her or him accept Task A? Of course, money or time would represent a much easier-to-understand "currency".

As you see, the main goal is to find out the value of different aspects of work. The more we have to "pay" for the task, the harder it is and, assumedly, the more it is perceived as a job demand. On the contrary, if we discover that an employee or manager is willing to have more of the task, we may assume that this task is associated with low job demands or even job resources.

[5] By the way, if you do not use the money equivalent but time, then it is called "willingness to trade". For instance, with our colleague, we estimated willingness to trade efficiency for different social costs related to digitalisation (Bogodistov and Ostern 2019).

Interestingly, while money is an easy-to-understand concept, it is indirectly (as we say "assumedly") related to job demands and resources. It may be a bit confusing, but you can measure the job demands and job resources directly. What if you formulate the DCE options like it is shown in Fig. 3.2?

You can even ask about activities that "bring you energy" to address job resources only, but we would not recommend it. Nevertheless, you have to take care of the confusion: first, people seldom think in "energy depletion" terms; second, the interpretation might be weird. In the example in Fig. 3.1, the interpretation is easy: "Participant prefers Task A over Task B. And in order to increase the preference, we need to offer … hours of Task A or increase the number of coffee breaks". In the example in Fig. 3.2, the interpretation would be "Participant perceives Task A as being associated with the lower level of job demands as Task B. And in order to compensate for the necessary energy investment, we need to offer … hours of Task A or increase the number of coffee breaks". For a practitioner, the second interpretation may sound too confusing, don't you think so?

By a sufficient number of "decisions" within your DCE, you may find relationships between different types of resources, i.e. you will be able not only to convert the value of each aspect of work in some units but also in other aspects of work. What if you know how many hours an employee would like to work on Task A in order to avoid/get one hour of Task B? Would you be able to organise work better? We are sure that the answer is "yes".

We are currently thinking about redesigning our processes. Examine the options below.

Which of the two options would **cost you more energy**?

Option 1	Option 2
Early shift	Late shift
3 coffee breaks	2 coffee breaks
1h task A, 2h task B	2h task A, 1h task B
In cooperation with department C	In cooperation with department D
☒	☐

Fig. 3.2 Alternative DCE example with the focus on job demands and job resources

If this method is too complex (it is not, you just need a bit of practice), you can propose to your employees to estimate the value of each additional unit of the investigated aspect of work. For instance, our team has recently proposed "to say 'thank you' for the fulfilled tasks". The idea is not bad but there is always a "but". What if we ask our team to estimate the perceived value of each additional "thank you"? Which of the graphs (as depicted in Fig. 3.3) would explain the added value best? What if the relation is a U-shape relationship or a reversed U-shape relationship (i.e. with each additional "thank you" people become happier; yet, their value starts diminishing after a certain point in time and may even become negative if people think that you mock them)? Thus, the utility of job resources is not always linear.

You can even try a more sophisticated approach where you propose graphs of different job demands and job resources and their conversion rate, whereby instead of "value" you offer a different job demand or job resource. E.g. how many "thanks" are you willing to give up in order to get a free working hour? This approach has two shortcomings, though: First, it is hard to understand for employees. Second, as there are various tasks and events, depicting all of them is a big challenge. That is why converting the focal job demand or resource to money, time, or mental effort is a better way to go. In the end, if you know the conversion rate for other job demands and resources into money, time, or mental efforts, you can easily convert job demands and job resources against each other.

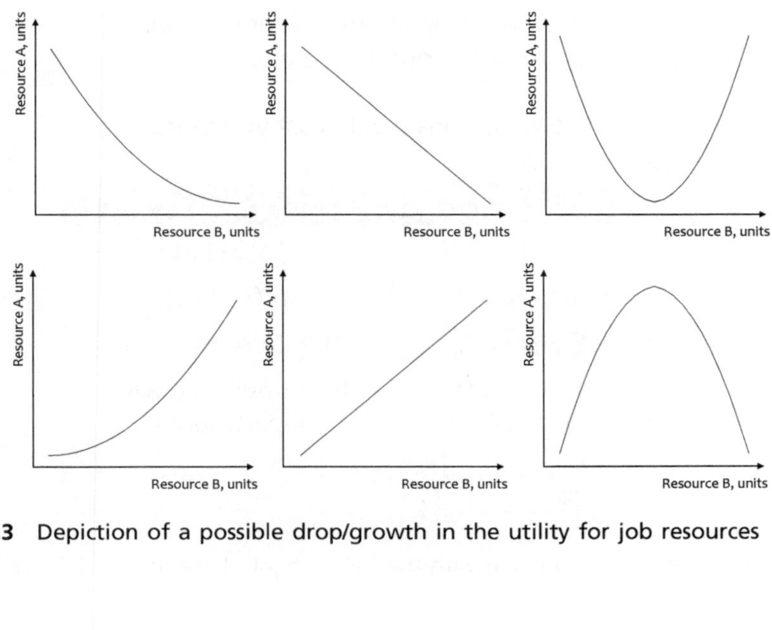

Fig. 3.3 Depiction of a possible drop/growth in the utility for job resources

3.7.2 Qualitative Approach to Job Demands and Job Resources

However, although we are both positivists who place a high value on the quantitative approach, we must admit that the qualitative approach is not only feasible but absolutely necessary under certain conditions. For instance, you can use interviews with open-ended questions to find out about the value and the current state of the job demands and resources. For instance, asking the question "What makes you happy at work?" may give you some insights about the job resources. If you formulate an even broader question, such as "How do you feel at work? Why?" you may gain further information or answers you did not even think about before. The more open the question, the more data you can generate. You can, for instance, discover new sources of energy and how your firm can provide those (i.e. job resources). The same applies to job demands.

The downside of the qualitative approach is that you receive raw data (text, video, sound, etc.) and extracting information from this data is a challenging and time-consuming procedure. Moreover, you will need to generalise to put the newly discovered resource into one of the existing categories. This means that you will bias the information through your understanding and assumptions concerning the meaning of what was said to you during the interview. Here, we recommend inviting a specialist in qualitative research to develop an interview guideline and learn qualitative data coding and analysis.

Finally, you have to take care when analysing data: the same task may be perceived as a job demand *or* a job resource, and the conversion of resources is an individual process. For instance, those who like to be thanked and acknowledged may value these job resources more than any other type of job resources. Can you "generalise" in this case?

This is not an easy question. On the one hand, you can calculate the average value of a certain job demand or job resource. This will help you understand the trends in the development of the emotional climate in your firm or unit. For instance, if you find out that 80% of your employees and managers disapprove activities related to the preparation of annual financial statements, then the last months of the year will be accompanied by a high level of organisational stress (even though some talented financial managers will feel happy and behave like the local heroes). Moreover, the average data might help you develop organisational rules of thumb (also known as heuristics) that will help make effective decisions in a much more efficient way (Bogodistov and Moormann 2020).

Yet, if you want to address a specific activity performed by a specific employee or manager, you should go for the individual (and not "on average") approach. The value for a specific employee or manager might differ from the average. Moreover, her or his utility from the job demands of job resources might have a different function.

3.8 Sustainability at Work

The concept of sustainability is a tricky one—it is too broad to be precisely defined and, consequently, to be efficiently and effectively addressed in this book. Let's focus on one of the Sustainable Development Goals (Sustainable Development Goals 2023)—Good health and well-being (SDG 3). It is one of our biggest challenges to develop new models of work where our employees and managers are able to be productive while maintaining their health. The employer organises the daily work and takes into account the activities that constitute a business process. But, does the employer take into account employees' and managers' well-being?

Think of a situation where the activities should be distributed among several employees. Usually, we look at the competencies, education, or experience of employees when distributing tasks. What we often forget to take into account is that each activity might be accompanied by strain or positive feelings, i.e. they can be seen as job demands or job resources. What if some activities are overloading the mental and psychological capacities of an employee, while for another one they would bring joy and self-confidence? Would a different allocation of the activities increase the efficiency of work? Based on the competencies, education, and experience it might not. But if draining and bringing energy is taken into account, an appropriate allocation of tasks would increase the well-being of employees without a decrease (and maybe even with an increase) in work results. Good (mental) health and employees' and managers' well-being are much easier to achieve than one might think.

Sustainability in terms of health and well-being can have different meanings ranging from "achieving long-term goals reassuring stable employment" to "making employees and managers feel good when working in our firm". In this book, we propose a way to combine the efficiency of process management with addressing the psychological aspects of work. Consequently, we argue, you will be able to achieve the whole range of sustainability-related outcomes.

References

Ahola, Kirsi, Jari Hakanen, Riku Perhoniemi, and Pertti Mutanen. 2014. Relationship between burnout and depressive symptoms: A study using the person-centred approach. *Burnout Research* 1: 29–37.

Armon, Galit, Samuel Melamed, Sharon Toker, Shlomo Berliner, and Itzhak Shapira. 2014. Joint effect of chronic medical illness and burnout on depressive symptoms among employed adults. *Health Psychology: Official Journal of the Division of Health Psychology, American Psychological Association* 33: 264–272.

Bakker, Arnold B., and Evangelia Demerouti. 2007. The job demands-resources model: State of the art. *Journal of Managerial Psychology* 22: 309–328.

Bianchi, Renzo, Irvin Sam Schonfeld, and Eric Laurent. 2015. Burnout–depression overlap: A review. *Clinical Psychology Review* 36: 28–41.

Bogodistov, Yevgen, and Jürgen Moormann. 2020. The role of information systems for firm-wide heuristics development. In *Proceedings of the 28th European Conference on Information Systems (ECIS 2020)*.

Bogodistov, Yevgen, and Nadine Kathrin Ostern. 2019. Digitization at Any Cost? Willingness to Trade Efficiency for Organizational, Human, and Relational Costs. In *AMCIS 2019 Proceedings*.

Creech, William A. 1966. Psychological testing and constitutional rights. *Duke Law Journal* 1966: 332.

Field, Andy. 2018. *Discovering Statistics Using IBM SPSS Statistics*. London: Sage.

Fiske, Alan Page. 1991. *Structures of social life: The four elementary forms of human relations: Communal sharing, authority ranking, equality matching, market pricing*. New York, NY: Free Press.

Gaskin, James. 2013. *SEM series*. YouTube. US: Gaskination's Statistics.

Goldberg, Lewis R. 1992. The development of markers for the Big-Five factor structure. *Psychological Assessment* 4: 26–42.

Gross, James J., and Oliver P. John. 2003. Individual differences in two emotion regulation processes: Implications for affect, relationships, and well-being. *Journal of Personality and Social Psychology* 85: 348–362.

Hakanen, Jari J., and Wilmar B. Schaufeli. 2012. Do burnout and work engagement predict depressive symptoms and life satisfaction? A three-wave seven-year prospective study. *Journal of Affective Disorders* 141: 415–424.

Haslam, Nick, and Alan Page Fiske. 1999. Relational models theory: A confirmatory factor analysis. *Personal Relationships* 6: 241–250.

Kristensen, Tage S., Marianne Borritz, Ebbe Villadsen, and Karl B. Christensen. 2005. The Copenhagen burnout Inventory: A new tool for the assessment of burnout. *Work & Stress* 19: 192–207.

Lancaster, Kelvin. 1991. *Modern consumer theory*. Northampton, MA: Edward Elgar.

Lee, Raymond T., Brenda L. Lovell, and Celeste M. Brotheridge. 2010. Relating physician emotional expression to shared understanding and shared decision-making with patients. *International Journal of Work Organisation and Emotion* 3: 336–350.

Lloyd, Chris, Robert King, and Lesley Chenoweth. 2002. Social work, stress and burnout: A review. *Journal of Mental Health* 11: 255–265.

Maslach, Christina, and Susan E. Jackson. 1981. The measurement of experienced burnout. *Journal of Organizational Behavior* 2: 99–113.

Maslach, Christina, Susan E. Jackson, and Michael P. Leiter. 1997. The Maslach Burnout Inventory manual. In *Evaluating stress: A book of resources*, ed. Carlos P. Zalaquett and Richard John Wood, 191–218. Lanham, MD: Scarecrow Press.

McFadden, Daniel. 1974. Conditional logit analysis of qualitative choice behavior. In *Frontiers in econometrics*, ed. P. Zarembka, 105–142. New York: Academic Press.

Pogrebna, Ganna, and Mark Skilton. 2019. *Navigating new cyber risks: How businesses can plan, build and manage safe spaces in the digital age*. Cham: Springer.

Rumsey, Deborah J. 2016. *Statistics for dummies*. Hoboken: Wiley.

Ryan, Richard M., and Edward L. Deci. 2000. Self-determination theory and the facilitation of intrinsic motivation, social development, and well-being. *American Psychologist* 55: 68–78.

Sterman, John D. 2000. *Business dynamics: Systems thinking and modeling for a complex world*. Chennai: McGraw-Hill Education Ltd.

Sustainable Development Goals. 2023. *United Nations Development Programme*. Accessed April 25. https://www.undp.org/sustainable-development-goals?gclid=CjwKCAjw9J2iBhBPEiwAErwpeX1iaA6bEkmYKImCETW9r6LzLua6xUZD5Iu-mm1txRbqbarfs36I3RoC3gMQAvD_BwE.

4

Identifying Burnout Using Process Management Inventory

Abstract In this chapter, we talk about how you can recognise that there are psychological problems in your organisation. We first provide you with some visualisation tools that can help you identify the problems, their strength, or their nature. Secondly, we present some methods from psychology, anthropology, and our professional lives. We explain why and how they work. We also deliver an overview of the "classical" tool to measure burnout—the Copenhagen Burnout Inventory. Sharing some insights from our lives, we explain what can go wrong and how to avoid the shortcomings. Finally, we talk briefly about how sudden burnout can occur.

4.1 Let's Make It Worse!

Usually, we don't want to make things worse. In contrast, we want to make things better. Interestingly, reverse thinking can really help us understand how burnout emerges. Let's illustrate this in the following way: Try to brainstorm on the topic "How to prevent burnout?". You may be more advanced in your ideas than we are. Yet, we would come up with some obvious ideas such as:

- Reducing workload,
- giving more freedom,
- avoiding unnecessary emotional labour,
- avoiding conflicts,

and other obvious but not helpful answers.

© The Author(s), under exclusive license to Springer Nature Switzerland AG 2024
Y. Bogodistov and J. Moormann, *Process Management and Burnout Prevention*, https://doi.org/10.1007/978-3-031-56615-8_4

We believe these answers are way too vague and do not really make us understand the real "pain points". Yet, what if we would ask you to brainstorm on a slightly different question: "How can we make sure that burnout appears?".

All of a sudden, the picture becomes much clearer: First, we notice that there are different ways to achieve the "best burnout results" in our team. Our academic colleague Andrew (the name has been changed) is a good communicator. Indeed, he is. He likes talking to students and may spend hours on this. So, adding more "people work" or emotional labour will not make burnout appear. But how could we make things worse for sure? Remember, we told you that job demands and resources should be approached at an individual level. Andrew' loves "orderliness"—he loves to plan and execute his work in a distinct order. So his main pain points are disorder and confusion. As this is his main pain point, we just need to add some chaos to his work routine.

What if we somehow create an issue with his software? This would greatly help achieve burnout! And here we don't speak about a computer virus—a simple slowdown in the work caused by our database would overheat his mind. However, if we want to achieve not just a temporary effect but long-term exhaustion, we need to add some deadlines which cannot be achieved due to, e.g. issues with software or chaos in processes. Try this exercise for your employees and managers and you will find out what causes their psychological problems at work, won't you?

For us (Yevgen and Jürgen), we would need to proceed differently. We are mostly exhausted if we have to work on too many tasks of different types at the same time. We are almost there if we add some administrative tasks, combined with teaching a new course, and two or three Revise & Resubmit decisions. Now we need to add some emotional labour. We usually like communicating with our students tête-à-tête. Such communication brings energy. Yet, a lecture with 50+ students requires us to act and perform at a high level. And, consequently, dries our emotional energy.

The good thing is that both of us are experienced professors, i.e. we recover fast. A good movie after the day of teaching and 8 hours of sleep and our energy is replenished. So, if we want to "make things worse" and achieve long-lasting burnout results, we need to add some other tasks. For both of us, deadlines will work—we hate deadlines, especially those tasks coming all of a sudden with the deadline "yesterday evening". But we also differ—Jürgen likes tasks requiring focus and attention. Proofreading papers calms him down. Yevgen likes creative tasks and hates attention-laden tasks. Consequently, to make things worse we need to introduce irregularly announced deadlines. Moreover, from now on, Jürgen gets all the creative tasks while

Yevgen has to proofread documents. The lack of perspective that things will get better leads to the deepest levels of burnout. Believe us, we were there! With only a few steps, we can make sure that we will be in a burnout state by the end of the month. Knowing what we've told you, you are ready, we bet, not only to make our lives hard but also to save us from burnout. Would you agree?

Let's take another example—our colleague Mary. For her, we would need an alternative approach. Mary loves students and dedicates a lot of emotional labour to working with them: she calls them regularly, passionately discusses their homework, and answers their emails even late at night. Indeed, she responds to emotion-laden requests of our students during vacation, late in the evening, or, sometimes, at night instead of sleeping. Consequently, her emotional energy has no time to replenish. If we don't let her replenish her energy and even increase her level of emotional labour, she will collapse quickly. For instance, we could add some emotional labour by encouraging her to answer students' emails during her vacation. We cannot ask for it directly due to the Right to Disconnect discussed in the EU Parliament (Chiuffo 2019), but we might find a workaround—we could *praise* her for her immediate response to students' emails even when not present in the office. This "social coercion" will nudge her to increase the workload even on vacation. The effect will be almost the same as criticism for ignoring students' emails. As a result, she will have no time to replenish her energy even when having a day off. Moreover, irregularity might help—if one cannot plan and, thus, prepare, she or he will get into stress due to immediate overload. The irregular nature of such emails (and students write their emails when they want, i.e. at any time of day or night) will introduce a lot of chaos in her life.[1] Then, let's add some other work which requires emotional engagement: discussion of the internal faculty affairs such as a new master programme combined with conflicts due to different points of view concerning our university curricula. Finally, let's postpone her birthday celebration[2] and, ta-da, we have a deep burnout state.

Actually, this exercise is not funny at all. Yet, it gives an overview of the weakest points in our department. You can apply this exercise to find your most burnout-relevant issues. If you look at our examples above, they had

---

[1] In the military, this is called "harassing fire". It is a form of psychological influence on your enemy via irregular and intermittent artillery fire that is performed at night. This harassing fire undermines morale, introduces stress, and prevents resting. We told you that the military knew it long before the JD-R model came up.

[2] In our team at the MCI, we agreed on a celebration day in the office, e.g. next Wednesday after the birthday. We raffle who is making a cake for whom and celebrate in a nice informal setting. We even have an informal position of a "Chief Cake Officer" who is responsible for the raffle.

something in common, e.g. stress due to chaos in organising work. You may find other aspects that are common for your employees and managers. But the examples above also indicate unique aspects of each person and her or his "path to burnout". The "Let's make it worse"-exercise helps you find the real issues in the team. Believe us, after a few months of work, you will develop a strong intuitive feeling about what makes people happy or exhausted. This exercise will help your intuition identify burnout-related aspects of your team members.

There is also something that we believe will *always* have an impact on the level of burnout in your firm: First, we need a negative or a lack of perspective in every case. The problem is not a sudden onset problem, but the fact that it will be a long-lasting or recurring problem. Temporary stress may be fine—our bodies are prepared to deal with stress in an ad hoc manner. However, constant (long-lasting) or frequent (recurring) stress undermines the performance of any employee or manager. Indeed, in the short term, we can replenish our resources. If we don't have the opportunity to do so immediately (we assume you had a situation like an exam for which you prepared all night), we believe we can replenish our resources with a delay (e.g. if we can sleep well after a sleepless night before taking an exam). As you can see, people hope to be able to replenish their resources. It is the hope that makes you work a little longer.

However, if we take away the perspective to recover from stress in the short-term perspective, people need to find a way to secure their resources. As long as the replenishment perspective is not given, they will start immediately saving on their resources (Hobfoll and Shirom 2001). This "saving" will lead to a lack of willingness or, if already all resources have been invested, to a lack of ability to emotionally engage in work-related activities. And this is one of the dimensions of burnout.

Second, we see that in all mentioned cases (Andrew, Mary, Yevgen, and Jürgen), we used different activities in order to increase the level of exhaustion. We showed that both the type and the number of activities overload people. The high number of activities makes your body "mobilise" all available psychological and physiological resources and, thus, increases the level of stress.

Remember that you need energy not only to talk to students, patients, or clients but also to switch between activities. It is hard to say what exactly requires so much energy—switching or the fact that one has to retain in mind different types of information or both. Anyway, frequent switching may be as exhausting as emotional labour.

Third, there was one factor that appeared in all our examples—chaos. Chaos can increase the necessity of switching between tasks. Moreover, chaos implies a lack of planning. Here, we would like to remind you of the monologue by Joker in the hospital (perfectly performed by Heath Ledger). "If something is not part of the plan, however terrible this plan might be, it blows our minds!"

Summarising, burnout is a very individual phenomenon—every person would have her or his reasons for experiencing burnout. At the same time, there are some common elements that one may find if he or she analyses the causes of burnout associated with his or her work. "Let's make it worse" is a scarily good tool for identifying both universal and individual predictors of burnout.

4.2 Individual vs Process Management?

In their book on foundations of strategy, Grant and Jordan (2015) write that a capability should be rooted in a firm's processes and not in individuals. If not, it is not an organisational capability: as soon as a certain individual leaves the firm (because of a better offer, sickness, or retirement), the capability disappears. In the event of burnout, the logic seems to be the opposite: it should not be rooted in the firm's processes as it is a very individual phenomenon, correct?

Wrong! Indeed, each individual might have her or his own propensity concerning job demands and job resources. But here is the trick: process-related tasks involve many informal interactions. For this reason, we think in a firm one should not focus on (formal) processes but on routines. Routines are rather the organisational habits (Cohen 2007; Winter 2013). These habits accompany the organisational processes. For instance, a process consists of a series of tasks. Formally, all can be found in a process description (tasks, roles involved, tools, documents to be used, etc.). Yet, who will accomplish these tasks, in cooperation with which person or team, and in which way is it a matter of rather informal mutual agreement of employees and managers? For instance, when we work on an academic paper, we have something like "internal specialisation". Some scholars take care of statistics and modelling, some focus on theory development, and some focus on the dissemination of the results among, e.g. practitioners. The process of academic writing became a set of habitual interactions and mutual role allocation. Technically, the process remained the same but the interpretation of the process found an expression in the form of an organisational habit.

Here is another example of Mary. She is very good at working with students. Indeed, we have our faculty quality assurance processes to help students with their studies. These processes are abstract descriptions and are interpreted differently in each department. Our colleagues from the neighbouring department might have more professors and research assistants who regularly interact with students. We have Mary. We think we all tried hard but she was the best in this regard. So, she focused on the role of a communicator and stayed at the interface with the students, while we took over other aspects of quality assurance with which Mary feels uncomfortable, e.g. documentation and official communication. Following this example, you may agree that every individual finds her or his place in the landscape of organisational processes. We develop our habits—we already know who is going to do what, when, and how.

Of course, if one of the tasks or roles is causing trouble for the person, we may focus on the issue. But wouldn't it be better if we dealt with the process at its core and not with the accompanying informal agreements? Moreover, those who are involved in specific tasks or roles (matching their expertise and psychological predispositions) might greatly profit from a systemic approach and reduce their burnout-related activities even further. If you refer to the formal process, you automatically have an impact on all the people involved and their mutual agreements.

Imagine that we find a way to reduce unnecessary interactions with students. There are a lot of interesting things to discuss with students, yet the discussion on the number of credit points for an internship abroad is not the most pleasant one. The countries and the internships are too different to make an easy decision. Since students have an emotional bias because they want to visit a certain country or company, and since we have a limitation due to available places at the partner universities or companies, the conversation becomes emotionally demanding. However, if we introduce a coherent table with detailed requirements, non-eligible students won't need to apply for internships and the problem would disappear. This would help Mary as well as other professors and research assistants in the neighbouring departments. Summarising, correct process (re)design may help systemically address burnout-related issues even though individuals differ concerning their perception of job demands and job resources.

4.3 Following the Process

There is an interesting exercise in process management—stapling. The goal of the exercise is to understand what a process looks like. Imagine that you would like to describe the process of hiring. You can try to depict the process but it will be easier and much more precise if you *walk* through the process in paper & pencil form, and apply the so-called "Process Stapling" approach (Wofuru-Nyenke et al. 2019; Lambert 2020). Let's assume you have a position to fill. What is this position? What are the tasks? First, you would probably need to talk to other employees involved in this process and ask about what work should be performed. Take a sheet of paper and go collect your first data. Each time you contact involved employees, "staple" their answers as a sheet of paper to your initial document with the initial vision of the vacancy. Second, you go back to your desk and produce a new document, which you staple to the others. Third, you would walk to the HR department to develop a profile fitting the expectations. Please add this step to the pile of process-related activities too. After you have a good description of the vacancy, you can post the vacancy on your firm's website. Then, you announce the new position internally to see whether there are candidates within the firm. Later, you would announce the vacancy on external platforms for job search. You can continue through interviews and the selection procedure until the new employee appears in the office and starts working in the firm.

The "stapling" exercise will help you delineate all activities within the process and understand the overall picture. Moreover, this exercise will help you find out about all interfaces and issues you have in the process. If you then draw a diagram, you might find a way to improve your process. Furthermore, a repetition of the exercise will help you discover variants in the process, media discontinuities, and process interruptions (you will find more on this in the section on process complexity analysis in the next chapter).

Theoretically, you can apply the same exercise to understand burnout-related issues. This time, you should be looking for job demands, i.e. psychological and physiological issues, accompanying each activity in a process. This would help you improve the respective process concerning employees' resources. Imagine that in the first step (when talking to employees involved in similar positions) you will also ask about how they feel and what activities are the most energy-draining. This knowledge would help you find employees and managers with a profile that not only matches the necessary expertise (e.g. "This vacancy requires knowledge of JavaScript and PHP") but also their psychological predispositions (e.g. "In this role, you will be required to interact with end users on a weekly basis and have conversations about the negative and positive feedback regarding the project progress."). This added line of text might discourage all those candidates from applying who suffer from emotional labour. Yet, those who like interaction with clients would find the vacancy appealing. Their level of emotional exhaustion will be lower at the end of the day as compared to a regular JavaScript and PHP programmer, wouldn't you agree?

Alternatively, you can apply this "stapling" approach and focus on any other process and employees involved in performing related tasks. What if you follow an employee during a workday and "staple" all activities? Observing her or his reactions, you might understand which activities are energy-draining. As you already know about job demands and job resources, you know what to focus on, when you perform the burnout-stapling exercise: interactions with other people (e.g. clients, partners, peers), especially those which require emotional labour; over-demanding or under-demanding tasks (e.g. boring work); high mental demands; bureaucracy; role conflicts; work-home conflicts, etc. (look for more details at the work by Schaufeli (2017) on the job demands-resources model).

After you have collected this data, you can apply two visualisation techniques. First, you can draw a process diagram using UML or any other modelling language. Here you should add information on burnout-related activities. For an employee, you can create a work description including indications of tasks which require a psychological or physiological investment from the employee. Feel free to add some colour codes, e.g. red for highly demanding activities, yellow for activities with moderate job demands, and green for neglectable job demands. You can take a further step and add information on job resources! As we previously discussed, some activities may bring energy to the employee. What if you mark these activities with stars? One star for slightly energising work, two stars for activities bringing a moderate level of energy, and three stars for activities that make one happy. You can use a five-star ranking if you want to be as precise as Amazon in its evaluation of products. Try to find your way to depict job demands and resources on a process chart. You can also look for our solution in Chapter 6 of this book (e.g. Fig. 6.26).

4.4 Visual Process Management

In process management, we use a variety of ways to depict tasks, activities, related IT systems, responsibilities, etc. We usually think in pictures. That is why we apply graphical notations (e.g. flowcharts) to describe processes. But we can also use visualisation to indicate issues with resource supply. Imagine that you have some tools (e.g. hammers, screwdrivers, scissors) which have to be present at a specific workplace. How to notice if something is missing? How to know if someone borrowed a tool or left the tool at the wrong place? A visual board may help you with this. Imagine that you have a board with mounts for the named tools. If you paint the board black and add the white contours of the tools, the missing tool becomes apparent. At the end of the workday, one would always notice that a certain tool is not in place (Fig. 4.1). This simple idea visualises a problem and allows addressing it immediately.

Theoretically, you can apply visual techniques for burnout indication too. If you visit Frankfurt Airport, you can find three buttons at the exit from each toilet: a green one with a happy smiley, a yellow one with a neutral smiley, and a red one with a sad smiley. In this way, Frankfurt Airport collects experience

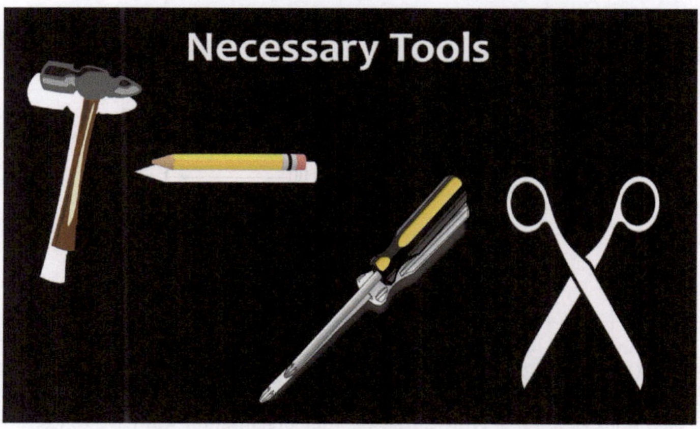

Fig. 4.1 Visual board for working tools

from visitors using their toilets. You can apply a similar technique too: for instance, you can introduce these three buttons in the office building. The issue is, however, that only a few people will make their way to express their emotions. That is why we propose a second option: introduce more buttons to your lift. What if when you come and have to go to your 4th floor, you can press one of three 4th-floor buttons? Each button has a smiley on it (Fig. 4.2).

Such an approach will help you not only capture the emotions of your employees and managers when they come to work or during the day. With an according algorithm, you can identify emotions when your employees move between floors. Even if you are not able to identify who pressed the button (which would not be allowed and is not wanted here)[3], you may find a sign for issues in communication between the floors. In one of the firms Yevgen used to work at, they had the floors dedicated to a specific department—top management was sitting on the top floor, beneath were the financial and controlling department, followed by the engineering department on the

Fig. 4.2 Capturing emotions in a company's lift

[3] Please pay attention to the General Data Protection Regulation (GDPR) in Europe, Regulation 2016/679 (lex-32016R0679) (Regulation 2016). According to the GDPR, you cannot collect and store individual data without explicit permission. The regulation also emphasises the existence of other legal bases for data processing for specific purposes. Your organisation will have to assess which lawful basis is appropriate for specific data processing activities and ensure compliance with the requirements of the GDPR.

next level down, and so on. The building of the Frankfurt School, where Jüergen works, follows a similar approach—faculty sits on the 3rd and 4th floor, bookkeeping and controlling on the 7th floor, and the president sits on the 8th (highest) floor. Usually, you can observe that the mood changes depending on the floor one has to go to. At Yevgen's firm, the highest level of distress was experienced by those who had to visit the top floor. Although it was obvious to all employees, the top management did not seem to notice the issue. Perhaps a system which delivers systematic data in this regard could help a management team reduce stress in the organisation by changing their behaviour or by delegating part of the work to middle-level managers who are closer to employees and able to manage daily issues with a lower level of stress.

4.4.1 Take a Smile—Give a Smile!

It is not easy to capture the emotional climate in an organisation. One reason is that the organisation is simply too big to make an easy estimation. As you can imagine this estimation might also differ between organisational units, locations, etc. However, sometimes the complex issue can be addressed in a very simple manner, as Yevgen's example below shows.

Once when I was working hard on my PhD in Frankfurt (Oder), I noticed a sheet of paper at the door of my colleague. She had written a simple note: "If you are happy, give a smile. If you are sad, take a smile." The lower part of the sheet was cut into stripes with smileys. In the middle, she had glued a small envelope. I tore a stripe and put it into the envelope—I gave her my smile (Fig. 4.3). *I noticed that there were fewer smileys in the envelope than the missing smileys. Obviously, some people "took a smile" with them. It was a funny and good way to estimate the emotional climate at the university. Can you imagine something like this in your organisation? What message would you write to find out the level of burnout? Hint: there are many types of smileys ...* 😈 🙂

4.4.2 Creative Students' Ideas

As a part of Yevgen's class "Business Psychology", he asked his students to apply their knowledge from process management to burnout prevention.

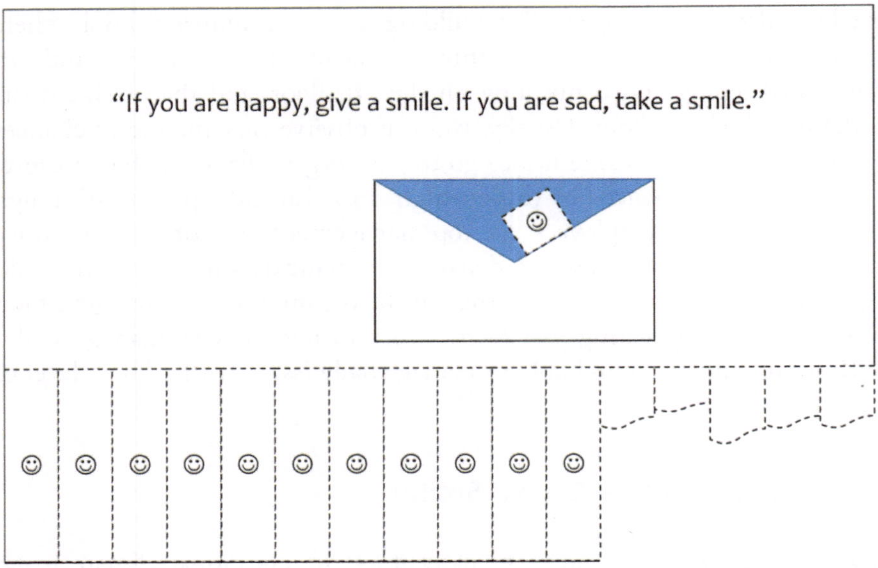

Fig. 4.3 Example of a simple data collection on emotional climate

He asked them to propose some simple visual tools that could help indicate (early) psychological problems. We would like to show you some of the solutions (of course with the students' permission).

Sarah Arrenberg suggested the creation of transparent tubes for "mood chips". Ms Arrenberg stuck to the theory of Herzberg (1974) and proposed to subscribe plates with tubes as "Hygiene factors", "Motivators", and "Private circumstances". Each group got three transparent tubes, each tube had the same inner diameter as a chip. The chips were provided in three colours: green ("everything is perfect"), yellow ("ok, but could be better"), and red ("improvement is needed"). Finally, she received a nice "bar chart" formed by chips. The bars indicated not only the mood but should also provide the management with ideas about which issues could and should be addressed first (Fig. 4.4).

Simon Drewes thought about the task in a different way. As coffee is something most people love and drink during the day (especially in Austria), he proposed to offer cups in different colours. If one is in a sad mood, she or he can take a blue cup. If one is happy, a green one would indicate her or his good mood. This tool would help display emotion at work. Maybe those who are sad might receive some support from their colleagues or, at least, not get overloaded by some emotionally demanding tasks (e.g. communication with problematic clients).

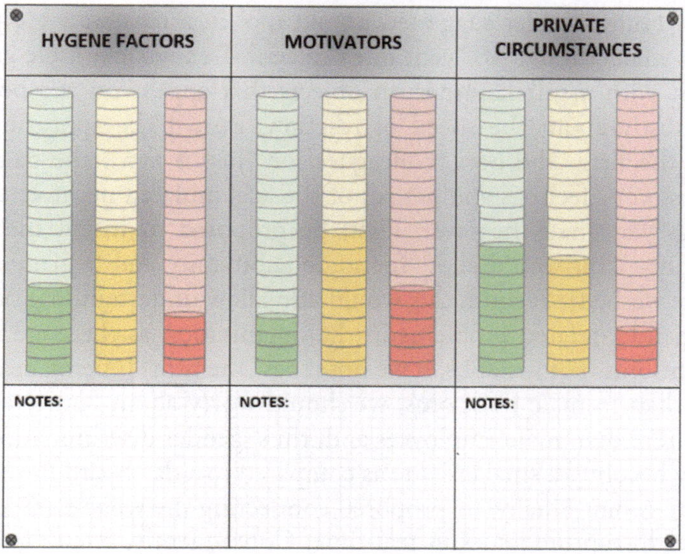

Fig. 4.4 Motivation indicator *Source* Drawing by Sarah Arrenberg

However, Mr Drewes went further—what if people wouldn't like to share their emotions with others? Not everyone is happy when being asked about her or his sadness. Mr Drewes proposed the cups may not be in a specific colour, but only have a coloured bottom. In this way, one could take the cup fitting the person's mood without showing it to others. At the same time, the staple of cups with specific bottom colours would become shorter, indicating to management and other employees how the emotional climate in the firm is.

Marco Hanser proposed to install a dart game. The dartboard should be divided into three segments: red for "very unsatisfied", yellow for "neutral", and green for "very satisfied" state. The darts should also be in different colours. To indicate "because of what": red for self, yellow for managers, and green for "overall".[4] Theoretically, one could build a statement like "I am very unsatisfied because of our management" or "Overall, I am very satisfied". Each employee could try "playing" darts. On the one hand, the game might evoke a willingness to engage in "surveying". It is fun. If one misses, she or he can throw again. On the other hand, the difference in colours makes the visual tool very "visual". Many green darts on the red field would indicate that it is time to work on job satisfaction in the firm.

---

[4] For us "overall" is a bit confusing, but Mr Hanser had his own vision about the tool. We would, by contrast, add the darts for "peers", "students/clients", and "no idea because of whom".

Thomas Hundsbichler suggested an old tool in a new way. He proposed to install a whac-a-mole[5] to "vent one's spleen". In a whac-a-mole game, you have to hit with a soft hammer on objects that appear on the board. The game is mostly about the speed of reaction. But, if the appearing objects would be the firm, the boss, colleagues, or "just 4 fun", the game might help express your feelings and get rid of the accumulated negative emotions. Two things were new, however. First, he proposed to install the game in the restrooms. This would allow for some anonymity and hygiene (after the hands were washed). Second, this would also allow understanding of whether there are gender-related problems in the organisation as there are male and female restrooms. For instance, if we note that "the firm" is being beaten more in female than in male restrooms, we should worry about female employees suffering more than male employees and, thus, gender discrimination. Third, anonymity becomes a smaller issue as compared to a dartboard in the kitchen or common room. Finally, he proposed connecting the whac-a-mole game to a computer to capture issues in real-time. Consequently, one might know if there are salient issues that should be addressed.

Finally, we would like to mention the proposition by Matthias Plank, who suggested installing boxes with chocolates. The better one feels, the smaller the piece of chocolate she or he should take. There are two advantages: First, chocolate is already a little cure—it makes (many) people happy. Second, you can easily see what kind of chocolate pieces quickly disappear.

As you can see, there are "plenty of ways to skin a cat". If you trust your employees, they may propose their own ideas to indicate issues with stress. Don't forget to think about anonymity: our emotions and our feelings belong to us. If you would like others to share their feelings, you have to reassure them that they will not be punished in any way for their honesty.

4.5 Tarot Cards: What About a Little Magic?

4.5.1 The Devil Is in the Details

Things are much easier, if you know what you are looking for and if you know how to measure it. But what if we don't know what we need? What if we need to discover something new? How can we approach the unknown issue? For this, we need to change the way we think. Instead of measuring what we intend to measure, we need to remain open and try to let the information

[5] https://en.wikipedia.org/wiki/Whac-A-Mole.

flow. Once we have acquired sufficient information, a certain aspect or a new phenomenon might become clear. In this way, you may discover hidden issues or new ways to handle the problem at hand.

Usually, observation or a survey with open-ended questions helps. However, we would like to recommend to you one more method for understanding the root of the cause: tarot cards. This idea goes back to a funny story: Once in Ukraine, Yevgen watched a TV series in which one of the actors used tarot cards. When he went to the bus station, he saw a street seller offering stationery: pencils, newspapers, cheap soft-back notebooks, and the tarot deck. It was just a cheap deck of cards (1 EUR?) but he wanted to have one. Yevgen bought it and put it in his bag and later forgot about it.

Some months later, Yevgen had a business trip to Kyiv. As the HR manager of a small firm, he needed to select personnel for our new Kyiv affiliate. He was accompanied by a colleague holding a PhD in psychology. Together they planned to conduct interviews and preselect five candidates.

The first part of the business trip was pretty easy: they interviewed a dozen candidates, discussed their capabilities and agreed on five candidates. Then they were invited into the room of the director of the affiliate: It seemed that the selection of candidates was only a reason to invite both to Kyiv. The other (main) reason was a problem with one of the employees. It appeared that some information had been leaked to one of the competitors. Something had to be done in this situation.

The situation was not clear at all: The director did not want to disclose all the details because the subject was sensitive to her personally. Both the director and the psychologists looked at Yevgen in expectation of a solution. And, all of a sudden, an idea sparked in his brain. Yevgen proposed to apply the "novel projective" method. He took the deck of cards and said that he would lay the cards in a cross—the card in the middle describes the current situation. He took one of the cards (he cannot remember which it was) and let the director speak what the card tells her. Interestingly, the psychologist joined the conversation. Yevgen received a wealth of information about the smallest details of the situation. Moreover, the director herself came up with new unnoticed aspects of the problem, e.g. process (in-)transparency, security issues due to low motivation, matrix structure of a rather small organisation, etc. Yevgen put the next card to the left with the words "This card describes the past and explains why the situation arose". He said only a few words and the discussion started again. When they got stuck, Yevgen explained an element of the card, e.g. "red colour stands for material issues, blue—for spiritual". It was enough to reignite the discussion. Then came the card on the right for "future awaiting us if we don't do anything". Then the card below for "This is how we could deal with the situation". Finally, the card on the top was for "What future awaits us if we do this 'anything'" (Fig. 4.5). It was one of the most productive data collections in Yevgen's life.

Fig. 4.5 Tarot deck for issue discovery *Source* Wikimedia

Fig. 4.6 Examples of tarot cards *Source* giftedMG at Pixabay

Imagine that you draw the card "Magician" or "Death" for the Future (Fig. 4.6). What would these cards tell you about your problem? Would "Magician" indicate your power over the situation? Or do you see some other manager ("Magician") pulling the strings of power? What does "Death" mean to you? Is it an indication that you should end your involvement or, vice versa, does the card want to tell you that the process, as you know it, is "dead" and you need to develop a new one? As you see, it is all about your interpretation. Put differently, your intuition might know the reason for the problem and may even have a solution. But to let your intuition speak, you need to give it a stimulus—a card with an abstract picture. Try it out!

4.5.2 Writer's Block

This method may help overcome other issues, we argue. Are you familiar with "Writer's Block" or any other situation when you get stuck in a task and don't know how to move on? It was Yevgen's second great application of this method. And it also has to do with burnout.

A friend of Yevgen was close to the state of burnout. She was in the late stage of her PhD thesis but she experienced writer's block, i.e. the state when she was unable to produce any text. Writer's Block was just a consequence of the difficulties in her life. Yevgen didn't know about that as she was always smiling and looked fine. Once she came to his office and, out of a sudden, told him that she didn't know how to proceed. Yevgen was surprised as he did not know the root of the cause. However, he remembered the tarot deck (which, by the way, was in the same bag and had not been used for 3 years, i.e. the story above). She agreed.

Yevgen made the same game—past, present, future, alternative present, alternative future. The effect was inspiring—she said that she understood what was the reason. She didn't tell Yevgen what it was but she understood it for herself. Only one hour later she wrote some pages for her thesis. And some pages the next day. And so on. Later she told Yevgen that it was the stress due to the overlapping of her personal and work life. So, maybe it was not the state of burnout but it was an imbalance between job demands and job resources at work accompanied by similar issues at home. Yevgen is proud that they identified it before the problem became serious.

By the way, this story has a sequel. Two years later, Yevgen changed his employer and worked in Bavaria. He received an unexpected call from her: "Yevgen, I am in trouble again and cannot write", she said. "Could you lay your cards, please?" Yevgen said that it might not work: it is important that she sees the cards and listens to his interpretation of the picture—is it upside-down or straight, and what are the colours? She responded that it wouldn't matter—she would google the cards and see them online. She tried it out and it worked again. So, it was not about Yevgen's "magical" deck, nor was it about what he said—she just needed a stimulus for her intuition to be able to write.

4.5.3 Why Does It Work?

As you can imagine, we do not believe in tarot. Yet, the effect is visible. We think it is not the future that we see but the art of projective psychological methods: each time we see a card, we "project" something from the unconscious part of our mind. We interpret and look for inspiration within ourselves. Instead of facing the same mind-walls we developed (e.g. "I know my problems well enough, I am just insecure"), we are forced to discover an alternative explanation (e.g. the card "Emperor" might remind us of the role of a parent, a good friend, or a manager in this situation). This small impetus may ignite a new argumentation for our brain. Again, if one gets stuck in the picture, there is the colour, the straight or the turned position of the card, the background, etc. Moreover, restriction by time (past, present, future) helps introduce structure to the thoughts. People love structure and look for it. We love to believe that there is a cause and an effect.

4.5.4 What Is the Problem with the Method?

We see two problems related to this method. First, we impose limits on individuals. Introducing a structure (time, form, shape, story) restricts individuals. Open questions would be much better for data collection and problem identification. Yet, our experience shows that open questions are not always the best choice. In some instances, cards work better. Maybe you have different experiences. If so, do what works best for you.

Second, we not only interpret the cards but also the answers. We filter out everything we cannot or do not want to understand. You could call it "interviewer bias"—not only the person reporting on the situation, but also the person laying the cards is running the information through a sieve of her or his beliefs, values, and mental models. Thus, the final result may be biassed. Furthermore, we may be restricted by the specific card (e.g. "Devil" or "Lovers" may draw attention to certain aspects of the problem and obscure other important issues). What if a card forms a thinking path and drives the interviewee in a specific direction? But, let's be honest, without the cards we would have no additional information at all. Consequently, we assume that having a part of the information is still better than having no information. Of course, one should try to remain open or even ask someone to suggest an alternative opinion or even try to repeat this game in a few days.

Finally, we have to think about the lack of faith. Indeed, some people might see "magic" in tarot cards and believe the cards work. Most people, however, do not expect a manager or a consultant to play a sorcerer. There are two good solutions for this: first, you can always say that you apply it as a "projective psychological tool" and you took exactly tarot cards and not other established tools because everyone heard about tarot and you can save time needed for interpretation and explanation. Second, you can try an alternative method. Below, we talk about the tool that we developed for our students to overcome writer's block. These cards are rooted in the theory of Joseph Campbell.

4.6 The Hero with a Thousand Faces

In his work, Joseph Campbell (2008) argues that all our stories follow a similar pattern. A hero lives in his ordinary world. Then something happens and he has to move away from his place and learn something new to save his place and the people around him. He finds a mentor and helpers, goes through several battles and faces the final ordeal. In this test, his personality dies and is reborn. Finally, he returns to his world and heals it with a new personality.

Which story have you thought of, when you read these lines? Bible and Jesus, or Star Wars and Luke Skywalker? Or maybe Anakin Skywalker? Or maybe Titanic and Rose DeWitt Bukater, who was perfectly played by Kate Winslet? The reason these stories are good, some people argue, is because they follow the "hero's journey" as described by Campbell (Fig. 4.7).

We tried to sketch some cards to depict each stage in the "hero's journey" and you can try to do the same. In contrast to tarot, these cards are rooted in the anthropological notion of Joseph Campbell's monomyth. Moreover, you can add your experience and the environment from your field. For instance, when we exchanged thoughts about the effect of tarot cards, we came up with the idea that we need something for our students. We focused on the

Fig. 4.7 The Hero's Journey, one of the interpretations *Source* Wikipedia; 4chan.org, thread about monomyths, aka the hero's journey

Fig. 4.8 Our Campbell cards, drawn by Veselina Ivanova: the "Ordinary (Students') World" (left), the "Supreme Ordeal" (middle), and the "Helpers" (right, first version of the deck) *Source* Drawings by Veselina Ivanova

Writer's Block and other studying-related issues. That is why our cards are simpler than regular tarot cards and depict situations from student life (see Fig. 4.8 for some examples). If you develop your own version of the deck, you may want to represent situations from business life or even specifics of your company, e.g. logistics, healthcare, or tourism.

4.6.1 Chronological Approach

We see two ways to use these (or similar) cards. The notion of the Monomyth by Campbell proposes a chronological order. The hero moves from the "Ordinary World" via "Refusal of the Quest" towards "Accepting the Call" and "Entering the Unknown", and so forth. This gives you a perfect opportunity to ask people to describe the issue as a "story" following the same steps. Later, you can ask them to use cards to figure out where they are now. As long as they know where they are, they can see the next stage and think about how to get there. Do you remember Negative Brainstorming ("Let's Make It Worse") where you had to conduct a thought experiment to achieve the worst possible results? Our card tool offers the opposite approach—we know the issue and need to overcome it. Moreover, we even know the next step and the whole plot. Theoretically, in the "Road of Trials" you can see the untackled job demands and their negative consequences; in the "Helpers" you may see the job resources that will help you reduce the negative effects of job demands; and the "Supreme Ordeal" might indicate the main battle, e.g. process redesign for burnout prevention. The "Reward" steps will help focus on the positive consequences of process redesign. Finally, "Return" might indicate the shift in organisational values where each person's well-being is valued and does not go at odds with the firm's performance.

Here is one of the visions with regard to the stages in the hero's journey, formulated as actions:

1. (Living in the) Ordinary World,
2. (Receiving the) Call for Adventure,
3. Refusal to Call,
4. (Receiving) Supernatural Aid,
5. Entering the Unknown,
6. (Walking the) Road of Trials,
7. (Facing the) Supreme Ordeal,
8. (Getting the) Reward,
9. Refusal to Return,
10. Return(ing),
11. Restoring the World,
12. (Becoming the) Master of the Two Worlds (Fig. 4.9).

Fig. 4.9 "Master of the Two Worlds" *Source* This is the final version of the card by Veselina Ivanova

You can also add cards for (finding) "Helpers", (standing for the) "Abyss", (crossing the) "Threshold", and other aspects that you find in the work of Campbell (2008).

4.6.2 Current Situation

A chronological order may require a lot of time which we do not always have. You can pick a card and ask the other party to describe it, similar to a tarot. The story should have a beginning and an end. And the shown card should reflect the "culmination" of the story. Here the use of any card helps promote creative thinking. Another approach may be picking cards associated with job demands or job resources may help you restrict the story and narrow it to the main cause of your investigation—burnout.

When telling the story, the interviewee will say something about the reasons for the situation's appearance. Thus, you may get some cues concerning the causes of the problem. The end of the story may indicate a possible solution or how the situation will proceed if a solution will not be found. Again, you have to give full freedom of storytelling to the interviewee and avoid any interference from your side. First, you have already intervened by showing the card. Second, if you intervene during storytelling, e.g. interrupting the story with the question "Do you mean that the process is not efficient or not effective?", it may bias the story. The interviewee will adapt the story to your desire and your vision. So, do not try to intervene or intervene with open questions only, e.g. "What would this mean for the process?".

4.7 Thematic Apperception Test

In the early 1930s, a group of Harvard scholars developed a test which used ambiguous pictures and required participants to write a story about the picture with a beginning and an end, where the picture shown is supposed to be the climax of the story. The scholars developed a set of pictures that were really hard to interpret: a boy looking at a violin with his head between his hands. This is, by the way, an adaptation of the photograph of Yehudi Menuhin—a young violin prodigy (Thematic Apperception Test Research 2004). The most important aspect of this picture is the ambiguous facial expression—is the boy struggling with playing? Or is he eager to start playing? Is he trying to concentrate? Or is he trying to take some rest after playing? This ambiguity gives plenty of room for interpretation. So when you describe this picture or place it at the centre of your story, you are more likely to reflect your own feelings.[6] The Thematic Apperception Test (TAT) is a projective psychological test based on the picture interpretation technique (Murray 1943; Morgan 2002).

There are many ways to proceed with the story. For instance, you may ask your interviewee to focus on

- what was the cause for the event shown in the picture,
- what is happening at the moment,
- what are the emotions experienced by the characters, or
- what is the outcome of the story?.

As you see, this method is similar to the one with Tarot cards or cards developed on the Theory of the Monomyth by Joseph Campbell. The difference is in the pictures: while the monomyth idea is rooted in a kind of chronological order, pictures for the TAT may not build a storyline. If you search for TAT pictures, you will discover, first, that the pictures are a bit outdated and, second, that the pictures do not always fit the topic of process management. For this reason, we would not recommend you use pictures from TAT. Moreover, there is a big debate on the validity and reliability of the method: there seems to be a large discrepancy between different raters concerning the test results (also known as inter-rater reliability). Moreover, those people who saw the same picture again came to different narratives (also known as test–retest reliability). As we cannot look into what happens in an interviewee's head, we cannot be sure that we are measuring what we attempt to measure (external validity) or that we do it in the correct way (internal validity).

Albeit true, the method is still interesting and may help induce creativity while looking for reasons for burnout resulting from our business processes as well as draw attention to previously unexpected unknown issues. You may sometimes lack an understanding of how people feel at work. A picture of a work situation (e.g. talking to clients, presenting, sitting at a desk) with some unclear (ambiguous) aspects may help reveal your employees' and managers' feelings. Therefore, we recommend you try it out. For this, you will need a set of ambiguous pictures which are up-to-date and somehow fit into the firm's background (i.e. if you investigate a logistics firm, using pictures from a bank branch might not deliver the intended results). Another concern that you will

[6] By the way, we know what the boy thought of. They found the main character who inspired this picture—Yehudi Menuhin. He said "*Actually, I was gazing in my usual state of being half absent in my own world and half in the present. I have usually been able to 'retire' in this way. I was also thinking that my life was tied up with the instrument and would I do it justice*?" (Thematic Apperception Test Research 2004).

have to deal with is gender. Apart from the prejudices in society (and there are many prejudices depending on the country or region you collect your data in), there might be a direct association with a specific person. Imagine that you investigate a team with mostly female employees and you show a picture of a male manager (e.g. Figure 4.10). Would the interpretation differ, if there were two female characters? What if the manager would be female and the employee male? How would one interpret the picture if it was the female manager putting her hand on the shoulder of the male manager? What if vice versa? As you see, such details matter and may bias the interpretation.

We see two directions the problem solution: First, prepare a set of similar pictures with different genders or gender combinations. Second, increase the level of abstraction, i.e. use pictures where some aspects (e.g. gender) are not seen (Fig. 4.11, b and c).

And this is the next concern which you have to be aware of: the level of abstraction. Compare the three pictures below (Fig. 4.11). What are the strengths and weaknesses of their usage for projective psychological analysis? Picture (a) is more concrete—one might even associate a specific male person from her or his organisation. Picture (b) is very symbolic. Consequently, one might not associate it with specific persons but with events (e.g. mergers & acquisitions, celebrations, peace, agreement, succeeding in a joint project, etc.). Picture (c) is somewhere in the middle—it is abstract enough not to

a b

Fig. 4.10 Gender issue in data analysis *Source* OpenAI, Dall-E

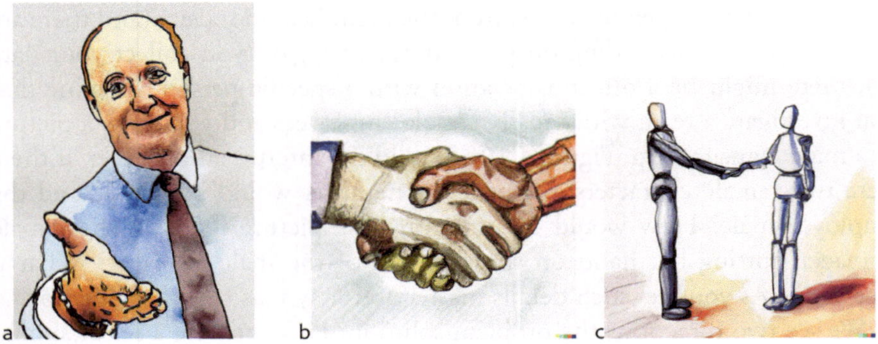

Fig. 4.11 Pictures with different levels of abstraction *Source* OpenAI, Dall-E

associate it with specific people and their gender. At the same time, it shows two people shaking hands.

What we recommend to you, is to work on your own picture set. You and your team have to learn how to interpret your pictures and the related stories. This requires experience. Introducing new pictures each time is not the best idea. However, if you develop a set of pictures that reflect common issues and use them regularly, you can improve your skills in this qualitative method. Again, it is not the most reliable and valid method as each individual has her or his own imagination. Yet, it is a great tool to narrow attention to a specific situation or issue while activating creative thinking.

4.8 Don't Promise when Happy, Don't Decide When Angry

The name of this section comes from a Ukrainian saying (there might be a similar saying in other cultures, we believe). You've got the main idea: emotions affect our decisions. Indeed, research shows that emotions activate a certain type of information processing—the so-called System 1 thinking (Stanovich and West 2000). Moreover, the Feelings-as-Information Theory (Schwarz 2011) assumes that we interpret our emotions as an additional source of information. For instance, fear makes us cautious about details and induces risk avoidance. Anger, by contrast, leads to careless, impulsive actions. Happiness can distort the assessment of the situation by interpreting the situation as more positive than it is (Bogodistov 2015). As you see, there are no simple answers to emotions: even negative emotions may have positive effects while positive ones may have negative impacts on our decision-making. For this reason, in academia, we avoid talking about "positive and negative" emotions and prefer to be more detailed referring to the discrete emotions of fear, anger, surprise, happiness, etc. (Solomon and Stone 2002).

Consequently, be it a good or a bad mood you or your interviewee are in, the information may be biassed. Usually, in process management, we talk about tasks, resources, roles, etc. In this book, we focus on the psychological aspects of process management. We argue that the impact of emotions is an inseparable part of process management. Imagine that you ask your interviewee about aspects of the process of bringing energy or stealing energy. "Bringing energy" might be associated with some types of happiness (joy, aspiration, "fiero" or feeling of having something done and succeeded, pride, etc.), while "stealing energy" might be associated with types of negative emotions (anger due to conflicts, fear due to a threat of failure, sadness because of losing established relationships, etc.).

Our experience shows that if talking about negative aspects of a process, the "negativeness" spills over to other aspects—one starts seeing more problems or related issues than there actually are. Vice versa, if happy, interviewees forget about difficulties or hold them for "less relevant aspects of the process". On the one hand, it is useful information—you can understand how certain aspects are perceived by this specific interviewee. On the other hand, it is still biassed information. The original assessment may be completely different on another day when the mood is different.

From bad to worse, if you are trying to reduce or eliminate burnout, the situation implies that some burnout is already there. Put differently, you may need to interview a person who is already close to burnout or is already in such a state. Can you guess what he or she will tell you about the process and the interactions in the team? Keep in mind that some scholars define burnout as a three-dimensional concept: emotional exhaustion, low self-efficacy, and cynicism are parts of what we call burnout. Consequently, what kind of data can you expect from someone who does not believe in himself or herself and does not see how he or she can positively influence the future (low self-efficacy)? Will cynicism help you collect objective data? What about estimating emotion-depleting aspects of a process by a person who is not willing or not able to show emotions?

As you may remember, there are some ways to cope with the issue:

1. "Time, the healer": you may interview each person at different times to experience her or him in different moods. In this way, you will understand whether or in how much mood biases the answer. If you hear about the problem under investigation in the morning after your coffee break, in the

evening when your psychological resources are depleted, on Monday and on Friday—can get an approximately objective picture of the matter.
2. Increase the sample: interview more people—the more people, the better the information about the process. It is unlikely that all employees involved experience burnout. So, the average understanding of the problem will be close to the objective one.
3. Try emotion regulation techniques such as reappraisal (Gross and John 2003). Try to bring your interviewee into a state when the communication is less biassed. You may ask your interviewee to think about something neutral. At least, you could interview the person not at her or his desk, but in a cafeteria—this small shift in atmosphere may help you collect data of better quality.

Finally, it is crucial to understand that the affective state of the interviewer matters even more. You as the interviewer will spread your ideas in all interviews. If you are in a bad mood, you may either ask biassed questions (e.g. "So, and how bad are things today?" which implies that something was and is assumed to be bad) or interpret answers in a biassed way. That is why we recommend you always make a break between data collection and data interpretation. And before using the information, try to put it aside for some time. It does help!

A Bad Reviewer

Once I was asked to review a paper. As always, such inquiries come at the wrong time: I urgently had to prepare for a new management course. Moreover, a paper of mine had been recently rejected, and my supervisor expected me to develop a new questionnaire for this study. Nevertheless, I printed out the manuscript and started reading it. Oh my gosh, the authors applied qualitative methods! Moreover, in a wrong way—they had a theory and instead of collecting quantitative data to prove/reject it, they started with interviews! And the number of interviews was way too small! Although the authors said that their interviewees were from top management, I did not trust them (e.g. in a small firm with 9 employees there may be three "C-level" managers as in Ukraine, you often have 1 CEO, 1 CFO, and 1 CTO even in tiny companies. But they are not comparable with managers of large companies). I was done with the review at the end of the day. Luckily, I had

not yet submitted it. The next day, I took the manuscript one more time in my hands. Actually, the paper was well written. On page 3, the authors said that they focused on three big market players. Consequently, my assumption about top managers was wrong. I read the paper again. Even the methodology was right—the authors aimed to find new aspects in the existing theory and not just to test it. I noticed that instead of being rejected, the paper was worth accepting with major revision (there were plenty of weaknesses, but not as many as I estimated initially). Thus, I changed my mind and my decision. Imagine how much time the authors spent on data collection and writing this manuscript. Imagine that this manuscript reflects a part of someone's PhD and the work of her or his life. Isn't it worth it, to put the job aside for some days and have a new look at it? It may not only make one happy, but it may also help the whole society.

4.9 The Root Cause

There is an interesting exercise in process management. Each time you encounter an issue which you would like/need to resolve, ask "why?". Example: If the thermometer shows a temperature which is way too high, you need to find out why. Is the thermometer broken or is it just hot in the room? Why is it warm in the room? Is the air conditioner not working? Why not? Is it a temporary issue or is it a systematic problem? Why? ...

With regard to a social issue, the procedure is very similar—you ask the question "why?" and look for the cause. What is different is the number of layers you have to go through. The rule of thumb of "5 whys" shows you how deep you have to dive into the case.

Let us take an example: Tamara, one of our best employees in the field of marketing, starts to underperform.

1. Why? She is tired of the stress of working from home.
2. Why? It seems that the number of tasks she has to accomplish has remained the same but switching between tasks has become more difficult. Earlier, on the way from the office, she managed to stop thinking about work-related issues and could focus on home tasks.
3. Why? The ride home and the related thinking time disappeared as in working from home you are sitting at your home office and your external office "simultaneously". There is simply no time for switching.

4. Why? It seems to be an ability or a skill to turn off thinking about work-related (or, vice versa, family-related) issues. This ability seems to be unevenly distributed among people. Tamara seems to lack this skill.
5. Why? It has never been the goal of the firm Tamara works at, to develop this skill. Before the Covid pandemic, it was not an issue, no one took care of it.

Now, having the "5 whys" answered, you got a much better overview of the problem as well as you found some hints for the problem resolution. For instance, on the individual level, you may want to offer Tamara support and give her more freedom in her job design. What if you offer her more of the tasks she can accomplish faster (and, thus, stop thinking about tasks in the pipeline)? What if you offer to focus on those tasks which are closer to family-related tasks? A task to develop a new commercial might be a good task you can accomplish not sitting at the computer but while walking your dog! For such tasks, the brain needs space and time and many creative ideas come up when you are on the Bus, in Bed, or Bath (3-B-rule [Michalko 2001]). Maybe you can use the lack of switching ability (between home and office) as a competence for creative tasks.

At the organisational level, you can, first, redesign processes to find an adequate variety of tasks for Tamara. No variety is as bad (i.e. boredom, monotone work, boreout) as too much variety (stress, overload, constant switch between tasks). Try to find the "golden mean"! Second, think about introducing training on task switching! If working from home is going to dominate the way Tamara works in the company, specific training in this regard is a good long-term investment! We can also think about an (online) meditation class and the introduction of 3 times 5 minute meditation breaks in everyone's work routine. Also, apps and online tools available for meditation may help understand what meditation is and integrate it into your daily routine. Simplified, meditation is a way to learn to manage your thoughts and shift your focus from "monkey mind" towards inner silence. They call our irregular state "monkey mind" because apes are very active and jump from one tree to another as you do when you jump from one task to the other. Focusing on breathing may help you "turn off" chaotic thinking. With some training, you learn to turn off thoughts that uncontrollably pop up, get into a state of inner calmness faster, and remain focused on what you want to accomplish. Studies show that meditation helps reduce stress in a variety of work situations (Tsai and Crockett 1993; Galantino et al. 2005; Bostock et al. 2019).

4.10 Why Not Simply Use the Existing Tools?

Of course, if you deal with burnout prevention in your firm you could apply existing tools for measuring the state of your employees and managers. There are several tools suggested in the literature. In this book, however, we will focus on the Copenhagen Burnout Inventory (CBI).

First, we are not in favour of the Maslach Burnout Inventory (MBI). It seems that the operationalised dimensions of the questionnaire are independent (i.e. they measure three different work-related aspects) and do not seem to deliver a strong construct of burnout (Kristensen et al. 2005). While emotional exhaustion is at the core of burnout, the dimensions of personal accomplishment and depersonalisation should be treated as separate constructs. Issues with personal accomplishment seem to be a consequence of emotional exhaustion and not a part of it. Depersonalisation is not a state but a mechanism of coping with work-related issues such as increased emotional job demands.

Second, we like it if a questionnaire is proven and openly available. The CBI can be found in an academic paper and can freely be used by anyone. We contacted Professor Kristensen via ResearchGate[7] and he expressed no concerns about usage and translation. Nowadays, you can find several translations on ResearchGate or request permission (via ResearchGate) from Professor Kristensen. There are also other questionnaires which you can find in academic papers. For the MBI, you have to pay as it is distributed by a commercial organisation.

Third, you should keep in mind that it is an ethical issue if you want to test some employees. It is more than suspicious if you pick those whom you expect to have trouble and ask them to take a test. We recommend you survey the whole firm or unit. With this, you may discover issues with those employees who never indicated signs of emotional exhaustion. Furthermore, it is less suspicious and no attention is directed towards specific employees. You can even try to make it a regular practice. For instance, we collect data on burnout among Ukrainian physicians on a yearly basis. Honestly, yearly is not sufficient but monthly would be way too often. We recommend a quarterly survey as a part of your organisational evaluation routine.

---

[7] ResearchGate is a social network for researchers. We publish our projects, latest findings, and papers there (if the publisher allows it); we also ask questions on theory and methodology and receive answers from our peers worldwide. Below each paper, you can find a comments section or you can contact the scholar directly if she or he is a participant of the network. And most of them are.

4.11 Can Burnout Appear All of a Sudden?

We would like to share an interesting conversation we had recently had with one of our students. He told us about a certain situation in his life. In his family, they had a rapid appearance of burnout of his father. No one noticed the problem until it happened, and the burnout seemed to come out of the blue—in a single evening. He asked us whether there are ways to predict burnout earlier and how to prevent it.

Once, Ernest Hemingway (2006) wrote: "How did you go bankrupt?"—"Two ways. Gradually, then suddenly". In fact, changes build up slowly but then appear quite abruptly. The Resource Conservation Theory by Hobfoll (2001; Hobfoll and Shirom 2001; Hobfoll et al. 2003) assumes that we have a certain amount of energy that we deplete during our work and recover at home (simplified explained). If you use the metaphor of a car's fuel tank, you simply use some fuel during the day and replenish the tank at home. If you use slightly more than you replenish, then one day the tank may be empty and the car will stop. How can you prevent this situation? There are several ways to predict burnout: First, there might be some early indicators of burnout (like the fuel gauge in your car). If someone is exhausted not only once but regularly or constantly, he or she is depleting too much energy at work (or at home if we talk about working from home). This "regular" appearance of fatigue and exhaustion is the first early indicator of burnout. The problem is that, in the event of a car, the manufacturers put the fuel gauge in front of your eyes, right behind the steering wheel. And if you get down to the last 5 litres, you even get an optical warning. It seems that in our society having enough fuel on the highway is more important than mental health, as we stigmatise talking about emotional and physical tiredness at work, don't you think?

Second, if you notice signs of low self-efficacy, according to Kristensen and colleagues (2005), this might already be a consequence of burnout. Self-efficacy is about your self-belief and belief that you will succeed in an endeavour. Understanding self-efficacy might be easier than one thinks. Simply ask your employees and managers questions like "Hey, what about introducing your new idea at work tomorrow?" or "What do you think about your role in the project?". You will notice whether the person believes that she or he can succeed in the respective endeavour. You will know whether she or he believes in herself or himself.

Third, if the person is distancing herself or himself from work and behaves cynically, this could be a sign of an approaching burnout. Do you remember the Resource Conservation Theory? Cynicism is a way to "save your resources", e.g. not to involve emotionally in activities and interactions with other people. While Maslach and followers would see cynicism as a dimension of burnout, Kristensen and followers see cynicism as a coping mechanism, i.e. people approach a burnout state and (intuitively) try to reduce the negative impact of job demands by behaving cynically. As we say in Ukraine "It is good to be cynical: you are either right or pleasantly surprised".[8]

Fourth, look at the work of this person. Are the processes clear? Are there any issues such as emotional labour involved? Is there any organisational change or are there other stress factors (new projects, new product launches, delays, etc.)? If yes, burnout will very likely appear if there are no countermeasures (provision of job resources) taken.

Fifth, it doesn't matter how exhausting the work is, you have to care about resource replenishment at home. Even if work is not very stressful, burnout can occur if the "tank" is not refilled or additional energy is used at home. Any indicator of "coming tired to work" is pointing toward problems. Count the number of cups of coffee the person drinks; count the number of times the person says "tired", "sleep deprived", "exhausted", etc.; or look at yawning or read eyes—there are plenty of ways to discover that the psychological resources have not been replenished.

Thus, the person may slowly move towards burnout and once the "tank" will become empty. This will happen all of a sudden to those who did not care about smaller indications earlier.

Here are some other thoughts you should worry about. Think of burnout at home. Burnout may not come from work. We know people who are happy to go to work as they find some rest there from home issues. The energy can be depleted in different places. So, for employees, it might be a good idea to look for signs of burnout "imported" from home.

Unfortunately, burnout is not the worst thing which can happen: clinical depression and burnout have very similar occurrences. There is still a debate about whether depression is the end point of burnout or whether these are two separate issues (Bianchi et al. 2015, 2016). Anyway, you have to be very careful in your observations as in the event of clinical depression simply a day off will not solve the problem.

[8] We heard this expression several times from Olksiy Arestovych—a Ukrainian blogger and x-advisor of the President of Ukraine. Yet, it seems to be a common saying. In his version, Mr Arestovych uses "sceptical" instead of cynical.

I remember an interesting story when I suddenly approached burnout myself. Since it was an organisational phenomenon, I would like to share the story with you.

In the firm I used to work at, we formed about four dominant informal coalitions. We had the "IT coalition", the "financial department coalition", the "logistics department coalition", and the coalition led by the HR department. I used to participate in three of them at different points in time. As you can imagine, each coalition had its goals which it tried to pursue. The whole firm's strategy appeared as a result of negotiations and compromises between these coalitions. The work was stressful but that is how business is done: everyone has an idea concerning the firm's future but only one of the ideas can succeed. This idea is then implemented. The other "coalitions" either accept the decision or sabotage it in all possible manners.

Once, I stood together with my colleagues in the kitchen, and the happy leader of the informal IT coalition entered the room. He announced that his services were recognised and he received a gift from the top management—a flat close to the city centre (which at that time amounted to 80 times of my monthly net income)! And here it comes: several people in our organisation got depressed. It was not because of envy but because of the signal the top management sent to all of us: the strength of the IT coalition grew enormously and the opinion of other coalitions seemed to be of less value. Or, put differently, our role in organisational decision-making became less important. From now on, when there was a discussion, it was expected that the top management would value the position of the IT coalition (and its leader) more than the others. Were the other coalitions and their leaders so wrong? Were their ideas now worse than those of the IT coalition? The gift of our top management skewed the power distribution. This redistribution of power led to negative feelings and a decline in self-efficacy among three-quarters of our employees. We lost the faith that we can shape and further develop the firm.

As you can imagine, in this event the rapid appearance of burnout is very likely. And I did not want to go to work the next day because I knew that whatever I would propose, would be rejected (since I was not in the IT coalition). Isn't it the depersonalisation and distancing from work which makes us feel burned out? Our work was exhausting but we all had hope. This hope disappeared after this disastrous signal.

If hope is one of the drivers for your employees or family members, its disappearance can cause an immediate worsening of the situation! Would you agree?

References

Bianchi, Renzo, Irvin Sam Schonfeld, and Eric Laurent. 2015. Burnout–depression overlap: A review. *Clinical Psychology Review* 36: 28–41.

Bianchi, Renzo, Jay Verkuilen, Romain Brisson, Irvin Sam Schonfeld, and Eric Laurent. 2016. Burnout and depression: Label-related stigma, help-seeking, and syndrome overlap. *Psychiatry Research* 245: 91–98.

Bogodistov, Yevgen. 2015. *Psychological microfoundations and activation of dynamic managerial capabilities: Influence of affective states on managerial behavior*. PhD thesis. Frankfurt (Oder): European University Viadrina.

Bostock, Sophie, Alexandra D. Crosswell, Aric A. Prather, and Andrew Steptoe. 2019. Mindfulness on-the-go: Effects of a mindfulness meditation app on work stress and well-being. *Journal of Occupational Health Psychology* 24: 127–138.

Campbell, Joseph. 2008. *The hero with a thousand faces*, 3rd ed. Bollingen Series 17, Novato, CA: New World Library.

Chiuffo, Facundo Martin. 2019. The "right to disconnect" or "how to pull the plug on work." SSRN Electronic Library.

Cohen, Michael D. 2007. Reading Dewey: Reflections on the study of routine. *Organization Studies* 28: 773–786.

Galantino, Mary Lou, Michael Baime, Maureen Maguire, Philippe O. Szapary, and John T. Farrar. 2005. Association of psychological and physiological measures of stress in health-care professionals during an 8-week mindfulness meditation program: Mindfulness in practice. *Stress and Health: Journal of the International Society for the Investigation of Stress* 21: 255–261.

Grant, Robert M., and Judith Jordan. 2015. *Foundations of strategy*, 2nd ed. Chichester, West Sussex: Wiley.

Gross, James J., and Oliver P. John. 2003. Individual differences in two emotion regulation processes: Implications for affect, relationships, and well-being. *Journal of Personality and Social Psychology* 85: 348–362.

Hemingway, Ernest. 2006. *The Sun also rises.* New York: Simon and Schuster.

Herzberg, Frederick. 1974. Motivation-hygiene profiles: Pinpointing what ails the organization. *Organizational Dynamics* 3: 18–29.

Hobfoll, Stevan E. 2001. The influence of culture, community, and the nested-self in the stress process: Advancing conservation of resources theory. *Applied Psychology = Psychologie Appliquee* 50: 337–421.

Hobfoll, Stevan E., Robert J. Johnson, Nicole Ennis, and Anita P. Jackson. 2003. Resource loss, resource gain, and emotional outcomes among inner city women. *Journal of Personality and Social Psychology* 84: 632–643.

Hobfoll, Stevan E., and Arie Shirom. 2001. Conservation of resources theory: Applications to stress and management in the workplace. In *Handbook of organizational behavior*, ed. R.T. Golembiewski, 57–80. New York, NY: Marcel Dekker.

Kristensen, Tage S., Marianne Borritz, Ebbe Villadsen, and Karl B. Christensen. 2005. The Copenhagen Burnout inventory: A new tool for the assessment of burnout. *Work & Stress* 19: 192–207.

Lambert, Robert. 2020. Process improvement—Staple yourself for brilliant insights. *Cultivated Management*. https://www.cultivatedmanagement.com/process-improvement/.

Michalko, Michael. 2001. *Cracking creativity: The secrets of creative genius*. New York: Ten Speed Press.

Morgan, Wesley G. 2002. Origin and history of the earliest Thematic Apperception Test pictures. *Journal of Personality Assessment* 79: 422–445.

Murray, H.A. 1943. *Thematic apperception test*. Cambridge, MA: Harvard University Press Thematic Apperception Test.

Regulation 2016. Regulation (EU) 2016/679 of the European Parliament and of the Council. *Official Journal of the European Union* 679: 1–88. https://eur-lex.europa.eu/legal-content/EN/TXT/?uri=CELEX:32016R0679.

Schaufeli, Wilmar B. 2017. Applying the job demands-resources model. *Organizational Dynamics* 2: 120–132.

Schwarz, Norbert. 2011. Feelings-as-information theory. In *Handbook of theories of social psychology*, ed. Paul A. M. van Lange, Arie W. Kruglanski, and E. Tory Higgins 1–2: 289–308. Thousand Oaks, CA: Sage.

Solomon, Robert C., and Lori D. Stone. 2002. On "positive" and "negative" emotions. *Journal for the Theory of Social Behaviour* 32: 417–435.

Stanovich, K. E., and R. F. West. 2000. Individual differences in reasoning: Implications for the rationality debate? *Behavioral and Brain Sciences* 23: 645–665; discussion 665–726.

Thematic Apperception Test Research. 2004. *The University of Tennessee Knoxville*. January 6.

Tsai, S. L., and M. S. Crockett. 1993. Effects of relaxation training, combining imagery, and meditation on the stress level of Chinese nurses working in modern hospitals in Taiwan. *Issues in Mental Health Nursing* 14: 51–66.

Winter, Sidney G. 2013. Habit, deliberation, and action: Strengthening the microfoundations of routines and capabilities. *Academy of Management Perspectives* 27: 120–137.

Wofuru-Nyenke, Ovundah King, Barinyima Nkoi, and Felix Ezekiel Oparadike. 2019. Waste and cost reduction for a water bottling process using lean six sigma. *European Journal of Engineering and Technology Research* 4: 71–77.

5

Burnout Prevention Using Process Management Tools

Abstract In this chapter, we show how to conduct process analysis. First, we explain the basic methods such as the "magic" triangle of process management, the eight wastes of Lean Management, and the process design. Second, we show how to apply the same methodology—i.e. the methodology used in traditional process management—to analyse psychological issues occurring in the processes of your company. Next, we introduce the concepts of process improvement and process innovation and explain how these concepts can be applied to your processes when addressing burnout and related psychological issues.

5.1 Finding the Bottleneck

Imagine that there is an order fulfilment process in your organisation. While all your processes work as usual, there is some emotional exhaustion that appears during the work. On the individual level, the SIPOC[1] view might help and works like this: there is a (C) customer—your employee. He or she is influenced by the activities during the day (P, process) which leads to an emotional outcome (O). There is definitely an input (I), i.e. activities which evoke certain emotions. You can call these inputs job demands and job resources. And there are those who provide this input—other processes, people, and the organisation (S, supplier). You can analyse this issue not

[1] SIPOC is a tool from the Six Sigma methodology. It is used to document the suppliers (S), inputs (I), process(es) (P), outputs (O), and customers (C) of a business process. The goal of the tool is to define the boundaries of a process at a high level.

© The Author(s), under exclusive license to Springer Nature Switzerland AG 2024
Y. Bogodistov and J. Moormann, *Process Management and Burnout Prevention*, https://doi.org/10.1007/978-3-031-56615-8_5

on the individual level only. Teams, departments, or specific roles can be approached in the same way.

There are many ways you can analyse process. If we were you, we would start with the bottlenecks. We know a lot about the analysis of bottlenecks from the Theory of Constraints (Dettmer 1997; Goldratt and Cox 2012). In this theory, one should look at the single activities within the process and identify which of these activities is slowing the whole process down. The core idea is that as soon as one discovers the bottleneck, he or she can arrange other activities in accordance with it. The whole process is as fast as its slowest element! Can you apply the same notion to the process of emotional exhaustion? Can we find a way to figure out which activities, situations, or persons drain the most energy? Actually, we can. If you look at the tools from the previous chapter, you can find a number of ideas on how to find the most energy-draining elements. As the whole process is slowed down, emotional exhaustion may impact all other activities this specific employee has to accomplish during the day. While the Theory of Constraints offers rather precise suggestions regarding process redesign, emotion-related aspects should be treated a bit differently. There are some important aspects that should be taken into account:

First, we have the issue of emotional contagion (Wild et al. 2001; Hennig-Thurau et al. 2006; Cropanzano et al. 2017). In contrast to regular processes, where the bottleneck has an impact on the investigated process, the employees transfer emotions to other employees involved in other organisational processes. I.e. the bottleneck for a single employee may produce spill-over effects on other employees.

Second, emotional exhaustion is an individual issue due to the perception of the activities, situations, or people. While the Theory of Constraints postulates that the process can be rearranged or changed, in the event of emotional exhaustion this might not always be the case. If you find a way to shift the perception with regard to e.g. specific events, the process may remain the same, while the impacted employee remains engaged in the same activities with a different point of view on these activities.

Finally, the Theory of Constraints proposes moving the activity towards the end of the process. For instance, if painting a car is the bottleneck as the whole production has to wait for the paint to dry, painting in later steps would be a part of the solution. In the event of emotional exhaustion, moving the emotion-draining components is an unethical step—the exhausted employee will take this state home and the spill-over effects will appear in her or his family. This approach is definitely unethical.

Nevertheless, we can learn a lot from the Theory of Constraints. First, there might be an activity in our meta-process which drains most of our energy and leads to emotional exhaustion. If we identify this activity and find a way to deal with it, all other activities might be performed with more energy and motivation. According to the JD-R model, the balance between job demands and job resources influences two important psychological aspects of our lives: strain and motivation. Moreover, by getting rid of strain in an activity, we reduce the negative spill-over effects mentioned above.

Second, the Theory of Constraints postulates that there are always constraints that reduce the throughput of a process. Although in their book Goldratt and Cox focus on the manufacturing process, the Theory of Constraints can be applied to any organisational process. The theory implies that (a) every process has also natural limitations due to e.g. capabilities of the equipment, and (b) as soon as one constraint is deleted from the process, the next one will appear. This would also apply to those processes that are associated with emotional exhaustion: (almost) each job is associated with psychological and physiological job demands and resources. If an employee is not in the "automatic" mode (see also *amotivation* as mentioned by Rayan and Deci [2000]), there will be some depletion of her or his psychological resources.

Yet, how can one identify the constraint? If you look at emotional exhaustion from the viewpoint of process management, you may find that (as activities are sequenced) emotional exhaustion appears gradually during the working day. We see two options: either all activities are equally emotionally draining (what is not to be assumed) or there are some activities which are associated with a higher level of energy depletion. The latter is a good case for investigation using the Theory of Constraints.

One should, for instance, interview an employee who experiences emotional exhaustion at the end of the day. Here, the interviewer can ask about the activities during the day and list those which were emotionally hard to accomplish. By the way, observation would also work. However, for observation, one would need specific skills in, for instance, a Facial Action Coding System (Ekman and Rosenberg 1997) or a similar instrument. Of course, intuition is also a good starting point, as we are well able to recognise feelings due to evolutionary needs (Damasio 2005).

As soon as the most energy-draining activities are listed, the investigator has to find out which of these activities have the highest impact—this will be the bottleneck. The investigator has to bear in mind, however, that there might have been spill-over effects and the first affective event has influenced the perception of the following events. As you know, we intuitively try to eliminate the unpleasant (energy-draining) activities. This creates a feeling of something unpleasant awaiting you, a kind of "sword of Damocles" that will shape your mood for the whole day. In their book on the Theory of Constraints, Goldratt and Cox propose to keep reorganising the process unless the less efficient activity (i.e. the constraint) is at the beginning. They argue that inefficiencies within a process can be avoided by moving the most inefficient parts forward whenever possible and/or addressing the throughput rate of the slowest element first. In any case, the entire (manufacturing) process is as fast as its slowest element. This leads to two important implications:

1. Have you heard about the "Eat that frog" rule? We know this rule from time management. According to the rule, you should start with the most complex and energy-draining activity ("frog"). Then, the rest of the day will seem to be easy.
2. Take care: following this rule could do harm in terms of psychological problems. If one starts the working day with psychologically draining activities, he or she might underperform in other activities. Moving this activity towards the end of the day is unethical (as explained above). Consequently, you have to estimate what is the optimal way for you. If the issue is assumed to drain a lot of energy, plan a break afterwards. Otherwise, try to solve the problems without changing the order of activities. In the next sections, you can find more information on how to deal with this type of issue.

Although the Theory of Constraints was mostly meant for the manufacturing process, the implications can be used for all types of processes and activities that are associated with energy depletion.

5.2 Make a Magic Tetrahedron from a Magic Triangle

We all know the "magic triangle" of process management: each process has to be viewed through the prism of three dimensions: time, costs, and quality. It is called "magic" because the dimensions are interrelated due to resource constraints. As we say in Ukraine "*We can renovate your flat a) cheaply, b) fast, c) in high quality—pick two out of three!*" Indeed, if you want to produce something cheap and fast, then the quality will suffer. If you want to have high quality for less money, then it will take a while until you get what you want.

You may have noticed that the magic triangle is dependent on resources. The problem we see in this process management approach is that we miss the psychological and physiological resources. Can we compensate them with money? Time? Quality? We assume that the emotional dimension plays a crucial role in process management. In our lives, we have seen too many projects fail and processes get stuck due to staff's inability to perform or manage stress and its consequences. It is the right time to transform the magic triangle into a "magic tetrahedron" by adding a dimension with regard to employees' energy.

If your employees experience burnout they may become detached from the process they work in and this might cause a delay in processing (time) (Maslach and Jackson 1984). Furthermore, if employees suffer from burnout they might get demotivated (Bakker et al. 2014) which will eventually lead to low-quality work. Finally, the costs of the project will increase as the combination of previous arguments and the fact that employees will get dissatisfied and might require a higher salary for the tasks they dislike (i.e. those tasks that require a higher emotional investment). Vice versa, a high workload, time pressure, and pressure with regard to costs may lead to higher psychological and physiological resource requirements and will eventually result in burnout. Shall we still treat business processes by using the lens of a "magic triangle"?

The JD-R model allows for incorporating psychological and physiological resources into process management. We need to use this opportunity to reduce the number of projects which never achieve good results as well as to improve processes (indeed, the notion of a "magic triangle" is used both in process and project management). When making a "magic tetrahedron" from a "magic triangle", we take into account additional factors crucial for the success of our work.

Is the JD-R model the most fitting one? Indeed, one can introduce any dimension to the tetrahedron, as some use a "scope" dimension for e.g. project management. One could go for motivation, level of emotionality, or any other concept from the field of social or cognitive psychology. Nevertheless, not all concepts are easily transferable into the language of process management. Moreover, not all concepts play a role in time-quality-costs relationships. For instance, the concept of psychological distance (Bar-Anan et al. 2006) might be of interest for communication within teams. Even though these concepts have an impact on organisational life, they are not directly related to the time, quality, and cost dimensions of the magic triangle, while the JD-R model can be easily applied without breaking the main assumptions of process management regarding the usage of resources.

5.3 Teach with a Case

What should you start with? We think the most promising way to start is to bring everyone "on board". Most managers were taught in terms of classical process management, where psychological and physiological aspects of work are treated rather tangentially. So how do you explain to them what you would like to focus on? How can you stress the importance of the JD-R model for your firm? Start with a teaching case!

When we are asked what a teaching case is, we refer to teaching with cases as a method of education. A professor provides her or his students with a description of a work situation that includes a problem. Students, in turn, have to solve the problem. This approach combines several cool elements: theory is good to have, yet personal experience plays a larger role. Students analyse the situation looking for clues for the case solution: they go through facts, analyse similar situations from their lives, and take the role of one of the managers involved in the case.

A teaching case is not about a correct solution—it is about the process of problem-solving. The method came from law students, who have a "case"—a controversial issue where each party has their own vision of who is right and who is wrong (Ellet 2018). Through the dispute, students learn not only to argue but also to understand the peculiarities of the situation, different points of view, and the use of different (theoretical) tools. In our context, you might need a similar situation, containing information on time, costs, and quality issues as well as on psychological aspects of the involved managers and employees. If you are successful, your team might come up with the need to introduce an additional axis into the "magic triangle" on their own. We recommend you stick to a short case (1–3 pages) from your (company's) own situation.

Here is a case we developed for such situations. Please bear in mind that the case is related to Yevgen's company and employees from his company can learn from it better than any other employees.

Short Case About the Tetrahedron Model

"Ok, Eugene, you will have to fire someone. Will you do it on your own or shall we take this over for you?" These were the last words in a C-level management meeting when I was asked to reduce the size of my team. It was really painful—we were all in stress and tried to organise our firm's structure. About three months ago our top management decided that we had to grow. It was not just about the number of employees—our logistics firm needed to develop new businesses and enter new markets. On the one hand, we moved from the regional to the international logistics market. On the other hand, we acquired several start-ups and small firms in the fields of ore mining, VoIP calling, and financial services.

Our firm was only five years old, had a strong market position and returns were increasing. Yet, the market of logistics services was saturated and the only way to become rich was to move into other markets. This meant that we had to, first, redesign established processes and, second, we had to introduce a new organisational structure. Indeed, processes are related to the company structure. But in this case, our top management wanted to introduce a completely new structure with the headquarters performing functions of finance, accounting, controlling, HR, and internal IT support. I was promoted to a COO responsible for the restructuring. And I failed.

*The process of change may be represented using the scheme by Kotter (*2011*). Following him, change has to go through eight stages:*

1. *Establishing a Sense of Urgency*
2. *Creating the Guiding Coalition*
3. *Developing a Vision and Strategy*
4. *Communicating the Change Vision*
5. *Empowering Employees for Broad-based Action*
6. *Generating Short-term Wins*
7. *Consolidating Gains and Producing More Change*
8. *Anchoring New Approaches in the Culture*

In our firm, we scored on all eight stages, yet the change did not appear: the top management stressed the need to grow, otherwise we would fail as more competitors joined the logistics market; my department was responsible for restructuring, whereby I immediately started creating a coalition of managers and key employees willing to perform the change; we had a clear vision and strategy, at least with

regard to restructuring; we were also constantly communicating the change; we empowered employees for broad-based actions by setting incentives (and punishment) for following the new values; we even opened a new affiliate and bought a new building (a part of it) for the new businesses which was a good example for a short-term win; and finally, we tried to consolidate gains to generate even more change.
Although we formally fulfilled these steps, we were all stressed:

- *Employees did not really accept the new values and (even being punished) tried to live the old way.*
- *The stress due to restructuring grew as we all had to conduct the old processes as usual whereby the new processes were introduced simultaneously.*
- *The restructuring process has reduced the clarity of roles, as new responsibilities have been accompanied by new subordinations. The existing supervisors and managers still performed old processes (and were expected to deliver profits from them) and—at the same time—new processes (and were expected to show profits there). This led to double or triple subordination.*

These issues are not unique—each firm which faces a change of such magnitude suffers from similar issues. The consequences are also very similar: the key players start leaving the firm, the newcomers are not familiar with the established processes, the quality of services decreases, and the level of exhaustion increases drastically. Eventually, our CEO and CFO decided to let someone go from my department because the change process was not as effective as they thought it should be. Although my whole department suffered from work overload, we were punished for not showing the desired results.

I would kindly ask you to always diagnose the root of the problem.

As you see, this case is a diagnosing case, i.e. you are asked to find the root cause for the described issue—an inefficient and ineffective change process. There is no simple or single answer to this question: the root cause might be the values, the rigidity of the firm, a too-long and "happy life" in an established market, or others. Yet, we would argue that in the case presented above the root cause was the ignorance of the "people issue".

In the plans regarding the new vision, we took into account markets, strategies, structures, and processes. Indeed, we spent a lot of time, money, and effort in designing new business processes that were scalable, profit-oriented, and adapted to the new organisational structure. We just forgot about people: those who work with clients, who suddenly lacked clarity concerning their current and future work, who could not manage a triple subordination, who needed time to learn but were penalised for mistakes in this complex transition. Put differently: from the point of view of process management, we addressed time, costs, and quality dimensions. Did we think about the fourth dimension—employees' energy (reflected in the balance between job demands and resources)? No.

All firms go through similar phases during change and they all face negative consequences of change. We argue, however, that if they would pay more attention to the psychological and physiological aspects of the change process, the negative consequences could be reduced substantially. For instance, one can look at our change process through the lens of time (number of months spent), costs (it was an expensive transformation accompanied by the implementation of a new ERP system), and quality (the envisaged structure is achieved and working). Yet, the introduction of an additional dimension of psychological and physiological demands and resources might have changed the outcome. First, we should have planned the change process in a different way. Second, we probably should have retained key personnel needed for the high-quality services we wanted to offer. Third, we could have saved losses that resulted from inefficient processes, staff turnover, conflicts, etc.

We recommend you to reflect on your own experience and find a good case from your firm where taking into account the psychological aspect could have drastically changed the outcome. If you remain objective, collect some data, and present your case to your team you may get support from their side for the new approach to process management in your firm.

5.4 Eight Wastes and Lean Management

In Lean Management, we talk about eight (seven[2]) wastes in processes which need to be eliminated. The entire Lean Management concept is about a continuous fight against these eight wastes (also known as the acronym TIM WOODS[3]):

---

[2] You may also find a conceptualisation with "seven" wastes. The reason is that "skills" were added later to the list.

[3] If you want to memorise a complex thing, you can apply the following technique. Take the first letters from the key terms and build a word or a phrase from these letters. TIM WOODS sounds like an easy-to-memorise name (and many of our students do believe that it was the name of the "inventor" of eight wastes). But TIM WOODS is nothing but an acronym made of the words Transportation, Inventory, Motion, Waiting, Overprocessing, Overproduction, Defects, and Skills.

1. Transportation, i.e. the unnecessary transportation of a product which the customer is not willing to pay for. For instance, a firm might decide to introduce an additional storage facility to store product parts. The newly created step—transportation to the intermediary storage facility—might not be seen positively from the customer's point of view.
2. Inventory, i.e. equipment or materials necessary for production. Wrong, lacking, or excessive equipment represents a "waste" in terms of time, costs, and quality. The same applies to excessive materials (e.g. a big box full of screws in front of a machine, whereby the place could have been used better as only a few screws are needed for each operation).
3. Motion, i.e. unnecessary movement of product components within a given process. For instance, you may think of a production line where the production units are located at a certain distance requiring each component to be relocated several times during the production process.
4. Waiting, i.e. unnecessary waiting time due to process inefficiencies. For instance, if your production requires painting works the whole production is impacted by the time of waiting for the paint to dry.
5. Overproduction, i.e. a too-fast manufacturing of a larger quantity of products than needed. These excessive products need to be stored somewhere leading to increased storage and transportation costs (as the product is transported not to the customer directly but to an intermediary storage facility).
6. Overprocessing, i.e. unnecessary operations within the process such as double checking. Overprocessing relies on the excessive usage of a firm's resources and leads to higher costs.
7. Defects, i.e. malfunctioning products or products not meeting customer requirements. Such products will be returned causing repair or new manufacturing. Costs are driven not only by the new products but also by the loss of credibility of the firm.
8. Skills, i.e. the wrong usage of employees' skills. This can be either the assignment of tasks to employees not competent in this specific field or the assignment of simple tasks to employees and managers who have a higher potential.

Let us look at these wastes from the viewpoint of the JD-R model. We can draw an analogy, as direct research in this field has not been conducted hitherto. We even asked our students to propose some ideas on which wastes ("muda" in the language of process management) would fit to each of the eight sorts of waste. However, there was no clarity concerning the categorisation of psychological aspects at work as initially wastes were associated with physical resources and processes. For instance, in our research, we discovered that switching between tasks when working from home may induce burnout (Bogodistov et al. 2023). Would you address this issue as a "motion waste" (i.e. switching between "desks" or between the kitchen and your computer), as a "skills waste" (i.e. lack of skills to easily switch between tasks), or as a "transportation waste" (i.e. moving your working process and resources away from the office to your home)? As you will see, the examples below are driven by analogy. We try to extrapolate from physical resources to psychological and physiological resources. Nevertheless, even this approach bears plenty of opportunities: thinking in terms of Lean Management about the psychological issues might help you bring your organisation's business processes to a qualitatively unprecedented level.

1. **Transportation.** There are two main aspects you may want to take into account: physiological demands and psychological demands. In Lean Management, transportation is related to the products or their parts but not to the movement of employees. Consequently, if your process requires a lot of physical load due to an inefficient product line (e.g. distance between production stations) or inefficient organisation (e.g. collecting signatures in different offices), strain might appear. Digitalisation solves some of these issues, indeed. Concerning psychological demands, we would emphasise the transfer of responsibility. Imagine that your product or service is generated by several employees each of whom has a responsibility for her or his activity. Each move to a new production station is related to a transfer of responsibility. One has not only to take over the responsibility for the specific task but also someone has to check that the previous employees managed their duties well. This can be a demanding process. Reduction of this "muda" might make the lives of your employees better. Did you know that one of the recommendations for organisational capability development is to bring involved employees together? Even though online meeting tools help bring people together, they cannot substitute for real communication. We can approach this issue as a transportation issue—the higher the distance between those who are responsible for the same capability (e.g. customer communication capability or dynamic capability), the weaker the capability is. This is due to the "transportation" of thoughts and ideas. Consider ways to reduce this sort of waste, such as creating pathways for thought and decision-making, making communication shorter and more efficient, and removing barriers to ideation.

2. **Inventory.** The physiological aspect is the easiest to investigate. You need to equip your employees with the necessary inventory to reduce physiological strain. For instance, good lamps and big screens may help your employees not only to perform better but also to keep some energy at the end of the day. Another helpful tool is "tabula rasa"[4] in its direct meaning. A requirement to have a clean table might not only reduce the physiological strain but also allow for a feeling of calmness and good organisation which is a perceptive, i.e. psychological, aspect of work. Furthermore, a variation in tasks might help employees reduce their psychological strain. We don't think we have to explain how demanding it is to sit the whole day in front of a monitor. Some variation in tasks, e.g. a short offline meeting, communication with people from another department or visiting the storage facility, might help employees cope with boredom and monotonous work. We would like to describe here another aspect related to equipment: A friend told us about the daily stress he had in the office. His manager decided to save on software. For this reason, he did not have a simple program (such as MS Excel/Google Sheets) but needed to produce all tables and related calculations in a word processor. You see the issue: due to the inventory issues, the whole firm had to perform "stupid" work while substituting the function through a bunch of alternative software. Was it necessary? How much damage was created due to this waste? Could it have been avoided?
3. **Motion.** In the event of motion, in process management we talk about the movement of a person. Physically, this aspect would be reflected by the inefficiencies due to needless movements at the desk (e.g. sorting documents, moving between desks and working places to reach colleagues). Another option would be to look at the distance between the employee's eyes and the monitor, and the position of the chair, possibly requiring constant repositioning of the body and leading to physical fatigue. A psychological equivalent would be the issue of bureaucracy, i.e. the necessity to collect signatures and permissions in order to fulfil a task. On the one hand, bureaucracy might be related to the transportation issue (i.e. physical movements between departments or buildings). On the other hand, we see bureaucracy as a psychological job demand. One has to accept the "weak position" of an "asker", while the recipient is a "giver" providing permission or a (digital) signature. Alternatively, one could

[4] "Tabula rasa" is a Latin phrase meaning "clean slate", i.e. before writing notes on a tablet ("tabula"), you need to clean it (make it blank, "rasa"). The phrase entered different parts of our life from "keeping your desk clean" to "denying of state succession for treaties" in international public law. Here, we refer to the simple usage of the term—"keeping your desk clean".

argue that motion can be seen as similar to work interruption (i.e. when a task needs to be interrupted and the mind has to switch to another task). "Mind walking" between different tasks may increase psychological strain as well.

4. **Waiting.** While it is relatively easy to find an analogy for physiological demands (e.g. boredom or work underload), it might be more tricky to draw a parallel to psychological demands. Indeed, boredom due to work underload or due to an inefficient process resulting in waiting till another employee finishes her or his task may lead to physiological fatigue. In the case of psychological demands, bureaucracy may be seen as a kind of waiting waste. The more hierarchical hurdles you have, the longer it takes to start with your actual task. This might lead to a feeling of low self-efficacy whereby you might stop believing that you can change anything. The locus of control is not by you but by someone else in the hierarchy. Responsibility and role clarity are also process management issues which are related to psychological exhaustion.
5. **Overproduction.** In the event of overproduction, we talk about components which are produced more than necessary. With regard to physiological demands, a good example would be producing more services than necessary. For instance, we have recently discovered that from the broad range of services we offer to our students (such as support with e-library, academic coaching, videos and podcasts with explanations for our lecture) only a few are used. Of the 30 or so videos dedicated to the "Discrete Choice Experiment" method, the students watch an average of four. As for the rest, they simply write us emails with questions. Nevertheless, we are required to produce plenty of learning materials that no one seems to be interested in instead of showing how many "cool things" we offer. Creating all these contents depletes our energy.[5] If the production of such services is accompanied by emotional issues, such as anger, annoyance, or fear of not meeting a firm's expectations, the psychological investment will grow. Other psychological demands that might reflect this waste might be the requirement for redundant communication with customers or introduction of unnecessary deadlines. An interesting suggestion comes from the Self-determination Theory by Ryan and Deci (2000), who suggest that deadlines are killing intrinsic motivation. A deadline is interpreted

[5] In each Learning Management System (LMS), when creating your course for the students, you can either offer just the basic information such as course structure and topics, or you can offer polls, videos, and interactive elements, such as small non-obligatory tasks, for fun. Would you like to guess how many students engage in interactive elements? If we reach 5% of them, we are more than happy. But we still develop these contents, trace and evaluate them, and give feedback to all active participants.

as "the task should be done independently from my state or capabilities" which destroys the locus of control, i.e. my capabilities have nothing to do with finalising the task. Unnecessary deadlines can be a burden on the psychological state of employees. Elimination of unnecessary deadlines and introduction of more freedom into work may help reduce this "muda".

6. **Overprocessing.** This "muda" is pretty straightforward: doing the same tasks twice because you have to review, reevaluate, or make sure of the result is exhausting on both a physiological and psychological level. Some operations require control indeed. However, if an opportunity to automate such processes (including control mechanisms) exists, one should go for the automation. Automation can reduce psychological and physiological job demands in your organisation.
7. **Defects.** As defects relate mostly to the evaluation of the product by clients, we can apply the same logic here. On the one hand, we can look at the customers of the organisation: if they are dissatisfied, the products will be returned followed by negative feedback. Physiologically, defects imply repairing it or producing the product anew. This might be exhausting but not as exhausting as the negative feedback, whereby the customer complains about an employee sharing negative emotions and putting the employees into a high-stress condition. On the other hand, one can look at employees as internal customers of the processes. Each dissatisfied employee indicates that there is a "defect" in the process. This might not necessarily be a defect in the sense of classical process management but in the sense of conflicts or other communication issues. If one finds a way to reduce these defects (e.g. conflicts), she or he might make life in the organisation better. Do not underestimate the issue of abusive supervision—this is one of the "communication process defects" leading not only to psychological but also to physiological exhaustion (e.g. insomnia) (Barnes et al. 2015; Zhang and Liao 2015).
8. **Skills.** Concerning physiological resources, we should take into account the skills to plan our time correctly, to know the correct posture for sitting, and to apply some exercises for our eyes, spine, or neck. In large firms, you often have a physician in your firm who is responsible for literacy in the field of organisation of work. We would also put your skills in the field of meditation into the category of physiological job resources, as mindfulness meditation helps with myocardial oxygen consumption, reduces blood pressure, stabilises heart rate, and, consequently, helps cope with stress at a physiological level (May et al. 2016; Pascoe et al. 2017). Developing these skills in the workplace can keep your employees healthy. In addition,

there are psychological skills which have to be developed and applied. For instance, employees should know how to deal with stress, how to resolve conflicts, how to communicate with other people without bothering them, etc. We would also highlight empathy as this skill is the key to successful communication and smoothly running business processes. You can call this skill Emotional Intelligence (EI) if you like, as empathy is at least a component of EI (Austin et al. 2007). Anyway, this skill can be developed (Serrat 2017) and will increase your organisation's chances of high performance (Côté and Miners 2006). Interestingly, Côté and Miners also show that EI is a compensator for the lack of cognitive intelligence: its effect on performance increases as cognitive intelligence decreases. Take this into account when deciding which "muda" to eliminate and which skills of your employees to develop.

The JD-R model assumes that it is all about balance. Putting it simply, if there are too many job demands, adding more job resources would be a good way to go. Yet, as we have already discussed, this logic might not always hold. For instance, employees might require different job resources to outweigh their resource depletion. This implies a growing complexity with each additional job demand. Moreover, one should bear in mind the issue of job resource inflation, i.e. an acknowledgement is very important but five acknowledgements in a row might not make the situation better or may even make the situation worse.

Consequently, we can apply the logic of process management, in particular of Lean Management, i.e. all wastes should be eliminated. This may bring the balance back. In addition, this approach could bring simple rules (like looking for Eight Wastes) to the complex interplay of job demands and job resources. And with a little creativity, you could find new ways to address an old problem—stress at work.

5.5 How to Eliminate the Eight Wastes?

There is no simple answer to this question. It all depends on the concrete waste you need to eliminate. Some improvements might require simply the installation of a proper table lamp, some might require a process restructuring. Below are some recommendations:

1. Start with those wastes that are easy to eliminate and produce the highest impact. If your observation shows that buying table lamps is easy, cheap, and has a great impact—go for it.
2. Continue with those wastes which have the highest impact on performance. Indeed, changing an organisation's culture is a long way but if you see that it resolves most of the waste, it might be a good investment with regard to time and effort.
3. If you decide to walk the long way through transformation, make a list of wastes that can be eliminated easily. In contrast to our recommendation #1, where we talked about the immediate effects, in a long-lasting transformation you should focus on the snowball effect. If the elimination of one waste enables the elimination of other wastes, the potential chain reaction is of bigger value than the immediate benefit. For instance, buying a lamp (to reduce physiological demands and increase concentration) is easier and the effects are more immediate than installing a new email software (to reduce data complexity and simplify work with information). Yet, if the email software allows you later to address work with clients, calendar planning, coordination of meetings with team members, etc., you should start with this waste first (to reduce the complexity of incoming information streams and overprocessing of data). It is extremely important to communicate the expected chain effects to your employees and managers to gain their support.
4. Always show the effects of your actions! Employees (and other managers) do not notice if things are fine. Consequently, it can happen that no one appreciates your efforts. Therefore, announce what has been done and what is the difference from the previous state.
5. Try to measure everything. Measure productivity (happiness, tiredness, job satisfaction) at the workplace before and after installing table lamps. The same holds for more abstract changes such as unnecessary meetings (overprocessing), bureaucracy (motion), or underqualified tasks (skills).

Waste elimination is an important part of continuous improvement. As soon as you are done with one "muda" the next one will become more salient or the third one will appear. We recommend continuous tracking of the various issues and their analysis in terms of the nature of waste. It is an idiosyncratic procedure, though. As previously noted, the "mudas" can be conceptualised in different ways. For one firm bureaucracy (as a form of standardisation) might be urgently needed, while another firm might suffer from unnecessary bureaucratic hurdles. One person prefers to have more emotional labour as it is her or his core competence, while the other person wants to avoid emotional labour at any cost. Depending on your experience, information access, and position (with or without managerial responsibility) your understanding of the wastes might differ. Accordingly, you will categorise and address the wastes differently. Yet, the task remains the same—eliminate the "muda" whichever name it has.

5.6 Analysis of Process Design and Its Complexity

There are two main ways you can proceed—the inductive and the deductive. Previously we primarily worked with an inductive approach—we looked at problems reported by employees. Then we tried to extrapolate and understand whether this problem is individual (e.g. personal characteristics) or systemic (e.g. failure of organisational processes). Let's start with organisational processes.

If you improve your organisation's processes, you usually perform the following:

- Analysis of process variations,
- analysis of media discontinuities,
- analysis of process interruptions, and
- analysis of interfaces.

5.6.1 Analysis of Process Variations

Each process can have several variations. For instance, if you want to open a bank account, there is a basic offline process with elements such as: collecting all necessary documents and going to the bank, the documents will be checked and forwarded to the back office where "a miracle occurs", and the account is created. Later, the front office communicates this to you. Now imagine that the marketing department discovers a new market opportunity—a student bank account with discounted conditions. First, we need to open the account. In this case, the bank has to check the status of the client. For you (as a student) it requires additional steps such as requesting an enrollment document from your university. This new variant of the process will need additional activities on the side of the bank, too—the bank has to prove the status and send an additional request to the university to ensure that the status is correct. Further, you have to be offered alternative conditions which imply that your account has to be marked as a "student account". This might require some additional steps on the side of IT. And voilà, the initial process exists in several variants. Now multiply this with special regional offers, accounts for elderly people, special accounts for those who use accounts for money saving vs those who need an account for daily payments tied to PayPal, and so on. A colleague of ours ran a process mining procedure to investigate how many variations of the account opening process a bank has and ended up with 188 process variations!

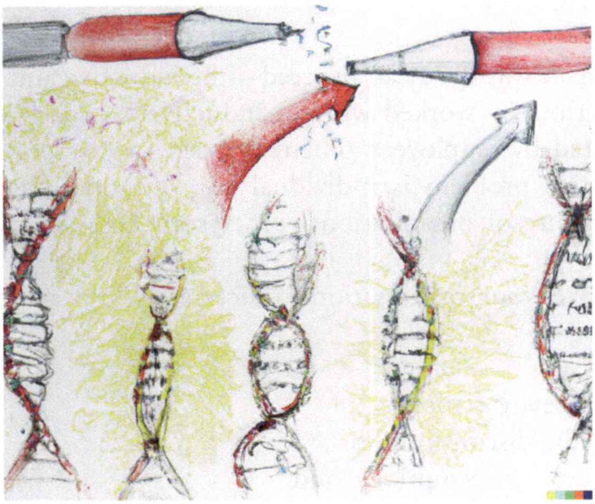

5.6.2 Analysis of Media Discontinuities

A media discontinuity is observed if the type of media within the process changes. Imagine our previous example of opening a bank account. Let's assume you bring all necessary documents in paper form. These documents will be checked by a bank officer. Next, these documents have to be scanned and stored in the system so the back office can work on them. If a bank clerk needs a signature (digital signatures are not always or not everywhere accepted, e.g. in Ukraine digital signatures are currently rather seldom), you need to print a document, sign it, scan it, and save it in the system. Moreover, you need to retain the physical copy of the document. Finally, the account is created and you as a new happy bank client receive mail in paper form. You can count the number of media discontinuities even in this simplified process. You can imagine what happens in less advanced organisations or organisations with a high degree of responsibility such as a ministry of defense.

5.6.3 Analysis of Process Interruptions

In terms of process interruption, we talk about situations when the whole process has to stop because a part of it depends on somebody outside of the firm. Going back to our example with the bank account: imagine that the bank offers bank accounts for widowed people. The bank will need confirmation from the local authorities that the husband/wife of the client has died. In the event of a student, the bank will need confirmation from the university that the potential customer is a student. In this case, the responsible officer will send a request to the university or the local authority. The process of opening a bank account, thus, comes to a halt. The needed activity (confirmation) does not lie in the hands of the bank. If you are lucky, you can still perform some activities in parallel. In all other cases (e.g. processes incorporating notaries, land registry, authorised persons, etc.), the whole process is delayed and you cannot prevent this interruption.

5.6.4 Analysis of Interfaces

Finally, when we improve processes, we look at process interfaces. This is the most promising approach for the improvement of processes. Under a process interface, we usually understand the movement between organisational functions (e.g. departments, groups, persons). Again, look at our process of opening a bank account. The customer meets our front-line employee. The employee collects the documents, checks them, and sends them to the back office. Here, IT, Marketing, and other departments come into play. Each time the process crosses the invisible border of a department or else, a conflict or at least a delay occurs. Such delays and conflicts are usually preprogrammed by the functional structure of firms that we usually refer to as "Tayloristic structure" or "silo structure". Each department does not only have people with very specific capabilities but also their own key performance indicators. If the organisational structure has not been transformed into a process-based structure yet, misconceptions (IT does not understand what the marketing department desires and the marketing department does not understand the capabilities of the IT system) or conflicts arise (IT sees each request as a "distractor" from their main activities or the marketing department sees technical requests as disturbing their primary activities). As part of process improvement, we try to minimise such interfaces. The best way to do this is to create a process-oriented structure for your company.

5.7 Analysis of Process Design Concerning Psychological Issues

When thinking about your processes, you can apply the same analysis to evaluate the strain generated by poor processes. Moreover, regular process improvement may happen at the cost of the psychological resources of your employees. If you want to have stable and smooth running processes, you have to take into account their job resources.

5.7.1 Analysis of Process Variations

A high process variation may impact your employees' well-being in different ways. First, it is not about the variety of tasks per se. Indeed, usually, it is recommended to have a high task variety to reduce counterproductive work behaviour (Morf et al. 2017). It is about variation within the same process. This variation increases complexity which may overload the cognitive capabilities of employees. Imagine that one has to constantly bear in mind all the names of all persons for each variation of the process. Second, as we noticed in our above mentioned example of a bank, variations were tracked using a process mining tool, i.e. the variations could be traced based on the digital footprint of activities necessary for opening a bank account. If there are different traces, there are different paths of communication, information processing, documentation, etc. The resulting bureaucratic burden might be an additional psychological job demand.

5.7.2 Analysis of Media Discontinuities

Each time the media changes, additional work appears. This additional work may result in psychological or physiological job demands or both. Media discontinuities might also evoke confusion as well as conflicts if one document is stored in the wrong place or in the wrong format. Each time we think about media discontinuities, we remember the anecdote about a professor who asked his assistant to print out all emails, read them aloud, dictated his answer, and asked his assistant to type it and send it. Another anecdote which comes to our mind is the work of a good friend. As it is a governmental institution, all fax messages and some emails have to be printed, stamped, then scanned and stored both in paper and digital form (as a picture such as without-PNG format). As you imagine, there could be a better way to engage employees as well as there are more interesting, challenging, and motivating tasks than reading aloud or scanning.

5.7.3 Analysis of Process Interruptions

For us, the interruption of processes is primarily associated with the place of control, or rather, with the absence of this control. Each time a process is interrupted and becomes the responsibility of another person, we have the feeling of losing control over the situation. Moreover, as in this situation we become dependent on someone else's will, the communication dynamic is formed by asymmetric relationships (I am the "asking side" and the other is the "giving side") and potential conflicts. Moreover, as the Self-Determination Theory suggests, intrinsic motivation disappears with the loss of control and autonomy. In the same vein, we cannot plan as we are not controlling the speed of the process and the quality of tasks performed by someone else. This is particularly true when the process (or a part of it) is passed to someone outside of the organisation (e.g. the customer needs to deliver necessary documents, a notarised confirmation, or similar). The effects on the psychological state of your employees and managers become particularly serious if there is time pressure (e.g. a loan needs to be closed before the end of the month). By the way, the control may get lost even if the process is interrupted within your organisation (e.g. you need permission from another department or headquarters). The lack of control may result in confusion and uncertainty leading to unnecessary stress.

5.7.4 Analysis of Interfaces

Interfaces between different functions are associated with information asymmetries and thus a deterioration in the quality of communication. Be it due to different motivation schemes within the functions or adverse selection and moral hazard issues which might result from information asymmetry, misconceptions and conflicts might appear. Each time your employee or manager has to cross the invisible border of another department, she or he may experience stress. If you are lucky, your employees have developed personal trust with the responsible party in the other department. Yet this is not the norm and classical process management does not necessarily imply trustworthy relationships. Consequently, if there are no established relationships, interfaces cause stress and are fruitful soil for interpersonal conflicts and processing errors.

5.8 Optimisation at What Cost?

All types of process analysis aim at optimisation or, better to say, improvement since mathematically we do not know where the optimum is. Thus, improvement would be the correct term. Reduction of process variations, elimination of media discontinuities, avoidance of process interruptions, and reduction of interfaces are performed to make processes smoother and faster. If processes run seamlessly and error-free, the quality of the final product or service will increase. You can see here the reference to the "magic triangle"—as long as the process is not in a perfect state one can increase quality or reduce costs or time without harming the process outcome. And here we would like to refer to the tetrahedron model which we postulated previously. If we forget about the psychological and physiological aspects of activities within a process, the improvement might not yield the required result.

Indeed, one can improve the (average) time a process needs. For instance, there might be an opportunity to reduce the time for a specific activity and from the point of view of classical process management such a decision would be legitimate. If the inefficiency is caused by wrong warehouse planning, new planning might speed up the process. Provided the other elements in the process can handle the new influx of inputs, the total process time will shrink. Yet, if this process element is not a robot or a machine but an employee, other aspects might come into play. A robot does not need to think about each operation, a robot does not get bored if the number of routine activities increases, and a robot does not get tired when the number of production increases. For a human, improvements might be an issue: speeding up work might cause stress, monotone activities might lead to boredom and a decrease in attention, and the increase in production might lead to physiological overload. Moreover, psychological demands are related to the sense of responsibility. In a process that is faster and produces a higher output of products or services, a mistake made by an employee might also lead to a higher number of losses as this slows down the process. This increases the (feeling of) responsibility of an employee. Thus, an employee would face the mentioned additional job demands. Therefore, improvement should be performed with care and should aim not only at process outcomes but also at job demand reduction.

That's why you have to be careful and not improve time, costs, and quality at the expense of stress and exhaustion. At the end of the day, you may lose your employees and managers—when they reach a burnout state, they will withdraw and mentally (or even physically) leave your company. Plus, the time needed to get them back to work after experiencing burnout will be very high. We would like you to keep in mind the chain reaction that might be evoked: if one employee or manager quits the process (e.g. due to burnout), the others will have to take over her or his responsibilities. This, in turn, will increase their psychological and physiological load and will reinforce the decay of mental and physical health in your organisation. Thinking of time, costs, and quality without incorporating the psychological resources of your team may lead to short-term process improvement but a long-term decay of the whole organisation.

Interestingly, burnout is the worst case of short-sighted process improvement. As a rule, you are confronted with minor problems along the way. If a process gets stopped or slowed down, we may speak of the loss of efficiency. Of course, not all employees get into a burnout state rapidly and at once. However, some may become demotivated which will decrease the quality of the outcome, the quality of communication, or the willingness to engage in related activities. These early signs of problems should be taken seriously. For instance, Sterman (2000) argues that we perceive most relationships that we observe as linear while they are non-linear. What if the problems in your organisation accumulate in an exponential way and you haven't noticed it? In his book on Business Dynamics Sterman (2000) proposes a "Paper Folding Challenge". He proposes to take a sheet of regular A4 paper and fold it in half. Then fold it in half again—the result will be less than a half millimetre thick. Now make a guess: if you could continue the procedure 40 more times, how thick will the final result be? Make a guess, without a calculator. You can find the correct answer and the explanation in the footnote.[6]

The negative effects of a short-sighted process improvement (i.e. ignoring the human aspect) may appear much faster than assumed. However,

---

[6] This task is used to show how often we underestimate non-linear effects. In the event of exponential growth (which is the case in the Paper Folding Challenge), the first effects seem linear if you depict them. But later they increase drastically. The correct answer is: after 42 folds the paper would be 440,000 km thick, i.e. longer than the distance from the earth to the moon. What if the problems within your organisation follow the same logic? If you think we are wrong, do an efficiency calculation assuming that all employees and managers are fully engaged in a process (i.e. they have few free resources). Then assume that one employee gets into a burnout state and quits and the others have to take over her or his tasks. How many will get into the same state and what will be the effects for the other employees and managers? If you add to this process time you need to find a new employee and time to explain the work, you will have an additional delay. How many new employees will you have to hire if, till the end of the job training, you will have lost another five employees?

observing how your employees and managers perform tasks may help you find a better way to improve your *status quo*. Haven't you noticed that sometimes process efficiency does not stem from a perfect organisation of activities within the process but from people, who managed to live with the *status quo* and who achieve great outcomes from this *status quo*?

Why We Should Start with Psychological Aspects

A friend of mine works in a large IT company. The internal processes are closely linked to a server where all the tools for environment-related statistics are located. One day, this company introduced an alternative server with a very similar name. From this point in time, all employees, who work with ecology statistics, had to use the new server and no longer the old one. It is still not clear why the old server had not been renamed and why it still appears in the systems if you search in the intranet for the correct server. As a result, about half of the employees and managers save their data on the wrong server. At the end of the month, my friend had to check all the data.

As you can imagine, 50% of the data is not found and my friend had to call all involved employees personally and ask them to transfer their files to the correct server. And here it comes: it is about personal communication. Those employees with whom my friend developed good relationships, store the data (mostly) on the correct server. They started caring about the task and its correctness because they care about good relationships. You can also explain it in terms of the Self-Determination Theory which we talked about earlier: "relatedness" is the factor that motivates the colleagues to cooperate. And if they forgot to perform the task, my friend arranges a short call (accompanied by positive emotions) and the work is done within minutes—the data appears on the correct server. We can say that the process defect was fixed on a psychological level—a pleasant relationship allows for compensation for technical inefficiency.

Yet, with the rest of the employees, there is an ongoing email ping-pong. What I am really surprised about is that the firm is satisfied with this process. As long as this (stupid) inefficiency is resolved on a personal level, no one notices the low level of quality or an issue with costs.

Two months ago, my friend changed departments. The new colleague who took over her role works hard on establishing personal contacts but it seems to be hard. Relationships always require time. The outlook for the next month is quite pessimistic—those involved in the process lack the willingness to transfer their files. Will the firm finally address the issue by, e.g. simply renaming the old server or making it inaccessible? My friend does not know. But we see that the workaround of the process based on the psychological dimension has been a very efficient solution hitherto. I wouldn't say that my friend was happy with the psychological solution—as a structured and well-organised person she would have been more happy to have the correctly named server. But her firm was satisfied, performance remained at the same level, and the firm's management did not even notice the bad process design.

5.9 Process Improvement and Burnout

There are many names for process improvement (process optimisation, incremental process innovation, or others). Important is that change matters and that each change of processes is related to innovation somehow. Of course, we differentiate between incremental and radical process innovation, whereby the latter term is related to the rethinking of the whole process and the creation of something completely new. We know that the line between incremental and radical process innovation is not very thick—it is hard to say where innovation starts being radical. "Radicality" of innovation, let's be honest, is a very perceptive measure. There are some attempts to introduce criteria for the differentiation between incremental and radical process innovation. Martinsons (1995, 266) suggests that process improvement refers to characteristics shown in Table 5.1.

As can be seen, processes may undergo a continuous yet small-scale change driven by the goal to improve certain process-related statistics. If you notice

Table 5.1 Characteristics related to process improvement

Aspect	Process improvement
Starting point	Existing processes
Nature of change	Fine-tuning of activities, culture, and structure
Time needed	Short
Effort needed	Moderate
Participation	Bottom-up
Scope of change	Narrow, within/between functions
Risks and rewards	Moderate
Primary enabler	Statistical control
Frequency of change	One-time/continuous

that your processes could be made better concerning psychological and physiological job demands and resources, process improvement is a good way to go.

5.9.1 Start with the Process

You need to start with an existing process. We assume that you have the necessary information about your process such as activities, resources, employees involved, etc. If you do not have a clear description of your process, start with the process description. In Table 5.2, you can find the adapted Process Observation Form by George and colleagues (George et al. 2005).

While George et al. (2005) focus on the distance between stations within a workspace (in feet) to improve the movements of the workers involved, we would rather focus on the employees' and managers' affective state. For this purpose, we would recommend using the Self-Assessment Manikin (SAM) (Bradley and Lang 1994). These scholars assume that there are three dimensions necessary to understand the affective state: valence (pleasant vs unpleasant), arousal (calm vs aroused), and dominance (dependent vs independent). For instance, fear would score low on the pleasantness scale, high on the arousal scale, and low on the dominance scale. Anger, on the contrary,

Table 5.2 Process observation form

Process observed:					Date:	Time:	
Step	Description	Employee	Affective state	Task time	Wait time	Work-in-progress	Observation
Totals:							

would score high on the independence scale, while being similar to fear with regard to pleasantness and arousal. Yet, the most interesting thing about the approach by Bradley and Lang is that they used pictures instead of words. This allows you, first, to avoid various interpretations of words (fear would certainly be experienced and described differently by each individual), second, to use it with employees with different language knowledge (which can be a problem if your process is multi-country or the team is cross-cultural, where emotions may be named and communicated differently), and, third, to produce fun for those who like answering such questions (example from our research can be found in Fig. 5.1).

Using this tool, you can easily fill out the Process Observation Form including the affective states accompanying each process step. You can use either the paper & pencil version of the scale or use an online tool to ask employees to estimate their affective state after (or during) performing the relevant step in the process.

5.9.2 Think About the Nature of Change

Take care of the nature of change. One should go for process improvement if the change is relatively small. Of course, it is a subjective understanding of what is small and what is not. Mainly, you should look at the change you plan to undertake. If you are not developing a completely new process (including new roles and differently allocated resources), we talk about process improvement. In the event of affective states, a small improvement can make a huge difference though. Imagine that employees involved in the process would leave their work happier and more relaxed. This would already be a great achievement. And here comes "culture and structure" into play: If you manage to change the perception of a certain task, you will improve

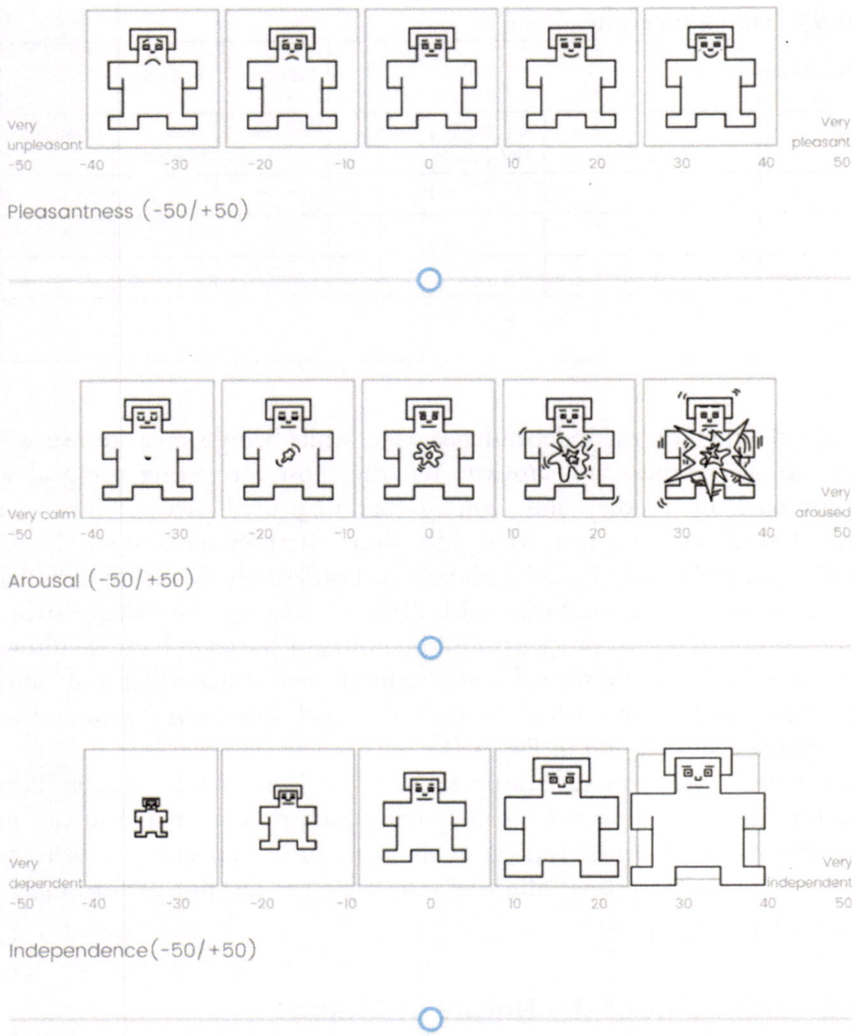

Fig. 5.1 Self-Assessment Manikin applied in our research (Bogodistov et al. 2021) (*Source* Adopted from Bradley and Lang [1994])

your process without further effort. Surely, this is easier said than done: To change the perception you might need to change the structure, e.g. to give more freedom and a higher degree of responsibility to your employees and managers.

Example of Work Distribution in a Researchers' Team

Often, one example is more helpful than a thousand words. If you remember, in one of the examples I wrote about how I changed my attitude towards statistics. I started loving them after I developed some interesting models and surprised my colleagues who were quite impressed by my (at the moment very basic) skills. Academic research usually involves several researchers who take responsibility for different parts of a research project. You can imagine that after I started to love statistics, I usually suggest focusing on data collection and analysis. This made the process of research very relaxed and accompanied by positive emotions for me. My colleagues, who are much more competent in writing or doing structured literature research, appreciate my role in the analysis part.

The process of academic research remains the same as it has been for dozens of years—we conduct a literature review to find a research gap, formulate our hypotheses, collect data to reject hypotheses, and submit our findings in the form of an academic paper. Theoretically, every researcher is capable of conducting all these steps on her or his own. In my team, however, it is much more pleasant and indeed more efficient and effective if we take the preferences of the individual team members into account. Conclusion: It is not difficult to change our attitude towards a person's expertise, which can be reflected in the way we assign tasks within a team. If you succeed, you can enjoy an increase in productivity without a large process improvement project. Isn't this cool?

5.9.3 Time Horizon

Remember that in the event of process improvement, we talk about short-term activities. We have to be clear about what "short-term" means. Here, it is not about the duration of the consequences—they can be long-lasting. It is about immediate action one can take without waiting for other actions. If a set of activities A requires the fulfilment of a set of activities B then we conceptualise the set of activities A as "short-term" and the set B as "mid-term" or "long-term". If you would like to improve the existing process, list the actions which you can immediately undertake. Think about the efforts which are associated with these actions. Then, list the expected consequences. Now depict it all on a graph with two axes: Effort and Impact (Fig. 5.2). As you can imagine, you should start with those activities which require the lowest effort and produce the highest impact. While this is easier done in

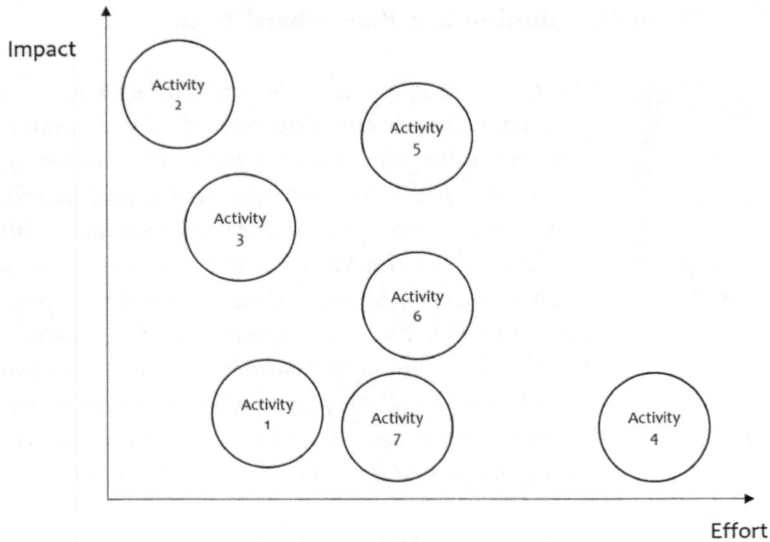

Fig. 5.2 Effort-impact analysis

classic process management, in our human-related version the analysis shown in Fig. 5.2 is the matter of individual talents of those who drive process improvement forward (i.e. what are you good at? Can you offer moral support or do you honestly acknowledge your employees' skills?) and those who are involved in the process (i.e. what is the channel of communication with a specific employee? What does he or she value most? What scares him/her and where can you immediately help?). The effort-impact analysis may be very individual but experience may help you excel in this exercise. You can improve your processes with just a small investment of your time, and psychological and physiological resources. In the end, improvement should not be an exhausting process but fun for you too.

5.9.4 Plan the Investment of Your Time and Efforts

Process improvement requires effort. You cannot create something from nothing. That is why any process change, incremental or radical, requires resource commitment. Change is always associated with costs, and you can decide on which or whose costs. If you try to improve a process, you have to find the necessary resources first. We do not only speak about tangible or intangible resources such as new equipment but also about the psychological resources of your employees. Even if you have found a way to reduce the psychological job demands by making some changes, it is psychologically costly to perform a familiar task in a different (albeit improved) way or to change daily routines. If your employees are already exhausted, a further emotional investment might not be feasible. It sounds like a shocking prospect—switching to a better way of working requires an immediate investment that will only pay off later. But do your employees and managers have the capacity for such an investment?

At the same time, you have to take care of your own psychological and physiological resources. Process improvement may not only be a long-term engagement but can also be accompanied by stress, misunderstandings, conflicts, etc. Even though you may aim at stressless but still efficient and effective organisational processes, the journey to this goal is likely to be stress-loaded. We recommend taking a few hours to analyse the existing capacities and their development trends (e.g. how fast will your team's capacities be depleted). Then you can implement your improvement plan. Here, we talk about the meta-level analysis, i.e. the necessity to step back and have a look at process improvement with a focus on psychological and physiological job demands. Try to focus not only on "how" and "when" the improved processes will run but also on the affective states which might appear on each step of the improvement project. Who is involved? Who will support you? Will they be happy or angry? Or maybe afraid? How can you change their affective states to get all on board? How long-lasting will their state be? Too often, we suffer from problems within our team, too much we think of the final result of our improvement project, and too often we forget about the psychological states of the team members involved in the improvement project itself. In Ukraine, we say "It is the shoemaker who has no shoes". Your team should be a model of how to do things to avoid psychological problems.

There are, of course, some other suggestions we can make. Since the improvement efforts are accompanied by both negative and positive affective states, you can celebrate positive events more and offer moral support in difficult times. Try to emphasise the fact that the immediate job demands related to the improvement efforts have a temporal nature, while the improved process will reduce the workload of your employees and managers. Finally, apply the techniques you read above to the project aiming at process improvement: conduct the effort-impact analysis, assign tasks to those who enjoy doing them, reduce the number of interruptions in your improvement endeavour, and so on. Most important: Don't forget to see the forest for the trees.

5.9.5 Who to Start with?

If it is about process improvement, it is usually about bottom-up participation. While new processes mostly are developed from the "top", process improvement is something that happens on the level of employees, team leaders, and the lowest line of a firm's managers. Concerning human-oriented process management you have to think about process improvement as a process driven by immediate comments and ideas of front-line employees. They know what is going wrong and, usually, only they know what is wrong with a specific process. You may not have the authority to conduct a big project with dramatic process changes, but you do have the power to make some small changes. Let the employees decide what can make their lives better immediately.

Unfortunately, we often think that process improvement should be driven by managers. Managers just have slightly more power, even if we talk about the lowest level of managers. We recommend creating an atmosphere of participation. Finally, you want your employees to speak directly about the psychological and physiological issues they encounter daily. Yet, you need neither constant non-constructive complaints nor complete silence. A state of cooperation is hard to achieve and easy to ruin. In Ukraine, we say "Trust is hard to establish but easy to lose". And, indeed, the readiness to cooperate and propose improvements is related to trust. Reward and punishment will not bring you far. The best way to proceed is to show personally that cooperation pays out. Support good ideas, ignore or mistrust "complaining for complaining". With time, employees will learn which behaviour is desired, supported, and leads to positive changes in their lives. Be very careful about punishment—ignorance of an idea may be considered as a sort of punishment. There are no easy answers here, but over time you will figure out how to proceed. If you have found it, stick to it, protect it, and embrace it.

5.9.6 Scope of Change

The scope of change within process improvement is rather narrow. Think about process improvement as a modification that starts with an improvement within one department (function). Even if you attempt to address the interaction between employees from different departments, keep in mind that you should focus on one specific activity first, e.g. the interaction of your employees with the IT support—an activity that drives some people crazy. Involving more than one department or function bears additional problems for the process improvement, as you will need support from an additional manager and you might run into unnecessary administrative struggles. Consequently, try to focus on what you can improve within a single department or what you can improve without involving too many people. At the end of the day, if you show how you succeeded with a specific improvement you will get some freedom and trust regarding further improvements.

Remember our examples where the perception of the activity as being a job demand or a job resource changed the affective state as well as the outcomes of the activity. This change in perception happens within an individual's brain and can be achieved without involving several organisational units. Consequently, some of the process-related issues can be addressed individually. Thus you might not need to include other people and organisational units. As long as the responsibility is not changing, you are fine. Yet, if you achieve a good result, fix it and communicate accordingly. When communicating results, think about the feelings of other employees and managers, as some of them might misinterpret your "soft intervention on the perception level" as a hard intervention on the level of personal responsibility and as a breach of the internal code of conduct or the established hierarchy. Always pay attention to the "stakeholders" of the process to be improved.

5.9.7 Risks and Uncertainty

While the rewards of process improvement are moderate, so are the risks. If you are working on a small improvement, the likelihood of major damage in the event of a mistake is relatively small. We would like to mention here that the little rewards should not demotivate you. A little but positive change in the affective states accompanying processes is of high value. And, the more often such small changes occur, the more positive side effects will occur. For instance, if employees and managers notice that your improvements bring small positive outcomes, they will be more willing to participate in further activities and will dedicate more energy to those. Apart from direct effects, you may observe indirect effects. These effects are actually less probable in classic process management, as the following aspects are simply missing in the framework of traditional process management: trust in the organisation and other employees might grow; discovered relational models might help reduce personal conflicts; motivation and positive emotional contagion might spread, etc. These are very positive spill-over effects which you might produce even with the smallest improvements.

5.9.8 Make It Stats-Driven!

How can you discover that you have something to improve? In traditional process management, you look at statistics of time delays, errors, missing materials and the like. In the best case, you develop a system of indicators to collect data on psychological issues. Without data you are doomed to trust your gut feeling which is a) not always the best and b) cannot be replicated by other managers or if you are on holiday leave. Consequently, we recommend you think about the data you can collect. In one of our previous sections, we offered some solutions in this regard (e.g. Self-Assessment Manikin to measure emotions, visual tools like cups of different colour or different sized pieces of chocolate that indicate the psychological state of an employee or manager—all these tools generate data that can be analysed). Yet, keep listening to your intuition—sometimes problems are not reported because they are too sensitive for the employees or because they do not realise that something is wrong. If your intuition helps you discover a problem, try to formalise the way of problem recognition.

Simple Signs of Psychological Issues in a Firm

It was 2009 in Ukraine when I joined a consulting team in a project on benchmarking. The idea of the project was quite simple but good: Our job was to compare different competing bank branches and find a way to rank them based on their quality of work. To do so, the team members had to go to a bank and open an account, a kind of "test purchase". While opening the account, we had to observe the process and take notes. We had to visit each bank branch about three times: to hand in the documents (ID card, application form, etc.), to pick up the documents after the account had been opened (account number, PIN, bank card), and, later, make one more visit to ask questions regarding the newly opened account to test the after-sales service quality. Each time after visiting the branch, we had to fill out a detailed survey. All questions were arranged in blocks, ranging from "experience while waiting in a queue" to "cleanliness of the table and presence of corporate culture symbols (e.g. posters with slogans, ties with logos)". Each team member from the consultancy had to open several accounts in different banks.

After several visits, I noticed that the questionnaire was not capturing the real situation. Some bank branches scored high in the survey but were definitely an unpleasant place to visit. For instance, one of the questions in our survey was whether employees were wearing business suits or dresses, wearing a tie/scarf with corporate symbols, and having posters with the bank's values on the walls. All aspects were to be answered with a "yes". But if you looked at how the employees were wearing their ties or how the posters were located the answer would be different. Some clerks had blots on their ties/scarfs; posters were there but inaccurately positioned and partly inclined; other corporate symbols were treated with the same level of disrespect. Including these aspects in the survey would have helped capture something that the clients really feel and pay attention to. Wouldn't you agree?

When you attempt to collect important data, think of Yevgen's experience within this consultancy project, where he "felt" for a long time that the variables "wearing corporate symbols" were not capturing the bad atmosphere he observed. Finally, Yevgen came up with an indicator related to clean, ironed, and accurately worn suits and dresses. This new indicator helped him delineate the problem in his future observations. Think thoroughly when developing your questionnaire—psychological aspects of work may be hard to capture. And trust your gut feeling—the longer you deal with psychological issues, the more intuition you will develop!

5.9.9 Where Is the End?

Process improvement is a never-ending story. Of course, you can conduct a one-time action whereby you solve a specific issue and the problem disappears. But believe us, there is always something you can do better. The constant search for improvements will constantly increase the quality of your processes with regard to psychological and physiological aspects. You have to bear in mind two important trade-offs of the continuous improvement approach:

1. We have a saying in Ukraine "Things left without active management tend to develop from good to bad, and from bad to even worse". We think this saying captures the dynamism of this world—the world is constantly changing: weather, politics, competitors, pandemics, wars, or simple ageing of employees cause a change of perception of the tasks and, consequently, of the job demands and job resources. Things which were fun become routine and boring. Tasks which were complex get learned and become simple (or automated). Customers who were happy with our services start requiring more. These changes require constant process change and constant improvement.

2. There is a trade-off between enjoying what is achieved and searching for a new aspect to improve. The more you seek, the more you get tired. If we talk about little improvements, a search for a new improvement opportunity and the stress related to putting this opportunity into life might cause more stress than simply ignoring this opportunity. There are no simple recommendations as the team might become tired even from their constantly improved processes. We think this is exactly the time to trust your gut feeling and make breaks in your improvement efforts. But not for a long time—the world is changing and so is your capability to improve processes. If not applied, it will become out of date making your sudden attempts to apply it doomed for failure. So, take breaks but regularly revoke your capability!

5.10 Process Innovation and Burnout

As you can imagine, process innovation is a completely different approach. An "innovation" implies either a radical change of a process or even the creation of a completely new process from scratch. When should one go for a radical change? There might be several starting points. Among those are the following:

1. The process runs efficiently, yet the goals are not achieved and cannot be achieved by introducing minor changes.
2. The process is not existing (e.g. because of new product demand) and needs to be created.
3. The whole work is changing (e.g. because of new technology) and the extant process does not fit into the work design anymore.

There might be more reasons. We would like to remind you that the border between incremental and radical process innovation is not clear and is a subjective matter. Yet, we are sure that everyone intuitively feels when we talk about a minor and a major change. To make this distinction clearer Martinsons (1995) proposed a number of characteristics of process innovation (Table 5.3).

Table 5.3 Characteristics related to process innovation

Aspect	Process innovation
Starting point	Clean slate
Nature of change	Radical restructuring and cultural transformation
Time needed	Long
Effort needed	Extensive
Participation	Top-down
Scope of change	Broad, cross-functional
Risks and rewards	Major
Primary enabler	Information technology
Frequency of change	One-time/periodic

5.10.1 Start with the Problem

If you have a problem which you did not manage to address using smaller changes or which cannot be addressed using process improvement tools, try to start from scratch. Write down the problem. While in traditional process management you start with a SIPOC analysis, try to think of your customers first and run a COPIS[7] analysis. This method assumes that you start with your external customers in mind when you design your processes because they are the reason why your company exists. However, also your employees are customers—they are "internal customers" having their own needs. Bringing these two perspectives together is a challenge: if you focus too much on your organisation's external customers, you might neglect the issues of your employees. The reason for this lies in the "Eight-Wastes Approach". For your external customers, all conflicts, psychological problems, and misunderstandings are not value-adding and, thus, a "waste", i.e. something they do not want to pay for. However, the more the external customers require (timely produced products or services of very high quality and, if possible, for free), the more psychological and physiological job demands they imply.

If you focus on your employees, however, the situation might not become better. Not all processes or activities within processes make your employees happy. The more you focus on the positive emotions of your employees, the more you might neglect your external customers. In the worst-case scenario, they will not be offered what they *want*, but what your employees are *willing* to produce. And there are many products and services all of us feel comfortable with—the known and trained ones. In the field of strategic management,

[7] When applying a COPIS analysis, you look at your process from the opposite direction of SIPOC: you start documenting customer needs (C) first, then outputs (O), process(es) (P), inputs (I), and at the end suppliers (S). Arguably, focusing on the customer first helps firms develop business processes that are more customer-centric.

we call this effect "path dependence" (David 1985; Sydow et al. 2009). In the field of psychology, we call it "habituation behaviour" (Ajzen 2002). Once individuals and firms develop a certain way of behaviour which appears to be effective (e.g. brings profit in the case of a firm), they repeat this behaviour with a certain degree of automaticity. However, the needs and wishes of the customers change and cannot be addressed with established ways of behaviour. An illustration of this issue can be the case of RIM—once the producer of Blackberry smartphones. After the introduction of the iPhone by Apple in 2007, the firm stuck to its business model and product, ignoring the shifting requirements of the customers (Himsel and Inkpen 2017).

We believe that the best way to look at both groups of your clients is to develop a matrix structure, where you map your internal customers' needs related to job demands and your external customers' desires. Usually, firms focus on external customers only. We recommend that you balance your activities concerning both groups until you find an "optimal" combination. Would it make sense if a critical element of a product or service would be produced by an exhausted or demotivated employee? Eventually, the external customer would suffer from a low-quality product or service. As you have noticed, we do not recommend doing only those things which your employee would like to do. We recommend "balancing actions" or, put differently, finding a match between the employees' and managers' attitudes and the customers' requirements and wishes. You may even think of hiring new employees if the activity is out of range of your current employees' capabilities. Again, a capability usually reflects what employees love to do. Maybe you should pay more attention to your employees' capabilities—as long as they do what they can do well, they will receive positive feedback from their team head/manager, their colleagues, or their customers and will start enjoying the new activities.

5.10.2 Changing Organisational Culture

Process innovation requires a cultural shift. If you change the processes on paper but employees behave in the same way as in the past, new processes will not come to life. In this case, you have two options: either you will end up with a slightly changed process (i.e. process improvement and not an innovation), or you will face a not properly working new process and the necessity to switch to the old one again.

This implies that you have to start with cultural change before process innovation or simultaneously with it. As the main idea of process innovation is to come up with new ways of approaching a problem, you cannot stick to habitual actions. Moreover, the roles and responsibilities will change.

We think this is the biggest issue in the cultural aspect of process innovation. Imagine that you will have to tell a manager that she or he will lose her or his managerial responsibility. Imagine that you have two or three departments which are in a constant clash and due to a new process one of those departments will increase its power. Imagine that you ascribe new roles to employees who have familiarised themselves with a specific way of working and now need to relearn their jobs. Process innovation is 20% of innovation, and 80% of activities are convincing, persuading, or even forcing people to act in a new way, live their new roles, and accept new roles of their colleagues.

5.10.3 (How Much) Time for a Big Change?

As discussed in the previous section, process innovation requires time. It is foremost a cultural shift and cultural change always requires time. In the event of countries, a cultural shift needs decades. Yet, sometimes this cultural shift can be reinforced. Think of the Covid pandemic—very suddenly all firms all over the world had to switch to remote working. The change was painful, but, on the other hand, in a very short period public institutions, business schools, and non- and for-profit organisations became digitalised and able to conduct their activities in a hitherto impossible format.

The same can be achieved within organisations. However, there are some aspects you have to take into account:

First, organisations are smaller. On the one hand, reinforcing process innovation should be much easier than reinforcing cultural change in a large corporation. On the other hand, if something goes wrong the firm will notice this immediately in its profit. Small firms might not be able to survive the consequences. You may look at small touristic agencies, which were not large enough to cope with changes due to the pandemic. The same would have happened if such firms decided to innovate their processes and, as a result, lost substantial parts of their income. Some firms are very sensible concerning their process outcomes and cannot afford a big change even if the current processes are inefficient.

Second, firms produce and deliver products based on the extant process. If they want to introduce a new product or service based on a completely new process, we talk about process innovation. An example might be the switch from traditional retail banking to online banking. Process innovation assumes a transfer from the old process to the new one. Such transfer requires a lot of resources, especially human resources, as the same employees have to partly run the old process and start learning the new way of acting. Overall, such an approach leads to increased job demands and, consequently, burnout (Bogodistov et al. 2018; Bogodistov et al. 2019).

Third, there is a big difference between the Covid situation and your firm. The pandemic was everywhere and one could not ignore the necessity to adapt to change. In the case of the firm, employees may simply decide to leave. It is not an easy process but employees are usually with a firm because they "like working there". It is not about the task but about the culture, friends/colleagues, image, etc. As soon as these cultural aspects start to change, they might easily consider leaving their employer. Is this bad? We do not know. On the one hand, losing experienced personnel is the worst thing you can experience in a firm. On the other hand, if you develop a new process from scratch, the old way of working may no longer work anyway. Losing ballast, i.e. those who are not able or willing to adapt to change is not the worst outcome. Although we usually avoid this option, in some cases it may be a virtue.

Be Consistent in Your Change

When our top management decided to transform our organisation, they started with the values. They wanted to change the way we work, starting with communication with clients and ending with a new market positioning. Our company should become the umbrella of several businesses and move from its niche to new markets. This implied process innovation. As a COO, I had to reorganise processes of internal communication within the new firm and find ways to introduce new businesses to our business model. So, I did not decide which direction our firm should go but I was responsible for incorporating the new paths into our way of acting.

Of course, the main issue were the employees and managers themselves—the habitual niche-thinking was predominant and the current firm was organised in a silo structure based on some departments. Our top managers started with the values. They looked at what was important for our firm hitherto and wrote down what should be important from now on, i.e. they wrote down the new values. For example, one of our old values was "friendly relations within a team". This old value was deemed obsolete and the new value of "making a profit" had to be implemented. Whatever decision had to be made, we always had to evaluate it from a profit perspective first. If generating revenue hurt employees' feelings, it was less important. These abstract values were implemented in a very harsh way, however. As we know, cultural change usually takes years. In our case, the top management reinforced the change process. It was a matter of reward and punishment—those employees whose behaviour was driven by the new values (e.g. making a profit) were rewarded, and those who put friendliness above profit were punished. Any behaviour in the old way was no longer approved.

After three weeks, the first employees and managers started to leave the company. After two months, we had an enormous turnover, whereby mostly the experienced "key players" had left. After three months, our company worked in a completely different way. Yes, at this moment, I left the company too, as it was no longer the company I had joined and I didn't share the new values. But new employees joined the company and it started functioning in a new way. This change is neither good nor bad—it just reflects how drastic and how fast a change in a few values can be.

With this example, we want to elucidate two aspects of process innovation: First, if you are persistent with your innovation initiative, the process of change runs faster than you might think. Second, process innovation changes not only the type and order of activities, it changes how an organisation is "felt". It means that not only the processes will change, but people and their self-esteem, communication, and interactions will also change. We believe that managers often underestimate what change means. Being shocked by the first results of change, they sometimes stop transforming the organisation. Stopping in the middle of the change is one of the worst things you can do—you neither enjoy the full change, nor can you go back to the old processes. Moreover, you may generate a feeling that change in your organisation is not feasible. Whatever your decision was, pursue it to the end.

5.10.4 Time and Efforts

John Kotter (1995) proposed an 8-step model for change. According to this model, you have to

1. create a sense of urgency,
2. build a guiding coalition,
3. form a strategic vision and initiatives,
4. enlist a volunteer army,
5. enable action by removing barriers,
6. generate short-term wins,
7. sustain acceleration, and
8. institute the change.

Kotter focused on radical change. If you plan to innovate your processes, this model is for you. Actually, this model is not meant for process innovation but for corporate transformation. Yet, as innovating your processes will lead to rethinking (a part of) your organisation, we recommend you applying it. The model reflects the high amount of time and effort which you have to invest in change. Creating a sense of urgency is a hard task—if you want to be successful in your change, you have to convince all or at least most people in your organisation. The same applies to building and guiding coalitions, forming a strategic vision, or institutionalising change. If we talk about process innovation, the efforts on your side are enormous!

If you look at Fig. 5.3, you will notice that corporate transformation is the highest level of business transformation. The higher you go on the Y-axix, the more you will need to think of the application of Kotter's model to make your innovation initiative accepted and implemented in your organisation. Process innovation is usually associated with the levels 3 and 4.

While the X-axis indicates the benefits, it also (partly) captures "efforts". No pain—no glory! Put differently, no efforts—no benefits. Think of it when you decide to drastically change or redesign your processes. When we talk about efforts, we also talk about psychological efforts (i.e. job demands): Local improvement of processes may lead to some increase in job demands, while process innovation related to business process redesign may have a significant impact on job demands. But corporate transformation inevitably makes coping with job demands a real challenge!

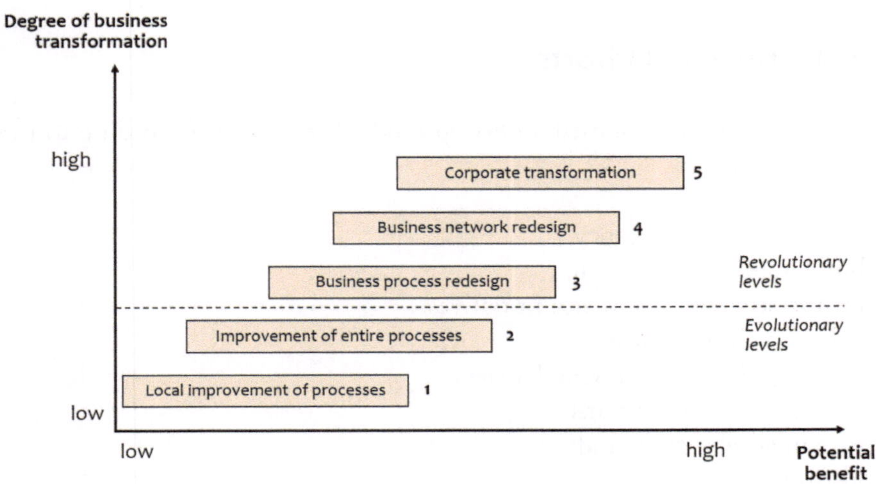

Fig. 5.3 Levels of change and their degree of business transformation (*Source* Adopted from Venkatraman [1994])

Conclusion: There is a big win waiting at the end but the way there might be strenuous.

5.10.5 But You Have Support ... Don't You?

In contrast to process improvement, in the case of process innovation remember the old Ukrainian saying: if you are between the hammer and the anvil, it is the hammer which hits on the anvil and not vice versa! So, if you have support from your top managers, you made the first step to success.

Indeed, process innovation is usually initiated at the top and, consequently, supported from the top. If you go through change and related conflicts with your back covered, the change journey is easier to follow. Yet, as soon as the change process yields the first negative consequences (conflicts among employees and managers), the support from the top may backfire. Change may become a political event rapidly and then the scapegoat will be needed. For top management, you might be the first candidate for this role.

Innovating the Patient Encounter Process

A few years ago, the Ukrainian Ministry of Health decided to reform the national health system. It attempted to introduce primary care to the outdated post-soviet health care system. It was a hard task, as it was not a minor improvement of the existing system but the introduction of a completely new process of interaction with patients, the separation of responsibilities between primary and secondary care, as well as the introduction of a new type of physicians—family doctors. Not so many managers wanted to lead this project as the outcomes were uncertain and the threats of conflicts on all levels (physicians, hospital management, local authorities) were real. But the project was supported from the highest level.

A friend of ours took over the task to manage the transformation in one of the largest Ukrainian cities. In the beginning, the work was stressful—but expectedly stressful. Conflicts were appearing all the time, resources were missing, and even the understanding of how the process innovation had to be implemented was lacking. Anyway, after four years the system worked sufficiently. And actually even better than expected—despite all organisational, financial, and technical issues.

The family doctors became drivers of the health system and showed other, not yet transformed levels how the transformation should run.

Before the next local elections, however, the political parties began to look for political points and took up all conflicts and critical issues. As we know, the usual "populist" approach is to criticise those who are in power. And to look for someone to blame when something doesn't work well. Our friend became such a scapegoat, although it was hard to legitimise because after the transformation the city was better off as compared to almost all other Ukrainian cities. Yet, in such a complex process involving so many stakeholders with different interests, some "sins" can always be found. And after an election, the new government has to show what it has "positively changed". Again our friend was the one who had to manage this "positive change". At the moment of writing this chapter, our friend is struggling with burnout. Although the work in the city was nearly perfect, the stress caused by the process of finding a scapegoat ruined his mental health. We recommend you think about how you can cope with emotions before you start process innovation. The job demands of process innovation are way higher as compared to process improvement!

5.10.6 Process Innovation Is Usually Cross-Functional

If you innovate a process, i.e. you want to make a radical change, several functions within your organisation will be affected. Of course, if we talk about a small process within one department, it might not impact other departments, i.e. functions. For instance, you notice that within your department meetings are performed ineffectively, i.e. you never come up with a final decision. In this case, you can achieve an improvement by introducing some time management techniques (*process improvement*) *or* you can decide to substitute all administrative meetings through alternative tools of communication and task planning. If there are decisions to be made, decision support systems come into play (*process innovation*). We would call this process innovation as the procedure of meetings is very different from the previous one. Yet, here we talk about a small department-internal communication process.

This might not work for business processes, where several functions are impacted and you are not the only "master and commander". Imagine that you discovered that in your organisation the procurement process induces a substantial number of psychological problems. This is the case in some large companies when one has to buy or lease a certain software via the IT procurement team. This process involves several departments as they have their own tasks for which they need specific resources and equipment. You may go for a process improvement and analyse where most psychological problems appear. If problems appear in a small part of e.g. the internal ordering system, a process innovation initiative might not be needed. A simple change of the interface may reduce the stress of the employees. However, if the psychological problems are caused by a number of overarching issues such as hierarchical thinking, shared responsibility, unnecessary dependencies between departments, struggles with funding, inappropriate KPIs and the like, it might make sense to completely redesign the process. Again, remember that you should start with the analysis of reasons for problems.

After the analysis, the change will impact several departments and also third parties. Digitalisation might help, yet it might create additional problems within the organisation and between your organisation and your partners (Bogodistov and Ostern 2019). The scope of change and of related psychological issues should not be underestimated. And think of the following: in our research, we showed that transformation projects do not (only) fail because of the price of the software, but rather because of the indirect social costs people associate with the change. The more radical the change, the higher the perceived costs. From our previous chapters, we know that job demands are often a matter of individual "perception" rather than of cost analysis. Think of these costs before you start a (cross-functional) process innovation initiative!

5.10.7 No Pain—No Glory

Unfortunately, the more innovative your new process, the higher the risks. If you perform just a minor change, the risk that a failure would lead to negative consequences is low. However, if you strive towards a new way of working and redesign activities, much bigger risks and higher degrees of resistance will appear. When we work with risks, we normally estimate the probability of their occurrence and the severity of their impact. If the process is running and you need a minor improvement, even if something goes wrong, you can quickly switch back to the old way of working. Moreover, most risks are easy to estimate as you have a history of the existing process. Consequently, you mostly deal with "known knowns". In the event of process innovation, your estimation will be much more vague. Moreover, if the new process is unique for your industry (e.g. there is no "best practice" that you are adopting from a competitor), you might face "unknown unknowns", i.e. events which are impossible to plan as no one thinks about them.

5.10.8 Driven by Information Systems

Radical change is driven by your information systems. Nowadays, designing a new process and taking into account all risks and peculiarities of a firm's daily life, is hardly feasible without strong information systems. Moreover, the new process has to start while the old one is still being executed or just in time with the termination of the old process.

Information technology itself may be a strong driver for process innovation on its own. Imagine that a new software appears on the market that allows you to rethink your processes completely. What about online banking? Three decades ago, online banking was absent. Most processes happened offline and even checking the account required a phone call or a visit at a branch. Remember, in the 1990s the fastest connection was GSM + EDGE with 384 kbps while this option was not even available everywhere. Simultaneous developments in the fields of Internet speed, programming languages, and hardware for mobile devices made online banking available, fast, secure, and desired. Yet, online banking requires a completely different logic. For instance, bank office hours, ways of data transmission, and requirements for cybersecurity have completely changed. Did this need for process innovation come from the banks' management? It came from technology and was pushed by the requests of customers. Consequently, information technology can both help you perform your planned process innovation and force you to go for a new process, even though it has not been intended hitherto.

5.10.9 Big Bang

In the case of process innovation as compared to process improvement, we speak about one-time changes. Remember the example of online banking. Once online banking appeared as a new service (process innovation), we continued with process improvement on a regular basis. For instance, security has been strengthened, speed has been continuously increased, reliability of the apps has been raised, etc. Maybe one day a new technology will substitute online banking as we have it today. At the moment, it is a good example of a one-time change, a "big bang".

In addition, process innovation (understood as radical change) and process improvement (understood as incremental change) alternate in phases. Many authors in process management advise against doing both at the same time. As a result, we always get more or less large "big bangs" at intervals in companies.

It should be noted that even after process innovation, efforts for continuous process improvement are necessary, as shown in Fig. 5.4 (right hand side). Empirical evidence shows that otherwise efficiency will fall again (left hand side of the figure). The reasons for this are declining attention in process monitoring, renewed hiring of personnel, increase in material costs, etc.

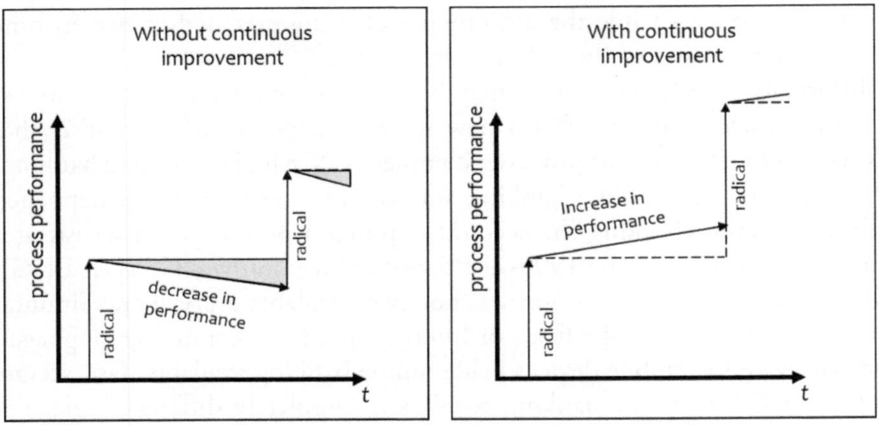

Fig. 5.4 Interplay between process innovation and process improvement

5.11 Burnout and Process Improvement/Process Innovation

Be it process improvement or process innovation, burnout is related to any type of change. First, burnout might result from process innovation as process innovation could overwhelm the psychological and physiological resources of those who are involved (Bogodistov et al. 2018; Bogodistov et al. 2019). Second, we have to bear in mind that tools for process management allow for addressing different organisational issues, e.g. bad psychological conditions or other issues appearing due to misuse of human resources.

5.11.1 Burnout Accompanying Process Changes

If your firm decides to change its processes, psychological and physiological job demands will increase. In the case of process improvement, the overuse of resources might appear as minor, yet continuous change, being at the core of process improvement, may lead to a continuous over-usage of individual psychological resources. At the end of the day, a continuous search for improvement opportunities requires an investment of resources in problem search, problem definition, risk assessment, and other related activities. Most of these activities have implications for the everyday work of your employees and managers. As a result, if you do not care about the balance between job demands and job resources, those employees and managers involved in process improvement will constantly deplete their resources.

The degree of change may be different and depends on your goals. Your employees and managers might think about improving their processes but also might think about the improvement of your products. The company Indesit, for instance, made searching for innovation a part of their daily life (Grant and Jordan 2015). Not only is the R&D department looking for new opportunities, but all employees in all departments are required to be innovative. This goal is challenging but also bears risks in itself—a continuous search and feeling an obligation to provide something innovative is resource-demanding. Creative tasks are those that bring you energy. But if you make creative problem-solving a routine, boredom might appear. Apart from boredom, other aspects might also be demanding. Imagine that each time you submit your report, you have to indicate what was "innovative" in your activities. There are many types of activities and not all of them are innovative by nature. Feeling a necessity to report innovativeness might create tensions as well as lead to dissatisfaction as an even perfectly performed task might lack innovativeness and, therefore, be estimated as "insufficiently good". As you see, even a minor process improvement (i.e. an inclusion in a short innovativeness report) may increase job demands and make employees feel bad.

In contrast to process improvement, process innovation requires a complete rethink and can therefore lead to an overuse of psychological and physiological resources. Often, not only the big bang has to be organised, because in addition to the new process, the old process also has to be continued, at least for a certain period of time. This is the case, for example, with the digitalisation of loan processing. Although the large number of loan transactions can be digitalised, special cases or loans that exceed certain amounts must continue to be processed manually for a while. There are many examples of this. Apart from resource overuse, other issues might appear such as risks and internal conflicts. The bigger the change, the higher the risks associated with the change. The higher the risks, the more severe the emotions elicited by these events or expectations of these events. Moreover, both radical change in the roles due to the process innovation as well as a (short-term) parallel execution of the old and the new process might (and most likely will) cause conflicts due to information asymmetries, power redistribution, and ambiguity of freshly defined roles.

Our overall recommendation is to include these considerations in any type of process change you plan to perform. The more radical the change, the more you should dedicate time and effort to think through all possible job demands which will accompany the activities in the transformation process. Plan carefully, as we have seen too many transformations that changed their direction somewhere in the middle or were completely stopped. The official excuses are "technical issues", "change in the conditions", or the like. In all of the negative transformation cases we experienced, the real reason for the lack of success was the psychological issues of employees, managers, clients, business owners, and so on. Does your experience go in line with ours?

5.11.2 Burnout Prevention as a Part of Process Changes

Actually, this book has two main goals: First, to illustrate how psychological issues appear at different stages in any organisation. Process management looks at all activities within an organisation through a prism of resources (including human resources). As human resources are reduced to simple entities with skills and eight hours of work, other psychological and physiological resources remain neglected. Second, in this book, we talk about different tools from the process management tools inventory which might be useful to provide a recursive look and remove the existing weaknesses.

Both process improvement and process innovation are helpful in this regard. Predominantly, process management should help firms allocate their resources in an efficient and effective manner. We must treat the psychological and physiological resources of employees and managers in the same way as the physical (material) resources of a company. The errors in allocation of these resources and their overuse should be seen as nothing but "muda" (waste) in the process that should be removed. As soon as they are removed, the same process should deliver better results, whereby employees and managers would get happier or at least protected from severe psychological consequences such as burnout.

Of course, if a process causes damage to the psychological health of your employees, you should think about process innovation. As usually process innovation takes the customer's perspective, you can do the same. First, you may look at your personnel as customers. This would be especially useful if you want to change your firm's internal processes. Second, if you have a process of producing products or services for your customers that you would like to redesign completely, you may conduct a needs and wishes analysis not only from the viewpoint of your (external or internal) customers but also from the viewpoint of employees and managers within your team or department. Why not only ask them whether they can perform certain tasks, but also how much energy these tasks bring or take away from them? If you include the calculation of psychological and physiological job demands and job resources during the process planning phase, you may not only make your employees happier or more resilient but also increase the probability that the procedure of process innovation will run smoothly. As long as your employees and managers see that you think about them and involve them in process design, they will show a higher willingness to act and support you during process innovation and later when the project is up and running.

And don't forget to constantly communicate with your team. First, many activities will be specified on the go, so you will need to define associated job demands and job resources also on the go. Second, often during the process of planning, activities are way too abstract. For this reason, as soon as you move on and specify activities, roles, and resources, the opinions of your employees and managers may change. We recommend regular discussions about activities throughout the process innovation initiative.

5.11.3 Changing Your Processes to Prevent Burnout

Kotter (1995) proposes eight steps which you need to follow to transform your organisation. In this book, we do not focus on the organisation but on business processes. However, if you address and change business processes, you will change your organisation too. As business processes are the DNA of an organisation, changing the DNA will inevitably result in how the organisation works. This change will alter the way your company is perceived by employees and the market; after all, the current change initiative signals to the world how your company will develop over the next few years. Based on Kotter (1995) we propose you follow the next steps to reduce burnout-related issues (Fig. 5.5):

1. **Create a sense of urgency**: Explain the urgency of burnout prevention (original: 'create the sense of urgency'). We believe that many managers underestimate the threat of burnout. We are all different and those who land on the managerial floor have usually developed a certain psychological resilience which helps them cope with the psychological demands of their job. This inevitably leads to an interesting consequence: we usually estimate other people through the lens of our capabilities. Consequently, those managers might underestimate psychological issues and overestimate the capabilities of employees to cope with them. The higher you climb the ladder, the higher the capability to resist psychological challenges and the lower the support for an initiative aiming at the reduction of burnout and related psychological issues.

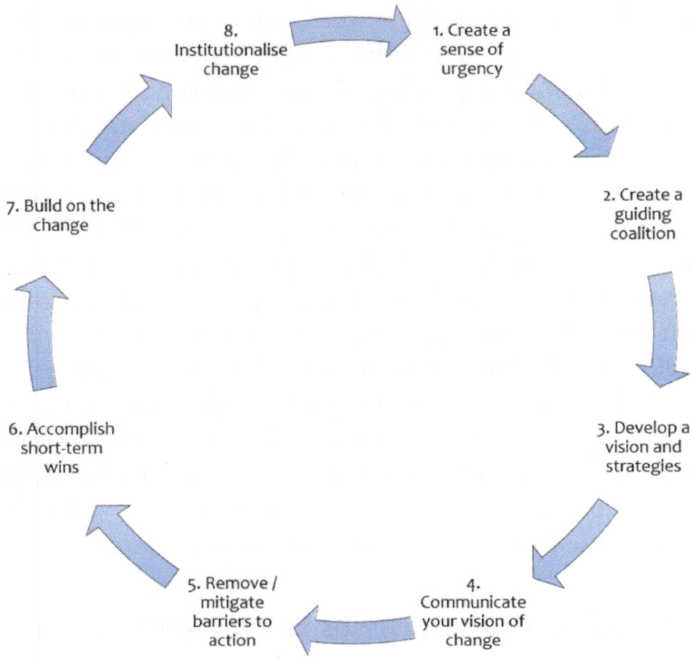

Fig. 5.5 Transformation model by Kotter (*Source* Adopted from Kotter [1995])

For this reason, a sense of urgency is extremely hard to generate. Look at any other process improvement or process innovation initiative: as long as you show what savings or earnings you can achieve with your process transformation, the sense of urgency will positively correlate with the amount of savings or earnings. But how would you argue about the "reduction of psychological costs"? The logic is the same—you should show why your initiative is helpful as well as why it is urgent. If the organisational culture and your country's culture are more prone to rely on money-related core values, you should argue using financial arguments. Try to calculate how much personnel turnover costs your organisation. Calculate the costs of absenteeism, low productivity due to fatigue or mistakes due to tiredness, or the monotone nature of the tasks. Make a measurement of the motivational profiles of employees and managers over a certain period (of course, anonymously) and relate this data to ups and downs in your organisation's profitability. Bring numbers and be sure that if you receive support, you will be able to show that the situation improves. Remember that all the data you collect will most likely become a base for your process monitoring KPIs.

If your organisation pays more attention to human-related values, you may directly address employees' well-being and how you can improve it. But even in most countries where the focus is on people, it's about money. For this reason, we recommend strengthening your arguments with additional savings/earnings arguments and data. Keep focusing on urgency: show that the long-term effect is worth investing time and money in. Advertise the immediate effects that will occur in the near future. Compare two versions of your organisation: the one, which continues to act as usual and the one, which will be transformed!

2. **Create a guiding coalition**: After you have created a sense of urgency, you might not be able to transform your organisation without a guiding coalition. You need support. For this, you have to find those who are willing to support you in this endeavour. First, you need people on the top, who will support you. Talk to your managers, especially those, who not only think about the efficiency of your processes but also about the feelings of your personnel. Usually, it should not be a problem—some of your managers experienced burnout probably on their own. Some have observed psychological issues intervening in your business processes. Those managers can help you communicate your initiative to other managers. Moreover, as soon as you have support on the top, you will find support on the bottom line of your organisation. Second, find employees willing to help you with your initiative. Most of your employees know about the psychological aspects of your business processes as they are involved in activities and related conflicts, misunderstandings, and psychological and physiological load.

   Now it is time to institutionalise—make a list of your change team and prepare a document which entails your group members as well as your vision and strategy. The more precise you are, the easier it will be for your firm to sign the document and create an official "task force" aiming at burnout prevention in your organisation. Moreover, the more precise your strategy and expected outcomes, the more willing your organisation's management will be to support the initiative. Remember, accountable goals and a clear timetable are what your top management wants to see. No one wants to support abstract goals—your management wants to know what will happen and when the first wins will be visible.

3. **Develop a vision and strategy**: Vision and strategy are the things that create clarity for your team. If you develop your vision, i.e. how the future of your organisation will look like after you succeed, and if you propose a concise strategy, i.e. how will we get there, half of your work is done. As we say in Germany, "a good plan is half of the work done". Yet, this is easier said than done. Many think that writing something like "prevent burnout

through the correct process management" is sufficient. But your organisation, as well as each member of your team, need to have clarity. First, they will trust you more if you know exactly what to do. Second, they need to see that their own experiences are addressed. For this, we recommend you run a Design Thinking workshop (see more on the process steps below). Through the creation of 'personas' and addressing the precise needs of "typical representatives" of your employees and managers, you look deep into the roots of the problem and propose strategies to address those needs.

After you have listed the basic needs and written down the operational and strategic steps to address those needs, you will be able to offer your team and your organisation a clear vision of your actions for the next months and, maybe, years. Don't forget that there are several ways to get to the same vision, i.e. you might need to develop two or more strategies. Having alternative ways to get to your goal will help you with the next step: when communicating your ideas it is always advantageous to offer more than one way to choose from. If one can choose, she or he believes in her or his power over the project, feels involved in the project, and develops a willingness to support your team.

4. **Communicate the change vision**: The best you can do to become successful in the process of transformation, is to communicate your vision to the rest of your organisation. Doesn't matter how good your ideas are, your organisation has to be able to absorb the results of your work. This willingness to absorb results depends on the organisation's absorptive capacity, on the one hand. On the other hand, the willingness to absorb depends on the understanding of the process. People are sceptical if they don't understand what is expected from them and why it is good for the organisation.

   If you want to be good at communication, you have to take a different lens—think of the psychological distance. You might be deep into your ideas and plans, i.e. you will definitely have a low psychological distance. This might lead to a specific way of arguing—you may rely on numbers, details, and concrete steps. Yet, the rest of the firm has a very abstract understanding of what you are trying to accomplish. So try to communicate the change from their perspective.

   We recommend three things in this regard. First, use visuals for your communication. Graphs, presentations, and diagrams help people better understand the status quo and your vision of the organisation and its processes in the future. We recommend using fewer pie charts and focusing on alternative visuals such as timelines, trends, and scatter plots.

   Second, use interesting data and facts which are unconsciously known to everyone but have never been presented as facts. What is the number of psychological issues? What kind of issues dominate the organisation's life?

Insomnia? Burnout? Tiredness? Complaints because of working conditions? By this, you show that you did your homework and that your ideas have their roots in real organisational problems. In addition, you create a basis for the measurability of your success. If you can show that in one year (month, week) the number of insomnia cases has dropped, you will know that you are on the right path.

Third, introduce a graph with quick and long-term wins. Don't forget to make a disclaimer that the wins will appear if the project is accepted in its current form. Changes may postpone or advance results.

5. **Remove barriers to action**: Whatever you plan to do, there will be hurdles which you will have to overcome. Mostly, the barriers are known to you in advance. For instance, many employees and managers will be sceptical with regard to the success of the project. Your project is not the only one, and often several other projects have failed before (this is normal, projects always entail risks), leading to negative memories of the involved and impacted persons. Imagine that you announce the main goal of your project—the reduction of psychological problems. The negative memories as well as the lack of willingness to discuss psychological issues of personnel will lead to scepticism and sabotage as the main barriers to action. You may also think of bureaucracy—your organisation is very likely to be present on the market for a while. As a result, rigid structures and bureaucratic processes have developed. You are trying to create something new, i.e. you will create new processes and change the existing ones. By doing so, you will have to intervene in power structures. Yes, bureaucracy implies the power of bureaucrats as those who decide are empowered to do so. Would someone like to give up her or his power? We are sure you know the answer. Here, your coalition and data-supported approach to the vision of success may really help you. As you see, if you make a mistake in one of the previous steps, you will face additional resistance in this fifth one.
6. **Accomplish short-term wins**: In one of the previous steps, we stressed the necessity of quick wins. Scepticism and internal resistance will not immediately disappear. Most likely they will accompany you through the whole journey and even after your initiative succeeds. There is always someone who thinks that "in the past everything was better". Each quick win which is clearly communicated reduces resistance and increases faith in your project. Therefore, make a list of possible quick wins and try to achieve those regularly. Yet, our recommendation is to be "not very regular". People get used to weekly win reports. But if wins appear in non-regular time then the novelty will be beheld. And you need this novelty to draw attention and remind others of your successful project.

Our good (academic) colleague uses this approach when reporting the success of his publications. Sometimes, he reports that the paper has been accepted for publication and then the actual publication of the paper.

Sometimes, he reports other steps, such as "paper has been submitted!" or "data has been processed!". If there are too many such wins, he reports only the final fact of the publication of his research. You can learn from his example: think of the bigger and smaller wins. A "running questionnaire" might be a small but necessary win. A reduction in the number of reported insomnia cases might be something valuable to report during the yearly presentation of your team's successes.

7. **Build on the change**: Unfortunately, the change has seldom an end date. Mostly, change initiatives keep running. In process management, we call this 'continuous improvement'. Believe us, after you achieve your goal, a dozen new goals (or ideas) will appear. Shall you stop here? No, you should continue and use the momentum—if your firm started believing in the success of your project, build on this change. Remember, believing does not always correspond to actual success. We certainly know of organisations where the actual cool results were not believed or perceived, or where these results were downplayed in political games. Again, burnout prevention is different from firefighting. The fire might disappear, but the job demands and constantly occurring challenges will not. So, why not use the same logic again: create a sense of urgency and accelerate your project, bringing it to a new level?
8. **Institutionalise the change**: Oh, yes, there is a reason why you cannot just jump to the next level. Before you start with step 1 from the beginning again, you need to make sure that the change you implemented will remain. People may enjoy the results of your project for a certain time and then, slowly, slip into the previously existing routine. This is especially the case in the event of psychological issues. We love our habits. Dewey (1922) sees habits as one of the key faculties of human actions. He argues that we perform more activities in a habitual way than in emotion-driven or cognition-driven ways. In organisations, routines appear and become permanent. A short-term change, if not becoming a part of the new routine, will be "overwritten" by previous activities. Here, you should remember the four signs of routinisation as conceptualised by Cohen and Bacdayan (1994): a routine is present when (1) you observe reliable results, e.g. no psychological overload of personnel in daily activities; (2) the speed of decision making and other related activities is increasing. This happens because in a routine we respond to stimuli in a learned (habitual) way without long considerations; (3) you observe repeated action sequences, e.g. managers always (or regularly) analyse new tasks with regard to their psychological and physiological load; and (4) the results are occasionally suboptimal. Yes, the more automatism you have in your activities, the more often you will make mistakes if the input into your process deviates. For example, you may overreact or underreact because you habitually

react the same way to changes, whereas the nature of the change may be different and a different response may be required.

When Change Initiative Result Is Left in Limbo

At this point, I would like to tell you a story. A good friend of mine used to work as an engineer at a plant. During the Soviet time, this plant produced different types of engines, mostly for non-military purposes. Once, he went on a business trip to visit an exhibition dedicated to recent developments in technology. There, he saw a drawing of a submarine and one of the elements drew his attention. As I am not into technology and cannot remember all the details, let's call this part a "boiler". It was just one of the elements but it was crucial for the survival of submarine personnel. He noticed that the boiler was not designed in the best way and could be improved.

When he came back, he proposed to address the detected issue. Being inspired and willing to show his capabilities, he found other engineers with whom he started a project. They spent plenty of time designing the new boiler. Finally, they produced a prototype and ran a trial. The final product was more reliable, more accurate, simpler and cheaper in manufacturing. Later, a visit from the Ministry of Defense followed. All engineers received some kind of award and then … nothing happened. It is hard to say what was the reason—no one delivered any explanation. After months of waiting for something to happen and trying to get information, all involved engineers were frustrated and completely disengaged. The spill-over effect was also present: no other team came up with new ideas from this point onwards. All have seen and felt what happens if the change has started but not been finished.

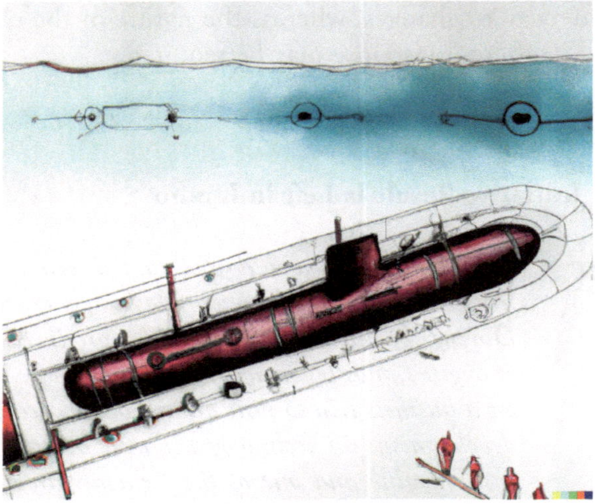

There are several takeaways from this story. First, communication matters. It could be the case that some features were not appropriate. Or maybe there was a long-term contract with a different company. Or even corruption was part of the game. It does not matter—however, knowing the reason for the lack of implementation could have helped retain the motivation of the involved and other engineers. Second, if the change does not get implemented, further change will hardly happen. If you run your project on burnout prevention and come up with a prototype of the solution, take care that it is implemented and that this implementation has a systemic nature, i.e. institutionalise change. Third, don't wait for a miracle to happen—start working on the next project, while the previous one is being implemented. Imagine that the engineers involved in the boiler design would have received the next important task. In only a few weeks they would be deep into the new project. Of course, not all projects succeed and this is normal. Continuing work on process improvement and innovation is a good cure against waiting for a miracle to come, especially if you consider that this miracle is often a matter of probability and not a sure consequence of even intensive project work.

5.11.4 Path Dependence

We have bad news for you—we are all path-dependent! Path dependence is a concept from the early 1980s. In his work, David (1985) showed that our technology development may not go optimally. Moreover, for some reason, we may end up in a "lock-down" state where we cannot change anymore.

The scholar sat at his desk looking at his keyboard and asked himself a question: How did it happen that the countries of the world that rely on the Latin alphabet have almost the same order of letters on their keyboards—QWERTY? Most people think this arrangement of letters makes for faster typing. Yet, the answer is the opposite: To avoid a mechanical problem ("jamming"), the inventor, who initially proposed to arrange letters alphabetically, decided to slow down the mechanical typing speed by placing letters often used in combination far from each other. When the writer was forced to slow down, the jamming did not appear. It was a simple solution with regard to the level of technology at that time.

Later, new technologies came but no one wanted to have a new arrangement of the letters. People got used to it, and several institutions were already equipped with QWERTY typewriters and were not willing to invest in new equipment. Finally, classes on 10-finger typing helped people become highly efficient despite inefficient technology. David concluded that there were three main factors which brought the development of technology into a "locked-in" state, i.e. a state where even high investment did not allow to change the technology for a better one. First, *technical interrelatedness* appears if other technologies start relying on the used one. Think of the software which is tied to the hardware. Shifting from one type of CPU to another may cause issues with software and require further software development. For this reason, many mobile phone producers stick to the same brand of CPUs as they don't want to force developers to invest too much time in software adaptation. Second, it is the *economies of scale* which drive the path dependence. Think of the example of the first typewriters. In the initial phase, changing technology to a better one was easy. But as soon as typewriters became mass products, change became expensive and way too complex. Third, it is the *quasi-irreversibility* or sunk costs. Not all investments can be returned if your project fails. If you build railways, the costs are enormous. If all of a sudden, you decide that you don't need railways any more, then the only thing you can do is to collect all pieces of the railway line and scrap it with the hope that you receive some payment for the scrapped metal. As you can imagine, this payment will be very small, while building a railway line is very expensive. And if you take into account all the human labour that was needed to build railways, the amount of irreversible investments is even higher.

Now let's think about burnout prevention. We have bad and good news for you: If your organisation got used to a specific way of working (e.g. ignoring the overuse of the personnel's psychological resources), it might be path-dependent and not willing to change. Why? This "used to" is a soft representation of technical interrelatedness (e.g. the hierarchies and established way of communication), economies of scale (e.g. broadly applied organisational practices), and quasi-irreversibility (e.g. working information system and described processes).

At the same time, research on path dependence has shown that change is still possible. For instance, in Finland the economy used to be highly dependent on wood processing and paper production. But as competition increased, Finns were forced to change their industry profile. Another example is the fossil fuels that our world largely relies on. Yet, the recent developments in climate and the response of the United Nations and most governments to this issue forced car manufacturers to shift from fossil fuels to cars using renewable energy. Consequently, the path dependency theory is not deterministic, it just predicts that the investment into change grows exponentially with every day (month, year) of using the new technology.

Now, think of your organisation and the current processes. Even though these processes may lead to psychological and physiological exhaustion, changing them to better ones might be hard. How can you change established structures, hierarchies, or habits that may even be reflected in your management information system? We propose the following approach: accept the *status quo* and communicate the enormous costs of the necessary investment. A high degree of pragmatism will help you allocate your change initiative resources wisely and evoke a feeling of trust from the employees and managers impacted. Then, try to gather a critical mass of those colleagues who would like your project to succeed and collect powerful supporters. Moreover, society and science are on your side—most countries and most researchers in the social sciences emphasise the importance of employee well-being. So, go on and you will succeed, even if the path will not be easy.

Further good news is that if you are successful, you will create a new path. The longer you stay on this path and continue to work in the new way, the less likely you are to fall back into the old, psychologically exhausting processes. Remember the exponential growth of switching costs. The longer you let your project run, the more you drive burnout prevention, and the harder it will be to switch back to the old mode. Every day without burnout increases the willingness of your employees to pay attention to their psychological and physiological resources. We hope that you will succeed in creating a self-reinforcing improvement process.

References

Ajzen, Icek. 2002. Residual effects of past on later behavior: Habituation and reasoned action perspectives. *Personality and Social Psychology Review* 6: 107–122. Sage.

Austin, Elizabeth J., Phillip Evans, Belinda Magnus, and Katie O'Hanlon. 2007. A preliminary study of empathy, emotional intelligence and examination performance in MBChB students. *Medical Education* 41: 684–689.

Bakker, Arnold B., Evangelia Demerouti, and Ana Isabel Sanz-Vergel. 2014. Burnout and Work Engagement: The JD–R Approach. *Annual Review of Organizational Psychology and Organizational Behavior* 1: 389–411.

Bar-Anan, Yoav, Nira Liberman, and Yaacov Trope. 2006. The association between psychological distance and construal level: Evidence from an implicit association test. *Journal of Experimental Psychology* 135: 609–622.

Barnes, Christopher M., Lorenzo Lucianetti, Devasheesh P. Bhave, and Michael S. Christian. 2015. "You wouldn't like me when I'm sleepy": Leaders' sleep, daily abusive supervision, and work unit engagement. *Academy of Management Journal* 58: 1419–1437.

Bogodistov, Yevgen, Moritz Martin Botts, and Martin Dinter. 2021. Learning from home: Can we learn better from stories than from textbooks? In *Remote and hybrid working: Variants, determinants, outcomes*, eds. Sevgin Batuk and Alev Özer Torgalöz, 187–210. Berlin, Germany: Peter Lang.

Bogodistov, Yevgen, Jürgen Moormann, and Mirjam Schweigkofler. 2023. Burnout im Homeoffice: Auswirkungen von Arbeitsanforderungen und Arbeitsressourcen im Homeoffice auf Burnout und Schlafqualität. *Zeitschrift fur Arbeitswissenschaft* 77: 375–389.

Bogodistov, Yevgen, Jürgen Moormann, and Rainer Sibbel. 2019. From openness to change to patients' satisfaction: A business process management approach. In

Proceedings of the Business Process Management Forum 2019, LNBIP Vol. 360, 195–210. Cham: Springer International Publishing.

Bogodistov, Yevgen, and Nadine Kathrin Ostern. 2019. Digitization at any cost? Willingness to trade efficiency for organizational, human, and relational costs. In *AMCIS 2019 Proceedings*.

Bogodistov, Y., Jürgen Moormann, and Rainer Sibbel. 2018. Beyond health care reform: How process management can alter patients' experience. *Academy of Management Proceedings* 2018 (1): 12544.

Bradley, Margaret M., and Peter J. Lang. 1994. Measuring emotion: The self-assessment manikin and the semantic differential. *Journal of Behavior Therapy and Experimental Psychiatry* 25: 49–59.

Cohen, Michael D., and Paul Bacdayan. 1994. Organizational routines are stored as procedural memory: Evidence from a laboratory study. *Organization Science* 5: 554–568.

Côté, Stéphane, and Christopher T. H. Miners. 2006. Emotional intelligence, cognitive intelligence, and job performance. *Administrative Science Quarterly* 51: 1–28.

Cropanzano, Russell, Marie T. Dasborough, and Howard M. Weiss. 2017. Affective events and the development of leader-member exchange. *Academy of Management Review* 42: 233–258.

Damasio, Antonio. 2005. *Descartes' error: Emotion, reason, and the human brain*. Reprint. London: Penguin Books.

David, Paul A. 1985. Clio and the economics of QWERTY. *The American Economic Review* 75: 332–337.

Dettmer, William H. 1997. *Goldratt's theory of constraints: A systems approach to continuous improvement*. Milwaukee, WI: ASQC Quality Press.

Dewey, John. 1922. *Human nature and conduct: An introduction to social psychology*. New York, NY: H. Holt and Company.

Ekman, Paul, and Erika L. Rosenberg. 1997. *What the face reveals: Basic and applied studies of spontaneous expression using the facial action coding system (FACS)*. Oxford University Press.

Ellet, William. 2018. *The case study handbook, revised edition: A student's guide*. Boston, MA: Harvard Business Review Press.

George, Michael, John Maxey, David Rowlands, and Malcolm Upton. 2005. *The lean six sigma pocket toolbook: A quick reference guide to nearly 100 tools for improving process quality, speed, and complexity*. New York, NY: McGraw Hill.

Goldratt, Eliyahu M., and Jeff Cox. 2012. *The goal: A process of ongoing improvement*. Great Barrington, MA: North River Press.

Grant, Robert M., and Judith Jordan. 2015. *Foundations of strategy*. Chichester, West Sussex: Wiley.

Hennig-Thurau, Thorsten, Markus Groth, Michael Paul, and Dwayne D. Gremler. 2006. Are all smiles created equal? How emotional contagion and emotional labor affect service relationships. *Journal of Marketing* 70: 58–73.

Himsel, D., and A. Inkpen. 2017. The rise and fall of BlackBerry. *Harvard Business Publishing Education.*

Kotter, John P. 1995. Leading change. *Harvard Business Review* 2: 1–10.

Kotter, John P. 2011. *Leading change: Wie Sie Ihr Unternehmen in acht Schritten erfolgreich verändern.* Munich, Germany. Vahlen.

Martinsons, M. G. 1995. Radical process innovation using information technology: The theory, the practice and the future of reengineering. *International Journal of Information Management* 15: 253–269.

Maslach, Christina, and Susan E. Jackson. 1984. Burnout in organizational settings. *Applied Social Psychology Annual* 5: 133–153.

May, Ross W., Mandy Bamber, Gregory S. Seibert, Marcos A. Sanchez-Gonzalez, Joseph T. Leonard, Rebecca A. Salsbury, and Frank D. Fincham. 2016. Understanding the physiology of mindfulness: Aortic hemodynamics and heart rate variability. *Stress* 19: 168–174.

Morf, Manuela, Anja Feierabend, and Bruno Staffelbach. 2017. Task variety and counterproductive work behavior. *Journal of Managerial Psychology* 32: 581–592.

Pascoe, Michaela C., David R. Thompson, Zoe M. Jenkins, and Chantal F. Ski. 2017. Mindfulness mediates the physiological markers of stress: Systematic review and meta-analysis. *Journal of Psychiatric Research* 95: 156–178.

Ryan, Richard M., and Edward L. Deci. 2000. Self-determination theory and the facilitation of intrinsic motivation, social development, and well-being. *American Psychologist* 55: 68–78.

Serrat, Olivier. 2017. Understanding and developing emotional intelligence. In *Knowledge solutions: Tools, methods, and approaches to drive organizational performance*, ed. Olivier Serrat, 329–339. Singapore: Springer.

Sterman, John D. 2000. *Business dynamics: Systems thinking and modeling for a complex world*. Chennai: McGraw-Hill Education.

Sydow, Jörg., Georg Schreyögg, and Jochen Koch. 2009. Organizational path dependence: Opening the Black Box. *Academy of Management Review* 34: 689–709.

Venkatraman, Nramanujam. 1994. IT-enabled business transformation: From automation to business scope redefinition. *Sloan Management Review* 35: 73–73.

Wild, Barbara, Michael Erb, and Mathias Bartels. 2001. Are emotions contagious? Evoked emotions while viewing emotionally expressive faces: Quality, quantity, time course and gender differences. *Psychiatry Research* 102: 109–124.

Zhang, Yucheng, and Zhenyu Liao. 2015. Consequences of abusive supervision: A meta-analytic review. *Asia Pacific Journal of Management* 32: 959–987.

6

Let's Practise and Make It Tangible

Abstract In this chapter, we look at tools from the process management field and try to apply them to burnout prevention. Tools like Design Thinking, House of Quality (i.e. Quality Function Deployment), or DMAIC are well-known in process management. The idea is that process management professionals learn to address the psychological and physiological demands using these tools. In turn, psychologists are given step-by-step instructions for some simple but rigorous tools that can help them address problems they are familiar with. Relying on years of experience from manufacturing, services, and quality management research, we show how to measure, improve, and safeguard the efficiency and effectiveness of your human-centred processes.

6.1 Design Thinking for Vision Development

There are many books dedicated to the topic of Design Thinking. The main idea of the approach is to take the customer's perspective. While in classical business process management, we focus on input, output, and throughput, Design Thinking stresses the necessity to start with the customer. Only when knowing her or his needs, we can design an effective process. Efficiency is of less relevance here and can be achieved in further stages of process management. But how to understand what a customer needs?

Recently, we received a request to help a process management group of a Ukrainian city council to develop a vision of change. The city still suffers from the Soviet inheritance, where strategies were developed top-down only by people who were seldom familiar with the problem "on the front line".

© The Author(s), under exclusive license to Springer Nature Switzerland AG 2024

Y. Bogodistov and J. Moormann, *Process Management and Burnout Prevention*, https://doi.org/10.1007/978-3-031-56615-8_6

The funny fact is that post-Soviet politicians and managers often don't know, that they don't know. In order to overcome this issue, we proposed a seminar where we showed some examples of problems from the daily life of a general practitioner and how to address them in a systematic way.

Below, we will describe our seminar step-by-step. Although it may sound like a seminar from a completely different field, it actually was not. Already in the first stages of the seminar, we discovered that most problems discussed stem from the situation of emotional and physical exhaustion of physicians (who were our target group). Furthermore, for you, the structure of the seminar is—we believe—of the highest importance. You can run this seminar for any problem you want to solve or process you want to improve.

6.1.1 Main Stages in a Design Thinking Seminar

During a Design Thinking seminar you go through five main stages:

1. **Empathise**—you need to take the perspective of your customer. Be it a patient or an internal customer of your IT support process, you need to understand her or his deepest needs.
2. **Define**—after you empathically approach your customer, you may be able to define the real (cause of the) problem. Usually, the real problem and the announced problem are "two different things". Yet, it is crucial to have a profound understanding of the customer before you move to the problem definition.
3. **Ideate**—if you know the cause of the problem as well as "the pain points" of the customer, you can start by searching for a solution. This is the main difference between Design Thinking and the classic approach—one is not allowed to propose a solution *before* this stage. The ideate stage consists of two substages—generating as many solutions as possible and then selecting the best-fitting solution.
4. **Prototype**—now you have some good solutions which cover the core needs of your customer. Here, you need to build a prototype—a working solution that you can test. At this stage, you discover which of the "fitting the needs" options might not be feasible due to technical, legal, or social reasons.
5. **Test**—finally, you test your solution. Apply it and look at the effects. Has the problem been solved? If yes, you generate a final product or service based on your prototype. If the goal has not or not fully been achieved (which is usually the case because of the complexity of the issue at hand), you repeat the previous steps until you have a working solution.

6.1.2 Preparation of the Seminar

For this seminar, you will need the following:

1. **Topic**. The seminar works best if people know what the seminar will be about. Communicate the topic clearly but do not tell the expected outcome—you cannot know the outcome for now. You can expect to have a solution to the investigated problem but what this solution is, will be the result at the end of the seminar. Take care that you communicate the duration and administrative aspects clearly. Once we had an issue: one part of our participants received an email with all the details. The second part was contacted using a messenger. As you know, in messengers, the details are not shown completely but only the first few lines with an opportunity to "click here to read more". Guess what happened? Most participants did not know that the seminar was planned for eight hours. They had made other plans and some even had to leave their groups in the middle of a discussion.
2. **Administration**. You need at least one contact person on the recipient side. This person is responsible for invitations, internal communication with the department/firm, tea/coffee and cookies, room preparation, etc. If you hold this seminar in an unknown place, even the smallest detail matters. The best way is to go with the contact person step-by-step through the whole seminar—if she or he knows what is going to happen, she or he can equip the room correctly as well as take care of flipcharts, food and drinks, necessary information, etc.
3. **Templates**. During a Design Thinking seminar, you will need to go through several exercises. For instance, you will need to create a persona (more information below). You can limit yourself to the use of flipcharts, but, as our experience shows, having printed templates for a persona will help the group work at their desk and then transfer their draft to the flipchart. We also prepared an adapted version of the Business Model Canvas (BMC) for non-profit organisations (Fig. 6.1). Our approach assumed that the found solutions would be implemented in the strategy of the city council. For this reason, we included fields regarding market segments, customer relations, value creation, actions, partners, communication channels, and key resources. In order to make the lives of our participants easier, we added in each field a few questions that should guide the brainstorming and help develop possible solutions. These solutions should come from the customer's needs that can be addressed using a depiction that we call the "Needs and pains graph" (Fig. 6.2). On

the right side of the graph, we depicted the customer's perspective—needs, desired gains, and existing "pains" (i.e. issues that cause trouble and negative emotions). On the left side of the graph, we addressed the resources and capabilities of the participants' organisations, such as products and services, actions that create gains, and actions that treat the customer's "pains". We printed both documents in A1 format and the persona templates in A2 format.

4. **Plan**. What helped us most in conducting the seminar was a good plan. Together with two colleagues, we developed a time schedule and the basic steps. Two things are unknown to you: the outcome of the seminar and the direction of thinking of the participants. First, it is the task of your participants to evaluate a situation and develop a novel solution, i.e. the solution is not given and you have to remain flexible with regard to the final step. For instance, in one of our first seminars, we expected the participants to come up with a solution which could be integrated into the city council strategy. But it was also possible that the participants remained on the operational level or even agreed on the status of the existing solution. You never know. As we say in Ukraine: "None of the wise men have seen tomorrow". Second, the direction of thought development is not controllable. In the same seminar, we attempted to develop some directions for the health system change in a large Ukrainian city. Of course, we assumed that as the result of the seminar we would receive a list of suggestions or even strategic options for the city council concerning health care management. Interestingly, *all* groups of participants found out that even though the observed problems appear in the healthcare domain, they are mostly consequences of shortcomings in other public or private areas. For instance, issues of children with disabilities could be addressed by the transportation system, e.g. specially equipped private taxis or public buses. As a result, be aware that the scope of solutions may lie far away from the initially observed field of problems.
5. **Backup**. As you don't know which direction the seminar is going to take, it is always good to have several tools and tasks for the participants. You can use these tools to change the view on the issue, deepen the analysis, or speed up or slow down the pace of the seminar. You can use these tools to help all groups speed up, or you can propose an additional (or an explanatory) task to a group, which is running ahead of other groups. It doesn't mean that the tasks should be stupid. On the contrary—you should see these tasks as an opportunity to deepen your understanding of the situation or as an enlightenment for those who lost their thread.

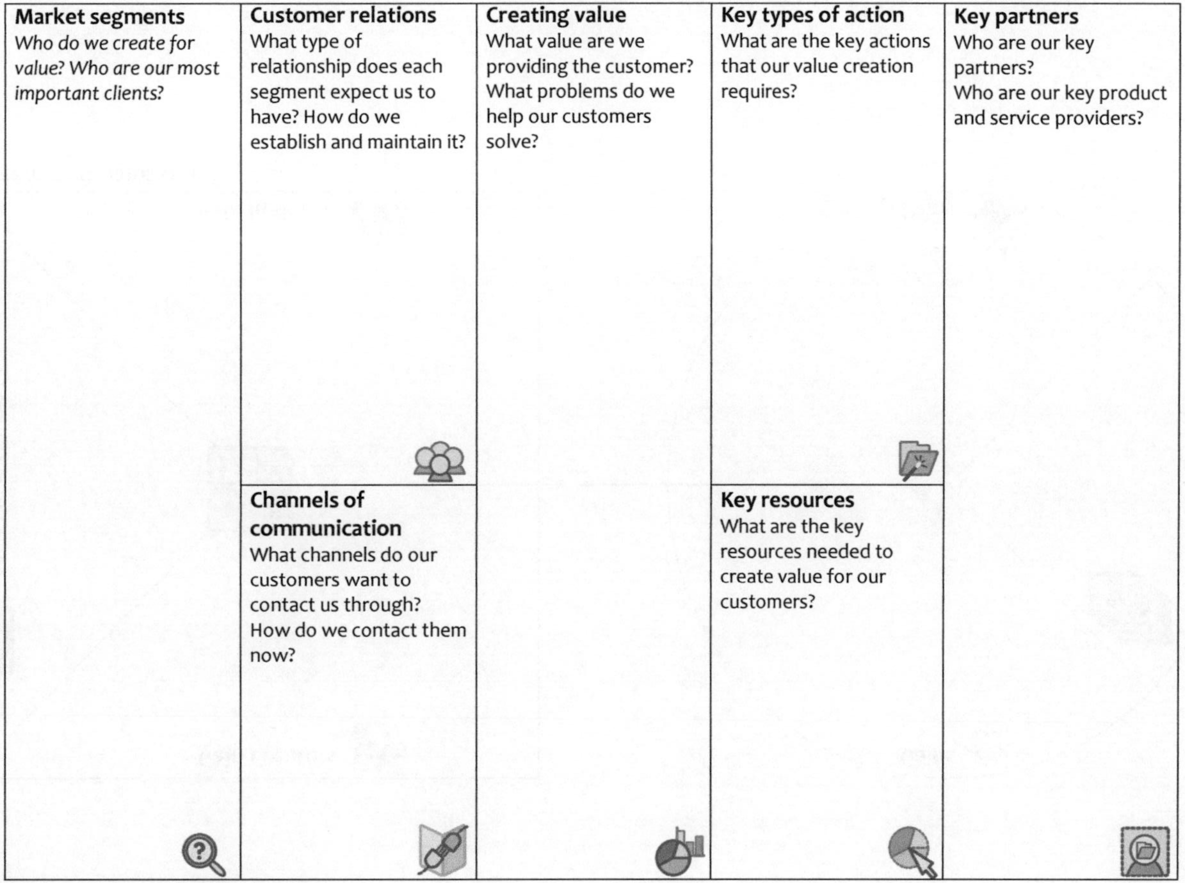

Fig. 6.1 BMC for strategy development

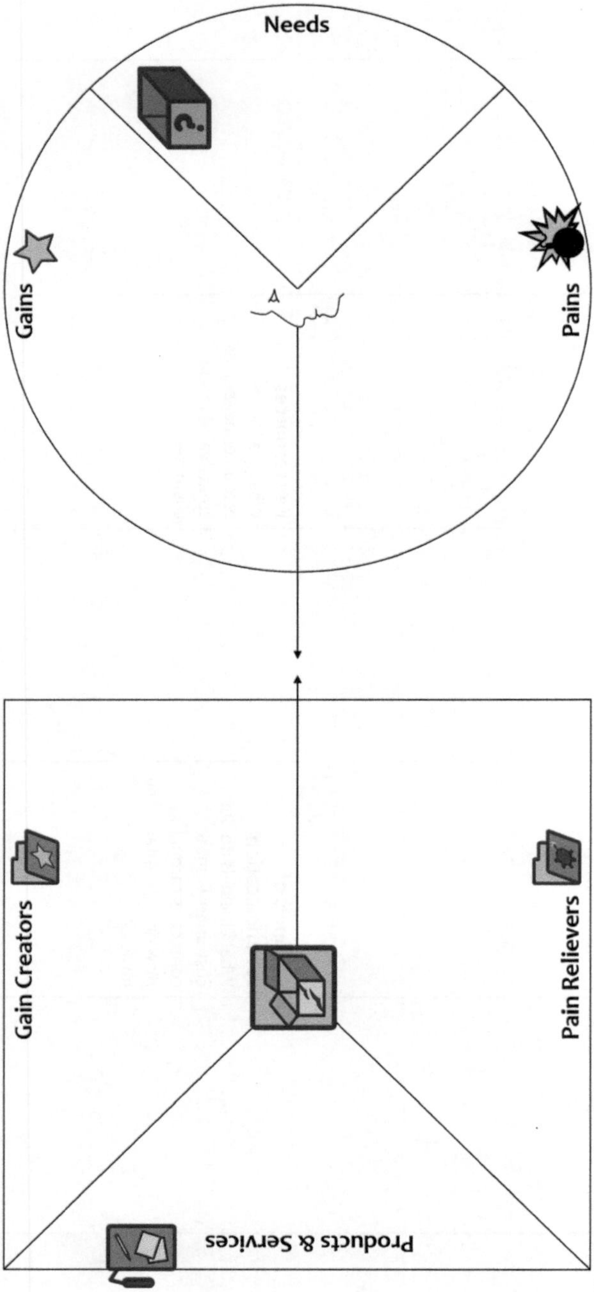

Fig. 6.2 Needs and pains graph

6. **Intermediate results and readiness to stop earlier.** As you don't know the speed, you should be ready to stop the session if necessary. Imagine that the discussion in groups becomes intense and is necessary for the problem solution. Although you usually make strict control of time, in this type of seminar you may encounter a need to give more time to the groups. Now, if you promised to finish at 17:00 and by 16:30 you are still in the ideate phase, what should you do? You can ask all the participants to remain one hour longer (which usually leads to turmoil). Our suggestion is: It is better to stop with a good idea and propose "prototyping" as homework or further self-study than to hurry up and make from a good idea a weak prototype. It is not a problem if you honestly tell your participants: "Hey, we had a great plan and wanted to see how far we can go with the problem solution today. We developed some great, really powerful ideas. The next phase would be 'prototyping'. In this phase, you should … Now, it is your voluntary homework. Will you manage to make a prototype from your idea or will you let it disappear?" Provoking is not a bad idea, in our humble opinion.

6.1.3 First Phase: Beginning with Empathy

Chris Voss and Tahl Raz write that empathy is the ability to understand the opponent. This means that you don't have to agree with the opponent. If you understand and agree, it is sympathy and not empathy. Empathy is the key to successful negotiations (Voss and Raz 2017). As negotiations revolve around a problem, empathy may help understand the other party and offer information and compromise in the way the opponent would be ready to accept them. Each party in a negotiation wants to be understood first and foremost.

Interestingly, the same logic applies to problem analysis. If you want to understand the root of a problem, you have to "look through the glasses" of each of the involved parties. In a Design Thinking workshop, we learn to focus on one particular party—our customers. Really, your customers pay you for your services and products. If you find a way to address their issues, you may count on a premium or additional customer loyalty. Consequently, we need to better understand the customers. But how can we do it?

1. ***Brainstorm about your customer segments.*** In our seminar, we asked all participants to list their customers (in our case: patients). We had an open discussion on segments and types and asked some questions about whether some customer segments can be merged into one bigger segment

or, vice versa, maybe a segment is too large and should be split into smaller groups. After a 20-minute discussion, we came up with about seven "problematic patient groups". As you see, we narrowed the task down. For instance, students, private entrepreneurs, and employees from big firms in the mining industry caused fewer problems during the patient encounter than pensioners, war veterans, children with disabilities, patients with a constant (opioid) drug prescription, etc. So, during the discussion, we switched from customer segments to *problematic* customer segments.

2. ***Use a whiteboard to write down the key customer segments.*** Then ask groups of your seminar to pick up one of the customer segments they are most interested in. You can even give the same customer segment to several seminar groups, but we would recommend you focus on different customer segments in order to reduce competition and increase the plurality of ideas.
3. ***Describe a persona.*** After each group received a customer segment for analysis, ask them to describe a typical representative of the segment. Who do they think of when they think of "pensioners"? It should be one or two so-called *personas*—an archetypical representative of the segment. For instance, the group working with "pensioners" said that the typical representative is a 67–70 year old woman, who is constantly "bellyaching". She always comes 1–2 hours earlier than appointed and complains unless one of the patients from the queue lets her visit the doctor. She seldom has a serious issue and rather comes to the doctor to talk, ask about an additional analysis, or ask for advice regarding a drug she heard about from an advertisement.
4. ***Ask the groups to give this persona a real name.*** From now on talk about this persona only calling her by name, e.g. Kate Smith. During the next 45 minutes, we ask the group to think about *Kate Smith*—how old is she? Where was she born? Who were her parents? Was or is she married? Children? How many? What is their age? Where do they live? Why? In our case, we prepared a document called "Persona Template" which we printed in A3 format—big enough to be presented but small enough to fill out empty fields carefully.
5. ***Present an example to the groups.*** Before they dived into this task, we presented our own sample persona. We did it to help groups visualise a persona as many have never done this type of analysis before. Initially, we thought about presenting one of the customer segments related to the topic of the seminar. However, we decided to choose a persona from a completely different field. We think it is better not to *prime* or skew your participants, yet give them an example. While the groups had to think about patient groups, we presented them with the persona of a bank

manager. We filled all the empty boxes such as "Life slogan", "Motivation drivers", "Demotivators", and even "Apps he/she is regularly using". The more detailed the characteristics of a persona are, the better. And feel free to add a bit of humour to this analysis. This creates a good mood and helps groups be more creative. For instance, the slogan of our bank manager was the phrase we heard from one of our students who described his team in one of the German banks—"*Morally flexible*". Although this is a joke, "there is a bit of truth in any joke", as we say in Ukraine.

This task is not only fun. The main goal is to go away from the rather abstract term "pensioners". The reason is that the more abstract our understanding of the target group, the harder it is to find a specific problem. But if you have a persona, then it is a concrete level and there the problems are easier to address.

It may sound confusing to you since if you address only one person's issues you hardly help the whole segment. Yes, but, first, it is not a concrete person, it is a *persona*, i.e. a collection of several people, an archetypal representation of the segment. Second, (and this is where the magic happens) if you address the issues of this persona correctly, the solution somehow holds for most representatives of the segment. Believe us, we tried it out several times. But how to "address the issue" and what is the issue? And here we move on to the next phase: "Define".

6.1.4 Second Phase: Defining the Pain Points

In the Define phase, you aim to understand the problems of your persona. What are her or his pain points? As we say in German "Wo drückt der Schuh?" (English: "Where does the shoe pinch?"). It is a relatively easy task since you just need to think about your *Kate Smith* and about problems she has. Of course, she can have a myriad of problems. Focus on those that relate to your situation. For instance, in our seminar with general practitioners, we focused on the patient-physician encounter and the often occurring conflicts. Write down those conflicts as "pains", and write down the arguments by *Kate Smith* to explain this pain to those who are not familiar with your group and your persona. Imagine that you have to explain the issue to a third person or even to a child (Fig. 6.2, "Pains").

If you brainstorm successfully, you will generate a list with 2–10 "pains". By the way, did you notice that if you brainstorm about your persona, your brainstorming does not look like the usual ideation where you try to generate as many ideas as possible, no matter good or bad? Here, you try to imagine(!) as if Kate Smith were a real person and you had really met her several times. This "imagining" may produce interesting insights into problems and help you turn off the oversimplification and heuristic processing of information usually related to a whole group of people such as "pensioners" or "veterans".

Yet, we know only the pains, not their cause. Creating a list of pains is a warm-up before you jump into the real task—finding the root cause of the problems. Have a precise look at the list with the pains. What could be their cause? Try to list all causes coming into your mind with regard to "needs". Isn't a cause something that people need and cannot get? Believe us, these will be only a few. Interestingly, our experience shows that the groups come up with 1–3 causes (needs) that spark or ignite all listed pains (Fig. 6.2, "Needs").

It is important to remember that although we started filling out a new field on our template, you are allowed to come back to pains and add new ones or merge the existing ones. While thinking about the needs, it is likely that you will discover even more pains resulting from a discussed need.

Actually, if you really want to be effective in this task, just call by mobile phone some representatives of the segment your persona is representing. For instance, if your segment is the retired people who visit a physician, just call some of them. In our event, general practitioners had mobile phone numbers of all their patients (yes, it is typical for Ukraine to respond to WhatsApp or Viber messages of your patients even at night or on the weekend. The general practitioners told us that it is easier than to stress the patients and self with an official visit if the problem can be solved immediately). Calling—although spontaneous—a few representatives of your target segment and asking something directly might help find new ideas, pains, and needs as well as eliminate those that appeared important to you. If we were you, we would ask open questions in order to find something new (e.g. "What are the problems that you encounter when you have to go to a hospital?" or "What causes negative emotions if you visit your physician? Why? What are these emotions?"). Then, after writing down all new pains, we would read the previously noted *pains* aloud in order to see how your interviewee reacts to them. Will she or he say that they matter or will she or he rather say "not at all" with regard to the respective pain?

However, we would like to caution you against reading the list of *needs* aloud! You can talk about pains but needs are seldom explicitly named, discussed, or even understood. How would your colleague react if you tell her or him that your conflict is a result of her or his Oedipus complex?! We don't mean that you need to go deep into psychoanalysis. We just mean that people seldom think about the real causes of conflicts or other pains if they lack knowledge from other involved parties. So, the root cause or the need may shock them and lead to a denial and feeling of being offended as a need is far behind the line of what a person would talk about publicly.

And here is an interesting example from our seminar. We talked about a persona—an old pensioner, Mrs Valentina Anatoliiyvna. The respective group did a great job of describing her life. Being widowed with three children, who grew up and went to Kyiv or Poland for work, she spends a lot of time visiting all kinds of public services. She starts early in the morning and goes by bus to the public bureau responsible for power supply. After a long conversation about the growing prices and a hard-to-understand pensioner payment app, she walks to the next public bureau. Finally, she visits her general practitioner (actually, she does it weekly although there is no real need for this). She wants to see the physician in priority to the long queue as she "is old and deserves to be treated with respect". She wants her general practitioner to spend at least thirty minutes talking. Mostly, she wants to discuss a new medicine she saw in a TV commercial or heard about from her friend. If this is not achieved (and physicians have to treat the long queue of patients with real problems and do not have time for Mrs Valentina Anatoliiyvna), she immediately goes to the hospital manager and submits an official complaint.

We know that the example may sound weird to someone from a different system: In Ukraine, you are state-insured and can visit the hospital as often as you want plus public transport is free for pensioners. But let's go back to the pains and needs. As can be concluded from the text above, there are several pains—conflicts in different instances with different people. Apart from being unpleasant and distracting, such conflicts cost the time of local authorities, physicians, other patients, and so on. When we asked the group about the root cause for a pretty long list of pain points, they came up with only two: First, Mrs. Anatliiyvna is alone and wants to be needed, heard, and held as important. All the family members went away, her husband died, and all her friends are at an age when most conversations are about illnesses and loneliness. Second, Mrs. Anatoliiyvna wants to be young and healthy. Partly because of this root cause, she has a problem accepting her ageing and approaching death. For this reason, she looks for all possible medications, suggestions, tests, etc. This may help her remain a bit healthier and a bit longer alive. "To see her grandchildren, to see how they go to school, or how they marry". As you see, two closely related needs appear to be the main causes of a big bunch of "pains". Even though there might be other needs, they are of less importance. Simply focus on the key needs and try to address these needs. The latter is the result of the next phase—"Ideate".

6.1.5 Third Phase: Ideate

As you have noticed, during this Design Thinking seminar the focus is constantly moving through two states: divergence and convergence. When you start thinking about the problem and who might be affected, you try to broaden your view. You try to remember as many target groups as possible. Then, you focus on only one of these groups. Then, again, you extrapolate and create a persona comprising features of the representatives of the target group. And, again, you focus on this single persona as if it is an individual and not a collection of attributes attached to all (or most) representatives of the group.

During the ideate phase, you repeat the procedure: First, you try to broaden the scope and create as many ideas as possible. Second, you reduce the number of ideas focusing on those which address the need(s) better and, thus, tackle most (or all) of the pains of the persona. For the divergence state, there is only one rule: *all ideas are good*! Do not think of the idea's feasibility, costs, negative consequences, collateral damage, excessive resource usage, and so forth. Only if the process of idea generation is not limited, new ideas will continue emerging. Acknowledge each thought, and write down the weirdest propositions even though you do not understand them completely. You may ask the author of the idea to explain it later in more detail. If you do it now, it will look like an evaluation of the quality (understandability of the idea) and will be perceived as a personal judgement. Avoid judgements, embrace freedom of thought and ease of communication.

After you are done with the list of ideas (i.e. you notice that the pace of idea appearance slows down and "new" ideas become indistinguishable from previous ones), it is time to have a short break and move on to the convergence phase. A break is necessary because you are going to change the nature of the activity. Instead of creating new ideas, all participants need to become focused on the feasibility and concreteness of only a few good thoughts—these are considerations where the entire group agrees on the importance and feasibility. Indeed, feasibility is one of the key aspects as there are plenty of impactful things that one can do if she or he had £1 billion. However, the resources are limited. Pick those ideas that are manageable based on your resources and still sufficiently impactful.

There are plenty of tools for idea generation and evaluation available "on the market". We are going to share with you the one that worked best for us. Our observation shows that after ideation, members of the group start defending their ideas as if they defend themselves. If it doesn't work, they would get frustrated and either demotivated about further work or destructive (overcritical) concerning other persons' ideas.

Our colleague, Professor Dr. Daniel Beimborn, proposed a specific form of "brainwriting" adopted from Rohrbach (1969):

> First, you give each group member a sheet of paper with a table. We suggest a 5 × 5 table (for a max. of 5 ideas in a 5-person group) with cells of the size needed to write down 10–15 words.
> Second, ask each participant to look at the list of generated ideas and pick 1 to 5 of those. Let them write the picked ideas into the cells in the first row of the table. Of course, each participant should add how she or he understands the idea. Some 10–15 words also allow a short explanation of why or how exactly this idea can relieve pain, address the need, or should be realised. Give the group about 15 minutes to do it.

Third, ask each group member to forward his or her sheet to the next member, for example clockwise. Now, every group member has to further develop the initial idea in the second row. If the idea is perceived as inadequate, she or he should write an explanation and propose an alternative. If the idea leads to a new problem, she or he may propose a new idea in a new column (just add another column for a new idea; for this, always leave some space on the sheet to stimulate the addition of upcoming ideas), starting it in the second round (to make other group members understand that it was a newly generated idea). The number of rounds is limited only by the time you plan for this phase. Give the participants about 10–15 minutes for each round and ask them to forward their sheets as soon as the time is over. Thus, if you have 5 participants in a group, within 1 hour you will have a reflection for each idea from each group member.

There is no clear recommendation on how many times to forward the sheet or how much time to give for each round. Our experience shows that it is cool if the sheet reaches the initial person to show him or her how his or her idea developed over time. We also noticed that sometimes the ideas get clarified pretty fast and there is no need to dedicate 15 minutes to each round. Yet, in one of the seminars, one group became fascinated by 1 or 2 solutions and they started writing more and more which required more time for the round. If we were you, we would flexibly manage this task. If one group needs more time for the stage—not a problem. Just send the other groups into the next round of sheet forwarding. The first group may skip one, but nothing bad will happen.

Finally, you will have a list of well thought-out ideas ready to be given a shot. How can you give an idea a shot? You create a prototype!

6.1.6 Fourth Phase: Let's Prototype It

In the event of a prototype, you have to create a "working version" of your solution. This working version will largely depend on the field of your work. If you are a programmer, the prototype might be an algorithm or a design of your new user interface. It means, the solution is not in its final form but allows us to test it and check whether it works. Consequently, if you came up with the idea that your software application requires a new graphical user interface, you don't need to write the whole programme. The initial page with newly introduced design elements might be sufficient to present it to (selected) customers and understand their reaction to the new design.

In our seminar, we tried to approach problems in healthcare management. The main goal was to develop a strategic, proactive approach to healthcare-related problems. "Strategic" is the keyword here. The prototype that our groups had to develop was some lines of text that could be included in the new strategy for the city's health department development. These lines of text should then be "tested" on several groups of customers: (1a) politicians from the governing party—they had to see the potential of the idea and how it can be implemented within the city strategy; (1b) politicians from the opposition needed to be asked—without a minimum of support or at least indifference the strategy would not be implemented; (2) physicians—although these were the physicians who developed the prototypes, they were only a small number. Our groups needed to know that their ideas were supported by a large circle of their colleagues; (3) patients—our groups selected very specific groups of patients. Testing (in our event, asking their opinion about the strategic proposition) had to consider these target groups.

Consequently, developing a prototype is a separate activity from testing. First, develop a solution with which your group is satisfied. Then define the procedure of testing. Remember the main principle—instead of supporting your idea, you should try to reject it. Develop a way to test your prototype in a way to discover its weaknesses as fast as possible. And remember that your assumed weaknesses might diverge from those perceived by your customers. Next, list the potential test persons. In our example, we listed the target segments mentioned above. But whom from these segments are we going to call? Make a list. Think about bias: if you select only your friends or those people who dislike you and criticise any of your ideas, the result will be skewed. Try to mix test persons and achieve a good balance.

Finally, how do you know that you collected the correct feedback? Develop a set of indicators and think of a way to ask for data matching these indicators. How will you know that the design is good? What about measuring the level of pleasantness and arousal using the SAM scale (Bradley and Lang 1994)? And how about the time needed to navigate the page? A good design is not only fun but also comfortable. Continue until you have compiled a list of indicators and questions/tools to measure them. And only now, you are ready for the test!

6.1.7 Fifth Phase: Testing the Prototype

There are many ways to test a prototype; they are just limited by your field and resources. Programming a new interface might take more time than calling some colleagues or asking them to write a few lines of feedback via messenger or email. You may plan weeks for this stage or only half an hour—it is up to you. On the one hand, the more time you spend, the better you test the prototype. On the other hand, more time leads to tiredness from the seminar and your participants might lose their motivation to continue. We suggest starting with a short pre-test of your prototype. If successful, look at the mood and motivation of your groups. Ask them about their vision and how much time they would like to have to test their prototype. If they use their freedom to decide on the time frame, they may become more motivated to test their ideas.

Testing means "rejecting". We would like to remind you that in science we don't try to support an idea, we try to reject it. Use the set of indicators that you developed in the previous phase and try to remain objective. Remember, people tend to defend their ideas, no matter how bad they are—their ideas are like children that they have to protect from the aggression of the outside world. You will likely run into the same situation. That is why you should try to find some weaknesses in your idea and then reduce them. Testing a prototype is about the process of further development of your idea and not about pitching whatever you have to other people. It is not marketing, it is rather "research and development".

As you can imagine, testing the prototype might be an unpleasant process—it doesn't matter how much effort your group has invested in the development of the idea—someone (or maybe almost everyone) will not like it. Developing new things is a risky issue. It is like entrepreneurship with all its risks but also with all its drive and possible success. The secret is simple: You should explain to your group that testing is not "pitching" and that the whole phase is similar to a cool game. You make your first move with the presentation of an idea. The others' move is to find a weakness in your idea. It is their goal. Your next move is to provoke as many criticisms as possible. Let the others believe they are winning through criticising. In reality, you are winning through the collection of as much feedback as possible. Because at the end of the day, you want to produce a new product or service. This needs a lot of trial and error. Why not speed up this process?!

Indeed, some criticisms are hard to withstand. And yes, there might appear some "knock-out" arguments eliminating the whole idea. Our experience shows that—independent of how bad they sound—most criticisms are easy to overcome, correct, or mitigate. And if the "knock-out" argument holds true … So what?! First, it is better to know it before you start investing your time and money into the implementation process. Second, you have a bunch of other ideas from the previous phases. Maybe it is time for your Plan B? Third, you now perfectly know how to analyse situations, how to develop new ideas, and how to create new prototypes. Consequently, there should be no worries. Relay and enjoy the prototype testing phase. Speed up the feedback, provoke criticism, put your idea under the most severe conditions and check whether it still holds. Enjoy this stage.

6.1.8 Repeat ...

Oh, the final section is the shortest one and we think you got the idea from the last paragraph of the previous section: repeat. You need to repeat all steps until you have gotten a great solution. Of course, this time it will be faster—you already have your persona. If you missed a need, you can add it to your initial set of needs. And if you need another persona (e.g. if you want to expand your solution to other target groups), you can create one based on the knowledge, templates, and routines you have just developed.

6.2 Design Thinking for Burnout Prevention

The previous sections of this chapter explained how to organise a Design Thinking seminar. This seminar can be dedicated to any topic. We propose you apply this method to the topic of burnout prevention. Try to address the existing organisational processes and the job demands and job resources attached to these processes. Look at the energy depletion. Look at the situations where employees and managers suffer from emotional exhaustion and show signs of cynicism and depersonalisation.

Design Thinking is usually applied to address the needs of customers. We propose you look at your firm's employees and managers as internal customers of processes and routines. How satisfied are they with their work? Even if you are the best employer on the market, the internal resources of your employees may get slowly (or quickly) depleted. It is too costly to let things go on their own. As we say in Ukraine: *Matters that are allowed to take their course develop from good to bad and from bad to even worse*. If we were you, we would dedicate plenty of attention to the psychological and physiological needs of your employees and managers.

In business, Design Thinking can even be used to develop a process from scratch. It would be great if new processes would take into account the psychological and physiological needs of your employees and managers. But this is hardly possible. And, at the end of the day, the customers of a firm's products and services pay for the work of all employees and managers. Consequently, we should start with the firm's external customers. However, you should introduce your employees and managers as one of the target groups or include them in the process design as early as you can. Remember our example: although the solution was meant for patients, only politicians may allow it to work. Why not include employees and managers in the idea development during the first stages of a process design—namely not only as developers but also as a group whose psychological and physiological needs should be addressed?

Start the process improvement initiative as early as possible. The earlier you start addressing the psychological and physiological job demands of your employees and managers, the earlier you learn to reduce the level of exhaustion and the faster you will make your firm's customers, your employees, and the top management happy. Design Thinking is a suitable method to uncover psychological problems hidden behind your beautifully crafted and formalised processes. Try it once and you will love it!

Some Suggestions from What We Learned During Our Study

We started the Design Thinking seminar mostly because of the burnout of physicians. The level of burnout was not critical but our regular data collection showed that, first, burnout harms the hospitals' performance as well as the performance of single physicians. Second, our research showed that transparency and clarity of processes matter (Bogodistov et al. 2018). We also found that interaction with patients might be very exhausting. For this reason, we proposed that the participants of our seminar (mostly physicians but also heads of hospital administration) focus on the meeting with the patient. We asked them to analyse the conflicts or other "problematic situations during a typical encounter with the patient".

We made two interesting observations (we have mentioned one of them earlier, sorry for the repetition): First, we discovered one more reason for burnout. The level of emotional exhaustion became obvious during the analysis of the pains of the personas developed. We had reason to hope for a better development of the situation after the seminar if the prototype would be implemented. Second, we noticed that most "root causes" were not lying in the field of health care, although at the beginning of the seminar, all participants and other parties (e.g. politicians) were sure that the core lies in financing and a wrong health system reform. The seminar revealed that several exhausting activities within the patient encounter process could be changed or simply eliminated. These processes are cross-functional and sometimes involve interactions with other public functions such as transportation, certification, verification, etc. This means that if the process could be improved for just one of the adjacent functions (e.g. transporting children with disabilities), the next patient contact would be more effective, efficient, and pleasant, i.e. each next encounter would be associated with lower psychological and physiological job demands. This in turn would free up more of the physician's resources. Of course you have to bear in mind that we talk about general practitioners (called "family doctors" in Ukraine) with whom we cooperate. A different group of doctors (e.g. surgeons) might need a different approach.

One more suggestion: As you don't know which direction the seminar is going to develop or what outputs will be produced, it may be a good idea to prepare additional tasks and exercises for your participants. What if they come up with a solution that is easy to build, let's say, in MS Excel or Google Sheets? Maybe they should build a prototype directly in one of these programmes. Or what if they can ask people using an online questionnaire? If you have 20 minutes, you can run a short hands-on task and show them how to use LimeSurvey or any other available software to help them in the test phase. You cannot prepare for everything. But you can have a card up the sleeve, can't you?

6.3 House of Cards … Sorry, House of Quality

One of the most beloved tools in the field of process management, especially process improvement, is the House of Quality (HoQ). The HoQ chart is the primary tool in Quality Function Deployment (QFD)—a broad set of techniques allowing firms to understand their needs, match them with the expected needs of the customers, and keep control of competitors trying to address the same customers. This tool has several advantages:

1. It is relatively easy to use.
2. It offers a clearly structured way to look at your problem.
3. It allows for a comparison of the quality of your processes against similar processes (services, products) of your competitors.
4. It is easy to interpret and understand. Thus, it may become the entrance ticket for your burnout prevention initiative.
5. Finally, it makes you look at the problem from a different angle. If you fill out all fields of the HoQ template, you will understand the burnout issue in a different way. You will look at it through the lens of related factors and their interaction. Moreover, you will need to compare yourself to your competitors (e.g. other firms or your firm's business units).

So, what are we waiting for? Let's dive into this simple but exciting and thoughtful tool.

6.3.1 Structure: Why Is It Called a "House"?

The HoQ is a graphical tool that brings together several topics, indicators, and analyses. The topics and indicators are grouped into "rooms". For instance, you have a "room" for your customer needs—a table where you list all the needs you managed to identify previously (via brainstorming, observation, or survey) (Fig. 6.3, Room 1). This is the "room" for "what" our customers need. Close to this room, you have a "room" for technical equipment, i.e. "how" the "what's" can be achieved or how our customers will evaluate that the "what's" have been achieved. Of course, you can introduce a third "room" on the corner of the two previously mentioned. You would then be able to map how much a "how" allows you to achieve the respective "what". What if you add a column for the importance of the "what's"? Now you can calculate a relative importance factor!

From these columns, rows, tables, and lists you build a big house as if they were bricks. Also, you may be interested in correlated "hows": you might then understand how to address the same "what" with different "hows" or whether you should expect synergies or inhibitive effects. The correlation table in the form of a roof finalises your "house" (Fig. 6.3, Roof). Thanks to this "roof" the tool received the name "House of Quality".

Have in mind that the HoQ is a creative tool and may look different in other firms. You can decide on your own which "bricks" you need and which you can neglect. For instance, in our example, we present a competitor analysis because we think it may play an important role in our attempt to prevent burnout. If you want to make a decision regarding different software solutions, an analysis of your competitors might not be as important as an analysis of the strengths and weaknesses of your hardware suppliers. Feel free to play with the rooms and build the house you need. We also recommend you search for different examples of HoQs for inspiration—sometimes you find a metric which never would have come to your mind. But, don't be biassed and don't feel restricted. In the next sections, we go through the "rooms" one by one and we will show you the logic behind our HoQ as well as provide you with options we decided not to include. Prepare to enjoy this elegant tool to understand and effectively address the targeted problem.

6.3.2 Room 1: What Do They Want?

In a regular HoQ, this "room" is dedicated to the needs of your firm's customers. Here you want to find out the desires of your customers and list them. Afterwards, you add priorities. For instance, if you work in a car

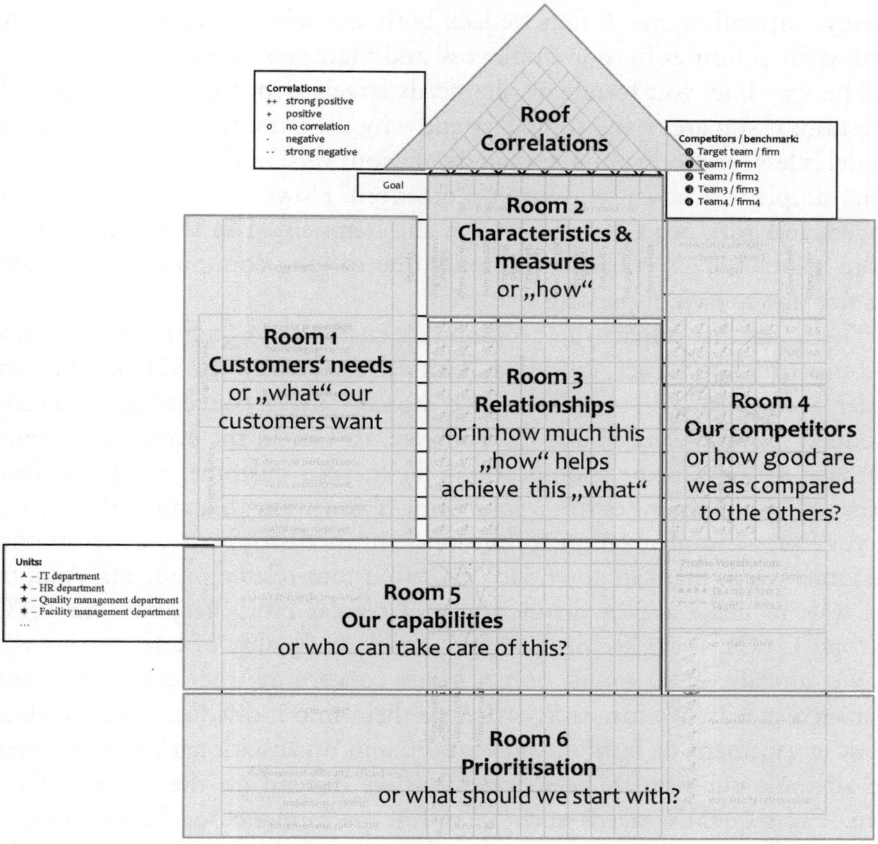

Fig. 6.3 Structure of the House of Quality

manufacturing company, you may discover that your most urgent customer needs are "better lateral impact protection", "a bigger rear mirror", and "a more powerful engine". If you apply the method rigorously, you should ask your customers, e.g. via surveying, about their priorities. You can also run a Discrete Choice Experiment (explained in Chapter 3; also known as Discrete Choice Conjoint) or conduct a qualitative analysis. If you don't have time, you may find already existing information on the priorities in literature—both scholars (in their studies on motivation and job satisfaction) and practitioners (in their HR and quality management departments) regularly address the needs of employees and managers. Sometimes you can even make estimations, e.g. that the power of the engine is more important than the size of the rear mirror. Data collection brings you a much better understanding of priorities and cures against biases. Yet, this method is the most time and energy-consuming one. Often we lack both and rely on our intuition while setting the priorities for our employees' and managers' needs.

The way how you formulate the needs largely depends on your research question: if you are trying to understand why the current version of your car model is less (or more) popular than its previous version the needs are possibly quite simple (e.g. advanced impact protection). However, if you are trying to understand why people use your cars, the items listed in this room will be more abstract, e.g. "enhanced mobility due to long commutes" or "smaller car size due to lack of parking spaces".

The needs that impact the decision of a customer to go for your (and not a competitor's) product are called "Critical to Quality" or CTQ. They are easier to formulate if you talk about customers' needs concerning a concrete product. However, burnout is less concrete, isn't it? In the event of burnout, we have to make some modifications. First, your customer might be your team or other employees from your firm. If you want to analyse the quality of your processes in relation to burnout, you need to focus on the internal customer needs that can potentially cause burnout-related problems. And, by the way, to make a clear distinction to a regular HoQ, let's call our CTQ factors "CTQL"—i.e. factors that are Critical to Quality of Life.

We already have found some hints concerning the employees' and managers' needs. We can easily structure them into individual needs, such as work engagement or burnout prevention, and organisational needs. Indeed, we all want our firm to be successful as we depend on the success of the firm. Consequently, needs such as In-role performance or Team commitment might be added to this room of our HoQ. Here, we want to make two remarks: (a) the logic of needs selection is the same as in the event of a car: you can be more precise and instead of using the abstract term "burnout prevention" say, e.g. "reduction of the level of emotional exhaustion at the end of the working day" or "remain emotionally attached to the team's task" (as an opposite to depersonalisation); (b) the focus may lie on an individual, process, group of individuals, or firm. In our example, we introduced two groups of factors—those that relate to the employees' and managers' well-being and those that relate to job performance. You are free to group the factors as it makes sense for you.

If you prepare a HoQ for your firm, you might enjoy the ease of data access. Moreover, many employees would be happy to share their feelings, needs, and concerns with you. Unfortunately, such data collection is emotionally exhausting. Apart from this, many managers might not want you to survey their employees about feelings and might even try to bias the employees (perhaps you have heard the phrase "Please report positively or we will all be in trouble" from your manager). Try to retain anonymity and use all your political skills when collecting internal data.

After you have prepared the list of customer needs, add a new column for the priorities. You may take the average values from your survey or round them off. Here, you have two options: (a) Take the numbers as they are. As your participants have already rated the items on a Likert scale (at least that is how we would do it), you can use the data as indicators of importance. This procedure allows you to use the subjectively rated importance for your employees. The larger the number of respondents, the closer are these values to reality, i.e. actually present and felt by your employees and managers. (b) An alternative option would be to take the average number and then rank the needs. I.e. you can say which of the items is the most important one (1st place), and which is the least important one (e.g. 10th place). This procedure allows you to simplify your approach, and make your decisions more salient (as the values 5.56 and 5.60 might be placed 1st and 2nd, thus making the differences appear greater than they are). This procedure does not only help in prioritising but also in curating several biases. For instance, people often tend to avoid the extremes of the scales and answer "8" instead of a maximum of "9" on a 9-point Likert scale. (c) Actually, there is another option available. You can normalise the value by dividing the mean value by the standard deviation. Being a bit more complex, this method gives you a more robust list of priorities and takes the best from the two previous options.

In our example, we used the simplest way, namely option (a) with rounded-off numbers. Again, this is an example. All numbers are made up (Fig. 6.4). Moreover, we renamed some items since we wanted the items to go in a clear direction, e.g. towards positive or negative. For instance, Work Engagement, Job Satisfaction, or In-role performance seem to be positive issues, while Burnout, Boredom, and Sleep Problems are rather negative outcomes. That is why we formulated them by adding "prevention". Make sure to be accurate: terms such as "prevention", "mitigation", and "avoidance" have different meanings. Select the one which is closer to your actual (internal) customers' needs.

6.3.3 Room 2: Characteristics and Measures

Now, after you know what the needs of your customers are as well as their relative importance, in a regular HoQ you would search for the list of characteristics, measures, or items that can help you fulfil the needs. For instance, if your customers need "better customer support", in Room 2 you may write

	Customers' needs	Priority
Employee well-being	Burnout **prevention**	5
	Work engagement	3
	Job satisfaction	5
	Boredom **avoidance**	2
	Sleep problems **prevention**	3
Job performance	In-role performance	4
	Extra-role performance	3
	Team commitment	5
	Organisation commitment	3
	Employee turnover	4

Fig. 6.4 Needs of (internal) customers, Room 1, House of Quality

different existing or desirable tools to support your customers such as "Hotline", "Chatbot", "FAQ", "Personal callback", or similar. If your company is a smartphone producer, you may want to write "High gaming performance", "YouTube videos", "Camera performance", and "Smooth work of social networks apps" in the list of needs. In Room 2, you would then add technical characteristics such as "Type of RAM", "Size of RAM", "Number of fast CPU cores", etc.

In our case, we need to add items that are related to psychological and physiological resources. As you can see in Fig. 6.4, all our needs are the outcomes of the Energy Compass as proposed by Schaufeli (2017). Based on our previous chapters, the notion by Schaufeli, as well as the job demands and resources model, we propose to focus on two groups of items: "job demands" and "job resources". If you follow the theory used in this book, these two groups of items would be the most obvious. A good alternative (also in line with this book) would be to focus on groups of items such as "psychological" and "physiological" demands. You can combine those or use any other way to structure your items. Moreover, the deeper you analyse the situation, the more precise your items will be.

By selecting your items, we recommend you apply qualitative surveys, observation, common sense, as well as literature. As you see in our example, we used a paper written by Schaufeli (2017) for inspiration. Yet, we have a big issue here: the more general you are in these items, the more issues you will have in the next "rooms" of our HoQ. The reason is simple: "Organisational change" is an abstract item and it is harder to measure than "Number of employees who changed their roles in the last month". The latter is much easier to understand and, actually, represents an easy-to-measure KPI. Unfortunately, it is too precise and does not capture the whole organisational change.

There are two solutions for this problem: You can (a) either develop a set of HoQs,[1] whereby you start with the higher level of abstraction and then deep-dive to the more precise HoQs. For instance, you can start with the HoQ that has the highest priority level; or (b) you develop a set of KPIs on a separate sheet of paper. For instance, a set with KPIs on "organisational change" may include indicators for role change, number of new employees, number of new products or processes, growth of market penetration, etc. Such a bundle of indicators might be a good approach, although you have to work hard on the weights of each indicator for the final KPI set. For example, you have to take into account that the "number of new employees" is a weaker indicator of organisational change than the "number of new products or processes", because the growth of an organisation is not really a "change". In contrast, the fact that an organisation starts new products or processes, appears like a big change. Moreover, new processes and products can also be introduced by the existing personnel, i.e. without hiring new employees.

On top of the row with all characteristics or measures, you should add a new row called "Goal". Here, you enter the KPI goal. If you look at the indicator "Number of employees who changed their roles in the last month" and you strive towards change, you may assume that as the result of change 70% of employees should have (partly) changed their roles. If your organisation has 100 employees, the goal would be 70. If you use the KPI set, you will have to make a more complex estimation but the logic is the same. To make it simple, we have used plain numbers for our imaginary KPI set (Fig. 6.5, Goal).

[1] It is recommended to develop several HoQs—you can start with a rough overview of the main issues, then you move to more precise activities and responsibilities of concrete people. We will describe the process in detail later in this chapter.

Goal		4	2,2	3,5	...					
		Job demands					Job resources			
Customers' needs	Priority	Organisational change	Work pressure	Time pressure	Emotional labour	Future job insecurity	Social support	Supervisor support	Autonomy	Task significance	Skill variety

Fig. 6.5 Characteristics and measures, Room 2, House of Quality (*Note* "Goal" shows the value of an imaginary KPI. For example, if your KPI "The maximum number of employees who have to change their role" is equal to four employees, the goal for "Organisational change" would be 4)

Let's bring these two "bricks" together (Fig. 6.6). We position Room 2 above Room 1. As a result, we have an unfilled space below Room 2 and on the right of Room 1. So, you may already understand what we are going to do next …

	Goal		4	2,2	3,5	...						
			Job demands					Job resources				
	Customers' needs	Priority	Organisational change	Work pressure	Time pressure	Emotional labour	Future job insecurity	Social support	Supervisor support	Autonomy	Task significance	Skill variety
Employee well-being	Burnout **prevention**	5										
	Work engagement	3										
	Job satisfaction	5										
	Boredom **avoidance**	2										
	Sleep problems **prevention**	3										
Job performance	In-role performance	4										
	Extra-role performance	3										
	Team commitment	5										
	Organisation commitment	3										
	Employee turnover	4										

Fig. 6.6 Positioning of Room 1 and Room 2 in the House of Quality

6.3.4 Room 3: Relationships or How to Best Achieve Meet Our Customers' Needs

As you have noticed, in Room 1 we talked about needs or "what our customers desire or require". Room 2 is actually about "how to get to those needs", e.g. if we manage our job demands and resources efficiently, we may avoid burnout and increase job satisfaction. Yet, how much will these "how" help achieve the "what"? Or, put differently, what is the power and direction of the relationship?

Now you see why we changed our items in Room 1 to only one direction—this step makes our life easier. If we had used "Burnout" (instead of "Burnout prevention"), then we would need to analyse the positive effect of "Work pressure" on "Burnout" and the negative effect on "Job satisfaction". "Positive" in this event means, the more of "how", the more of "what". "Negative", on the contrary, implies that the more "how" is present, the less of "what" we would have. As "Work pressure" increases "Burnout", the relationship is positive. In the same vein, as "Job pressure" reduces job satisfaction, the relationship would be negative. It is not a big issue to introduce positive and negative numbers, but when you perform further calculations (e.g. importance index), you need to sum up values. Having only positive or negative values is not a problem. High negative values and high positive values indicate high importance. But when summing them up, you might end up with something close to zero. To prevent the issue, just sum up the absolute values.

We decided to use the "way round" and formulated our items in Room 1 in a way that they all go in the same direction. Thus, we just need to calculate how strong the relationship is without using negative numbers. We decided that our lowest value is "0", i.e. no influence at all. The highest value is "10", i.e. "very strong influence". Where did we take these values from? Well, in this example, we made the numbers up. In real life, you have three options: (a) You use your gut feeling. Of course, you should not make this evaluation alone but together with experts and some involved employees and managers. The higher the number of those who evaluate, the closer the number to the objective one. The main advantage of this procedure is the speed. But, of course, it is just an estimation. (b) You can run a quick survey and find out what the involved employees and managers think. You don't need to ask them all—as long as you create a correct sample representing your team, you may extrapolate and draw conclusions that are very close to objectivity. The main advantage of the procedure is that it brings you close to the current status within your firm. (c) You may look for academic papers. Researchers have usually done all the job for you—they know how to select the correct sample and how to run the correct statistics. However, they usually collect data in their domain of interest and this may differ from your domain. For instance, we work a lot with data from general practitioners from Ukrainian hospitals, i.e. in a non-profit domain. Will our relationship data be the same as in your Austrian, British, or Canadian firm? We are pretty sure it will deviate. The question is only "in how much". The main advantage of this procedure is its closeness to objectivity. Even though the numbers might not be the same as in your firm, they will most likely be free of biases and measurement errors as scientists are usually more rigorous in data processing, otherwise they will not be accepted by the academic community.

So, consider these three options carefully and select the one which best fits your needs, capabilities, and available resources. Enter the values of the strength of the relationship in the appropriate fields. To be more precise, under "strength" we understand the power of impact and not the statistical significance. At the moment, we would like to know how well the "how" allows us to achieve the respective "what" (Fig. 6.7).

	Goal		4	2,2	3,5	…						
			Job demands					Job resources				
	Customers' needs	Priority	Organisational change	Work pressure	Time pressure	Emotional labour	Future job insecurity	Social support	Supervisor support	Autonomy	Task significance	Skill variety
Employee well-being	Burnout **prevention**	5	⑤	⑧	⑦	…						
	Work engagement	3	⑥	⑦	⑥							
	Job satisfaction	5	⑦	⑤	④							
	Boredom **avoidance**	2	②	③	⓪							
	Sleep problems **prevention**	3	③	⑦	⑨							
Job performance	In-role performance	4	⑧	⑦	⑨							
	Extra-role performance	3	⑨	⑩	⑥							
	Team commitment	5	⑨	④	⑥							
	Organisation commitment	3	②	⑤	③							
	Employee turnover	4	④	⑥	④							

Fig. 6.7 Relationships, Room 3, House of Quality (we filled out only a few columns as an example)

6.3.5 Room 4: Whom Do You Compete with?

In a regular House of Quality, you use Room 4 for comparison against your competitors. Of course, it depends on what you use the technique for. For instance, you can use an adapted version of the House of Quality for decision-making: you may want to analyse the pros and cons of different decision options. Room 4 would be used, in this event, for a comparison of different decision alternatives. In a regular analysis, you add basic information on your competitors, i.e. you continue evaluating your customers' needs concerning the way the needs are addressed by your competitors.

In the event of burnout or other needs related to your employees' well-being or job performance, the competitors are hard to define. We propose two options:

First, you can compare yourself against your main competitors in the market. This approach will show how good you are not only in products, services, and sales, but also in your HR policy, values, and other aspects of organising work. Unfortunately, this approach has several difficulties. One of these is the complexity of data collection. Your competitors might not be willing to share with you information on their employees' well-being. The second difficulty is defining your competitors. As in our version of the HoQ, we do not strive towards understanding the strengths and weaknesses of our production process but of the way we work with personnel. Thus, our competitors are not firms who compete with us in a certain market but firms who would be glad to headhunt our employees. And this might be a much broader market, hard to estimate.

For this reason, second, it might be a good idea to perform a comparison between your firm's departments. Data collection is relatively easy and employees working in other departments are those people whom your team members compare them with. The disadvantage of this approach is the fact that even if other companies around you are much better/worse, you will not take them into account. Easiness in data collection goes at odds with the objectivity of your position determination.

Now let's talk about the steps you should take. To begin with, estimate your department's relative position as compared to other departments. Simply rank all departments with regard to each customer need on a 5-point scale. To increase the readability of the HoQ, we use different fonts (Figs. 6.8 and 6.9). After you have rated all customer needs, connect the numbers of each firm/department with a line. This simple step visualises "the profiles". In our example, you can see that Firm 1 is much better in indicators related to employees' well-being, but shows lower success concerning the job performance-related indicators. Use different lines or colours for the profiles.

The next column is the "sales point". This data helps us understand and structure what our customers are willing to pay for. Or, put differently, this indicator helps us identify the most powerful customer requirements that address the problems best. You can understand this indicator as "What will help me 'sell' my solution to my customers?". For any marketing or PR campaign it is important to have about three sales points, i.e. the message should root in three strong arguments, or at least one very strong argument and two minor arguments. Here, we use the values ranging from 1 (does not play a significant role as a sales point) to 1.3 (helps convince our customers)

		Goal	4	2,2	3,5	...													
			Job demands					Job resources											
	Customers' needs	Priority	Organisational change	Work pressure	Time pressure	Emotional labour	Future job insecurity	Social support	Supervisor support	Autonomy	Task significance	Skill variety	Internal (External) benchmark, 1 (low) – 5 (high)					Sales points	Improvement ratio
													5	4	3	2	1		
Employee well-being	Burnout **prevention**	5	⑤	⑧	⑦	...							❶	❹	❷	❸	⓿	1.2	1.5
	Work engagement	3	⑥	⑦	⑥								❹	❶	❷	⓿		1.0	1.5
	Job satisfaction	5	⑦	⑤	④								❹	❶	❷	⓿		1.7	1.7
	Boredom **avoidance**	2	②	③	⓪								❶	⓿	❹	❷		...	...
	Sleep problems **prevention**	3	③	⑦	⑨								❹	❶	❸	❷	⓿		
Job performance	In-role performance	4	⑧	⑦	⑨									❷	❶	⓿	❸		
	Extra-role performance	3	⑨	⑩	⑥									❶	⓿	❷	❸		
	Team commitment	5	⑨	④	⑥									❶	❷	⓿	❸		
	Organisation commitment	3	②	⑤	③								❶	❷	⓿	❹	❸		
	Employee turnover	4	④	⑥	④								❶	❹	❷	⓿			

Fig. 6.8 Competitors, Room 4, House of Quality

Competitors / benchmark:
⓿ Target team / firm
❶ Team1 / firm1
❷ Team2 / firm2
❸ Team3 / firm3
❹ Team4 / firm4

⓪ - no relationship
①
②
③
④
⑤ - moderate relationship
⑥
⑦
⑧
⑨
⑩ - very strong relationship

Profile visualisation:
Target team / firm (solid red line)
Team1 / firm1 (dotted black line)
Team2 / firm2 (dashed blue line)
...

Fig. 6.9 Legend for symbols used for the relationships and analysis of competitors

with weaker arguments 1.1 and 1.2 in between. The main idea behind this is when we use this importance as a factor for future calculation, a multiplication by 1 will leave things as they are, and a multiplication by 1.3 will increase the targeted value.[2]

The next column refers to the "Improvement ratio". If you want to calculate this value, look at your competitive position and decide where you would like to be. For instance, in our example (Fig. 6.8) the firm is not good in the field of burnout. Burnout prevention is a very demanding issue—it has a high priority and it is our minor sales point. We think it is plausible to move from rank 1 (where we are now) to 5 (where firm 1 is positioned). So, we need to move four steps forward (from rank 1 to rank 5). Consequently, we calculate the Improvement ratio as 1 + 0. 1 for each step in the rank, i.e. 1.4. Concerning work engagement, we decided to catch up with most competitors who are ranked at 3. For us it is only one step ahead in the ranking, so the Improvement ratio would be 1.1. Concerning Job satisfaction, our main sales point, at least two steps are necessary—we should be not worse than the strongest competitor in this domain, so we go at least for 1.2.[3]

You can find our HoQ below. We filled out only a few lines and, please remember, the numbers are made up and are not rooted in statistical analysis.

6.3.6 Room 5: Our Capabilities or Who Takes Care of What?

In Room 5, analysts usually show either risk assessment (e.g. type of risk, risk coping strategy, probability, impact) or, more often, the competitive technical assessment. As the HoQ stems from manufacturing, this "room" may include materials, technological details, know-how, etc. and a depiction of this data in comparison to our main competitors. Practically, Room 5 defines the "how" from Room 2 in terms of concrete data. For instance, if we propose Organisational change as a "how" for Burnout prevention, how can we measure Organisational change? Here, we come back to the issue: the more concrete the "how", the easier it can be transferred into a simple scale. In our case, we focus on more abstract "hows" and suggest these sets of KPIs. While many scholars propose to start Room 5 with the specification of the target value

---

[2] It also means that you can use a range from 1 to 2 with 1.5 as a value for minor sales points. The numbers play an arbitrary role. It is important that you remember which role you have given to them.

[3] Actually, as this aspect is so important for our customers and the main sales point, an improvement ratio of 1.3 would be even better. What do you think?

(ReVelle 2004), we propose to add a field dedicated to organisational capabilities,[4] i.e. "a firm's ability to perform repeatedly a productive task which relates either directly or indirectly to a firm's capacity for creating value through affecting the transformation of inputs into outputs" (Grant 1996, 377).

There are three reasons for referring to organisational capabilities. First, we can identify which team or department is best capable of dealing with the problem. This might help us develop our KPIs and understand what data would be of greatest interest. E.g. the HR department might not be so happy to receive plenty of raw data from your survey, observations, and KPIs measurements if these require comprehensive statistical work, while our firm's data analysts might not be happy with an oversimplified data representation. Second, we may estimate power distribution: if most tasks related to psychological and physiological demands and resources end up in the same department, this department may play a larger role in our process improvement and should be better informed, represented in our process improvement team, and enjoy the privilege to have an "ambassador" who may organise our collaboration. Third, if we discover that a certain department is responsible for most aspects of our work and if these aspects are worse than those at competitors or lacking to fill the customers' needs, we may have discovered a bottleneck, i.e. a constraint which does not allow our processes to run properly (Dettmer 1997; Goldratt and Cox 2012). This finding may give us a hint of where to start the process improvement.

In our example, we reformulated the concept of the organisational capability to "Unit to handle this issue best". This is, of course, an oversimplification of the notion of capabilities. Yet, this approach might capture the necessary elements of an organisational capability (Bogodistov and Moormann 2019). Moreover, we introduced the organisational units that might help address the issue. We used stars to make this "room" easier to distinguish from other "rooms". To make the capabilities obvious, we connected the stars with a line. As you can see in Fig. 6.10, the Quality management department seems to have the strongest capability. The overall picture looks, for now, as shown in Fig. 6.11.

6.3.7 Room 6 (Basement): What Should We Start with?

We know that all HoQs are different: one tries to be more accurate to make an action as clear as possible, and the other tries to be more abstract to address a broad set of issues and prefers creativity. The more concrete you are, the easier

---

[4] We will talk about organisational capabilities in the next chapter and explain them in more detail.

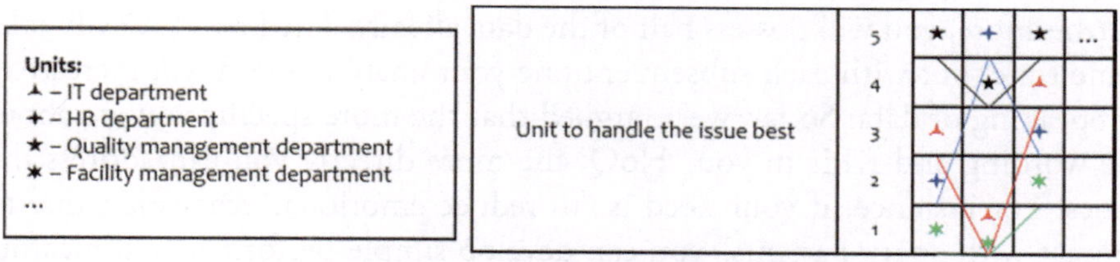

Fig. 6.10 Distribution of necessary organisational capabilities among departments, Room 5, House of Quality

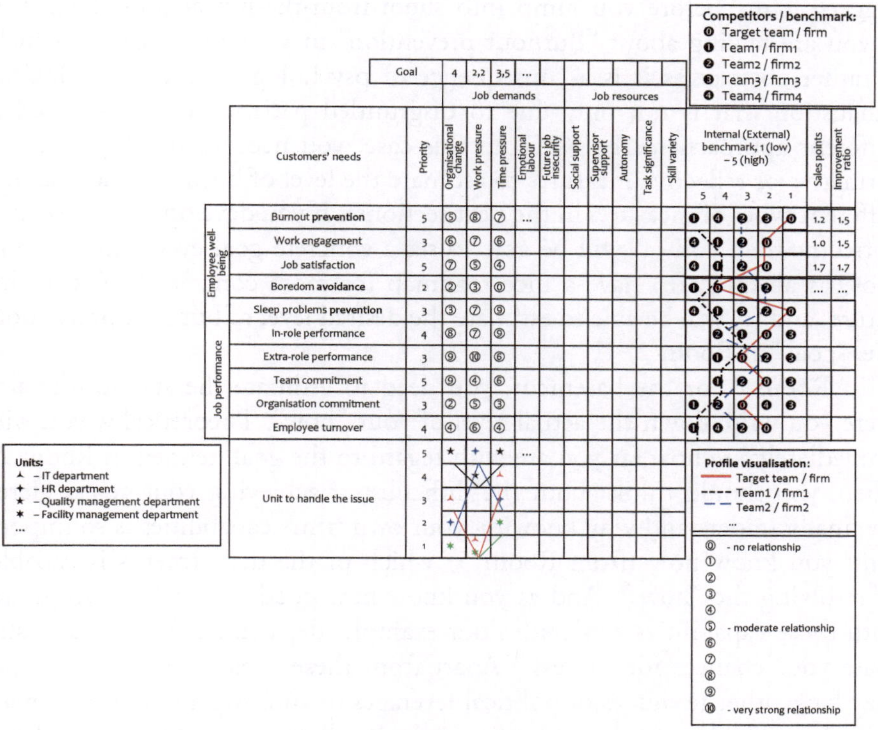

Fig. 6.11 Rooms 1 to 5, House of Quality

is your HoQ to implement as you know all the details. The more abstract you are, the more creative you have to be as you need to fill all the gaps with your knowledge and novel solutions. But remember, the one approach does not exclude the other one—you can start with a more abstract HoQ at first and then develop more detailed HoQs, e.g. focusing on the specific solution and its implementation. No worries, the first HoQ will take some time, but all the others will be developed faster because you know the methodology.

Furthermore, you will possess half of the data already. The first HoQ will take some time, but with each subsequent one your analysis speed will increase.

Speaking of data: So far, we've argued that the more specific you are about the wording and KPIs in your HoQ, the more directly you can address the issues. For instance, if your need is "to reduce emotional exhaustion due to contact with angry patients" you can develop simple performance indicators to track the meetings and your state after them to measure the level of anger of your patients or to measure the way you feel after each such encounter. Yet, staying at a more abstract level makes sense if you want to see the bigger picture before you jump into shoot-from-the-hip actions. Example: If you are talking about "Burnout prevention" in your organisation, which is rather abstract as it is a consequence of psychological and physiological exhaustion that is not only due to disgruntled patients, then you need a different approach to the KPIs. In this case, you need to develop a set of formative or reflective measures to estimate the level of burnout (more about different types of measures in the next sections). If you develop such measures correctly, then you (a) will be able to set a concrete goal even though your HoQ is abstract; (b) have a nice roadmap for more concrete HoQs in the future, and (c) will be able to estimate the desired level of burnout prevention (i.e. "goal" in Room 2).

In Room 6, or the basement, you need to estimate the state-of-the-art. Here you write down the actual level of your "how". Theoretically, you will immediately see how far you are with regard to the goal defined in Room 2. Then, you should think about the difficulty of achieving your goals. Here, we finally understand why knowing your own firm's capabilities is so important: you know now (from Room 5) which of the departments is capable of resolving the "hows". And as you know how good your relationships are with those capabilities carriers (in our example, departments), you may estimate your chances for success.[5] Apart from these capabilities carriers, you may have other resources or political leverages in your organisation that may shift the difficulty of achieving your goals. Finally, you should not only have a list of priorities with regard to customer needs but also your own priority with regard to ease of implementation. It is always cool to know your simple wins, i.e. actions that take few resources and effort from your side but make our customers satisfied very fast.

[5] And here is a simple homework for you: Try to change our version of the HoQ by introducing your own or your project's relationships with the carriers of the relevant capabilities (Room 5) and your competitors (Room 4). Room 5 will allow you to add these relationships as a factor to estimate the shift in probability of success of your internal improvement; room 4 will help you estimate the level of objectivity of your estimations.

Now it is time to move on to the next row—Importance rating. In order to be as objective as possible,[6] you need to sum up all relationships of the respective "how" (e.g. column "Organisational change"), multiplying each of them with the noted priority in the column "Priority". Consequently, to calculate the importance rating of "Organisational change" we need to sum up the relationships between "Organisational change" and "Burnout prevention" multiplied by the priority, "Organisational change" and "Work engagement" multiplied by the respective priority, and so on. The whole calculation for the importance rating of "Organisational change" equals $5 \times 5 + 3 \times 6 + 5 \times 7 + 2 \times 2 + 3 \times 3 + 4 \times 8 + 3 \times 9 + 5 \times 9 + 3 \times 2 + 4 \times 4 = 217$. If we calculate the rating for the other items, we will see which of them has the highest potential. Or, put differently, with which of the "hows" can we address the needs of the customers best?

Finally, we add a row called Improvement ratio. This row shows how far we have to go with our improvement. For instance, if we set the goal to "4" (or any other value fitting our developed KPI set) and the actual KPI is "3", then we have some work to do. How to calculate the amount of change? Just divide the goal (from Room 2) by the actual KPI (from Room 6). If the number equals or approximates zero, then we are good and don't have to change much. If the value is higher than "1", then we should work hard on the issue.[7] The higher the distance from "1", the more work is to be done. However, if the value is below "1" (i.e. the goal lies below the current state), we can relax and move to the next important issue.

In our example (Fig. 6.12), we came up with values of 1.14, 0.63, and 0.88 for "Organisational change", "Work pressure", and "Time pressure" (Improvement ratio, JD-R[8]). As we can see from our made-up example, we should focus on "Work pressure" prevention as it is the most important issue (Importance rating of 230). Luckily, our KPI indicates that we are good at preventing "Work pressure"—the value of 3.5 (Fig. 6.12) is far above the target value of 2.2 (Fig. 6.11). Consequently, we can skip "Work pressure" for now. Instead, we need to start with the next urgent issue which

---

[6] You should remain objective in this field; yet, if your estimations of priorities of the customers' needs and their relationship to "how" were subjective, this row might be nothing more than an objective interpretation of subjective data. You see how important it is to feed in data that is as objective as possible.

[7] Here, we assume that the higher the value of the KPI, the more it is needed.

[8] We added "JD-R" to "Improvement ratio" because we have to bear in mind that it is about the balance between job demands and job resources.

is “Organisational change” (Importance rating of 217, KPI = 3.5, whereas 4.0 is needed).

See for the overall picture Fig. 6.13.

Actual KPI*	*Organisational change = 3.5	*Work pressure = 3.5	*Time pressure = 4.0	…						
Achievement difficulty, 1 (low) – 5 (high)	4	4	3	…						
Importance rating	217	230	174	…						
Improvement ratio, JDR	1.14	0.62	0.88	…						

Fig. 6.12 Prioritisation of actions, Room 6, House of Quality

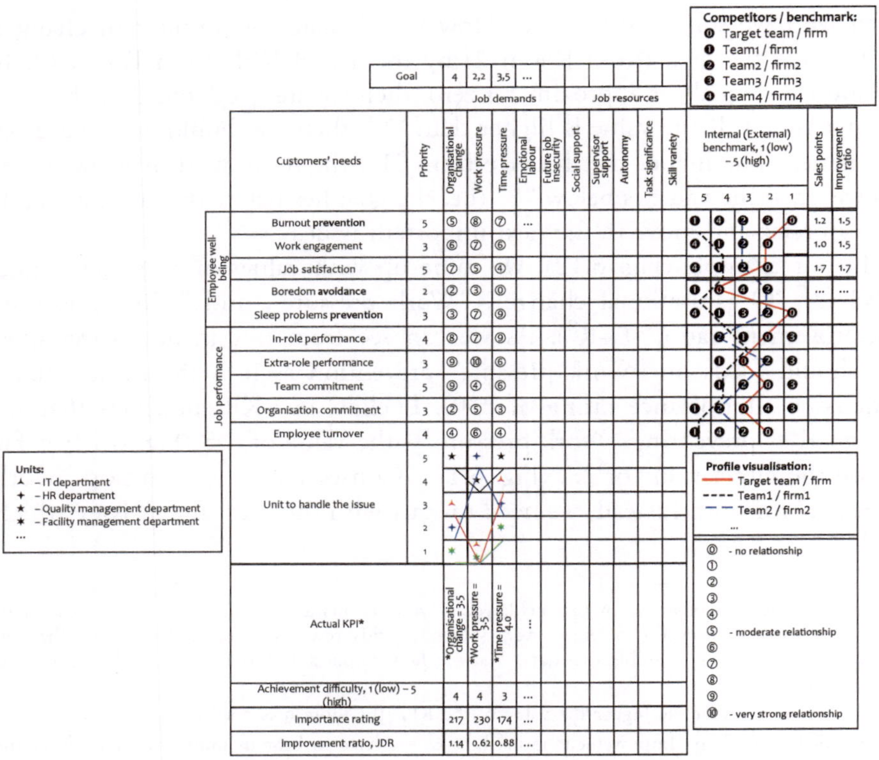

Fig. 6.13 Overview of the House of Quality, Rooms 1–6

6.3.8 Roof: Correlations of "Hows"

Now, it is time to look at the correlations among characteristics and measures. Indeed, some of them might be positively or negatively related. Understanding the degree and direction of the relationship will help you understand several important things:

1. If the characteristics or measures are highly correlated, it might be due to the fact that they are measuring the same or parts of the same construct. This may have interesting implications such as (a) sometimes you might be able to satisfy several needs by focusing on only a few characteristics and measures, or (b) sometimes it may be a trade-off as you have to decide which characteristic or measure to focus on, although they both might be needed and important for your customers.
2. The opposite is true for negatively correlated items: If the characteristics or measures are negatively correlated, you might avoid the trade-off situation but you might not enjoy spill-over effects when focusing on one characteristic or measure.
3. If the characteristics or measures are correlated, you might be able to group them and develop, for example, a firm's strategy for burnout prevention. The stronger the positive correlation, the easier items can be integrated into a new policy. On the contrary, if the items are negatively correlated, conflicts may appear.
4. The correlation matrix may help you double-check your previous assumptions. For instance, if you have assumed that the first measure has a positive effect on a customer's need and that the second measure has a positive influence on the customer's need, then the measures should be positively correlated. If by filling out the Roof of the HoQ you notice that they are negatively correlated, you need to double-check the data entered. Indeed, it can happen that you will not find a correlation but double-checking is always good.
5. Always look at these "hows" with the eyes of your customers, not yours. Even though some characteristics require more attention or higher investments of resources, if they are crucial for your customers, focus on them.

Again, you can make a fast analysis by entering the intuitive estimations, or you can conduct a short survey, or you can look into the literature. As with all previous "rooms", you will find a trade-off between speed and quality.

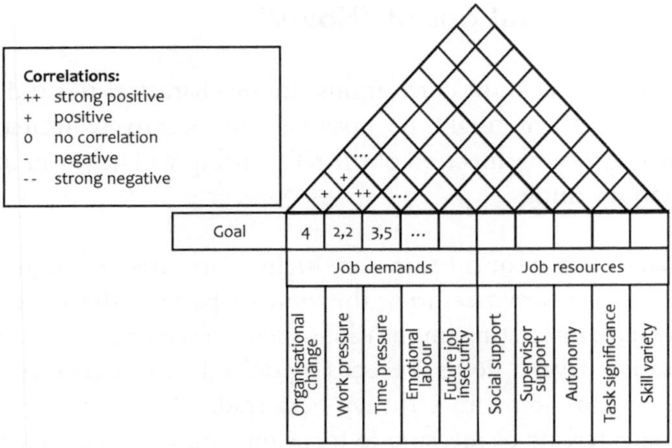

Fig. 6.14 Example of a correlation of characteristics or measures, Roof, House of Quality

If you depict the correlations, you can use different symbols. We prefer to use something obvious, e.g. "++" for a strong positive correlation, "+" for a weak positive correlation, "0" for no correlation, and "-" and "- -" for negative correlations (Fig. 6.14). Of course, you can introduce a more complex scale corresponding to a 7- or even 9-point Likert scale, ranging from "- - - -" to "++++". The granularity of the approach is up to you. And here is another trick: "+" and "-" make your Roof easy to understand. Sometimes we feel that consultants are trying to be more confusing in order to keep some "magic" in their methods. This approach is easy to follow: the less your buyers understand your actions, the more they are willing to pay (Grant and Jordan 2015). If you feel similar, just use some funny symbols for relationships in your table, e.g. "◆", "◇", or "◈" for "positive", "no", or "negative" correlation. Or something like this: "◐", "◑", "◒", "◔", "◕", etc. Anyway, the Roof is the last component to fill out in your HoQ. Now our "house" is constructed (Fig. 6.15).

6.3.9 Drilling Down and Moving Forward

First, we would like to remind you of what we previously wrote: there are several ways to approach the needs of your customers—you may remain on an abstract or move to a concrete level. Second, we would like to highlight that if you want to be rigorous about addressing the issue of burnout by using the HoQ, you need to make the next steps and develop some additional matrices. You can even draw them as a series of HoQs.

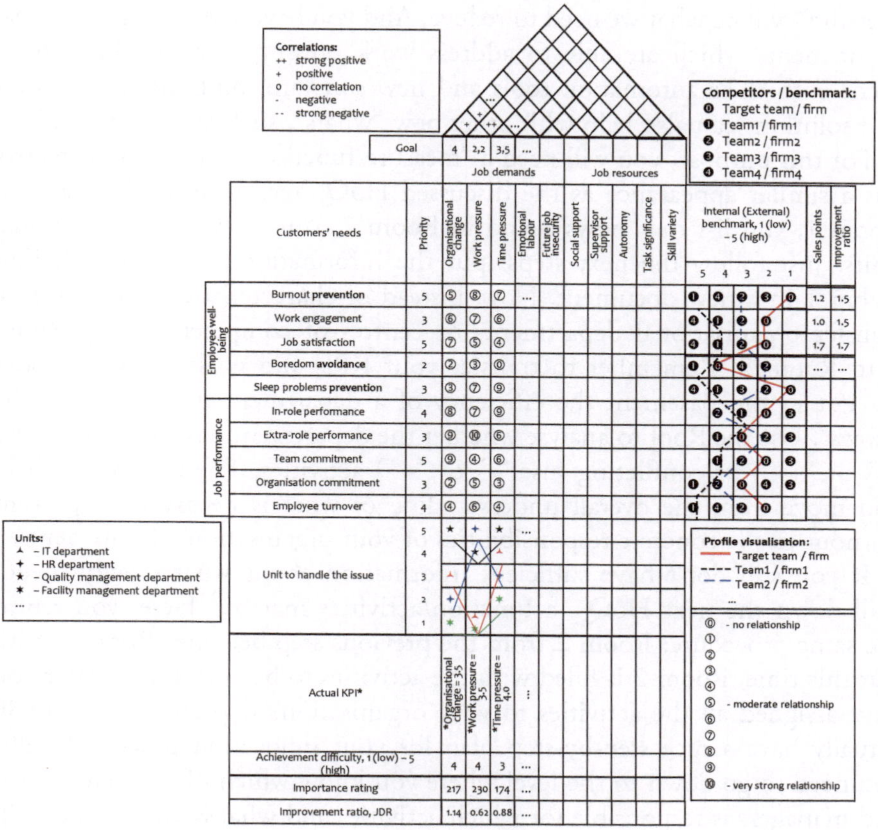

Fig. 6.15 Overview of the final House of Quality

You can go deeper or go further. For instance, you may take all abstract characteristics and measures and make them more concrete. "Organisational change" can be split into several items, all of which might be integrated into the previous scheme. Theoretically, you may apply the same logic to the customer needs—the need for higher "Job satisfaction" can be described by a number of underlying motivators, such as the wish to be acknowledged and the wish to be recognised. Consequently, "going deeper" would mean expanding the existing HoQ by adding more underlying factors for your needs ("what") and adding more steps to your "hows".

However, if you think you are precise enough and the "whats" and "hows" are clear and don't need a deeper explanation, the most common approach is to take your Room 2 and transform it into Room 1. This is "going further", i.e. moving towards the implementation of your initiative and setting concrete steps. Your "hows" will become "whats". For instance, "Work pressure" will be what we need to reduce. And you have several organisational departments which are able to address work pressure, e.g. the IT department with their automation tools and new software solutions. These tools and solutions can also help with other new "whats", such as "Autonomy".

For this purpose, you will need a "measure/functions matrix". This matrix has a similar appearance as the discussed HoQ. Yet, instead of "whats" in Room 1, you list the "hows". And in Room 2, you list your organisational units. Just follow the next steps: put the information from Room 2 into Room 1 in a new document. Now, instead of characteristics and measures, transfer organisational departments or centres of competence from Room 5 to Room 2. Remember to transfer your KPIs and goals (now in Room 4). Put in the Basement the efficiency of a department in performing the "hows". Use the Roof to analyse whether the department has a matching (use "+" or "++") or conflicting (use "-" or "--") activities. The matrix will help you move from the overall understanding of what is necessary to prevent burnout to the concrete responsibilities of your organisation's departments.

If you still don't have sufficient information about what exactly to do, drill down the next HoQ—a function/activities matrix.[9] Here, you repeat the same procedure: Room 2 from the previous step becomes Room 1 now. But this time, Room 2 is filled with the activities to be performed. After you have assigned all the activities to your organisation's departments, you will actually have a nice step-by-step plan for your innovation process. Ideally, you need to go down to the level where you know which of your employees and managers is responsible for which activities and what resources they will need for these activities. Practically, you will have a set of prioritised activities assigned to specific employees and managers. Moreover, you will be aware of synergy effects and possible conflicts. This information is also necessary for the process control in the future.

The deeper you go with your HoQs, the more you will have to simplify their structure. Complex topics like "Burnout prevention" become a set of simple activities that don't require complex KPIs or correlation tables. The Roof (where you enter correlations of the items from Room 2) might still be helpful to show synergies and conflicts, but the deeper you drill down, the more effortful it will be to collect data. So, look at your situation. The level of depth of analysis is dictated by the common understanding of what to do. If your organisation is small and/or your employees and managers know

[9] The idea is that you always go into depth until you know what you have to do. If you're making a HoQ for a small department, then one HoQ should be enough. If it's a large organisation with multiple levels and complex tasks, then you have to drill deeper until everyone knows what they are supposed to do and what the KPIs should be.

what to do from the first HoQ, don't waste your time on additional analyses! If there are no inconsistencies or obvious issues—start implementing your change. You can always go back and add an additional layer of analysis if you encounter implementation issues.

6.3.10 What to Do Next: Implementation

Actually, we have learned a lot about the House of Quality tool. This tool allows for a simple but rigorous approach if you want to improve your process quality. And having balanced processes with motivated and willing employees is a goal firms should strive to achieve. There are two more aspects to mention before we move on to the next useful process management tool that can be applied for burnout prevention.

First, as you have noticed, the HoQ is nothing but a way to better structure a problem and look at it through the prism of customer needs, competitors, performance indicators, organisational capabilities, and so on. Moreover, if you map all these aspects, you receive a systemic view. Academics work for a long time on the interrelation of different elements of complex systems. They proposed approaches such as Systems Thinking (Vester 1988, 2001), System Dynamics (Forrester 1971), or Modern Systems Theory (Luhmann 1987, 2004). The HoQ is a practitioner's instrument which goes in line with this stream of thought. For instance, Vester (1988) argued that focusing on a single aspect may be wrong as only the overall systemic view can shed light on what happens with a system (e.g. a firm, a business unit, or a business process). The HoQ incorporates several views, plenty of items, and their interrelation. Filling out these documents might help you see the forest behind the trees. Our experience shows that this is the bigger picture which should guide us in turbulent times. Knowing the interrelation will help you avoid unintended consequences, find workarounds using related but not directly involved items, and use your firm's resources and capabilities to their best.

Second, a deep elaboration on the HoQ, i.e. developing a series of HoQs each building upon the previous one, will generate a good understanding of the concrete steps you need to make to implement change. As you have seen, the HoQ is a tool simple to understand and apply, i.e. if you do your "homework" well, you are in a position to easily explain to all employees and managers what to do and why they should do it. Implementation is way easier with a good plan at hand, where you not only see the important milestones but also all relevant interrelations.

Yet, we have to admit that there are different ways to analyse the situation. The HoQ is only one of those ways. Furthermore, there is no clear prescription about how to apply it. For instance, we added the aspect "Organisational capabilities" while others may focus on risks or technological capacities. Did we make a mistake? No! And we recommend you to think about those aspects that fit your needs. Remember the Systems Thinking approach: it is important not to look at single relations (e.g. what your customers need) but also on how to achieve it, who is involved, your capabilities, etc. To receive a full picture, why not add risk management, other stakeholders' needs, principles and values of your organisation—or whatever you think is important for you? Of course, in the beginning, we recommend you use the regular HoQ as we suggested in this chapter. However, as soon as you have the feeling that you can fill out the HoQ quickly and in a reliable manner, you should try to improvise and focus on those aspects which are relevant to you or your firm.

Finally, not only the structure of the HoQ is flexible. So is the field of applying the tool. Do you plan to buy a new smartphone or a car? Do you need to decide which of the software solutions is best for your firm's digitalisation? Try to apply the HoQ: Write down your needs and write down the important characteristics. Instead of your competitors, you may put in alternative products. Follow the same logic for other "rooms" in your decision-related HoQ. We believe you got the point.

House of Quality: An Example from Practice

We would like to share with you the HoQ from the homework of one of our students—Mr Markus Pircher. He designed the HoQ for a bank. He started by sending a survey with his questions to 200 bank employees from five departments which he used for benchmarking. When developing the questions, he combined the Job Demands-Resources model with the Effort-Reward Imbalance model (Siegrist 2016). He also used a free QFD template from QFDOnlin.com. As you see, you can be very creative when designing your HoQ (Fig. 6.16).

We would also like to share with you a few sentences from the Discussion section of his work: "*The template clearly shows that the perceived implementation of the various customer requirements is assessed very differently within the various departments and staff members. It can therefore be assumed that the level of mental and physical energy exhaustion is not the same in the various departments of the firm. In the credit department, which is one of the most important departments of the bank, the support is primarily rated as poor. After defining this as an important customer requirement, it is imperative to act in order to*

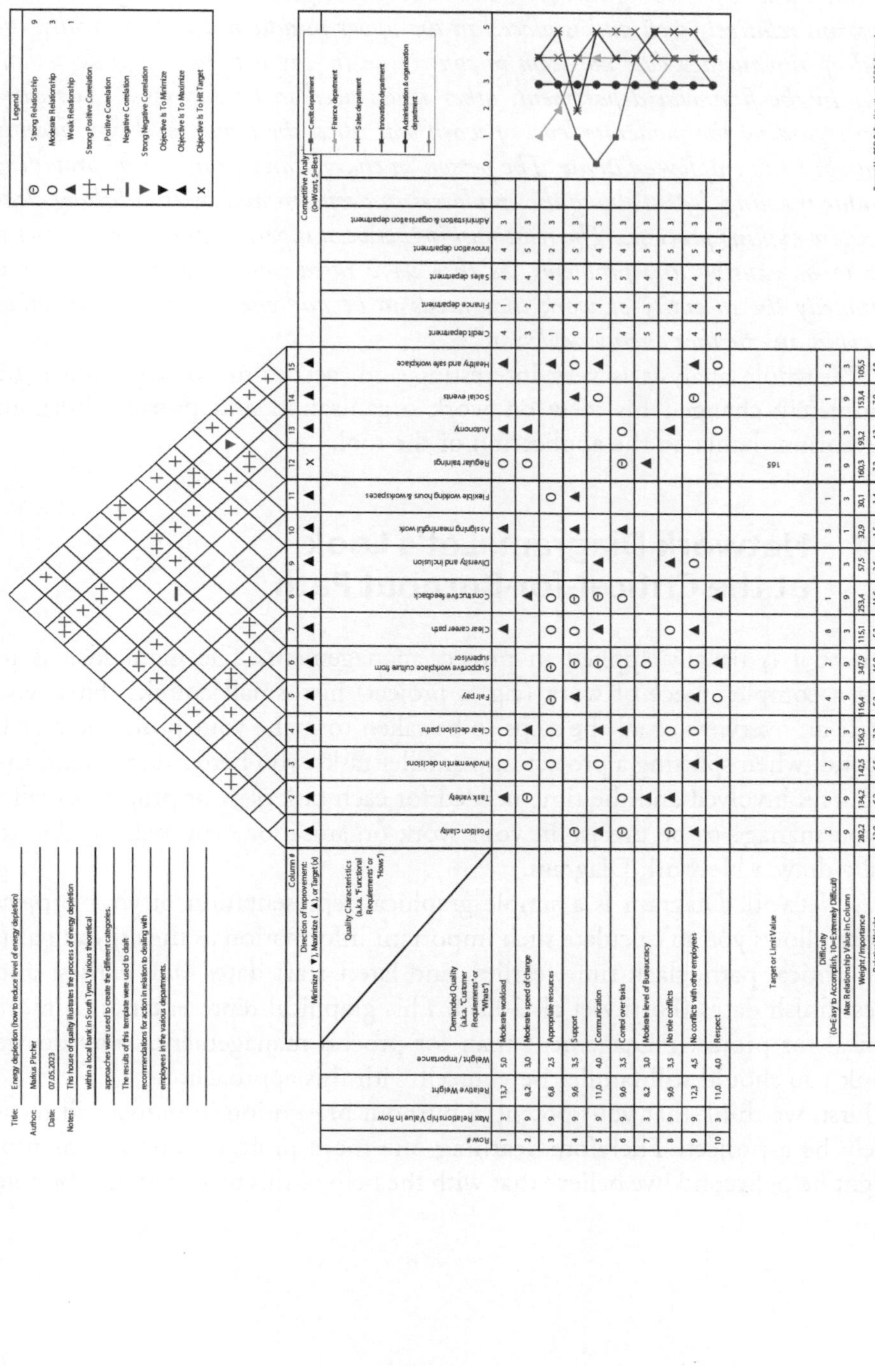

Fig. 6.16 Practical example of the House of Quality (*Source* Pircher [2023])

reduce the level of energy depletion. This can be achieved primarily through a supportive culture on the part of managers and continuous feedback. A change in this component would lead to more autonomy in the workforce and also to a healthier and safer workplace. [...] In the other categories, the credit department performs relatively well and is placed in the upper middle range. Specifically, the level of bureaucracy does not seem to contribute in any way to energy depletion. [...] In the financial department, other issues need to be addressed. The category regarding the moderate level of work was rated the lowest and significantly contributes to employee fatigue. The person in charge can counteract by providing regular training, by involving the employees in decisions and by establishing clear decision-making processes. The relationships between superiors and colleagues seem not to be causing any problems, as they were rated positively. Therefore, it is primarily the quantity of work that needs to be addressed or tackled in order to avoid any further energy depletion."

The whole analysis is very interesting and, according to Mr Pircher, he completely changed his view on work organisation and possible burnout prevention thanks to the application of the tool.

6.4 Network Diagram: Let's Look at the Critical-for-Burnout Path

This tool is usually applied in project management. The main idea is to split a complex piece of work (e.g. a project) into small chunks. First, you create an overview of all the steps to be taken to make your project succeed. Second, when splitting a project into smaller tasks, you better understand the resources involved and the time needed for each task of your project. Finally, if you manage to be precise in your work organisation, you will be able to easily draw a Network Diagram.

A Network Diagram is a simple graphical representation of your project which allows you to calculate such important information as the critical path, non-critical path, slack time, earliest and latest start dates, and earliest and latest finish dates (Portny et al. 2007). This graphical representation is more typical for project management than for process management. Why do we think you should still familiarise yourself with this approach?

First, we think that your potential burnout prevention initiative will most likely be a project. Therefore, learning one more project management tool might help. Second, we believe that with the help of this tool, you may be able to understand when and why burnout occurs. If you know the reason, you may cure it directly. Believe us, curing a reason is much more effective than addressing the symptoms, i.e. the consequences of the reason. Even though the diagram is simple, it may help you describe the main elements of your activities that lead to burnout or other psychological issues.

6.4.1 Main Elements of a Network Diagram

A Network Diagram is a simple flowchart containing only two types of elements: boxes and arrows. Apart from these elements, in a classical Network Diagram, you add a name for each task/milestone and the time you need to accomplish the task in the respective box. This simple tool helps depict complex projects, shows the order of tasks, and helps plan the overall project time as well as the time needed for subprojects. Once you have represented your project in this form, you can determine the critical path and calculate the slack time.

Although this tool uses only boxes and arrows, there is an easy way to differentiate between the tasks and milestones: while tasks require time, i.e. $t > 0$, a milestone does not require time, i.e. $t = 0$. For instance, having your homework submitted to a university portal is a milestone ("Work submitted", $t = 0$), whereas preparing your work for submission is a task which may require days ("Submitting your work", $t = 4$ days). Below, you can find a simple representation of a Network Diagram (Fig. 6.17).

If you want to analyse such a diagram, there are two rules to follow: (1) all activities have to be performed in the order indicated by arrows. Consequently, you can proceed with Task 3 only after finishing Task 2. (2) You are allowed to start the new task only if all tasks with arrows leading to the task are completed. Of course, the same is true for milestones. By the way, there are two milestones in Fig. 6.17: "Project Start" and "Project End". You can see it by looking at the time $t = 0$.

Now, knowing this, we can depict some important things. First, let's look at the longest path leading from the beginning of the project to its end. It

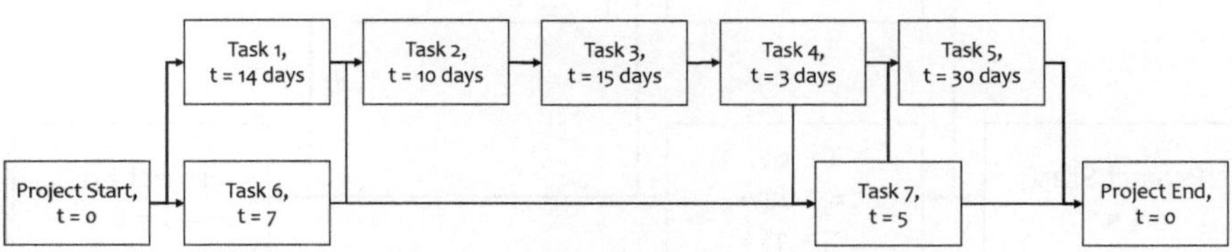

Fig. 6.17 Structure of a simple network diagram

seems that you need to accomplish Tasks 1, 2, 3, 4, 7, and 5 to finish your project in 77 days. At the same time, Task 6 needs 7 days to be completed and runs simultaneously with Task 1. The latter needs 14 days. This means that Task 6 has 7 days of *slack time*—but this delay will have no impact on the length of your project. However, only 1 day delay in Tasks 1, 2, 3, 4, 7, or 5 will lead to a delay in the whole project. If this is the case, we call this path a "critical path". Task 6 is not on the critical path. Knowing the duration of each task and knowing all tasks' interrelations helps you plan the earliest start and end date as well as the latest start and end date. For instance, the earliest start date for Task 6 is 0, i.e. immediately after the milestone "Project start". The latest end date is 14 days, i.e. when finishing Task 6 within 14 days, the overall project time will not be affected. These 14 days include the time needed for Task 6 (7 days) and 7 days of slack time. The latest date for the start of Task 6 is day 7, otherwise, you will not manage to finish your project at the planned time (14 days—7 days needed for Task 6).

6.4.2 Network Diagram for Psychological Issues

Now we have a question for you: Can we apply the same approach in order to identify the critical-for-burnout path? We can. Let's make some modifications to the initial Network Diagram. First, we need to add a variable, namely resource depletion. Let's call it "r_d". But according to the JD-R model, the resources cannot only be depleted but also replenished, "r_r". Most activities are related to an employee's or manager's psychological and physiological resources, "r". As a result of an activity, the resources will be either depleted or replenished and this state will depend on the perception of the activity by the employee (Fig. 6.18). If we assume that an employee or a manager has 100% of energy, at the end of the task they might have lost some of the energy. This loss represents the difference between job demands and job resources.

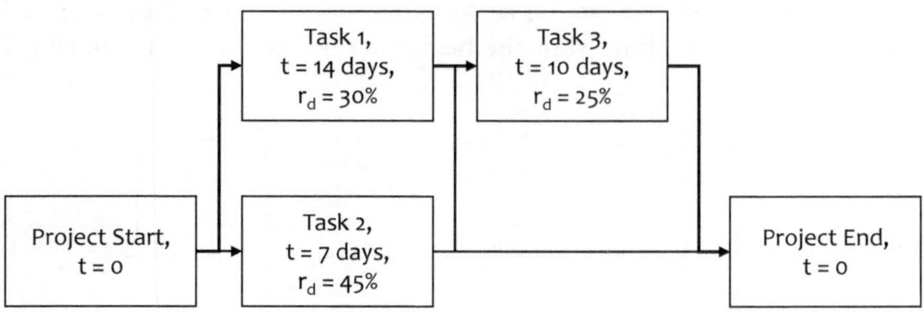

Fig. 6.18 Network diagram for resource depletion, if replenishment is ignored

You probably observe an issue with this diagram: At the end of the project, the involved employees and managers have less than zero psychological resources. Indeed, in real life, the resources are not only depleted but also replenished. Yet, the replenishment of resources usually happens after we leave our job and go home. We get energy when we take a rest, celebrate with friends, sleep, read, or similar. But the regular Network Diagram captures only the work activities. Consequently, if we want to see what happens with our psychological resources we have to include additional activities.

Moreover, there are other ways to replenish psychological resources. As we discussed in previous chapters of this book, acknowledgement, social support, feeling of security, and other aspects of human attention might help employees cope with complex tasks. Even though some activities are strenuous and consume almost all energy, organisations can intervene and support employees during difficult times and/or when completing challenging tasks (Fig. 6.19).

As you can see in Fig. 6.18, tasks are not only draining energy. After the work is done, an employee or a manager goes home and takes a rest. The next morning, he/she can continue with replenished energy. This relationship should be balanced. If something happens and employees have to stay longer in the office, they will not only work more (what managers for some reason see as a good idea as more work is done at the end of the day), but they will also spend more of their psychological and physiological resources. And this is not the end: they will have less time to sleep, exercise, or communicate, and their resources will not be fully replenished.

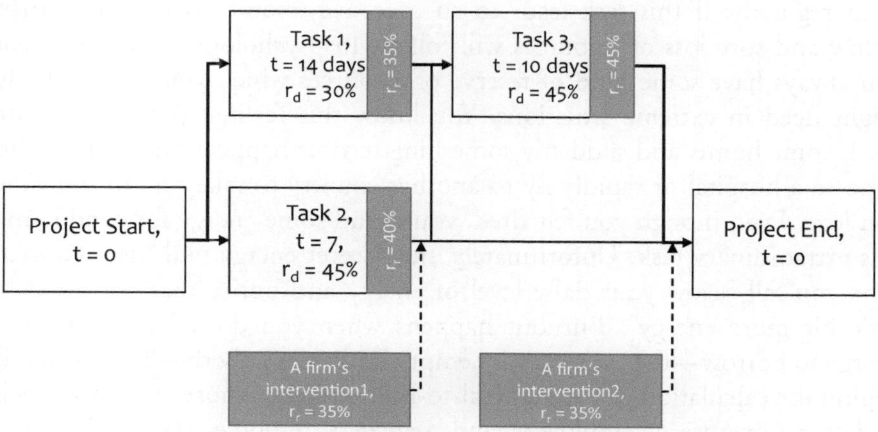

Fig. 6.19 Network diagram with depletion and replenishment of psychological (and physiological) resources

You have certainly noticed that we have an issue with our Task 2—it drains more energy than employees or managers can replenish. It may indeed be a big problem—your team will not have sufficient energy for Task 3. The tiredness may lead to costly mistakes. If you want to understand the seriousness of the issue, imagine that some of the employees, after having completed Task 2, will have to work with dangerous goods or drive colleagues home. This puts the health and safety of personnel at risk. The risk, thus, outweighs the problem of exceeding the project deadline.

Therefore, we propose our firm intervenes at this point. Remember from our previous section, depictions that Task 2 is not on the critical path. Moreover, there is some slack time. If we were the firm's managers, we would use this slack time to offer employees some rest after completing Task 2.

When does burnout occur? The main idea behind the concept of burnout is that it results from a long-lasting deployment of psychological and physiological resources. I.e. if employees feel exhausted after a certain task but have an opportunity to replenish their resources, burnout would not appear. Look at Fig. 6.19: While Task 2 drains your resources, Task 1 seems to be an easy task which may bring fun to the employees involved or it may be a task requiring work from home where everyone can take a nap when tired. This results in 5% more resources replenished than spent (40% − 35% = 5%). If work on a project deploys more energy from employees and managers than they can replenish, burnout or at least a state of deep exhaustion will inevitably appear.

In the event of a process, the situation is a bit more complicated. As a process differs from a project in particular by its repetitive nature, a task will recur regularly. If this task leads to an excessive resource deployment then a slow and sure loss of resources will follow. In psychology, we assume that you always have some kind of reserve of resources which you or your body might need in extreme situations. You know this feeling: Assume you are tired, come home, and suddenly something terrible happens and you have to drive to a hospital or rapidly fly to another country to take care of someone you love. Even though you felt tired, you found some energy for conducting this extraordinary task. Unfortunately, this "secret energy tank" is used each time you fall below your daily level of energy and notice that you need "a little bit more energy". Burnout happens when you don't have any more energy to borrow—the resources are empty. This is exactly the thought that is behind the calculation of your critical-to-burnout path: those elements which lead to an overuse of employees' and managers' resources (especially if not outbalanced) lie on this path.

A project can be seen as a planned work with a one-off target achievement. When the goal is achieved, the project is over. Yet, if the work of the project needs to be repeated, the project may become a process. Processes are permanently running, in the same way, with more or less the same tasks. Thus the Network Diagram shown in Fig. 6.19 would become a loop and instead of reaching the End, you would just jump back to the Start. If some of the tasks drain your energy, they will not disappear because there will be no End of Project anymore. The slightest imbalance between job demands and resources leads to an increasing loss of energy. It is just a matter of time when you will end up with burnout. Process management requires much more precision when taking into account psychological and physiological resources.

And now comes the most fascinating thing about this tool: If such an approach becomes your organisation's standard (you may be the one who makes it a new standard), your management will have to constantly pay attention to the balance of job demands and resources, organise their replenishment, and even include job demands-resources imbalance as one of the key risks in their risk management system. Regular and well-thought interventions and a holistic approach may change your organisation's life if only you find a way to depict the process of exhaustion and calculate (or even simulate) possible losses. By the way, the same would hold for job resources and possible gains. If you manage to understand, depict, and increase your job resources, you will develop a positive working climate which, according to the JD-R model, will result in a high level of motivation and willingness of your employees and managers to walk an extra mile.

6.4.3 More Complex Notation of Psychological Resources in Process Management

In process management, several notations are used. Yet, they all have the same goal—describe the repetitive activities as well as the conditions in these activities. Consequently, in the most basic form of notation, we only need figures, representing activities and decisions. Additionally, we need something to indicate a beginning and an end of the process. And yes, we need to have a flow, so arrows would be an adequate element to show the direction of the process flow (Fig. 6.20).

For instance, the process of brewing tea would look as shown in Fig. 6.21.

First, as you see, there is no simple rule about how detailed you should do the process documentation. It depends on your needs. Imagine that you

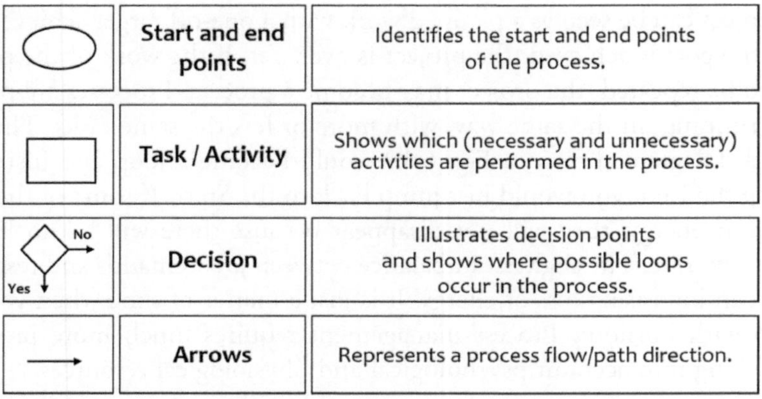

Fig. 6.20 Basic figures of a process flow notation

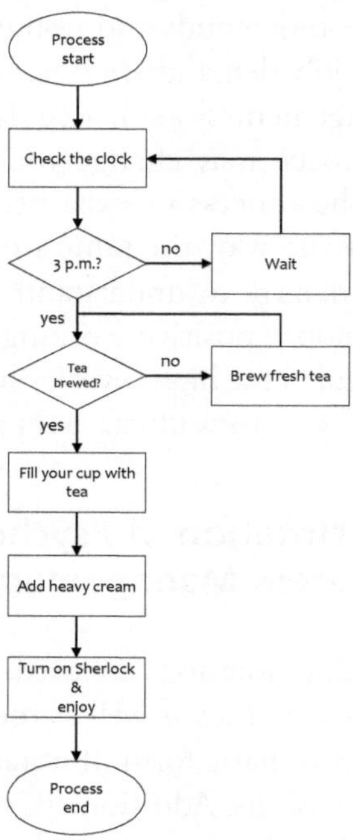

Fig. 6.21 Exemplary process of brewing tea

explain to someone who has never brewed tea how she or he has to do it. And now imagine that the king is going to visit you during your teatime. Probably, in this event, you should be much more precise with regard to brewing tea: what tea to choose, how to set the table, how hot should the water be for the selected type of tea, and so on. Yet, for your regular business, a simple, more abstract process notation would be sufficient. We recommend you not to mix different levels of abstraction within one flowchart. By the way, this is a very common mistake beginners make. If you are unsure which granularity of the depiction is adequate, ask yourself three questions (inspired by Portny (2020)):

1. Can you achieve a clear (and measurable) result from this activity?
2. Are you able to estimate resources needed for this activity with a sufficient level of precision, i.e. that any third person can understand with which and with how many of these resources she or he has to accomplish the activity?
3. Can you specify the exact time required for this activity?
4. If you delegate this activity, will a third person understand the activity correctly and completely?

If you answer one of these questions with "No", you should go deeper and be more precise. On the contrary, if these questions would have been answered with "Yes", your granularity of depiction is adequate. As you see, it is about understanding, communication, and resource planning. This also means that the same process may be depicted differently for different stakeholders.

Second, the notation shown in Fig. 6.21 is a bit too simple. In real-life scenarios, employees and managers need more information about different aspects of the process they are involved in. They may be interested in documents at different stages of the process, storage mediums, or data inputs. Moreover, from the viewpoint of process analysis, it may make sense to look at how the investigated process involves different organisational functions. If depicted, the unnecessary interface (e.g. activities within the same process are performed in different departments and/or an object or a product is moved between departments) may be better understood and avoided (Fig. 6.22). In this example, we assume that the only office kitchen available is the one in the IT department. Consequently, if we want to brew our tea before watching an episode of Sherlock (again, we assume that we can do it during our lunch break), we need to walk to another department, brew our tea, and walk back. Brewing tea in another department's kitchen is rather inconvenient and inefficient. Yet, in a business process, if you cross the invisible line of a department, you usually have to get their (and your) manager's approval, schedule an appointment, and think of their interests as they might not be the same as yours. In our example, installing an electric kettle in your department would reduce the complexity of the process and increase its efficiency.

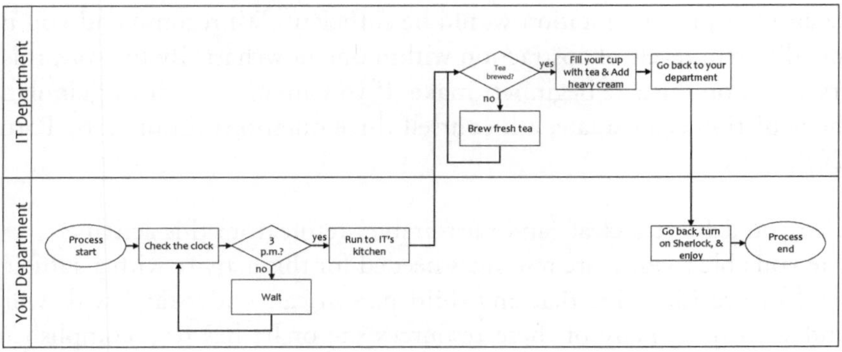

Fig. 6.22 Cross-functional tea brewing

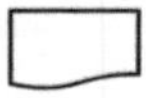	**Document**	Identifies an input or output of a document.
	**Storage medium / Server**	Shows the data that is stored on a storage service that can allow for user searches and filters.
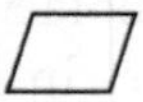	**Data**	Illustrates input or output from a data source.
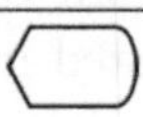	**Display / Screen**	Indicates that information is being shown to the user.

Fig. 6.23 Additional symbols used in flowcharts

Third, if you need to add more information to the graph you may use additional notations. For instance, you may want to indicate that after a certain process step a document has to be created or that information has to be stored on a server to be available to all employees of your firm (Fig. 6.23). There are several symbols used in flowcharts. Also, there might be differences between different notation languages. So clarify the rules for notation before you read the flowchart and start interpreting it.

6.4.4 Notation for Tracking of Burnout-Related Issues

As you can imagine, it is advantageous to use specific process notations to describe your processes in relation to burnout. If you add specific symbols to depict job demands and job resources, you will better understand how burnout appears in your organisation. If used correctly, it may help estimate the psychological and physiological job demands as well as job resources.

There is no precise description of which symbols to use or how exactly to apply them. Remember that a flowchart is a graphical representation. Its main goal is to provide the "bigger picture", logic, relationships, and flow. Using advanced symbols will help you add human, tangible, and intangible resources, document flow, location of human–computer interaction, and so forth. For sure, we need to add additional symbols for psychological and physiological job demands and resources (Fig. 6.24, symbols are our own creations).

We also need to introduce some rules:

Rule 1—The JD-R symbols indicate different levels of job demands and resources (Fig. 6.25).

Rule 2—Although we usually associate JD-R as attached to activities, a certificate of achievement (i.e. marked by the document symbol, Fig. 6.23) can add some positive energy (e.g. symbol "lightning" in the first row of Fig. 6.24), while a complex decision (symbol of a diamond, Fig. 6.20) might drain a lot of energy (e.g. symbol "skull" in the second row of Fig. 6.24).

Consequently, we can depict a simple process, showing how job demands and job resources are attached to certain process elements (Fig. 6.26). In this

	**Psychological Resources**	Identifies an energising activity, bringing you energy.
	**Psychological Demands**	Shows that the activity is draining your energy.
	**Physiological Resources**	Illustrates the activity that adds you physiological power.
	**Physiological Demands**	Indicates that the activity is physiologically exhausting.

Fig. 6.24 Set of symbols indicating psychological and physiological job demands and resources (*Note* "Lightning" stands for energy boost, "skull"—energy exhaustion, "head"—psychological resources, "biceps"—physiological resources)

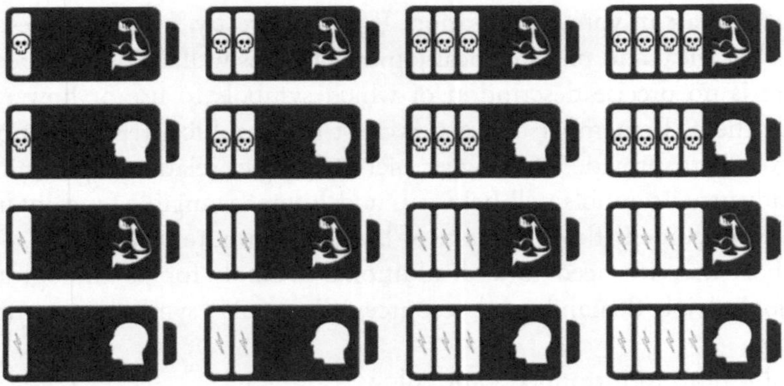

Fig. 6.25 Set of symbols for the gradation of job demands and resources (*Note* The number of "skulls" indicates the level of exhaustion; the number of "lightnings" indicates the level of energy received; both are ranging from 1 [very low] to 4 [very high])

example, we assume that waiting is boring and costs you some energy. We also assume that calling your supervisor costs you more energy than seeing him or her in person.[10] Reporting might also be a demanding activity, whereas getting positive feedback may bring some energy.

From Fig. 6.26, we can learn several things: First, it is a subjective representation of the job demands and resources related to the process. Indeed, reporting is just a neutral activity from the perspective of traditional process management. Yet, if conflicts appear within our organisation or if the workload is so high that an additional report stresses your project manager, the event becomes energy-draining. On the contrary, if your relationship with your manager is just perfect, each report and each call can energise you. Consequently, adding job demands and job resources makes your process description more subjective but also tailored to your current situation. This implies that the flowchart should be regularly reevaluated—any change in roles, workload, or other personal aspects may change your process for the better or for the worse.

Second, you may have noticed that there are two pathways, one taking more energy than the other one. Indeed, some people prefer calls (e.g. they might feel more secure and safe) while others prefer personal meetings (e.g. they better understand emotions and, thus, have a higher feeling of control over the situation). If two pathways exist, the improvement idea is obvious:

[10] Of course this depends on your individual perception. We have had different experiences—sometimes a phone call is the "least of all evils", but sometimes a face-to-face meeting is more pleasant than a phone call. So, it is about your perception of the activity. The job demands and resources are a matter of perception and can be highly subjective.

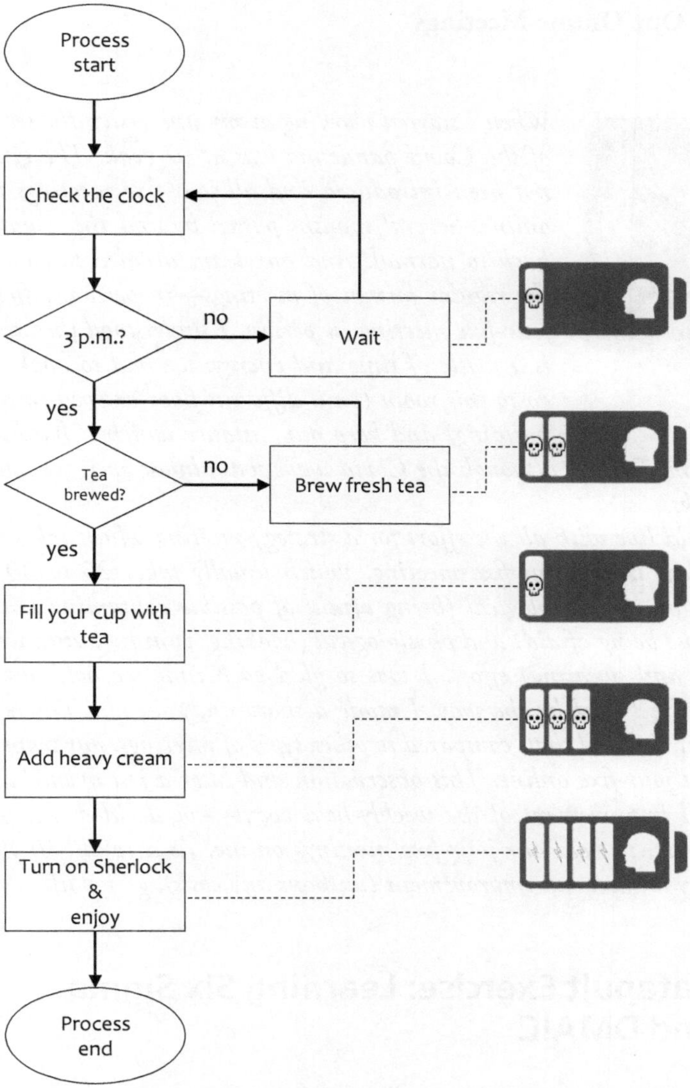

Fig. 6.26 Simple process including an indication of job demands and resources

take the less energy-draining path. By the way, we unconsciously tend to select this path. Now you can do it consciously.

Example: Our Online Meetings

When I started working at my university, the second wave of the Covid pandemic was at its peak. The vaccine had not been introduced and all jour-fixe meetings were held online. Several months passed by and the situation went back to normal. And our team decided to come back to the regular format of meetings—in person. After my first jour-fixe meeting in person, I understood that this format is a waste of time and energy: we had to book the room, go to this room (on a different floor or even in a different building) and keep our distance which is hard if you are a large team. Finally, although the Covid wave was almost over, we had to wear facial masks.

I could live with all the effort for a strategy meeting which takes the whole working day. But a jour-fixe meeting, which usually takes 20 to 30 minutes, meant too much psychological (being afraid of possible contamination or being tired of those being afraid) and physiological (booking, running, distance keeping, breathing, and sweating) effort. I was so glad each time we held our jour-fixe meeting online! And by the way, I made a short study using a Discrete Choice Experiment. I found that, compared to other types of meetings, our team preferred to attend a jour-fixe online. This observation and later a test opened an avenue for a small improvement of the weekly-held event—we decided, till the end of the pandemic, to hold our jour-fixe meetings online. As a result, iIf there is an opportunity to make an improvement (without any costs), go for it!

6.5 Catapult Exercise: Learning Six Sigma and DMAIC

Those who discover Six Sigma are usually fascinated by the simplicity and power of the method. While often people are scared when hearing "sigma" and "standard deviation", the method is much simpler than they might have thought. There are a number of books available about Six Sigma and its relatively new spin-off Lean Six Sigma. Yet, on the next pages we want to introduce to you the method in a very superficial manner. This book section should be sufficient for you to try it out and, if you like it, deepen your knowledge by reading a book that is fully dedicated to this topic. In the following, we will describe step by step a catapult exercise. If you have time and opportunity, stop reading after each subsection and try to recreate what we have written. For this, you will need a catapult.

6.5.1 Building a Catapult and Setting the Target

If building a catapult shocks you—no worries. We gave it as homework to our students and we built a catapult on our own. It should become a small device able to shoot little missiles up to a range of 1–4 m. As a missile, we initially took little wooden cubes (10 × 10 mm), and then a colleague recommended that we shoot "Gummibärchen"—gummy bears or jelly babies. The advantage is that if you play this exercise with students, they eat the missile after the shooting is finished. Just take care of hygiene and ethical issues; they may differ from country to country.

There can be different mechanics and dozens of ways to bring a catapult to life. The most complex one we saw was made by one of our students at the Frankfurt School of Finance & Management. The device contained so many screws and bolts that it was about 1 kg (ours has a weight of about 400 gr). Another student brought a tablespoon and a bottle. He tied the spoon at the neck to the bottle with a scotch in a way that the spoon became an arm, and the bottle became a fulcrum. By hitting the handle, a missile is shot from the bowl. While simple, this construction is not helpful for our exercise.

Next, you will need a surface on which you can draw your target. Usually, we use three tables pulled together. But you can also play on the floor or any other surface. You will need about 3 m of length to shoot your missiles. Then choose your missiles, e.g. Gummibärchen or gummy bears. They are available in many colours (one colour for each participant). This will help you track the individual results of your team members. Finally, you will need a ruler.

In the next step, we set a target. Last time, we took a white adhesive tape and made a cross at a distance of about 2.5 m. Draw a square of about 50 × 50 cm around this cross. Then, we asked our students to position their catapult at the edge of the table and shoot. They should get as close as possible to the cross. On the one hand, you want to give the participants a chance to try out their devices and show their shooting capabilities. On the other hand, it is about fun and motivation. If students are motivated, they enjoy shooting and later the evaluation procedure. Important is that the task is simple and correct, the target is clear, and all students get a chance to shoot. By the way, here comes your "Gummibärchen" into play. Not only that you can colour-code your shooters and immediately see who is shooting better. You can also suggest the shooters eat their missiles afterwards. Before the Covid pandemic, this was the most fun. Nowadays, many hesitate to eat the missiles even though they were the only ones who touched them.

By the way, if it is not your first catapult exercise, you can set more complex targets. These allow you to show how process improvement works especially if processes are complex. You can offer a team task: a team has to go through, e.g. four "stations". Each station is a marked square with a size of 50 × 50 cm and a distance of 2–2.5 m among them. One team member uses her or his catapult to shoot from Station 1 to Station 2. The next team member has to shoot from Station 2 to Station 3 using her or his catapult.[11] Yet, she or he is allowed to shoot only those missiles that landed within the marked square. Consequently, the worse the result of the first shooter, the fewer missiles the second shooter will have. The same applies to the following stations and assigned shooters. In the end, you are interested in how many missiles land in the last square. It usually brings more fun than regular shooting and helps students understand teamwork as each team is dependent on the other one and each shot elucidates the state of dependence, trust, and degree of happiness about cooperation.[12]

As you understand, the whole game is not about shooting. It is about understanding the process, its impacting variables, and improvement of the

[11] You can also work with one catapult per team and just move it after the first round of shooting.

[12] By the way, this version of the catapult game can be used to demonstrate information asymmetry. If you assume that the initial pool of missiles is the "full information" and shooting stands for "communication", you can show how the quality of communication impacts the amount of information finally received by the last employee or manager in the chain.

way of working. The first analysis is about the dispersion of the missiles fired and understanding the basics of statistics. And, obviously, we start with the mean.

6.5.2 Intended and Actual Mean

We start with a simple analysis and ignore some aspects that might be important. For instance, we ask our students to take a ruler and measure the distance from the catapult to the landing point of each missile. Here, we ignore two things: first, how far to the right or to the left they flew. We are interested only in the length of the flight. Second, we ignore the landing and the rolling position. Be it a cube, ball, or a "Gummibärchen", the missiles roll after landing. Balls roll far away, "Gummibärchen" jump in different directions, and even the small wooden cubes do not end their journey at the place of landing. At the moment, we can ignore these aspects and return to them, when we are in the debriefing stage at the end of the seminar.

Here, we introduce the two notions—the intended and the actual mean. As you can imagine, the *intended mean* is right in the centre of our adhesive tape cross. The *actual mean* is the mean distance for all missiles fired. If you play this task in teams—the intended mean is the same, but the actual mean might differ for every team. And most likely, it does not match the intended mean. At this point, you may draw a conclusion based on the actual mean and reestimate the results of the shooting. Indeed, some students will have some missiles landed almost exactly on the cross—you can see it by the colours of the missiles. Moreover, if you compare teams, you might find that some teams have not a single missile landed on the intended position, yet their average (actual mean) will be mathematically close to the intended mean. By contrast, some teams might have several missiles landed right where they had to. Yet, the average of the team (actual mean) may lie far away from the intended mean. It is a good moment to introduce the concept of quality and explain what quality in this exercise means.

6.5.3 Upper and Lower Specification Limits

In the Six Sigma methodology you need to know the upper and lower specification limits for your KPIs in the process. In our exercise, after which distance the missile counts as an "acceptable hit"? And after which distance would the missile count as "missing the target"? You have probably wondered why we asked you to mark a square around your cross. This square represents the upper and lower specification limits for our exercise (i.e. upper and bottom lines of the square). As long as a missile lands within the square, it can be used by the next team, remember? Put differently, all missiles that land outside the square do not meet the quality criteria (they are beyond the specification limits) and are considered as "missed the target".

If you ignore, as we proposed, the distribution of missiles to the left and to the right and focus on distance only, you may ignore the left and right sides of the square. By the way, for the sake of simplicity, you may draw two lines instead of squares. If you prepared everything correctly before you start the catapult exercise you already know the intended mean (your cross), the lower specification limit (LSL, the line closer to the catapult, in front of the cross) and the upper specification limit (USL, the line farther from the catapult, behind the cross). If you follow our suggestions, the intended mean will be 2.5 m exactly, the LSL will be 2.25 m, and the USL will be 2.75 m.

6.5.4 Distribution, Variance, and Standard Deviation

Usually, each time our students hear the words "standard deviation" or "distribution" they stop thinking. For whatever reason, they are afraid of statistics. And, as we know from psychology, fear causes an escape or freeze response. Consequently, students stop listening, talking, and understanding. Our exercise may change this pattern.

First, don't talk about distribution, variance, or standard deviations. It is like the "Fight Club" rules: The first rule of a fight club is that you don't talk about the fight club. Second, we ask our students to come closer to the target and have a look at how the missiles lie. And ask them how they estimate the area where the missiles landed. Third, you could come to the conclusion that the farther the missiles are spread, the worse the quality of shooting. "By the way"—you add—"this spread of missiles is nothing other than the variance!" In this way, you may evoke interest in statistics and avoid the fear of statistical terms. In a simpler representation (caution, it is not completely statistically correct), you may say that the variance is close to the "area". It is like having single points, and then connecting them with lines to the mean and assuming that this line is the side of an imaginary square. To find out the square's area, you square the sides. Finally, you take all your areas and divide them by the number of squares. This average gives you something like the average area covered by missiles.

In the next step, you propose to think of a measure to estimate the average of how good or bad the spread of missiles is. Our students quickly realised that the larger the area, the worse your shooting was. But if you would like to understand the average dispersion of missiles relative to the mean, you should take a square root from the variance, the so-called standard deviation. As you see, these metrics are closely related—if the variance is about the area covered by your missiles, the standard deviation is more about the distance. In both cases, the lower the value, the better.

The only thing left to explain is the distribution. Here, we ask our students to take a ruler and measure the distance from the shooting point to each missile in cm. Then, we ask them to enter these values into a spreadsheet. Usually, as the number of shots is low, it makes sense to round numbers up to 5, i.e. instead of 173, 175, 176, 180 and 183 cm, they should enter 175, 175, 175, 180 and 185 cm. Now, create two columns in your spreadsheet: in the first one you enter the distance, and in the second one add the number of times the missile landed at this point (Fig. 6.27). Having this data, you can easily create a distribution plot. Use the distance as your X-axis and the frequency as your Y-axis. Create a bar chart. By the way, don't forget to click the bar chart and add a "trendline" (if you use MS Excel).

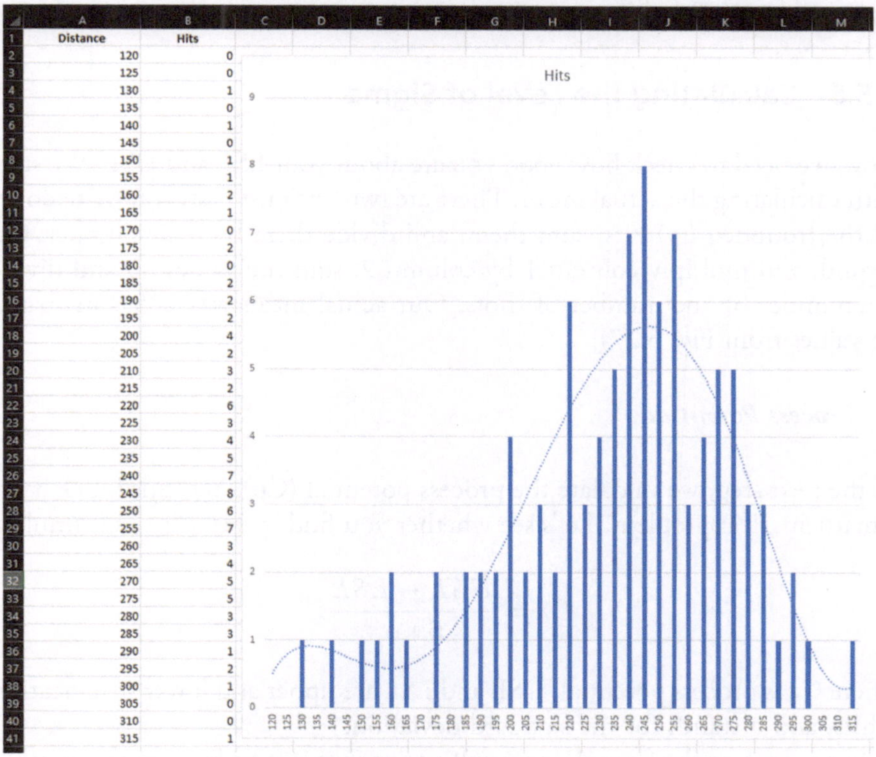

Distance	Hits
120	0
125	0
130	1
135	0
140	1
145	0
150	1
155	1
160	2
165	1
170	0
175	2
180	0
185	2
190	2
195	2
200	4
205	2
210	3
215	2
220	6
225	3
230	4
235	5
240	7
245	8
250	6
255	7
260	3
265	4
270	5
275	5
280	3
285	3
290	1
295	2
300	1
305	0
310	0
315	1

Fig. 6.27 Results of a catapult exercise including a superimposed curve (MS Excel "trendline")

As you can see, the trendline looks pretty close to a normal distribution. Of course, it can also look like an exponential distribution—it all depends on the quality of shooting (some people just tend to "overshoot", i.e. to pull harder than necessary) or on the location. Imagine that you shoot in front of a wall. Although the cross is set to 2.5 m, if the wall is at 2.90 m, then all overshot missiles will land at 2.90 m. This will create something similar to an exponential distribution with a big peak on one side of the distribution line.

The concept of distribution is important. If it happens to be not normal-distributed, you might need a completely different statistical procedure for the data analysis. Luckily, in our catapult exercise, the normal distribution is usually the case as you do not shoot in front of a wall and as you allow your participants to make several shots. So, if someone overshoots the goal, she or he can immediately adjust his or her shooting. If you apply this procedure in practice, you might need to make adjustments for your further analysis (e.g. for the exponential distribution as all missiles will land before the wall). This information lies beyond the scope of this book but it is not complex—you just need to select a different procedure in your stats programme.

6.5.5 Calculating the Level of Sigma

Now, we need to check how good you are about your LSL and USL. We start with calculating the actual mean. There are two options: first, you write down all the (rounded up) hits, sum them, and divide them by their number. Or, second, you multiply column 1 by column 2, sum the values up and divide the number by the number of shots. Our actual mean was 235.9 m (based on values from Fig. 6.27).

A. ***Process Potential***

In the next step, we calculate the process potential (Cp). Yet, this index bears a mathematical problem. Let's see whether you find it. Here is the formula:

$$C_p = \frac{USL - LSL}{6 * \sigma},$$

where C_p is process potential, USL and LSL are upper and lower specification limits, and σ stands for the standard deviation.

If you look at the formula, you will notice that it is addressing the number of "errors". The broader the range between the upper and the lower specification limits and the lower the standard deviation, the higher the process potential. Put differently, the more tolerant we are about the rules (i.e. what we count as a hit or as a miss) and the better we shoot, the higher the potential of our process (i.e. what we expect our process to deliver). After having calculated the standard deviation of 37.53 using the STDEVA command in Excel for a standard deviation of our sample, our process potential is:

$$C_p = \frac{275 - 225}{6 * 37.53} = 0.222$$

The result is far from being good. Let us think logically: the numerator is the acceptable range, whereas the denominator shows how good we shoot. If our shooting (denominator) lies within the interval (numerator)—we are just great. A larger numerator divided by the smaller denominator would result in values larger than 1. If our numerator is equal to the denominator, our process is in an optimal state—we are well within the range, although we can do even better. Yet, if our denominator is larger than the numerator, we end up with numbers below one. The smaller the number, the worse the process potential.

However, as we have mentioned above, this approach has a mathematical issue. It only works under the condition that the process is centred, i.e. the mean is located exactly in the middle between the LSL and USL. Otherwise, the process potential will be estimated wrongly. Let us assume that our observed process of shooting was (almost) centred. And, actually, it is close to the truth—the actual mean was 235.9 (the intended mean was 250) and the distribution looked close to normal.

To illustrate the mathematical problem, let us manipulate our data as if our mean was far from the middle between LSL and USL. For this, we can simply subtract 20 cm from each landing point. We pretend that all missiles landed on average 20 cm closer to the catapult and further away from the intended mean. You can find the manipulated shooting data in Fig. 6.28, with the green bar showing the previous actual mean and the red bar showing the manipulated actual mean. As shown on the second diagram (Fig. 6.28), the quality of the shots has deteriorated massively. Even our previous actual mean was below the intended mean. Now, the discrepancy has become even larger. But what about the process potential C_p?

$$C_p = \frac{275 - 225}{6 * 37.53} = 0.222$$

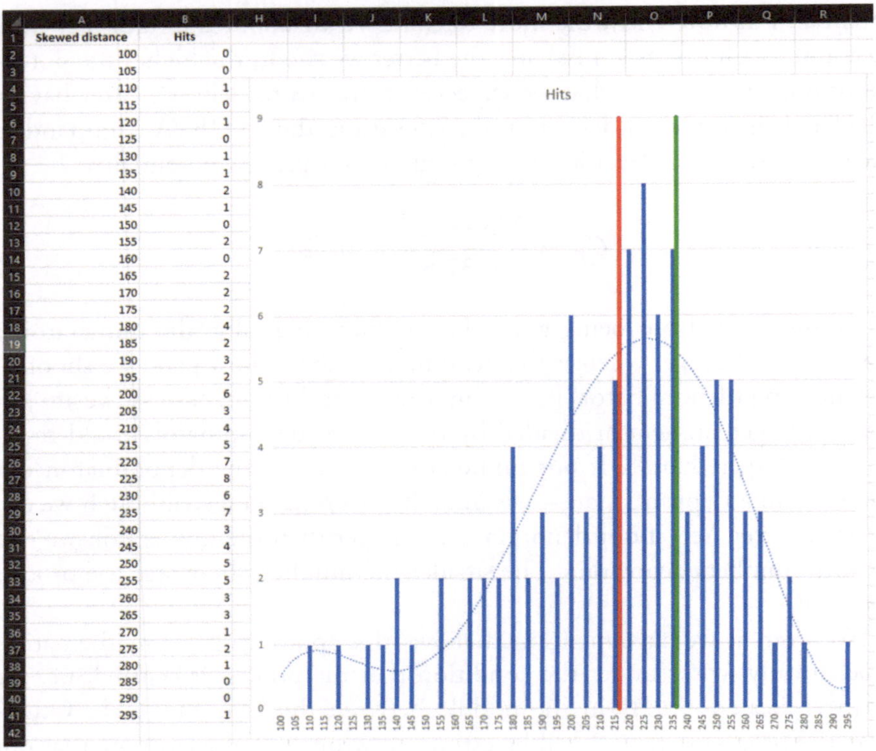

Fig. 6.28 Results of a catapult exercise with manipulated data; 20 cm are deduced from each of the previously noted hits

It did not change! As the LSL and USL remained unchanged, so did the standard deviation. Consequently, the result of the formula did not change although we observed a worse result of shooting (Fig. 6.28).

Now, you can see why the process must be centred, i.e. the mean value should be equidistant from the LSL and USL, if you want to apply this formula and calculate the process potential. And, by the way, processes are often skewed. Think about an assembly line. Let us assume that some robots work on different elements of a car. The speed is programmed and, usually, the assembly line works within the robots' capabilities. Due to possible upcoming problems, most robots can slow down or stop working. Yet, they might not start working faster. If you shoot your catapult close to a wall, the missiles will not fly farther than the wall. But they can use the whole distance between the catapult and the set target. Therefore, there is a simple explanation for the fact that most processes are skewed: we try to use the full potential of the equipment and improve the processes to the best we can. We can slow them down, but we can hardly speed them up as they mostly work with the highest possible efficiency. But is there a way to calculate the quality of our processes if they are skewed?

B. ***Process Potential for Skewed Processes***

Some practitioners focus on *process capability* (C_{pk}) instead of process potential (C_p). Here is how you calculate it:

First, you need to calculate how well three standard deviations fit within the range between the USL and the mean:

$$C_{pU} = \frac{USL - \bar{x}}{3 * \sigma},$$

where $\bar{x}$ represents the mean value.

Second, you perform the same calculation for the three standard deviations (σ) fitting into the range between the mean and the LSL:

$$C_{pL} = \frac{\bar{x} - LSL}{3 * \sigma},$$

Finally, you take the *lowest of the values* as a rigorous indication of process potential:

$$C_{pk} = min(C_{pL}, C_{pU})$$

Let's take our two examples: the one with little skewness and the one skewed for 20 cm for each shot. Let's start with the process that we artificially skewed. We receive:

$$C_{pU} = \frac{275 - 215.9}{3 * 37.53} = 0.525,$$

$$C_{pL} = \frac{215.9 - 225}{3 * 37.53} = -0.081,$$

$$C_{pk} = min(0.525, -0.081) = -0.081.$$

Wow! Look at the difference in the process potential from the previous section, where C_p was 0.222! As you see, first, the indicator C_{pk} allows us to capture the skewness of our model (C_p does not). Indeed, if the value is below 1, the quality of the process is very bad. Second, we produced a negative number. So, it is easy to see that something is wrong with the process. A negative number indicates that the actual mean lies outside the specification limits. Put differently, the process is so bad that we should not care about the reduction of variance but, first of all, about getting the mean into the wanted range.

We think you might be interested in calculating the C_{pk} for our less skewed process:

$$C_{pU} = \frac{275 - 235.9}{3 * 37.53} = 0.347,$$

$$C_{pL} = \frac{235.9 - 225}{3 * 37.53} = 0.097,$$

$$C_{pk} = min(0.347, 0.097) = 0.097.$$

The result is closer to 0 than the previously calculated C_p value of 0.222. This discrepancy indicates that the initial process was not perfectly centred, i.e. the mean was not equidistant from the LSL and USL. Yet, the result is close to the previous one and indicates that the process is not perfect but much better than its artificially skewed version—the one where we manipulated the data by subtracting 20 cm.

C. ***From Process Potential to the Level of Sigma***

Now we need to convert our process potential (or process capability as some would call the indicator) to the Level of Sigma. This would show how many standard deviations fit within the specification limits. Remember, the higher the value of the process potential, the better your process is. You can formulate it also this way: a high value of the process potential indicates how well your hits lie within the specified range.

Here, the process potential $C_{pk} = 1$ indicates the three standard deviations of your hits fit into the specified range. $C_{pk} = 2$ indicates that six standard deviations fit into the range. As you remember, the number of standard deviations fitting shows how many errors (or defects) will occur. To make these calculations readable, we report the number of Defects per Million Opportunities (DPMO) (Table 6.1).

Using Table 5, the table, you can estimate how good your process is. If you are not satisfied, move on to the next step in the catapult exercise, the DMAIC analysis.

Table 6.1 Conversion of process potential into the level of sigma and defects

Process potential C_{pk}/C_p	Level of sigma	Process output (%)	DPMO	Defect rate
0.333	1	68.27	317,311	1 in 3.15
0.667	2	95.45	45,500	1 in 22
1	3	99.73	2,700	1 in 370
1.333	4	99.99	63	1 in 15,873
1.667	5	99.9999	1	1 in 1,000,000
2.00	6	99.9999998	0.002	1 in 500,000,000

6.6 DMA(G)IC

Actually, the method is called DMAIC [də-MAY-ick]. The letters D, M, A, I, and C represent an abbreviation of the key steps in the analysis: Define, Measure, Analyse, Improve, and Control. Once we visited a consulting firm, which used its own version, called DMAGIC [də-Magic]. It slightly reminded us of the Harry Potter series and Gilderoy Lockhart with his book "The Magical Me". They added the new step—Generalise—which, by the way, is usually part of the "Analyse" step. On the one hand, this step added unnecessary complexity. On the other, it added something magical and unique to one of the most applied tools procedures in the field of process management. There is no magic in the tool—it is nothing but common sense. Let's try to work with our catapult exercise.

In the previous steps, we made the first measurement and calculated the process potential and process capability. We discovered that they are far from being efficient. Obviously, we need to make improvements, but where should we start?

6.6.1 Define

In the first step, we need to define the key factor having an impact on the quality of our result. We usually brainstorm with our students. There are not so many factors influencing the quality of shooting a catapult, e.g. length of the arm, angle, the weight of the missile, the form of the missile, the person who is shooting, etc. In class, we are interested in the most influential factors. In the event of our small self-made catapult, this is the angle of launch. But who shoots as well as other factors might be also important. At the moment, let us start with only the launch angle and the shooter.

In this step, we not only define the variables but also the assumed relationship and its strength (also called "hypothesis"). For instance, the launch angle has a strong negative relationship concerning the shot distance—the lower the angle, the further the missile will land. With regard to the shooter, we may proceed exploratively, i.e. simply assuming that shooters shoot differently. Or, if your previous observation allows you to do it, you may develop hypotheses such as "Mr A shoots too far", "Ms B is very good on target", and so on.

6.6.2 Measure

A. ***Operationalisation***

In this step, you have, first, to understand how to test your previously developed hypotheses. In academia, we call this *operationalisation*, i.e. the way to approach the hypothesised relationship. For instance, if our hypothesis is related to the difference between the two shooters—Mr A and Ms B—we may simply ask these two shooters to make about 20 shots. Then, we can compare the results using an appropriate statistical test (no worries, these are only a few clicks in MS Excel). If we find a statistical difference—our hypothesis has been supported. If not—we have rejected our hypotheses. We apply the same logic to the launch angle: we just make 10 shots from the angle of 0°, 10 shots from the angle of 10°, and repeat the procedure till 80°. You can even be more precise and try the step of 5° between trials: 0°, 5°, 10°, …, 85°. In real life, however, you don't have so much time for this exercise and you save your time making only 5 shots with the interval of 5°, starting from 0° and finishing at 35°. You also may speed up the measurement by asking your two shooters to shoot from different angles. You simply ask both Mr A and Ms B to make 3–5 shots from different angles.

You should take notes for each shot: who was shooting, what was the angle, and where did the missile land?

After you have collected the data, you can analyse it: we need to apply the appropriate statistical tests. Usually, the correct statistical test is defined by your variable types and the distribution of the shot results. For instance, if your results are not normally distributed (when depicted they do not build a nice bell curve), then you have to apply non-parametric tests. Unfortunately, it is beyond the scope of this chapter. However, you can search for more information on how to test the normality of distribution and what kind of tests to apply (Field 2018). In this chapter, we assume the normality (which is most likely the case) of the distribution of your data.

B. ***Types of Data***

Then, you look at the type of data. There are four main types of variables in statistics: categorical (nominal), ordinal, interval, and ratio. In very simple terms: categorical variables simply depict different groups, e.g. "male, female, diverse", or "Kyiv, Kharkiv, Odessa, Dnipro". These groups allow for a comparison between them, e.g. what is the average population density in Kharkiv and Odessa? Yet, you cannot convert one into the other: even though you code female as 1, male as 2, and diverse as 3, you cannot say that diverse is three times female.

Also, ordinal variables do not allow you a conversion of one group into the other one but at least you can rank the answers. An example would be "young, adult, elderly" or "completely disagree, disagree, neither agree nor disagree, agree, completely agree". This approach gives you additional power of analysis—you cannot only compare two groups, e.g. young vs adult but you also know that adults are older than young people and younger than older people. You also know that "completely disagree" is more negative than just "disagree" and "neither agree nor disagree". The additional power lies in your ability to test hypotheses related to the power of the investigated relationship. The statement "The more of A, the stronger B" is very powerful.

This power of relationship can be addressed even better if you use interval or ratio variables. The difference between them is that the interval scale has a clear limit. Age is a good example: it cannot be negative, i.e. zero is the limit of this scale. Yet, the upper limit is not set. Temperature is another example—it cannot be lower than −273.15 °C (i.e. absolute zero). Ratio variables do not have limits. In both cases, you can test the smallest changes in e.g. temperature, and how it impacts the willingness to pay for an additional ice cream cone.

Long story short: you usually have two types of variables in your analysis—independent and dependent variables. An independent variable is the one that you manipulate and/or the one that has an impact on the missile flight. The dependent variable is the one that is dependent on the change in the independent variable. Based on the type of variables, you can select the correct statistical test (Table 6.2). For the sake of simplicity, we will assume that we are allowed to treat ordinal, interval, and ratio scales similarly. Please pay attention that it may work only by a correct development of the ordinal scale, i.e. if intervals between answer options are comparable. E.g. the use of an established Likert scale[13] might help you avoid most problems.

---

[13] Likert scales are established psychometric scales. They were named after their inventor—Rensis Likert. There are now many types of Likert scales that can meet all kinds of requirements.

Table 6.2 Simplified scheme for statistical test selection

Independent variable	Dependent variable	Test
Categorical	Categorical	Crosstabs test in SPSS©, Chi-square test
Categorical	Ordinal, interval, ratio	ANOVA
Ordinal, interval, ratio	Categorical	Logistic regression
Ordinal, interval, ratio	Ordinal, interval, ratio	Linear regression

Now, let us look at the variables we have in our little experiment. Our *dependent variable* is the distance. If the distance lies between 2.25 and 2.75 m, we have a hit. Otherwise, we have missed it. Distance is an interval variable—it cannot be below zero as zero is the point where our catapult stands. Our *independent variables* are the shooter and the angle. The shooter is a categorical variable: it is either Mr A or Ms B. The angle is an interval variable—it cannot be lower than zero, i.e. the point of maximum tension at which the catapult arm is stretched to the maximum possible position.

Since we have assumed that the data is normally distributed, we can apply the tests shown in Table 6.2. We would need an ANOVA test to check whether shooters differ in their capabilities. We would need a linear regression to check whether there is a relationship between the angle of the arm and the flight distance of the missile.[14]

C. *Linear Regression*

You can run both tests with almost any software, starting with MS Excel and finishing with R. The simplest and most available option for most users is MS Excel. To run such an analysis you have to activate the pre-installed plug-in. Go to File → Options → Add-ins → Excel add-ins. After clicking, you will see a small window with checkboxes. Select the checkbox "Analysis ToolPak". Now, if you go to the tab "Data", you will see an additional button on the right—"Data Analysis". That was it, the plug-in was activated. If something does not work, search for instructions on YouTube, there are plenty of them. Now add your measurement and we are good to go. We made a sample measurement with five people, each of whom we asked to make two shots from angles of 40°, 35°, 30°, 25° and 20° (Fig. 6.29).

[14] If you use SPSS©, you can use the univariate analysis which will make a kind of a combination and calculate both the ANOVA and the linear regression. Actually, it is recommended to analyse all dependent variables in one model—you can check whether some of these variables explain the dependent variable "at cost" of another dependent variable. Some significant single direct effects might disappear if other independent variables explain the dependent variable better.

	A	B	C
1	Angle	Result	person
2	40	120	1
3	40	118	1
4	40	130	2
5	40	125	2
6	40	117	3
7	40	118	3
8	40	127	4
9	40	115	4
10	40	118	5
11	40	127	5
12	35	145	1
13	35	150	1
14	35	150	2
15	35	139	2
16	35	134	3

Fig. 6.29 Sample shots for the analysis phase

For the regression analysis, you go to Data, then Data Analysis (that appears after activating the "Analysis ToolPak"), then Regression. In the new window you are asked to provide the variables (range) for Y and X. Y is the dependent variable or the one which we want to estimate, e.g. distance of the missile flight. X is our independent variable or the one that influences the dependent variable, e.g. the angle of the arm during a shot. If your first row contains the names of the columns, select "Labels". Then, decide where you want to have the results—on the same sheet, on a new one, or even in a new workbook. The rest of the settings may give you additional information about the quality of your prediction. But for now, leave these checkboxes untouched (Fig. 6.30).

After clicking "OK", the new worksheet is created. In this worksheet, you will find three tables: "Regression statistics", "ANOVA" and "Regression". We are mainly interested in the first and the last tables. The first table offers you a very interesting indicator—R^2. This indicator shows how much variance in the dependent variable is explained by your model. In our event, we have only one independent variable—the angle. Consequently, you can see how much the angle of the arm explains how far the missiles fly. The R^2 of 0.97

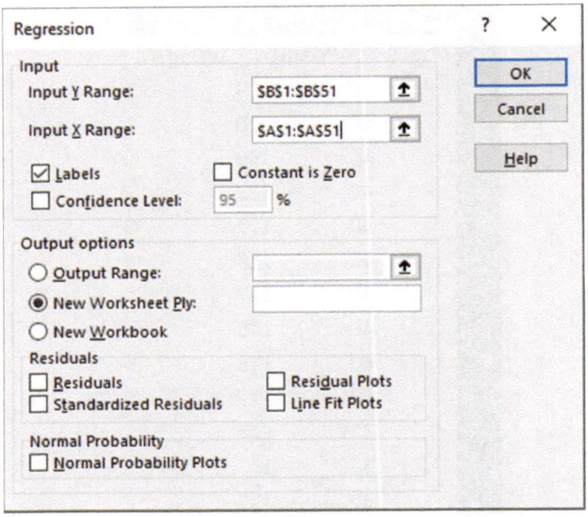

Fig. 6.30 MS Excel regression settings

means that about 97% of the variance is explained by the variable "Angle"[15] (Fig. 6.31).

Before we interpret the results, we need to make p-values (i.e. statistical significance) easier to read—for some reason, MS Excel shows the level of significance in the format "2.34499110850842E-51". To correct this situation, right-click on the cells "p-value → Format cells → Number" and set 3 decimal places. Now we can read the values: $p < 0.1$ means "weakly significant" or showing a trend towards significance; $p < 0.05$ means "statistically significant", i.e. if you repeat the same procedure 100 times then in 95% of repetitions you will observe similar results; $p < 0.005$ and $p < 0.001$ indicate a strong statistical significance. If the p-value is even lower than 0.001, we report "$p < 0.001$" without specifying the precise value (Fig. 6.31).

[15] Actually, the R^2 values are usually not that high. The reason for our high values might come from the fact that the data is made up to illustrate in a simple way how statistics work. What we observe in real life is the following: In social sciences if your R^2 value is 20–30% you are very good. If you find out that adding a new variable has increased your R^2 for 6% ($\Delta R^2 = 6$), that is already good. In chemistry, we can expect much higher R^2 values, as the models you work with are based on the laws of chemistry that are more precise and indefeasible. If hydrogen burns, it produces the amount of water that is perfectly predicted by the amount of hydrogen and oxygen. Consequently, if the R^2 value is below 60%, the reviewers of an academic journal would criticise the quality of your work. However, in social sciences, most models depend on perception and reflection and are constantly evolving as the actors evolve over time. Having an R^2 value higher than 40% is an indication that you might have done something wrong. E.g. there might be discriminant validity issues between your dependent and independent variables.

	A	B	C	D	E	F	G	H	I
1	SUMMARY OUTPUT								
2									
3	*Regression Statistics*								
4	Multiple R	0,987003767							
5	R Square	0,974176437							
6	Adjusted R Square	0,973638446							
7	Standard Error	9,08756042							
8	Observations	50							
9									
10	ANOVA								
11		*df*	*SS*	*MS*	*F*	*Significance F*			
12	Regression	1	149539,9798	149540	1810,768	0,000			
13	Residual	48	3964,02021	82,58375					
14	Total	49	153504						
15									
16		*Coefficients*	*Standard Error*	*t Stat*	*P-value*	*Lower 95%*	*Upper 95%*	*Lower 95,0%*	*Upper 95,0%*
17	Intercept	426,5926995	5,701960225	74,8151	0,000	415,1281401	438,0572589	415,1281401	438,0572589
18	Angle	-7,853578057	0,18455942	-42,5531	0,000	-8,224659642	-7,482496472	-8,224659642	-7,482496472
19									

Fig. 6.31 Regression results

Now, let's look at the table with the final results. While the first table of Fig. 6.31 shows how good our model is, the second elucidates the dependence between the variability in our dependent variable and the variability in our independent variable. I.e. if the *F*-value is significant, a change of our independent variable (angle of the arm) is related to a change in the flight distance of our missile, i.e. our dependent variable.[16]

The last table of Fig. 6.31 shows the precise impact of our independent variable. As the (linear) regression is about finding a line which reflects how much the change in the independent variable impacts the change in the dependent variable, the coefficient tells you how much of the distance of missile flight (dependent variable) will be added/distracted by each degree of the catapult arm. The coefficient column tells you the power of the relationship, i.e. in how many cm the distance will grow for each 1°. The *p*-value indicates whether this result is significant, i.e. if you repeat the catapult exercise what is the chance that you will receive the same result?

Can we check the analysis somehow? Yes, we can. First, look at the linear regression formula:

$$y = intercept + coefficient * x$$

As we know the intercept (third table, first row, coefficient in Fig. 6.31), the coefficient for our shooting angle, we can check the flight distance for each

[16] Imagine a situation in which it doesn't matter how you pull the arm of the catapult—the missile would land at the same position. Or imagine that you constantly shoot from the same angle, yet all missiles land randomly. In both cases, variability in the dependent and the independent variable is not related. The *F*-value would then be insignificant. By the way, this is a good way to ensure that the selected factors impact the final result.

x. Let's assume that we would like to shoot from an angle of 30°:

$$distance = 426.59 + (-7.85) * 30 = 191.09$$

This result is of course only an approximation, but it seems to work. With this in mind, we can make our first predictions with regard to shooting and become much more successful in shooting.

D. ***More Complex Regression***

By the way, you can make the calculation a bit more complex. What if there is a non-linear relation, i.e. with each degree the power of shooting increases not linearly but exponentially? There is a simple way to test it and you have all the knowledge necessary.

First, you need to calculate the additional variable x^2 (Fig. 6.32).

In MS Excel you can add several variables as independent variables. In the next calculation, try to add both "angle" and "angle squared". And here are the results (Fig. 6.33):

Hey, our suspicion that there might be a non-linear relationship appears to be true. First, look at the R^2 value: it became slightly higher. It is only about a 1% difference but the model became better. Consequently, adding the

	A	B	C	D
1	Angle	Angle^2	Result	person
2	40	1600	120	1
3	40	1600	118	1
4	40	1600	130	2
5	40	1600	125	2
6	40	1600	117	3
7	40	1600	118	3
8	40	1600	127	4
9	40	1600	115	4
10	40	1600	118	5
11	40	1600	127	5
12	35	1225	145	1
13	35	1225	150	1
14	35	1225	150	2

Fig. 6.32 Calculating an additional variable to check for non-linearity

SUMMARY OUTPUT

Regression Statistics	
Multiple R	0,991784197
R Square	0,983635894
Adjusted R Square	0,982939549
Standard Error	7,310667994
Observations	50

ANOVA

	df	SS	MS	F	Significance F
Regression	2	150992,0443	75496,02214	1412,57	0,000
Residual	47	2511,955727	53,44586653		
Total	49	153504			

	Coefficients	Standard Error	t Stat	P-value	Lower 95%	Upper 95%	Lower 95,0%	Upper 95,0%
Intercept	538,6832186	21,98845938	24,49845208	0,000	494,448144	582,918293	494,448144	582,9182931
Angle	-15,71376767	1,515276872	-10,37022867	0,000	-18,7621115	-12,6654238	-18,76211154	-12,6654238
Angle^2	0,130436028	0,025024285	5,212377845	0,000	0,08009366	0,1807784	0,08009366	0,180778395

Fig. 6.33 Results including the squared independent variable

squared value of the angle makes your estimation more correct and precise. The F-value remained significant. Important: both coefficients for "angle" and "angle-squared" are significant. Let's perform a prediction with the new model. Here is our formula:

$$y = intercept + coefficient1 * x + coefficient2 * x^2$$

Consequently,

$$distance = 538.68 + (-15.71) * 30 + 0.13 * 900 = 184.38$$

As you see, our estimation for the arm angle of 30% shifted for 6.71 cm. This is a lot if you remember that all missiles that landed more than 25 cm from the intended mean are considered "missed".

E. ***Analysis of Variance (ANOVA)***

The ANOVA allows you to compare means between categorical variables. E.g. you can compare means between male and female shooters or between different persons. Remember, for the analysis, we asked five people to make a number of shots from different angles. What if we compare the means? If one of the shooters pulls stronger than the others or pushes the trigger earlier or later, he or she will systematically differ in her or his shooting.

In order to analyse this data in MS Excel, we need to slightly restructure our data set: we need to introduce a column for each shooter and copy her or his shooting results there. If you have data organised as we did in Fig. 6.32, you can simply select the column "person", sort it, and expand the sorting to other columns. After you have sorted the results by shooters, you can simply copy the results and paste them into a new table, as you see in Fig. 6.34.

Now we are ready to perform the analysis. Go to “Data → Data analysis → Anova: Single Factor”. Select all five columns, indicate that the first row contains labels and click “Ok” (Fig. 6.35).

If we look at the results (Fig. 6.36), we notice that the comparison between groups (in our event, between shooters) is not significant ($p > 0.05$). It is not even weakly significant. Therefore we conclude that shooters did not generate a systematic error in our results. Thus, no improvement is needed. You can also find some additional information. Although there is no statistically significant difference among the shooters, Person 1 has the lowest variance in her or his shooting. Moreover, as we have our regression analysis results, we can calculate the intended mean. For this, we calculate our distance for 40°, 35°, 30°, 25° and 20°. Then, we calculate the average, which equals 191.18 cm. Person 2 was closer to the intended mean. Of course, you

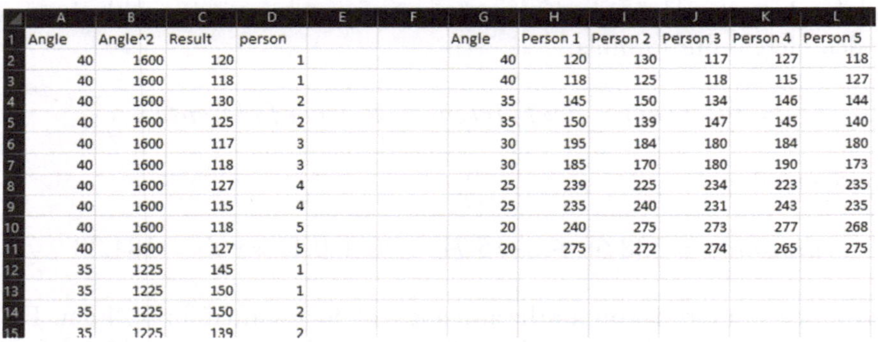

Angle	Angle^2	Result	person
40	1600	120	1
40	1600	118	1
40	1600	130	2
40	1600	125	2
40	1600	117	3
40	1600	118	3
40	1600	127	4
40	1600	115	4
40	1600	118	5
40	1600	127	5
35	1225	145	1
35	1225	150	1
35	1225	150	2
35	1225	139	2

Angle	Person 1	Person 2	Person 3	Person 4	Person 5
40	120	130	117	127	118
40	118	125	118	115	127
35	145	150	134	146	144
35	150	139	147	145	140
30	195	184	180	184	180
30	185	170	180	190	173
25	239	225	234	223	235
25	235	240	231	243	235
20	240	275	273	277	268
20	275	272	274	265	275

Fig. 6.34 Data prepared for the ANOVA

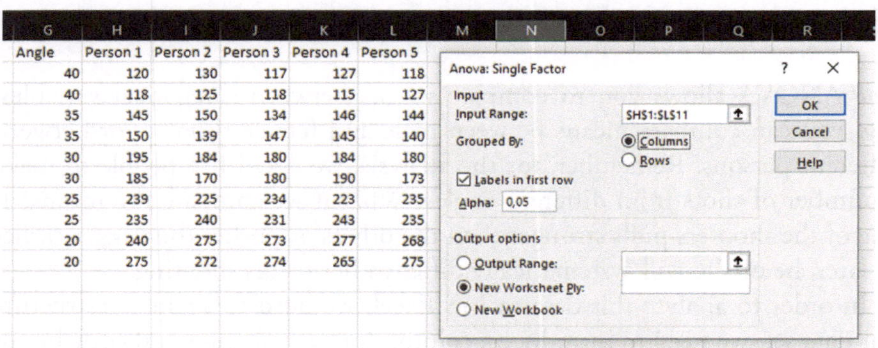

Angle	Person 1	Person 2	Person 3	Person 4	Person 5
40	120	130	117	127	118
40	118	125	118	115	127
35	145	150	134	146	144
35	150	139	147	145	140
30	195	184	180	184	180
30	185	170	180	190	173
25	239	225	234	223	235
25	235	240	231	243	235
20	240	275	273	277	268
20	275	272	274	265	275

Fig. 6.35 Running the ANOVA using MS Excel

	A	B	C	D	E	F	G
1	Anova: Single Factor						
2							
3	SUMMARY						
4	*Groups*	*Count*	*Sum*	*Average*	*Variance*		
5	Person 1	10	1902	190,2	3101,067		
6	Person 2	10	1910	191	3347,333		
7	Person 3	10	1888	188,8	3693,956		
8	Person 4	10	1915	191,5	3406,722		
9	Person 5	10	1895	189,5	3501,611		
10							
11							
12	ANOVA						
13	*Source of Variation*	*SS*	*df*	*MS*	*F*	*P-value*	*F crit*
14	Between Groups	47,8	4	11,95	0,003504	0,9999745	2,578739184
15	Within Groups	153456,2	45	3410,138			
16							
17	Total	153504	49				

Fig. 6.36 Results of the ANOVA in MS Excel

can continue the analysis and calculate precisely who should be shooting the catapult in future. But even this simple look at the ANOVA table may help you plan your process improvement.

F. *More Complex Models*

The analysis we did indicates that at least one of two hypothesised relationships holds: the angle has a strong significant impact on the quality of our shooting. Yet, the shooter itself has no significant impact. In statistics, we try to run more complex models that contain all independent variables at once. The reason is simple: some of the variables may explain more variance than others and even "grab a big piece of the pie" in the variance of the dependent variable. I.e. in a more complex model, some of the effects may lose their significance due to other, more powerful explanations.

Moreover, we include several control variables in the final model since we want to check whether alternative explanations hold. For instance, a good researcher would not only check the hypothesised factors such as the angle and the shooter, but also the gender and age of the shooter, weather conditions and light, experience in shooting, and so on. All these variables might be alternative explanations of the final result. For instance, what if experience in the shooting has more impact than the angle? What if an experienced shooter has an impact on shooting through the triggering technique or similar? And, again, the inclusion of these variables into the model may help explain more of the variance, thus making the model better. Yet, the effects of each separate variable may become weaker or even non-significant. Imagine a situation in which you want to test the effects of the shooters on the final result (e.g. "Who is the best shooter?") and find that two of them shoot much better than the others. Then you add "shooting experience" as a control variable. If the two best shooters simply have more experience than the others, their experience will predict shooting results better than just being "John" or "Jane". Consequently, the model will become better but the independent variable "shooter" will lose its significance. Making more complex models may be beneficial.

Yet, how can you do it? The best way is to apply professional software such as SPSS©, Stata®, or R (the last one is for free). These programmes allow you to enter all variables into the analysis in a very simple way. For instance, in SPSS© you can run an "univariate analysis" and add all categorical variables as "factors" and all ratio variables as "covariates". The output will comprise all necessary ANOVA and regression tables. With regard to MS Excel, we tell you a trick. You just need to recode your categorical variables into "ratios". We call such variables "dummies". For our table shown in Fig. 6.32, you create five additional variables—one for each shooter. If the shot was made by person 1, you recode this variable as "1", if it was someone else, you recode this variable as "0" (Fig. 6.37).

Now you run a regression analysis, whereby you choose as your dependent variable the distance, and as your independent variables the angle, the angle squared, as well as the five dummy variables for shooters.

One more issue: usually, one of the dummies is automatically sorted out. The reason is that in ANOVA you compare different shooters against one

	A	B	C	D	E	F	G	H	I	J
1	Angle	Angle^2	Result	person		person1	person2	person3	person4	person5
2	40	1600	120	1		1	0	0	0	0
3	40	1600	118	1		1	0	0	0	0
4	40	1600	130	2		0	1	0	0	0
5	40	1600	125	2		0	1	0	0	0
6	40	1600	117	3		0	0	1	0	0
7	40	1600	118	3		0	0	1	0	0
8	40	1600	127	4		0	0	0	1	0
9	40	1600	115	4		0	0	0	1	0
10	40	1600	118	5		0	0	0	0	1
11	40	1600	127	5		0	0	0	0	1
12	35	1225	145	1		1	0	0	0	0
13	35	1225	150	1		1	0	0	0	0

Fig. 6.37 Introducing dummies

shooter (the so-called "reference value"). The programme skips one of the variables automatically, e.g. Shooter 5. This has two implications: First, you must plot the results in order to see the differences. If two shooters are located far away from the reference Shooter 5 and/or from each other, you need to repeat the test skipping another shooter. Second, the statistical significance has to be interpreted with care. If one of the shooters is really bad in his/her shooting, then if you compare other (assumedly good) shooters against him/her, the results will be highly most likely statistically significant. Yet, if you compare other shooters against a good shooter, only one will show a statistically significant difference in the quality of shooting—the bad shooter. All other shooters may be equally good and do not differ much in their results.

Both MS Excel and SPSS© sort out one of the variables automatically. So, how can you make different comparisons? It is very simple: do not include the reference variable in your calculations. For instance, if you do not include Person 1, both MS Excel and SPSS© will compare the leftover variables against the missing variable (Fig. 6.38). Repeat the measure again and skip the variable Person 2. Now, you have a comparison of Persons 1, 3, 4, and 5 against Person 2.

As you see in Fig. 6.38, Person 3 and Person 5 tend to pull the catapult arm (weakly significantly) less than our reference person – Person 1. The coefficients are negative, indicating e.g. that Person 3 is short of the target by 6.35 cm on average. Look again at the results: Person 1 shoots further than all other shooters. The highest deviation we find at Person 3. Let us run the test skipping Person 3 (Fig. 6.39). Compare the regression results for

	A	B	C	D	E	F	G	H	I
3	*Regression Statistics*								
4	Multiple R	0,9925814							
5	R Square	0,9852179							
6	Adjusted R Square	0,9831552							
7	Standard Error	7,2643058							
8	Observations	50							
9									
10	ANOVA								
11		*df*	*SS*	*MS*	*F*	*ignificance F*			
12	Regression	6	151234,884	25205,814	477,653	0,000			
13	Residual	43	2269,115957	52,770139					
14	Total	49	153504						
15									
16		*Coefficients*	*Standard Error*	*t Stat*	*P-value*	*Lower 95%*	*Upper 95%*	*Lower 95,0%*	*Upper 95,0%*
17	Intercept	545,936	22,172	24,622	0,000	501,221	590,651	501,221	590,651
18	person2	-4,153	3,255	-1,276	0,209	-10,718	2,411	-10,718	2,411
19	person3	-6,353	3,255	-1,952	0,057	-12,918	0,211	-12,918	0,211
20	person4	-3,653	3,255	-1,122	0,268	-10,218	2,911	-10,218	2,911
21	person5	-5,653	3,255	-1,737	0,090	-12,218	0,911	-12,218	0,911
22	Angle	-15,935	1,510	-10,553	0,000	-18,981	-12,890	-18,981	-12,890
23	Angle^2	0,134	0,025	5,373	0,000	0,084	0,184	0,084	0,184

Fig. 6.38 Calculation with dummy variables

	A	B	C	D	E	F	G	H	I
1	SUMMARY OUTPUT								
2									
3	*Regression Statistics*								
4	Multiple R	0,992581							
5	R Square	0,985218							
6	Adjusted R Square	0,983155							
7	Standard Error	7,264306							
8	Observations	50							
9									
10	ANOVA								
11		*df*	*SS*	*MS*	*F*	*Significance F*			
12	Regression	6	151234,884	25205,814	477,652981	0,000			
13	Residual	43	2269,115957	52,7701385					
14	Total	49	153504						
15									
16		*Coefficients*	*Standard Error*	*t Stat*	*P-value*	*Lower 95%*	*Upper 95%*	*Lower 95,0%*	*Upper 95,0%*
17	Intercept	539,583	21,972	24,558	0,000	495,272	583,894	495,272	583,894
18	person1	6,353	3,255	1,952	0,057	-0,211	12,918	-0,211	12,918
19	person2	2,200	3,249	0,677	0,502	-4,352	8,752	-4,352	8,752
20	person4	2,700	3,249	0,831	0,411	-3,852	9,252	-3,852	9,252
21	person5	0,700	3,249	0,215	0,830	-5,852	7,252	-5,852	7,252
22	Angle	-15,935	1,510	-10,553	0,000	-18,981	-12,890	-18,981	-12,890
23	Angle^2	0,134	0,025	5,373	0,000	0,084	0,184	0,084	0,184

Fig. 6.39 Repetitive calculation with a different variable skipped

Person 1 and Person 3: The coefficient has simply changed its direction but the value and the significance levels remained the same. Indeed, if Person 1 shoots about 6 cm further than Person 3, then Person 3 shoots the same 6 cm closer than Person 1.

In the same way, you can include other variables in your research. If the variables are scalable, e.g. the number of months of catapult shooting experience, you can include these variables directly into your regression analysis. If the variable is categorical (e.g. having plenty of managerial responsibilities vs having some managerial experience vs not having them), you can introduce dummies. In this event: dummy1—managerial_experience_present, dummy2—some_managerial_experience, and dummy3—no_managerial_experience. All these dummies are coded with 1 if the option is available and with 0 if the option is not available.

6.6.3 Analyse

Actually, analysis is a very simple thing. You just need to look into the tables and find, first, statistically significant results and, second, sort them according to their impact. If some of the variables that you have assumed to have an impact on your process are not statistically significant, you may ignore them. The reason is simple: it doesn't matter whether the effect (i.e. coefficient) is large—this effect seems to be a coincidence and not the rule. The insufficient *p*-value indicates that if you repeat the measurement, the result might differ each time.

But if the *p*-value is significant, move on to the coefficients. The larger the coefficient, the greater the impact of the focal variable on the final result. However, you need to pay attention to another important element of our analysis—the nature of the variables. Look at our variables in Fig. 6.38. The coefficient indicating a difference between our shooters, namely Person 1 and Person 3, seems to be the second largest value in the analysis. At the same time, the angle squared adds only 0.134 to our analysis. Remember, the angle squared indicates the accumulative power of the catapult due to higher spring tension. Maybe this example is not the most obvious one, but it indicates an important aspect: although changing the shooter (Person 1) might increase the results by an average of 6 cm, the spring tension remains very important. The reason is that it is 1° which increases the flight range of the missile. A tension accompanying 10° of the arm angle results in a 1.34 cm deviation, 30° in about 4 cm, and so on. If your goal is to shoot at a distance of 2.55 m, you will choose an angle of 22° that may add pretty much of a deviation to the final result. We know that it would be more obvious if the effect of the variable would be a bit more powerful. For instance, in artillery, where you shoot for up to 20 km, a change in angle of 1° would lead to dozens of metres of deviation from the target, while having a different shooter who triggers the shot would have (almost) no impact at all. Here, even the small value of the barrel angle would be more important than some categorical coefficients like "shooter".

6.6.4 Improve

Now, pick the most important variables and think about how to improve them. We (and most process management experts) recommend starting with one variable at a time. The reasons are simple: You can, first, ensure that your model is correct—if the effects of change appear immediately and to the expected extent, then you should continue. Second, there is an advanced aspect of research models that we neglected so far: what if the effects of several variables are related? What if changing one variable impacts not only the dependent variable but also the independent variables (e.g. in the event of an unnoticed mediation relationship[17]) or the joint effect of several independent variables on the dependent variable (e.g. in the event of an unnoticed moderation[18])?[19] In a perfect world, we would have enough time to define all possible variables and their relations. In this simplified example, we can only improve the results one by one while repeating measurements and noticing the change.

Ok, let's be honest—in most organisations, people will try to improve all they can at once and as soon as they can. This will deliver good results. Even though you won't be able to understand the precise mechanism and all complex relations, you will enjoy the immediate improvement of the known relation. If you are under stress and pressure from your supervisor (or professor), this might be a good option. You can make your model even more complex later when you have familiarised yourself with the approach and (of course) when you need it.

6.6.5 Control

The final stage of the DMAIC cycle is to control the process quality. First of all, it is about continuous measurement. Even after you increase the efficiency and effectiveness of your process, you need to be reassured that you did everything correctly. But besides that, there is a "big secret" all process management experts know: you can *always* improve something. After you have achieved a great improvement, the next ones may be smaller but still they are improvements. Keep looking for new improvement opportunities! And yes, now we come back to the beginning—go back to the Define stage and repeat the DMAIC cycle.

---

[17] Above, we used the example of shooters and shooting experience. This is exactly the case of an unnoticed mediation. In our example, shooting experience is a better predictor of shooting than just being Shooter 1 or Shooter 5. Shooting experience is, thus, an explanatory variable (or a mediator) as it explains why some shooters shoot better.

[18] We did not provide an example, but here you have one: shooting in bad light conditions would lead to bad results by all shooters as they won't be able to aim sufficiently and see the angle they are choosing. Adding good light would increase the preciseness. Light is independent of shooters while shooting experience is. So, we talk about moderation and not about mediation.

[19] If you want to know more about it, you can find information online, either in Yevgen's podcasts (www.mci4research.podbean.com) or in books on the basics of statistics. These effects are easy to understand. However, as they distract us from the main idea, we don't want to go into them in this book.

6.6.6 DMA[G]IC?

Shall it be DMAIC or DMAGIC? Remember, at the beginning of the chapter, we told you that some firms call the DMAIC cycle *DMAGIC*. First, it sounds a bit cooler than the usual DMAIC. Second, they argue that "Generalisation" is an important step of the cycle. But what is this generalisation?

In academia, generalisation is the ability to draw a conclusion from an observation that applies to all similar situations. For instance, we would like to conclude that our catapult exercise would hold for all catapults all over the world. If we manage to do that, then what we have done is of great importance for many people and not only for the firm investigated. Indeed, our observation concerning the angle and the range of flight of a missile might help others in designing their catapults. Unfortunately, those who introduced generalisation into the DMAIC cycle hardly thought of academia, didn't they? Otherwise, the generalisation would have appeared at the end of the cycle and not in the middle of it. A researcher would, as we argued, improve the variables one by one and wait until the control phase supports his or her theory.

In our case, we assume that the model is a good approximation to real life. Our catapult is not bad, but we are not sure that it would have helped Roman warriors in their fight. Nevertheless, our catapult achieved the set goals—hitting a target of 2.25–2.75 m distance. Our measurement seems to be helpful in explaining how our dependent variable behaves (remember the R^2). Based on our measurement and calculation we can "generalise", i.e. claim that our calculations in MS Excel are applicable to the real process of catapult shooting—the one we are aiming to improve. In this specific understanding, "generalisation" is the correct word. However, we would rather include it in the step of analysis (R^2 calculations) and not create a separate stage.

By the way, we encountered other options for "G", such as "generate and prioritise ideas for improvement" (van Beek 2022) or "green it up (before you invest in new ideas)" (Hill 2012). We think it's a matter of your imagination and intention to turn a not-so-funny DMAIC cycle into something magical. Should you do it? It depends on what your goal is. If you want to show others that you made something different from mainstream process management, it might be an option. If you want to be understood, then stick to the common terminology.

6.7 What About Burnout?

As you see, usually the exercise described above has several goals:

1. You can show how to build a research model.
2. You can teach stats in a simple and funny way.
3. You can learn the DMAIC cycle—one of the core elements of process improvement.

But in this book, this exercise has an additional role.

Can we approach the issues of burnout in the same way? Why would you think that burnout resulting from badly organised processes cannot be approached as a catapult? Why not apply DMAIC to eliminate burnout in our organisations?

Indeed, there is a big difference between organisations, their processes, and a catapult. If you apply the notions from the Systems Theory (Luhmann 2004), a catapult is not a self-referential autopoietic system. We know this formulation might confuse many. Simply said: a catapult remains a catapult and will not evolve over time (except through regular wear and tear). Humans do. Organisations do. And even the processes do (i.e. due to the adoption of new regulations or due to routinisation and different organisational habits). The word "autopoietic" means that a system is capable of creating new versions of itself. Think of your team—you currently have a constellation of people you know and know how to work with. But only a few months/years ago they were in other departments or other firms. Moreover, your team will change over time when some team members leave and new team members come. From the philosophical point of view, your team will recreate itself, will partly change its form, or perhaps it will become the core of a new project.

6.7.1 Defining Burnout-Related Aspects

If you go back to our example with the catapult, you will notice the difference: in the case of a catapult, the main predictors of success or failure will not change. But in your team, they will. Nevertheless, the main idea behind the catapult exercise remains the same: if you understand the mechanism and define the main predictors of the efficiency and effectiveness of the mechanism, you will find a way to measure them, analyse, improve, and control the functioning of the system.

Luckily, from our previous chapters we know the overall mechanism of burnout occurrence. Moreover, we know that the system (be it a team, a department, a firm, or a society) should take into account the individual aspects of each of its members (team members, citizens, etc.). The larger the system, the harder it is to include everything as the complexity of interactions of individuals or groups with each other and with the resources grows exponentially. But every journey begins with a first step.

Each organisation is unique. Even firms that compete in the same market and offer similar products or services have different routines and organisational habits. Consequently, you will have to start with a description of your processes and a search for potential sources of burnout. In the event of the catapult exercise, the predictors of success are obvious. In more complex systems you will need to do much more homework in order to define a list of predictors of burnout. But why not start "where the shoe pinches"? In our Chapter 4, we offered you some tools for identifying psychological problems in your company. Indeed, in a company, we may have many processes with sub-processes. If you manage to locate those employees and managers with a high number of complaints or other indications of psychological issues, you can understand which processes you should improve first. Mapping the complaints or discovered psychological issues to activities within the process, will help you understand where to look for *systematic* issues that may lead to burnout.

With all this information, you start collecting data in a systematic way (as complaints can be isolated or random problems). At the next step, you can use a qualitative approach and ask about the issues directly. Knowing the process and personnel involved, you can conduct a semi-structured interview in order to find out

- what exactly causes distress,
- who is impacted (most), and
- what are the individual preferences of the personnel involved.

Now, you can start "sketching" the mechanism of your "catapult". As the system you investigate is complex, the definition phase might require some time. Our first suggestion is to try to accept that you cannot know everything, at least not in a given time. Remember what we wrote about a complex social system? If you spend too much time on the definition phase, the system might change again and you will need to redefine the main predictors. On the other hand, if you hurry up, you may miss an important aspect.

Our second suggestion is to try to stop when you receive the first indication of information richness. In qualitative research, we call this "saturation". Each new talk with an involved employee does not bring new information or the amount of new information decreases rapidly. The first indication tells you to start "depicting" your model and looking for the model's components that you need to measure.

Our third suggestion is to trust your intuition with regard to interpersonal communication and mistrust it with regard to understanding complex mechanisms. With regard to communication, humans developed a strong mechanism of empathy. With regard to complex relationships, we tend to oversimplify. That is why it is wise to stick to the information from the interviews, observations, or visual tools of process management.

6.7.2 Measuring Social Systems

With regard to measurement in social systems you have to take care of the following aspects:

- Time and internal development
- subjectivity of answers, and
- all possible types of respondent-related biases.

Time and internal development. In the event of a catapult, the system is mostly stable and does not change over time. I.e. you can make a measurement shooting your missiles today, tomorrow, or the day after tomorrow and nothing will change—the measurement will remain reliable and valid. In the event of humans, this might not be the case. The longer the periods between measurements, the more the participants will change. It is actually not a big issue: you made your measurement and made your analysis. Two weeks later, you repeat the measurement and repeat the analysis. If there is a difference between the results, this is due to some internal evolution of the system or external factors (e.g. Covid pandemic). The problem appears mostly in two cases:

- Imagine that you collected data in one department during this week. Next week you survey the second department. In the third week, you survey your firm's management. It can happen that while you needed a week to move from one department to another, the situation has changed. Finally, you might start comparing apples with oranges. And if in the third week, your firm's management has made a new decision (i.e. it has incorporated some of the issues that you were initially about to measure), then, when you are done with your calculation, your results will be deprecated. It is like making a measurement with one catapult and when you receive the result you discover that you need to shoot with a different one.

- A better situation is if you manage to collect all the data immediately, but you need time to process the data. If the time span between data collection, data processing, and final analysis is too long, you might end up in a situation similar to the one described above. Why is this situation a bit better? As you make your data collection in the whole firm simultaneously, you will be able to know the reliable historical data. In contrast to the previous situation, where the data is useless, you will have data that can be used to understand the root causes of the problems or trace how your firm evolved over time.

Subjectivity of answers. We are all human beings and we all make mistakes. Moreover, most of us desire to control. We want to be liked by others. We believe that we control our life. We could continue with this list of (wrong) beliefs. You all know them. These beliefs, however, have a huge impact on our behaviour while being surveyed. For instance, if you ask people to remember something, they might start generating their memories as if they really attended an event, experienced certain emotions, or saw something they couldn't have seen. If we ask people about something associated with socially important topics, we will most likely receive an answer that is "socially desirable" but not necessarily true. And you have certainly been asked "Why did you do that?" and you explained why, although in the moment of doing it, you did not think about the "Why". The latter shows that we try to do so as if we control everything, whereas it is seldom the case.

What we want to tell by this is that participants will only approximately report the true state of the system. Each answer will entail not only the state of the system but also the current state of mind of the respondent, her or his beliefs, her or his interpretations, her or his mood, etc. This implies that in the event of social systems, the measurement is much less precise than in a catapult and we have to accept it. Luckily, researchers have developed plenty of tools to avoid or control for these confounding effects, ranging from "How to formulate the questions correctly" to "Running common method variance tests".

All possible types of respondent-related biases. There are already many biases known to the researchers. Below, you will find a list of most of the biases you will encounter:

- *Social desirability bias.* As you can guess by the name, it is about the desire of your respondent to be liked by society. People tend to give "desired" answers and avoid giving answers that might be "misunderstood" (i.e. not accepted by society). Of course, there are questions that are strongly related to this type of bias. "Do you have some racial prejudice?" or "Do you think that democracy is overvalued?". Even if one has a prejudice or disagrees with the political system, she or he would most likely not answer this question with "yes". In earlier times, questionnaires often included specific randomly distributed questions to evaluate the quality of the answers of each respondent. Questions such as "Have you ever been late for work?" were often used. Let's be honest, it has happened to us at least once in our lives. So if someone answers "No" to these and similar questions, it could be an indication that his/her bias is high. Nowadays, we no longer check the trustworthiness of our participants as this could be seen as ethically incorrect.
- *Habituation bias.* This bias is usually a consequence of too long and way too complex questionnaires. The longer the text and the more complex the questionnaire is, the more people tend to reduce their efforts and simply answer in a patterned way. As an example, they are checking all the boxes on the right with some minor deviations. For a while researchers added reverse-coded items, i.e. questions that state the opposite of the previous question. "I feel tired at the end of the day" vs "I feel full of energy at the end of the day". Unfortunately, such questions caused more confusion than they helped avoid bias. Consequently, in research, we try to find other ways to reduce this bias, e.g. keeping questionnaires short, items clear and easy to understand, and putting not too many questions on one page of the survey.
- *Acquiescence bias.* This bias becomes even more evident as the level of respect increases. Usually, people tend to say "yes" and avoid explicit contradictions. Imagine that they know that the question comes from a well-known researcher or a somewhat important person. The tendency to agree will grow immediately. There are many cures against this bias, ranging from making the distribution of the questionnaire less personalised (e.g. in the name of your department but not of a certain person) to formulating the statements in an explicitly neutral way.
- *Recall bias.* This bias is the one we criticise our students for. Many students like psychology and pick a topic for their Bachelor's or Master's thesis from this domain. As a methodology, they prefer to use questionnaires, whereby they ask questions about beliefs early in life, how people felt a

year ago, or what they thought when they performed something. Unfortunately, recalling is inappropriate in this event: We believe that our values and beliefs do not change over time (which is not true, by the way) and we react from our current point of view, which we confuse with our values and beliefs from the past. Thus, we transfer our current feelings to a previous situation. Consequently, when measuring memory, feelings, and other psychological aspects, we need to focus on the current situation, apply different methods (e.g. observation, experiments), or repeat our measurement later to ensure that the answer remains the same after the mood has changed.

- Finally, *self-selection bias is* of high importance. At the end of every course, we ask our students to give us a grade for the quality of teaching. Due to self-selection, the final grade is always skewed: those, who dislike the course, take their time to give a negative grade, while those who like the course do not bother with evaluation as "everything is fine anyway". Finally, positive grades are underrepresented if you don't do something proactively. For instance, we ask our students to share what they liked in our courses so that we can keep good elements (case studies, simulations, or exercises) and remove some boring elements for next year. For example, if a professor speaks very fast (as Yevgen does, by the way), he or she can hardly change it. Consequently, criticising the pace of speaking is not constructive. However, a professor can change the contents of the slides.
- The same will happen in your case. If you want to evaluate the psychological issues at work, you may have three main groups: first, those who are satisfied with everything. They will most likely see no sense in one more questionnaire. Second, those who are already in a burnout state. They will not answer your question due to their disengagement and lack of belief in the success of your initiative (cynicism). Third, those who would like to share their negative feelings. They will participate in your survey massively. Now, let's guess, whose answers are the most useful. It would be great to know what led to the burnout state (i.e. the group of employees in the burnout state) and why some people were not affected (i.e. the group of employees not suffering from burnout). But we will most likely have answers from neither of these groups. Consequently, you need to develop a strategy on how to motivate the members of these two groups and reduce the negative effects of the "willing-to-participate group". Here, we have no suggestions as you know your team better and know what to do.

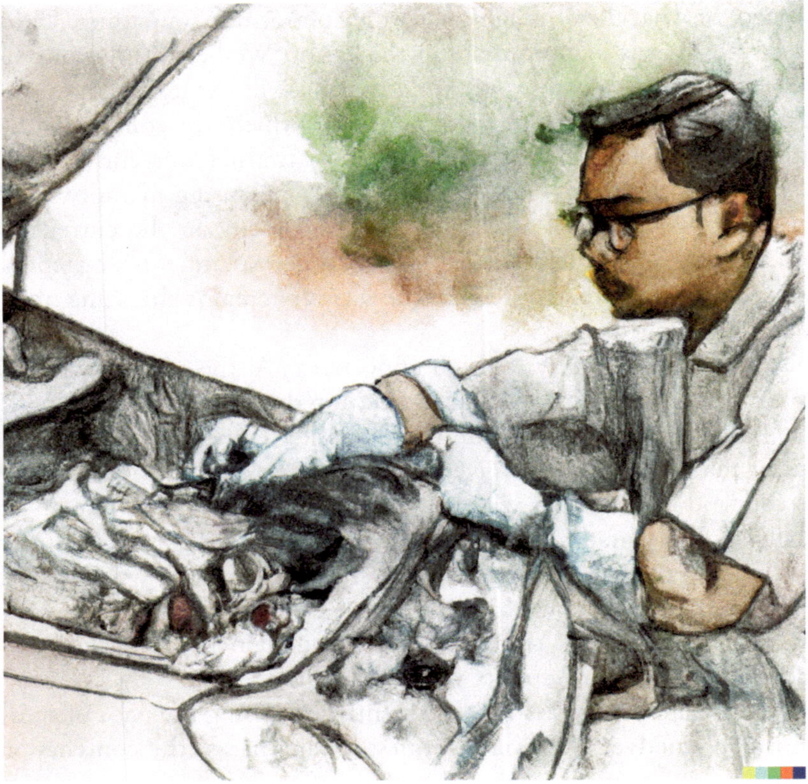

Consequently, how hard is it to measure a social system compared to a catapult? Here, we remember the Ukrainian joke when a mechanic meets a cardiac surgeon and says that a motor is much more complex than a heart. So, the mechanic asks, why is he paid less than a surgeon? And the surgeon answers that he would be paid better if he managed to repair a *running* motor.

Finally, we should mention two other aspects of data collection "on a running motor". *Maturity* is an important aspect that you need to take into account when working with people. People learn over time, they get used to many things, and develop a new view of things. Consequently, the longer the period between your measurements, the more it looks like you work with different people. Even after the first (hopefully) successful burnout prevention initiative, they will get used to the quality of your work and demand more. At the same time, they will know some questions and, thus, may become bored. Another important aspect is *mortality*. Of course, we mean mortality in the statistical sense. If you start your study with a hundred people, you would want to repeat your measurement in the control phase with the same people. Yet, some will have changed their place of work, some will be on vacation, and some will find no time to participate. We call this phenomenon "mortality" as you lose people on the go. The lower the turnover of participants involved, the more precise your results.

6.7.3 Analysis of Far Too Complex Relationships

As you see, the phase of measuring becomes quite complex in the event of social systems. It is similar to the phase of analysing. Namely, you have to

- add more variables,
- increase your sample size, and
- think of interactions.

Adding more variables. If you work with an unstable system that is impacted by several external and internal factors as well as by self-development (autopoiesis), you have to control for the impact of these factors. It sounds more complex than it is. You have to take two steps: first, list all possible impact factors that you can find, and, second, measure them and include them as additional variables. For instance, let's assume that the system has evolved. What variable do we have to include? Yes, time! Just introduce the variable "measurement_time" into your analysis and *violá*—if there is an impact of time, you will notice it in the regression table.

Listing all important factors does not mean listing all possible variables. You need to pick those that *matter*. In the case of our catapult, we focused on the angle and the shooter and ignored humidity, height over the sea level, and so on. Adding too many variables would confuse you and would worsen the final results. Yet, control for external factors such as a change in management, change of tasks, roles, and responsibilities, or even inflation—the fact that your employees notice that their income is declining may lead to burnout as well.

Increase your sample size. The reason is very simple—the more complex your model, the larger the sample size which is required to verify the model. The sample size depends on several factors. First, it is about your population, i.e. all persons about whom you want to make your conclusion. If we are talking about a small firm with 20 employees, then it is easy and feasible to work with each of them. If we talk about a large corporation with thousands of employees, we need to find a representative sample, i.e. all groups of employees should be represented (e.g. different departments, different ages, different genders, different levels of managerial responsibility). With a sufficiently large sample, you can run your statistical tests and obtain reliable and valid results.

Second, the sample size is influenced by the strength of the relationship you are assuming to test. The smaller the assumed effect, the larger sample is needed to capture the effect. If the effect is strong, then even a smaller sample size might work. For instance, if we talk about the impact of temperature on the effectiveness of office workers, you might need a very large sample size as the effects are probably minor. However, if you want to check the impact of the new manager, a smaller sample size might suffice. For students, we propose a rule of thumb. It is not academic (if you want a fully academic approach, use the freely available GPower app of the Heinrich Heine University Düsseldorf): If we assume average effects, we propose the students use $n = 60$ for a single relationship (Faul et al. 2009). If they plan to test two relationships, they need to add another 30 participants. For the next, they need to add 15 more participants. Further, add another 10 for each new relationship. Theoretically, one can continue but the rule of thumb is meant to be simple, isn't it? Consequently, if you assume there are five variables in your model, you need to survey $60 + 30 + 15 + 10 + 10 = 125$ participants. If the effects are minor, you will notice it by the statistical significance (p-value is close to 0.1). Then just increase the number of participants or focus on the variables that have a stronger predictive power. We wouldn't apply this rule to the control variables. Theoretically, if you add any variable, your statistics programme sees them as a relationship to test (it does not distinguish between what you mean by each variable). Yet, as you assume that the main effects come from your key variables and control variables are assumed to have no effect, this should not be an issue for the sample size. In the worst-case scenario add more participants to your study.

Think of interactions. Finally, social systems are so complex that many variables may interact. Think of the following example: Salary has an impact on some types of motivation (external regulation). Yet, research has shown that it is not only the salary that impacts an individual's behaviour but also her or his social comparison (Salovey and Rodin 1984; Gilbert et al. 1995). As soon as your well-paid manager discovers that she or he is paid 1,000 EUR less than a colleague in a similar position, she or he will become demotivated. Vice versa, if she or he discovers that she or he receives 1,000 EUR more than her or his colleagues, she or he will become proud and highly motivated. As you see, it is not only the salary that you should include in your final calculations but also the "knowledge about others' salaries".

Interaction is easy to test. Your statistics programme (e.g. SPSS©, Stata®) will do it for you if you not only want to analyse direct effects but also their interaction. The interaction variable will be created automatically. You just need to indicate that you want to see the interaction between your independent A and B that predict C. In this case, SPSS© or Stata® would test the direct effect of A, the direct effect of B, and their interaction: A*B. In MS Excel you can calculate your regression with interaction variables with a tweak. Here you will need to create another independent variable D that will be the result of multiplication A*B. Then, you add independent variables to your regression analysis A, B, and D, and your dependent variable remains C. If the variable D shows a statistically significant value, you have found a moderation.

6.7.4 Improving a Running Motor

Actually, there is not so much we can add about improving the system if you follow our previous comments on social systems. As you know about the complexity and the constant self-development of the system, you need to take into account the

- constant reflection on the state of the system,
- constant awareness of new variables, and
- appearance of new interactions.

Constant reflection on the state of the system. While you are improving your system, involved people will co-evolve: they will develop a different understanding (i.e. perception) of the relationships, they will change their point of view on the situation and adapt their beliefs, and they will build up new organisational habits. For you, it means that while you expect your improvements to have a specific impact, they might produce (completely) unexpected results. If we were you, we would constantly monitor the situation and compare it to the initial state. This will help you understand whether the result you observe comes from your intervention or other internal or external factors. Moreover, consider regular reflection meetings to know whether the planned intervention is still up to date. If the situation has changed, you may need to change your plan.

Constant awareness of new variables. This aspect comes directly from the previous point: If you notice that something has changed indeed, you can measure it. Find out what exactly happened and what are the (root) causes for this change. Transfer this observation into new variables and add them to your calculation. What if you discovered a new reason for dissatisfaction while you were improving some other aspects of your process? Will this discovery impact your running improvement efforts? Is it critical for the current improvement or can you improve the newly discovered aspect after you have finished your current measure? Are employees and managers dissatisfied because of your improvement or because of the newly discovered issue? The inclusion of additional variables into your analysis will help distinguish between the real impact and your or others' biases in this regard.

Appearance of new interactions. Since we assume that the perception of the involved personnel might change, some of the variables might play a reinforcing or dampening role. Imagine that you run a process improvement initiative and introduce a tool for process simulation. Yet, as this tool is running on Linux, many will struggle to use it. Since Linus has adapted some aspects of MS Windows with regard to the graphical user interface, PC users might have fewer issues than Mac users with the new system. I.e. it is not only about the new system that might be efficient and effective for your goal. It is about the reinforcing (in the event of PC users) or dampening (in the event of Mac users) effects on the relationship between "new software" and "better processes". Of course, it is a made-up example, but you've got the point.

6.7.5 Control: Quis Custodiet Ipsos Custodes?[20]

In the event of a closed system, such as a catapult, you control the mechanism, the repetitive actions, and the outcome variables. In the event of human beings, you want to control humans. And humans seldom like to be controlled. If you try, you will run into two problems:

- You undermine trust and, thus, motivation of the personnel, and
- You might generate the Hawthorne effect.

Trust and motivation. Even though you focus on some key indicators to check the effects of an intervention, people will see it as more than just a measurement. They will take it to mean that you want to monitor them and control their private lives. In their Self-Determination Theory of Motivation, Deci and Ryan (2002) distinguish between extrinsic (coming from outside, from someone else) and intrinsic (coming from inside, an innate wish) motivation. In a firm you almost never find intrinsic motivation—the

[20] Latin phrase meaning "Who will guard the guards themselves?"

reason employees and managers go to work and the reason they engage in their activities is a need to earn their living and get security for themselves and their family, i.e. external factors. Yet, the scholars suggested that within this extrinsic motivation, there are several "regulation types", e.g. reward and punishment as well as being asked by someone whom you respect are external factors but with deviating consequences—performing an activity asked by someone we respect leads to much better outcomes than if the same activity is driven by reward and punishment.

As you can imagine, reward and punishment are the less efficient regulation types. What do you think the employees will believe if they see you running around and collecting data? If you are lucky, they will understand that you work on their processes to reduce their psychological and physiological strain. But, if you are not lucky (that happens more often than one thinks), they will feel monitored. One gets the impression that you want to know where you can prove them wrong. This state is immediately associated with reward and punishment (why else should you be monitoring them?!). This association may result in a drop in trust and a decline in willingness to cooperate.

Do you remember our story with the young football players in Chapter 2? Paying for participation in data collection (as Dr Smith from our story did to the kids playing football) would lead to a similar result as punishing employees—the lowest possible level of motivation. For this reason, you must be very careful and (where possible) should explain what you are doing and what is the goal. Ryan and Deci (2000) also showed that the best result can be achieved if people understand what has to be done, and why it matters, and they incorporate the goal as their desired goal. In this case, the motivation will be hardly distinguishable from the intrinsic one.

***Hawthorne effect*.** This is one of the fascinating biases in the field of research. If you want to find the original story, search for it online. Here we share a summary only: A researcher collected data in the American firm Hawthorne Works. Yet, as the employees knew that they were being observed they started performing better. Maybe to look better (social desirability?) or to avoid the disappointment of researchers (acquiescence bias?), in any way they started working harder. The results of the experiments, therefore, were not due to the hypothesised effects but due to the researchers themselves.

While the feeling of being observed might reduce performance, the Hawthorne effect may drastically increase it. To be honest, you can observe both tendencies at the same time: While employees work hard under observation (productivity spikes), they "retaliate" with low performance in other activities, such as absenteeism or poor performance when they are not observed. Unfortunately, there is no simple cure for these problems. However, if you know your team, know your competencies, stick to common sense, and rely on academic tools, you might be able to avoid these effects in the control phase. In the end, this phase is the input for further improvements. It is crucial to remain calm and focused, avoid biases, and get the job done by approaching your goal step by step.

6.8 What If You Redesign the Process?

Process management has many faces—from the introduction of a new tool for a certain process step (i.e. a small, incremental improvement) to the complete redesign of a business process (i.e. a comprehensive, radical change). The latter may also be called process reengineering. Should you aim for a more comprehensive approach, you should go for the DMADV cycle instead of DMAIC:

1. **Define**: You have to define the goal of the process and the desire of the customers. Be it external or internal customers (i.e. your employees or your colleagues), you need to direct the process towards their needs and wishes.
2. **Measure**: In this phase, you address the critical-to-quality requirements of your customers and think of a way to measure the requirements. It is suggested to create a metric for each of the critical-to-quality requirements.
3. **Analyse**: Here, you try to compare different process design elements based on the measurement you have conducted. You should not only find the best design in general but also investigate every single element of the new process regarding its contribution to efficiency and effectiveness.
4. **Design**: In this phase, you develop a process prototype. Think of all the roles, resources granted, and interactions expected.
5. **Verify**: Now it is time to test-run your process and observe whether it is working and whether the goals set have been achieved.

Here, we would like to add the following advice: **Repeat**. Often the newly designed process does not work as expected. I.e. you will need to iterate the whole process design. Nevertheless, you will eventually achieve a satisfactory result. Then, you get back to the DMAIC cycle and start working on the continuous improvement of the process.

History Matters

It happened to me only recently. In our team, the charged atmosphere was clearly palpable. The level of dissatisfaction was constantly growing but the reasons were not clear. Definitely, there were no issues with motivation and engagement. Based on Herzberg's (1974) Two-Factor Theory of Motivation, a clear problem with the hygiene factors was recognisable. Maybe something was wrong with the clarity of rules, feeling of security, status, or interpersonal relations. Anyway, the level of dissatisfaction and, consequently, of emotional and physical exhaustion became high and kept increasing. After some consideration, our management decided that it was all due to work overload caused by irregular distractions (e.g. spontaneous emails, colleagues requests, phone calls). At this point, I wished they had read our book to apply any type of root cause analysis, e.g. the one with "5 whys". Yet, we remained at the first and obvious level of analysis, the distractions. The solution to the current problem was reduced to the introduction of "quiet hours" during which all distractions are prohibited: no phone calls, no email checking, no meetings, and so on. My question to you: Did we succeed in reducing work stress?

"Yes and no" would be my answer. Further analysis would reveal that we were treating symptoms instead of the core issue. When employees notice that the management is doing something, the mood becomes more positive. However, this happens for a short time only. After one symptom is healed, the next symptom will appear as the core problem remains untackled.

We can discuss for a long time, what was the root cause. I would like to share my opinion in this regard and tell you why this specific process improvement—"quiet hours"—hardly works in this situation. Let's start with the initial problem—the growing level of dissatisfaction. Now, let's try to find out why it happened:

Level 1: Why did we have clearly sensed dissatisfaction among the whole team? Indeed, our team was dissatisfied. Essentially, the dissatisfaction was found at the assistant level. Yet, the more they were dissatisfied, the more it became a problem for all other team members.

Level 2: Why did it happen? It happened because of the overload of physical and psychological resources. The team was under constant pressure dictated by a high number of tasks.

Level 3: Why? There might be several explanations. Yet, the most obvious was the wrong planning and the lack of resources due to the poor planning.
Level 4: Why? At first glance, the problem was the low level of resources—only a few assistants and other office workers were not sufficient for all the tasks. However, other similar organisations manage to handle even bigger loads with the same size of teams. Why?
Level 5: It seems that our business school has developed some processes that no longer fitted the old form. When the business school started, the main goal was to introduce business administration to relatively small groups of practice-oriented students (in contrast to the larger public university in the city—the University of Innsbruck). Accordingly, the contents should be more applied than the ones of public universities. The initial structure comprised administrative personnel only, while lecturers were hired on a short-term basis, as adjuncts. The administration was seen as the key to success, research was beyond the horizon of possibilities, and teaching was outsourced. Yet, with each year the business school grew and became more institutionalised. More and more it focused on its own teaching curricula, unified quality criteria (triggered by accreditation agencies), and high-quality research. However, high-quality teaching can hardly be achieved with adjuncts only. Also, research cannot be outsourced, otherwise the results would belong to one of the competitors. Moreover, research became not only desired but necessary for the school's survival (international ranking, accreditation, employer branding, etc.). The role of the administrative staff began to resemble that of an established university, whereas the role of lecturers, their spectrum of work, and the range of responsibilities became more pronounced. The new cohort of researchers took over a key role in business school affairs. At the same time, the role of teaching and research assistants is radically changing—from "being the core of the administration of a small business school with many adjuncts" to "taking care of assistance in teaching and research in a mid-size university with a strong faculty". For instance, at other universities in Austria and Germany, research and teaching assistants work in temporary positions in order to achieve their doctorate in this way. Yet, in our university the assistant positions are mostly permanent, they require personnel with BA or MA (as in other comparable universities), while the concept of earning a doctorate at the same time is optional or non-existent. You can imagine the level of disorientation of people with high potential and no clear academic growth perspective.

But what about the processes at the business school? They hardly changed: the way we process applications of potential students, the way we organise exams and how we administer the learning management system was "slowly getting out of hand" or, put differently, did not reflect the needs of the "new" institution.

Let's look at the problem through the lens of our last "whys":

- *We are still involved with entire teams in the interviews with potential students (skill waste, overprocessing). Setting up a separate, permanent interview team for all intakes from all departments would save our resources enormously. The team could also take on some marketing tasks, such as organising student fairs.*
- *We still manually copy all the content from previous years when we hold the same class this year (waste of skills, overprocessing, motion waste). Automating this procedure will help us avoid boredom (copying) and save valuable time.*
- *We are still siloed in how we administer exams (overproduction, skill waste). As all exams run at almost the same time, why not make a permanent team of administrators? By the way, as exams run at a different time than intakes, one team can help address issues of all faculties, not only ours.*

And if we want to reduce the dissatisfaction, we should look at what our team members are good at. Many love teaching while hating research. The others love research while hating administrative tasks. Wouldn't it be a good idea to arrange our internal processes in a way that everyone gets what she or he likes and minimises undesired tasks? The dissatisfaction was mainly caused because the resources were wrongly allocated, overprocessing was at every step, and struggles because of the office spaces for the personnel became wars of interest. In terms of Bulgakov: "The housing problem has corrupted them."[21] *All these problems, if tackled at their core, can not only avoid dissatisfaction but also increase motivation.*

Will "quiet hours" reduce the level of dissatisfaction? To some extent yes—as it addresses the first level of "why". Can the problem at its core be solved by introducing "quiet hours"? Probably not. Indeed, Lean Management and the elimination of "Seven Wastes" would help. However, when I look at many of the current processes, I become eager to redesign them. Addressing the dissatisfaction factors at the beginning and taking care of the psychological and physiological resources of each team member would be the best way to proceed.

[21] In Bulgakov's novel "The Master and Margarita", Satan said "… they're people like any other people … they love money, but that has always been so … Mankind loves money, whatever it's made of—leather, paper, bronze, gold. Well, they're light-minded … well, what of it … mercy sometimes knocks at their hearts … ordinary people … In general, reminiscent of the former ones … only the housing problem has corrupted them …". The phrase fits so well to the office space problem—at any university or firm.

References

Bogodistov, Yevgen, and Jürgen Moormann. 2019. Theorizing on operational excellence: A capability-based approach. *Academy of Management Proceedings* 2019: 12174.

Bogodistov, Yevgen, Jürgen Moormann, and Rainer Sibbel. 2018. Beyond health care reform: How process management can alter patients' experience. *Academy of Management Proceedings* 2018 (12544).

Bradley, Margaret M., and Peter J. Lang. 1994. Measuring emotion: The self-assessment manikin and the semantic differential. *Journal of Behavior Therapy and Experimental Psychiatry* 25: 49–59.

Deci, Edward L., and Richard M. Ryan. 2002. *Handbook of self-determination research*. Rochester, NY: University Rochester Press.

Dettmer, William H. 1997. *Goldratt's theory of constraints: A systems approach to continuous improvement*. Milwaukee,WI: ASQC Quality Press.

Faul, Franz, Edgar Erdfelder, Axel Buchner, and Albert-Georg. Lang. 2009. Statistical power analyses using G*Power 3.1: Tests for correlation and regression analyses. *Behavior Research Methods* 41: 1149–1160.

Field, Andy. 2018. *Discovering statistics using IBM SPSS statistics*. London: Sage.

Forrester, Jay W. 1971. Counterintuitive behavior of social systems. *Theory and Decision* 2: 109–140.

Gilbert, D. T., R. B. Giesler, and K. A. Morris. 1995. When comparisons arise. *Journal of Personality and Social Psychology* 69: 227–236.

Goldratt, Eliyahu M., and Jeff Cox. 2012. *The goal: A process of ongoing improvement*. Great Barrington, MA: North River Press.

Grant, Robert M. 1996. Prospering in dynamically-competitive environments: Organizational capability as knowledge integration. *Organization Science* 7: 375–387.

Grant, Robert M., and Judith Jordan. 2015. *Foundations of strategy*. Chichester, West Sussex: Wiley.

Herzberg, Frederick. 1974. Motivation-hygiene profiles: Pinpointing what ails the organization. *Organizational Dynamics* 3: 18–29.

Hill, Rod. 2012. Dear valentine, DMAIC? A Six sigma analysis of love. *Process Excellence Network*. February 6.

Luhmann, Niklas. 1987. *Soziale Systeme: Grundriss einer allgemeinen Theorie*. Frankfurt a.M.: Suhrkamp.

Luhmann, Niklas. 2004. *Einführung in die Systemtheorie*. Heidelberg: Carl Auer.

Pircher, Markus. 2023. House of Quality (HoQ): How to reduce the level of energy depletion in a local bank in South Tyrol, seminar paper, Management Center Innsbruck.

Portny, Stanley E. 2020. *Project management all-in-one for dummies*. Hoboken, NJ: Wiley.

Portny, Stanley E., Samuel J. Mantel Jr, Jack R. Meredith, Scott M. Shafer, and Margaret M. Sutton. 2007. *Wiley pathways project management*. Hoboken: Wiley.

ReVelle, Jack B. 2004. *Quality essentials: A reference guide from A to Z*. Milwaukee, WI: ASQ Quality Press.

Rohrbach, B. 1969. Methode 635, eine neue Technik zum Lösen von Problemen. *Absatzwirtschaft* 12: 73–76.

Ryan, Richard M., and Edward L. Deci. 2000. Self-determination theory and the facilitation of intrinsic motivation, social development, and well-being. *American Psychologist* 55: 68–78.

Salovey, Peter, and Judith Rodin. 1984. Some antecedents and consequences of social-comparison jealousy. *Journal of Personality and Social Psychology* 47: 780–792.

Schaufeli, Wilmar B. 2017. Applying the job demands-resources model. *Organizational Dynamics* 2: 120–132.

Siegrist, J. 2016. Effort-reward imbalance model. In *Stress: Concepts, cognition, emotion, and behavior*, ed. George Fink, Chapter 9, 81–86. San Diego, CA: Academic Press.

van Beek, Daan. 2022. Kaizen. *Data science for decision makers and data professionals*. Passioned Publishers. Accessed May 10, 2023. https://www.passionned.com/ci/improvement-methods/kaizen/.

Vester, Frederic. 1988. The biocybernetic approach as a basis for planning our environment. *Systems Practice* 1: 399–413.

Vester, Frederic. 2001. *Die Kunst, vernetzt zu denken. Ideen und Werkzeuge für einen neuen Umgang mit Komplexität*. Stuttgart, Germany: DVA.

Voss, Chris, and Tahl Raz. 2017. *Never split the difference: Negotiating as if your life depended on it*. London, UK: Penguin Random House.

7

Can a Firm Develop a Burnout Resilience Capability?

Abstract While in the previous chapter we went down the rabbit hole and became very concrete regarding the application of tools from process management, in this chapter we go back to the organisation's level and try to show the bigger picture of your burnout prevention activities – development of burnout resistance or even a burnout resilience capability. First, we discuss what an organisational capability is. Second, we talk about how one can measure an organisational capability. Finally, we give some advice concerning capability development. This chapter is designed to help you *convince your executive board or those responsible for your organisation's strategy* of your change initiative, as top managers think in abstract terms of organisational capabilities (also called "competencies") and not in terms of tools, exercises, or local (e.g. team or department) problems.

7.1 Being Capable, Being Able, Being Competent, Having Power, or Having Potential?

The topic of organisational capabilities is one of the most fascinating in strategic management—many scholars work on the concept and they are unable to understand what a capability is. Please, don't get us wrong—there are many definitions and approaches but they all lack conciseness and clarity. For instance, we know that a capability is what we can do with a certain resource, i.e. if two distinct firms have the same resources, they will most likely utilise them differently and, thus, achieve different outcomes. In our

© The Author(s), under exclusive license to Springer Nature Switzerland AG 2024
Y. Bogodistov and J. Moormann, *Process Management and Burnout Prevention*,
https://doi.org/10.1007/978-3-031-56615-8_7

classes we ran a thought experiment: we asked our students to imagine a situation when we give them 25,000 EUR, a car, and a flat in the city centre of Frankfurt (or Innsbruck). Yet, we would not make a gift, but we would invest these financial resources and expect an appropriate return. Then we asked them what they would do with this investment. It is really funny to hear investment ideas ranging from setting up a start-up business for financial advisory to buying a very expensive business suit because it will help you make the desired impression at a job interview and get a job that will pay back the investment very fast. And we have plenty of options in between. During the last couple of years, we collected about a hundred unique ideas. In fact, we collected about fifty ideas each year but they often overlap. By 'unique' we really mean unique and unexpected ways to use the three resources provided. This thought experiment illustrates the difference between a resource and a capability—having the same resources and a similar education (the students are from the same year of study and of more or less equal age), the participants create completely new ways to utilise these resources.

If you present this example to one of the scholars from the Resource-based View (RBV), they will argue that the above mentioned novel ways to utilise these resources can be explained differently. First, they would argue that a capability is also a resource, i.e. we don't need a new concept of a capability as we can treat them as regular resources. Second, the RBV assumes that the utilisation of resources is defined by the individual resources of each student, i.e. their skills, knowledge, education, etc. Consequently, it is not about what the students would do with the resources but about what kind of education and background they have. Those who were good in finance would probably tend towards financial advisory as a business idea, whereas those whose parents found their job thanks to their perfect outfit might overestimate the importance of a business suit at a job interview. This is one of the ways to argue. Well, we don't think this approach is very useful: we could ask ourselves questions such as "What explains why some students use their skills and others don't?" or "What made them study at this university and take this course?". In order to explain this, we would need to dive into the topic of psychology, sociology, history, or even genetics. The RBV may have to go all the way back to the Big Bang to explain why certain activities occur.

Alternatively, a spin-off of the RBV could help—the Capability-based View (CBV). This approach focuses on the function of a resource and is, in our humble opinion, a much more promising approach to understand why some individuals and firms become successful while others hardly manage to survive. Assumedly, the reason lies in their individual (for individuals) or organisational (for firms) capabilities.

Both individual and organisational capabilities are harder to understand than one would think. Try to answer the following questions:

- What are your capabilities?
- *For firms:* Do you own this capability or will it disappear if Mrs Smith leaves your organisation?
- *For individuals:* Are these your own capabilities or are you relying on someone else to get the result? E.g. you have a great paper writing capability but only if someone processes the data for you.
- How did you develop these capabilities? Can you develop them again?
- Can you teach others to develop a similar capability?

One of the definitions of a capability, delivered by Winter (2003, 991), says "An organisational capability is a high-level routine (or a collection of routines) that, together with its implementing input flows, confers upon an organisation's management a set of decision options for producing significant outputs of a particular type." From our perspective, this definition is very good. It incorporates both a routine as a microfoundation of a capability, incorporates the notion of input and output as we know it from process management, and says that a capability is about a potential but not about a specific result. The aspect of potential is really important for theorists and practitioners, even though the latter seldom think about it. The trick is that most people try to define a capability tautologically, e.g. a *logistics capability* means being good at *logistics*. However, this is wrong as one can have a capability but not activate it or as one can be successful by luck. If you coincidentally made money by investing in a favourable share, can we call you a competent financial investor? Not really, but many firms and managers are described by the press as "gurus" or "centres of competence", even though they are not.

A capability is more about a potential or, in terms of Winter, a set of decision options that is available to an individual (in the event of an individual capability) or a firm's management (in the event of an organisational capability). Think of your individual capability: if you learn to play a song on a guitar or if you learn how to run an ANOVA test in Excel, this could give the impression that you are a good guitarist or a good statistician. In real life, this "capability" might bring more harm than use. If you recall the phrase by Abraham Maslow "If the only tool you have is a hammer, you tend to see every problem as a nail", you know what we mean. Playing the same song at all parties or applying an ANOVA test to all situations, will destroy the final result (happiness of your listeners or your statistics professor). However, if you learn to play different songs over a longer period of time you will:

1. Learn to handle the guitar and even play guitar solos,
2. Develop a feeling of playing and changing chords, and
3. Get a feel for music, etc.

As a result, you develop a set of decision options from which you can choose in different situations. You will become good at something and you will be free to activate this capability or not. If you don't like a party, you can decide whether you are willing to amuse people with your songs or not. The opposite is shown in a dialogue:

– Are you good at playing the violin?
– I don't know—I've never tried.

We know someone's capability if one has never tried, don't we?

7.2 Understanding a Capability

7.2.1 Consequences of a Capability

Interestingly, there are several ways to approach a capability. We can approach a capability through a reflective or a formative measurement (discussed in the next section). Usually, we use reflective measurement as we look at the consequences of a capability or its "reflection". It is like observing ripples in the water—we know they are a result of a stone falling into the water. Based on the size of the ripples and intervals between them, we may estimate the size of the stone, where it landed, and even when it was dropped. The ripples reflect the fact of stone falling. Similarly, we may look at the consequences of a capability to understand its state.

In their work, Cohen and Bacdayan (1994) investigated routines. As routines are at the core of a capability, we can apply their arguments to understand a capability. The authors emphasise four reflections of capability.

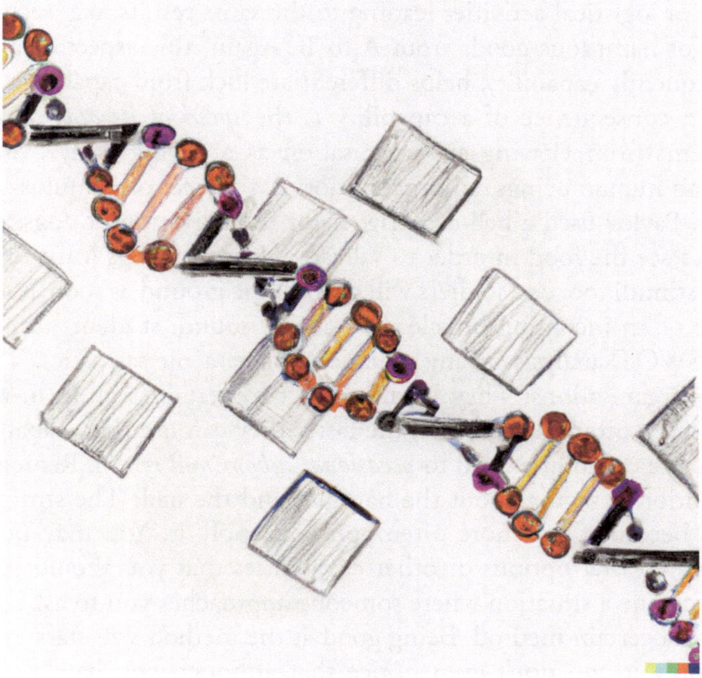

First, a capability should be represented by a *patterned sequence of actions*, i.a. actions that are repetitive, recognisable, and carried out by multiple actors. It is not about taking a guitar in your hands once; the path to mastery lies in the repetition of the activity, over and over again. Only then will you learn different ways of handling your guitar and develop a routine of playing that might become a capability. In our case, however, we look at the reflection of a capability, i.e. its consequence. So, if we know that there is a sequence of actions that precede an outcome, we can be sure that the observed outcome is not a coincidence or luck. This, by the way, is a reason why we can be sure that someone who has never played a violin (as in the dialogue in the previous section) will most likely fail if she or he tries. Remember what we wrote about the DNA of an organisation? Scholars in the field of process management say that business processes are the firm's DNA. But maybe it's not the processes but the routines that create the uniqueness and idiosyncrasy of an organisation. Routines are not far away from processes—they just (additionally) include the informal interactions between employees and employees and resources.

Second, a capability would produce *reliable results*. Do you remember that reliability is about achieving the same or a very similar result when repeating an action? A capability in, let's say, logistics will be reflected in a reliable repetition of logistical activities leading to the same results, e.g. secure transportation of hazardous goods from A to B. Again, this aspect of a routine, and consequently capability, helps differentiate luck from capability.

Third, a consequence of a capability is the *speed of its application.* This notion stems from viewing an organisation as a "living body". Similar to animals and human beings, an organisation is a subject of stimulus–response behaviour. Pavlov used a bell as a trigger for the salivation of dogs: dogs did not have to see the food in order to salivate. Human beings learn to respond to certain stimuli too: e.g. soldiers will drop to the ground as soon as they hear the whine of an incoming missile or a similar sound; students immediately think of SWOT analysis in any situation (okay, a bit sarcastic). The same applies to organisations: They learn to react to certain stimuli in a certain way. The more often they do this, the faster they can use their capabilities.

Fourth, the capabilities lead to *occasional suboptimal results.* Remember the above-mentioned saying about the hammer and the nail? The stronger your capability becomes, the more often you will apply it. You may not notice that there are other options or other capabilities that you should have used instead. Imagine a situation where someone approaches you to ask for advice in applying a certain method. Being good at the method you start explaining how to apply it and don't even notice that although you have been asked about the method, the problem at hand might need the application of a different method. Or, what also happens often, a person does not need advice but attention and compassion. Yet, you haven't noticed that as you were fully in the tunnel of your competence. If it never happened to you, lucky you!

As you see, the approach by Cohen and Bacdayan (1994) does not only allow for the delineation of a capability from a non-capability but also gives hints about how to measure a capability: we need to find out whether we have a patterned action of behaviour, whether we produce reliable results, whether we are fast in providing these results, and whether some suboptimality occurs as we apply our capability to non-related tasks. Can we find indicators for these four consequences? We are certain that yes.

An organisational capability is a latent construct, i.e. we cannot measure it as it is unobservable. But the four consequences that we took from the work of the scholars are. Can we estimate the reliability of the results, e.g. that stressful situations or burnout cases (almost) disappeared? Yes, we can. Can we measure the speed of response to a challenge, e.g. that we perform a process change after we have discovered some cases of burnout? We can. Can we indicate a sequence of actions that repeat over time, e.g. that we have a team that repeatedly shows its competence and willingness to apply its skills to improve organisational processes to reduce psychological issues? Oh yes, the whole field of process management is dedicated to this goal. Finally, will we notice if firms sometimes make mistakes due to a wrong application of their capabilities? We are pretty sure, we will. Consequently, we can measure organisational capability by its consequences. But what if we want to estimate the capability not based on its consequences, i.e. after it has been activated, but during the capability has started to occur? Here, we do not need a reflective but a formative approach.

7.2.2 Antecedents of a Capability

When we need to explain to our students the difference between a reflective and a formative measurement we take the example of a drunk person. So, how can you know that someone is drunk? Usually, a drunk person shows signs of deviating behaviour: he or she cannot walk straight, cannot pronounce words correctly, may smell alcohol, may behave aggressively, and so on. As you see, these are the reflections or consequences of being drunk. And if you want to be sure, you have to observe several of these reflections. Otherwise, you might be wrong in your judgement. Did you know that the smell of alcohol also appears after drinking buttermilk or eating an apple on an empty stomach? Also, people can have problems walking when injured or simply tired. Tiredness and some other physiological issues may lead to problems with pronounciation. However, the more reflections you find and the more they are pronounced, the more you can be sure that a person is drunk. But what if there was a more precise way of knowing the state of the person in focus?

We think you have found the solution already—we just need to take the blood of the person and measure the amount of alcohol! Yet, it might be a hard (and illegal) way to do this. How about a legal way—sitting in the bar and counting the number of beer mugs the person under investigation has drunk? And here we come to an important point: if you want to look at antecedents or predictors of the state of being drunk, you need to take into account all important aspects. Counting the beer mugs is not enough if the person also drank wine. Consequently, you need to count all types of alcohol consumed. Moreover, whiskey has more alcohol than beer. So we need to count the amount and type of drinks.

Did we miss something? Oh, yes, we did. First, we need to control for time—the longer the duration of alcohol consumption, the greater the decay of alcohol in the blood. The one who drank two beers over two hours will be less drunk than the one who recently drank two beers. And finally, we need to measure the body weight—the bigger the body, the lower the concentration of alcohol.

Now, we believe, you see the problem with the formative measurement—it is hard to conduct and missing a single element (e.g. body weight) may lead to wrong conclusions. At the same time, a formative measurement is more precise and has a certain predictive power—you can say about the person's state at the time of ordering a drink. For the reflective measurement, you would need to wait for the occurrence of the state.

Now that you know the characteristics of a formative measurement, we can put together the antecedents of an organisational capability as suggested by Grant and Jordan (2015):

1. Organisational capabilities have to be anchored in the *processes* of the company itself. The authors stressed this notion to delineate an individual from an organisational capability. If your capability disappears with a manager who decides to continue her or his career in another organisation, then this capability obviously has been an individual one (even though your firm prospered from using it for a certain period of time). If you want to be sure that you possess an organisational capability, ensure that it is really part of your processes and is clearly described. In this event, if an employee or a manager leaves your firm, another one can perform her or his activities so that the capability is not affected.

   We have to keep in mind that processes are not the same as routines. The latter is less formal or completely informal. Therefore, tracing a capability might become a hard task, as informal interactions are harder to capture. If a manager leaves your organisation, those who interacted with her or him might be able to replicate the biggest part of his/her tasks. Consequently, the capability will not disappear. Retaining the capability will depend on the number of people involved in the interaction as well as your awareness of informal routines within your firm.
2. If one wants to develop an organisational capability, she or he has to establish the appropriate *organisational structure*. Usually, scholars argue that the best way to develop a capability is to bring those people, who are involved in the capability, together and let them develop the routines and processes necessary that increase the range of possible decision options for the firm (see Winter's (2003) definition of a capability). The further apart the people involved are, the more complex the collaboration and the weaker the capability. It is not a dogma, though. While it helps to communicate directly, the Covid crisis showed that meeting your colleagues

online is not a big obstacle. Firms learned to interact and develop/activate their capabilities even if they are thousands of kilometres apart.

Here is a well-known example of how IBM worked on its innovation capability. IBM brought their developers into an office and allowed them to ignore some of the organisation's rules to develop a new product—the personal computer. An alternative example is Whirlpool which tried to disseminate the innovation capability and spread the requirement for innovativeness throughout the whole organisation. Both succeeded. So, it depends on your organisation and the capability that you intend to develop. The usual suggestion is to focus (see IBM), but with an investment of time and money, Whirlpool's approach can also be useful.

3. The next component of an organisational capability is the *motivation of the personnel involved*. It is an easy-to-understand idea: even if you have an established routine or a well-running process, even if you have an appropriate organisational structure, without the willingness of the personnel to perform the capability will hardly be activated. In the end, it is up to people whether to interact with each other or to underperform. Think of the "work-to-rule", i.e. a type of strike when employees follow the minimum requirements of their work contract? It is a way to strike without announcing a strike. If your employees and managers lack motivation, they might sabotage any organisational capability, may never generate it, or may not activate it if already developed.
4. Finally, we need to think about the bigger picture for an organisational capability, i.e. the *readiness* of the firm to use this capability, i.e. *to absorb* its results. Imagine a situation when a talented and motivated R&D team proposes a new way to manufacture a firm's product that is of high quality with lower production costs and times. Yet, to implement this new approach, other departments of the firm would have to adapt their software. Moreover, a little restructuring within the firm would be needed. These are the two painful topics we have observed in our research (Bogodistov and Ostern 2019). A firm's management might not be ready for such a change, even though the quality improvement is obvious. There might be myriads of reasons for this. Yet, the result is the same: The organisational capabilities will not be used at a firm's level, even if they are activated at a team's or department's level.

Consequently, if you want to formatively assess your firm's capabilities or even predict its strength, you have to look at the above-mentioned antecedents. But there is one more aspect to mention. In contrast to the reflective measurement of an organisational capability (or, actually, of any other construct), all consequences need to be correlated. The reason is simple—as they are a reflection of the latent construct, they all should reflect the same construct. If some reflections are not correlated or only weakly correlated, then we assume that the measurement was inconsistent.

This logic does not hold for the formative measurement. As we measure different aspects contributing to the final latent construct, they should not be related. Remember our example of measuring whether a person is drunk? We suggested counting the number of drinks the person consumed. The number of beers a person has had may not be correlated with body weight—people of all sizes can drink different amounts of alcohol. But for the correctness of the final measurement (the level of alcohol in blood) we need both the number of beers and the body weight. Imagine the difference of three beers on people weighing 48, 98, and 148 kg! The difference will be huge, i.e. ignorance of one important antecedent (although not correlated with the other antecedents) can completely change the result. Consequently, the effects of each antecedent on the formation of the organisational capability can be very different.

The latter explains why researchers usually use reflective measures. First, it can be easy to overlook some of the formative dimensions. What if we haven't told you about body weight? What would you think of it? Second, formative factors require a different type of analysis. The most popular statistics software is not able to work with formative factors. Some programmes, e.g. the variance-based structural equation modelling programme SmartPLS, work with formative measures but are less known. Finally, sometimes established measures can entail mistakes. Therefore, keep your mind open and remain critical. For instance, would you treat the three dimensions of burnout as proposed by the Copenhagen Burnout Inventory (personal, work-related, and client-related burnout) as formative or reflective dimensions? In literature, they are assumed to reflect the latent construct of overall burnout. But, they can also be seen as formative dimensions that create or form the latent construct of burnout. As you see, even the established measurements may entail mistakes or be wrongly understood.

Whether to use a reflective or a formative approach to your firm's capabilities is up to you. Both approaches will give you a reliable result if you apply the measurement correctly. There are books written about measurement development and its legitimation. We advise our readers to search for good sources as this endeavour lies behind the scope of this book (e.g. DeVellis and Thorpe 2021).

7.2.3 Structure of a Capability

Strategic management scholars always tried to understand how capabilities work. The mechanisms underlying an organisational capability are usually called "microfoundations". The notion of microfoundations comes from microeconomics—as supply and demand are the base of our understanding of economic models, scholars are trying to find something similar in the context of organisational capabilities. Because then, we would be able to fill the black box of an organisational capability with a clearly described function. Consequently, we would be able to teach managers how to develop a capability and how to retain it. As you have seen from the two sections above, we succeeded to some extent in this regard. However, the initial search brought us something different, but also very useful—an organisational capability to adapt to change (the so-called *dynamic capability*). We do believe that what we learned from literature related to dynamic capabilities, holds for all other organisational capabilities, e.g. a capability to prevent burnout.

After the introduction of the concept of dynamic capabilities in 1994 and then, in a refined version of the paper in 1997 (Pisano 1994; Teece et al. 1997), Teece and his followers started looking for a better explanation of why dynamic capabilities actually work. Our feeling is that the papers in 1994 and 1997 were a "brave suggestion" rather than a thought-through concept:

First, at that time we lacked a profound understanding of an organisational capability, not to mention a higher-order capability to change other capabilities. Second, at that time we lacked mechanisms explaining how a dynamic capability functions. For this reason, Teece started working on the microfoundations of a dynamic capability. What he found was not a microfoundation but a well-accepted structure of a dynamic capability.

A new paper by Teece (2007) became one of his most cited papers in the field of strategy indicating the importance of his idea. Interestingly, the idea is usually referred to as "elements", "components", or "pillars" of a dynamic capability, while the victory wreath for the explanation of microfoundations went to those scientists who investigated routines and their dynamics. So what did Teece propose?

Teece approached the topic of capabilities by using evolutionary logic. Think of a firm as an organism. As we know, all organisms interact with the environment using stimulus–response logic. If there is a stimulus (e.g. a noise that gets louder) we show a certain response (e.g. we look in the direction of the noise, cover our ears, or lower our head). It is similar in the business world: If there is a change, e.g. a new technology coming up or a competitor bringing a new product to the market, we respond with attention, analysis, and maybe even with an own product to outbalance shifts in supply and demand. In biology and psychology stimulus–response logic is simple, in business the response is less automatic. Firms make a "decision", i.e. the process is a deliberate and controlled one. For this reason, an organisational capability of any type should contain three main pillars:

1. A capacity to *sense* the trigger, i.e. discover events, products, and technologies that require our attention. E.g. for a burnout prevention capability, some discovered cases of burnout of employees or managers involved in a specific process should draw the attention of your team.
2. A capacity to *seize* an option, i.e. selection of a possible response. E.g. after you have discovered some burnout cases, you need to understand which cases represent a systemic issue and stem from work and which cases come from other sources such as family affairs. You may decide to respond to systemic work-related issues first.
3. A capacity to act via resource *reconfiguration*, i.e. transforming the existing resources into the desired end result. E.g. after you have decided to respond to discovered systemic issues, you calculate the process capabilities, apply the DMAIC cycle, and provide a clear solution to your problem (as proposed in the previous chapter).

In the case of a dynamic capability, i.e. the capability to deal with new opportunities and threats, the three pillars have the following form:

1. A capacity to sense (and shape) opportunities and threats for the firm.
2. A capacity to seize an opportunity or a threat to respond to.
3. A capacity to reconfigure the resource base by establishing new routines and processes, adapting the existing routines and processes, or getting rid of unnecessary or inefficient routines and processes.

Although Teece (2007) called the three pillars "capacities", they are actually capabilities or sub-capabilities if you want. Sensing, seizing, and reconfiguration are not about a number of resources or potential—they are about actions that a firm has to perform to deploy its dynamic capability. For example, as a dynamic capability is meant to respond to opportunities and threats, a logistics capability will be activated by requests of your customers to transfer goods. Similarly, a burnout prevention capability will be triggered by discovered cases of burnout. The logic is the same for all organisational capabilities.

7.2.4 Measuring a Capability

Knowing the structure of an organisational capability, let's combine this knowledge with what we know about the two types of measurement: the formative and the reflective one. In the end, we want to know how to measure an organisational capability whatever type it is.

7.2.4.1 Approaching an Organisational Capability Using Reflective Logics

Actually, it is quite simple: we need to look at each of the three pillars and observe them through the lens of

- patterned sequence of actions,
- reliable results,
- speed of its application, and
- occasional suboptimality (Cohen and Bacdayan 1994).

The simplest (but not the most correct way) would be to ask questions about each of the reflective elements, e.g. "Can we observe a pattern of actions in how people discover the need for activation of the capability?". The better way is to develop a set of questions addressing the patterned sequences of actions. This approach is more correct as the patterned sequence of actions (or a routine) are a latent construct that has to be addressed in a subjective way. You might need to ask several involved people to understand whether a pattern exists. For this, you need to develop several questions that reflect that there is a pattern of actions. You will need to pretest these questions and run an Exploratory and Confirmatory Factor Analysis to know that your questionnaire works. This requires some basic knowledge of statistics. For this reason, you might be interested in finding established questionnaires. We provide you with some ideas in the Appendix of this book (Table A1). You should develop 3–5 questions for each of the dimensions to measure an organisational capability.

7.2.4.2 Approaching an Organisational Capability Using Formative Logics

This approach is a bit different from the previous one. You need to focus on the four antecedents as mentioned before, i.e.

- organisational processes, i.e. reassure that the capability is embedded into a process and is not a capability of a single person,
- appropriate structure, i.e. people who develop a capability are located close to each other and have reliable ways of communication,
- motivation of the personnel involved, i.e. the persons are ready and willing to perform, and
- readiness to absorb the results of your capability.

Again, as a simple test, you can ask yourself a question of whether the motivation is present or not. Yet, if you want to be more rigorous, you have to address each of the antecedents as a latent construct. The good thing is that even though these antecedents form the organisational capability, you can apply the reflective approach (as explained in the previous section) to address them. Look at the sample items that we offer you in the Appendix to this book (Table A2).

7.2.4.3 Final Analysis

For data collection you will need a correct sample. Long story short: there are two main concepts in statistics—population and sample. The *population* represents all the people about whom you want to make your statement. A *sample* is a subset of the population. Usually, you cannot test all the employees and managers involved, e.g. due to time limitations or because you do not want to distract so many people from their daily work. We have the same issue in science. Also, political analysts may run out of time and money if they ask each and every citizen about their preferences with regard to presidential candidates. Yet, statistics teaches us that we can avoid this issue if we have a representative sample. For instance, if we assume that there are some key demographic variables that describe your population, e.g. age, gender, and income, then in order to represent the population our sample should comprise the same proportion of people of certain age, gender and income. If your population comprises 40% of female employees, then your sample should also comprise the same proportion of female employees.

Consequently, if you want to be sure that your results are valid, you will need to define the key variables that might impact the investigated process. We would start with the department, age, gender, and type of activities a person is performing in the company. I.e. even though you cannot ask everybody, you can take care that each department, different ages and genders, as well as each type of activity is represented proportionally and that the sample mirrors the population. The collected data will inevitably deviate from the population, but the deviation will be minimal and neglectable.

The final statistical calculations are beyond the scope of this book. We can give you some hints though: You should calculate the latent (the so-called "second-order" construct as each consequence or antecedent is the "first-order" construct) reflective or formative constructs and work with them for your further calculations, e.g. regress them on your performance variables and find out whether and in how much your organisational capability increases performance. For the reflective latent construct, you can work with SPSS© and AMOS©. For the formative latent construct, you might need SmartPLS©. Although there is a difference in how these programmes work (AMOS© has a covariance logic behind it, while SmartPLS© is a variance-based software), both will work for your needs. Luckily, there are several tutorials on YouTube on how to work with latent constructs for both of the programmes. We recommend James Gaskin's tutorials.

7.2.5 Making Conclusions

Have in mind that an organisational capability is not a static but a dynamic concept. As soon as external conditions change, the capability will also change. If motivation disappears, the capability disappears. If your top management team runs into a conflict with managers involved in the capability, the readiness to absorb the outcome of the capability will drop. Consequently, a capability requires a constant reassessment.

The fact that an organisational capability is a "thing in flux" implies that the relationships between the capability and your firm's performance are not "written in stone". This means that you will need a regular reassessment of all aspects relevant to your processes. Moreover, as social systems (be it individuals, groups, departments, or firms) evolve you will need to capture the system's actual state in order to be up to date with your data.

There is also a positive aspect, though. An organisational capability does not change too fast and not too often as it involves too many resources and people, relying on (psychological) contract relationships. This rigidity allows you to make conclusions that hold over some time and allow for improvement activities. Later, the process has been changed anyway and you need to collect data about its (completely) new state.

We recommend you communicate directly that the processes are evolving and this is the normal situation. Make your measurements and analyses a recurring, normal, expected, and planned activity. We believe that all employees must develop a "process view" with regard to their daily activities—and with activities it is the same as with processes: they are not static but dynamically evolving in a planned and controllable way. The earlier your employees and managers understand dynamism as normal and not as a deviation "from good old times", the stronger your capabilities will be, e.g. concerning burnout resilience.

7.3 Burnout Resistance Capability

Let's combine the knowledge about organisational capabilities from the sections above and our knowledge about burnout and prevention tools from the previous chapters. We may define:

> A burnout resistance capability is a set of organisational routines aiming at early recognition of the disbalance of job demands and job resources, development of a solution for balance restoration and implementation of this solution.

A burnout resistance capability, if activated, increases the chances to avoid burnout appearance.

Developing this capability is a far more complex task than simply analysing your processes and finding a way to make them both customer-centric and at the same time tailored to the resources of your managers and employees. A capability is about a recurring event, i.e. we talk about the regular use of your process management tools to detect signs of burnout occurrence. This is achieved by a constant, proactive analysis of psychological and physiological job demands and job resources. Put simply, being one-time successful in burnout prevention does not make the capability.

Yet, we may talk of a burnout resistance capability if a firm

- manages to establish a set of routines and processes involving several people,
- provides a motivational fundament,
- installs an appropriate organisational structure, and
- is ready to acknowledge, support, and implement your burnout prevention initiative.

Developing such a capability is a difficult task. However, such a capability may become one of your (sustained) competitive advantages.

A capability is hard to copy. Imagine that other companies realise that your company attracts applicants from all over the world because your processes perfectly match the skills of the employees and the current demand. They will assume that you have an ability to deal with psychological problems and will want to develop it. Yet, the more complex the relationships within a capability, the more problems will your competitors have when trying to replicate the burnout resistance capability. I.e. while other firms will continue to have problems with burnout, tiredness, as well as emotional and physiological exhaustion, you will enjoy a competitive advantage by becoming a magnet for employees. Indeed, the new age is becoming an age of high speed and constant distractions (due to a flow of news, emails, SMS, or advertisements at every step) (Crawford 2015). New technologies help us achieve our goals. These achievements are at odds with our mental health, though. Nowadays, employees have to juggle dozens of tasks, do it fast, and be constantly available for the always-eager-to-have-more clients—be the clients external or internal. All this multitasking, stress, and pressure increase the psychological and physiological workload. Not for nothing, burnout has become one of the "fashion illnesses" of this century (Kitze 2021). Employee turnover increases constantly. Developing the burnout resistance capability might help your firm avoid personnel loss and become a magnet for talents. People appreciate it when you take care of them. Those who manage to offer this service—not as a free gym but as a part of their daily employee treatment—will have a great advantage in the job market.

7.4 Burnout Resilience Capability?

What is the difference between resistance and resilience? Resistance is about not making something happen. Resilience is about restoring, reviving, and repairing the self after a problem has occurred. Indeed, burnout at the individual level as well as other psychological problems at the team, group, or organisational level is unavoidable. We mean that even if you are very good in your burnout resistance capability, due to the occasional suboptimality (mentioned above) problems will appear time after time. Additionally, we have to take into account the unpredictability of external change. Whether it is a new technology or an unexpected move by a competitor, the situation could change in such a way that your capabilities are not sufficient to cope with it. This means that even if you develop a strong burnout resistance capability, from time to time you will face burnout or other stress-related issues.

Interestingly, you will need to develop an additional capability that helps you eliminate encountered issues. Put differently, you need two capabilities to be perfectly equipped against events that are draining energy from your team. There is good news, though. When you start systematising and implementing knowledge from this book, you start from the status quo, i.e. a situation of several psychological and physiological issues bringing your employees and managers down. Theoretically, by codifying your actions and practising them for future use, you will develop the required burnout resilience capability. However, the necessary capability is only acquired if you manage to train a routine and repeat it from time to time to keep your knowledge up to date.

Here we want to mention an interesting discussion about organisational capabilities by Winter (2003), who wrote about his understanding of one of the organisational capabilities—a dynamic capability (i.e. a capability that allows a firm to adapt to change). Winter wrote that a dynamic capability is not the only option and there are many ways to achieve change. In contrast to a routinised and structured dynamic capability, he proposed a "firefighting mode", i.e. "a high-paced, contingent, opportunistic and perhaps creative search for satisfactory alternative behaviors" (Winter 2003, 992). Following Winter's logic, burnout can be addressed in an opportunistic or creative search for new solutions. We partly agree with Winter: Indeed, completely new problems have to be addressed in a way that we could not have developed before the problem appeared (e.g. as an "unknown unknown" in terms of risk management). After the first occurrence, the way of responding can become the core of a new routine and, eventually, a capability. The latter will happen if the firm manages to establish the four aspects that we refer to as formative components of the capability (organisational processes, motivation of the personnel involved, appropriate structure, and readiness to accept your work on burnout prevention). Otherwise, your firm will have to redevelop this capability or face costly and unpredictably successful firefighting.

7.5 Criticism of the Capability Approach

7.5.1 Do Firms Need Capabilities to Withstand Burnout and Similar Issues?

This question is relatively easy to answer as it is a matter of common sense and a simple calculation. Common sense would say that to have employees who are not suffering from emotional and physical exhaustion, who are not cynical concerning their peers, and who are engaged in the firm's processes is a good thing. A cost calculation takes into account the number of hours lost due to the consequences of burnout. It is not only the question of hiring a new employee, it is the question of loss of knowledge—of someone who has been trained, who possesses the tacit knowledge, and who is a part of the working team. The fact of leaving due to burnout combined with the lack of attention from the side of the firm may lead to a huge drop in motivation by other employees. You should also take into account that the knowledge that your firm will lose, will very likely appear at the doorfront of your competitor.

Another good argument to develop a capability to cope with burnout is your employers' branding. Not only are the markets turbulent, but the firms also start losing their ground as calm havens where employees can feel secure and needed. Consequently, many employees are in a constant search (or a half-passive observation) for new positions. A simple approach from strategic management says that one has to have either a cost or a differentiation advantage to be attractive to customers (in this event, potential candidates) (Grant and Jordan 2015). Our experience shows that it is mostly not about money. Of course, income is very important. But only a few will change from an organisation with very good relationships to an organisation where they will have to suffer for a (slightly) higher salary. And those who go for such an option, usually do it for a very limited time: to earn money for a house/car, get experience, and develop a network of relationships. Afterwards, most of them (actually, we could not find an exception) found their own company, join firms with an opposite (i.e. very positive) emotional climate and strong organisational culture, or go back to their initial organisation in a new role. People seem to prefer to spend the third part of their lives in conditions that are good for their mental health.

Don't get us wrong, we don't ask you to underpay your employees. We argue that as the markets become competitive, salary has a very limited impact on the decisions of your potential employees. Under conditions of personnel deficit, firms try to offer a higher salary to become more attractive. Yet, there are two boundaries: first, from a certain point in time, employees might become too costly for a firm, i.e. making the final product so expensive that the customers will not be willing to pay for it. Second, money (as actually any product) has a diminishing utility. It is not as pronounced as in the event of cars: a car might make you happy, and the second car will also add something to your comfort and, thus, happiness. The fifth will be probably as useless as the seventh or the hundredth. Employees who are satisfied with their jobs would switch only if the gap is huge. If you organise your processes wisely and pay the average salary on the market you will still be able to retain personnel. Moreover, if you increase the level of salaries in your firm, you will become highly attractive to other potential employees currently working for your competitor.

7.5.2 Is Positive Psychology Enough?

Positive psychology is one of the streams of research in (organisational) psychology that aims at employee well-being. Arguably, if employees experience positive emotions, work in a pleasant atmosphere, and are engaged in organisations striving for the well-being of their employees, they will avoid mental illnesses and live lives they enjoy. However, if we focus on positive aspects of organisational life only, will we be able to avoid psychological strain?

We believe that, first, our daily life cannot be associated only with positive emotions as we experience the full range of emotions, starting from surprise and ending with contempt. Moreover, we need this full range of emotions as they are natural coping mechanisms. Their evolutionary functions helped the human species survive. Today, emotions help us navigate this complex world full of different situations that require different coping strategies.

Second, our research shows that positive emotions can have negative effects on performance, while negative emotions can be quite useful (Bogodistov 2015; Bogodistov and Moormann 2019a, 2019b). Consequently, to be successful, employees and managers need to be able to experience different emotions and the emotional climate should correspond to the respective situation. It can happen that a fearful atmosphere might be useful when a firm needs to activate analytics capabilities, while a cheerful atmosphere is required to implement decisions that have been made (Bogodistov 2015).

Third, we think it is not about emotions and feelings as they are a response to certain triggers. Indeed, a conflict due to a wrong allocation of process-related resources or a high amount of emotional labour might be accompanied by anger, fear, or happiness. Focusing on the triggers (antecedents, affective events) is more important in the long run than focusing on the consequences.

Positive psychology has been and will remain important for organisations. In this book, we argue that focusing on job demands and job resources should precede the analysis of employee well-being, and a pleasant atmosphere is best achieved if the processes and the associated job demands and resources get balanced.

7.5.3 What If We Increase the Resource Base?

This is an important theoretical question. When we talked about organisational capabilities, we talked about the actors and resources involved. A capability is about the interaction of individuals with each other and with dedicated resources. The more resources and personnel we have, the stronger the capability, isn't it? What if we hire more employees who have nothing to do until a problem occurs and then immediately jump in and save the firm? Put differently, the capability is limited by available actors and their resources. If we increase organisational capacities and add more personnel and resources, we could theoretically increase our flexibility and would be able to assign more resources to novel problems, e.g. burnout. Instead of a masterful organisation of routines and capabilities, we could have the "brute force" of resources and money.

We have some arguments as to why such an approach would not work. First, if we assume that you work in a competitive field, then every penny matters. The more intense the competition, the fewer opportunities you have to freely allocate resources. Second, assuming that (some) employees and managers are underutilised, this leads to boredom or lack of motivation due to boredom, lack of recognition of achievements, lack of personal development, and other aspects. Does this approach help your firm in an emerging situation or is it more likely to harm it in the long term? We assume that the latter is the case. Third, our lives are about social comparison. That is why we usually don't tell peers about our salary. Even the smallest difference can demotivate people—"Do I work 20 EUR worse than my colleague?!" If we hire employees who have a lower workload or have to wait for a certain order to come in, we create a social bomb. Those who work more will compare themselves against those who work (at the moment) less. Those who work now will compare themselves against those who will have to perform their tasks in the future. And so on. Finally, we must admit that the primary assumption can be wrong—research shows that it is seldom about the resources but about what we can do with these resources. Consequently, instead of adding personnel and resources, you might be interested in training the existing routine and/or investing in employee development. Education of any type increases the potential of employees concerning their resource deployment.

References

Bogodistov, Yevgen. 2015. Psychological microfoundations and activation of dynamic managerial capabilities: Influence of affective states on managerial behavior. PhD thesis. European University Viadrina, Frankfurt (Oder).

Bogodistov, Yevgen, and Jürgen Moormann. 2019a. Influence of emotions on IT-driven payment process design: Shorter, simpler, and riskier. In *ICIS 2019 Proceedings*.

Bogodistov, Yevgen, and Jürgen. Moormann. 2019b. Cash means control. *European Journal of Management Issues* 27: 55–62.

Bogodistov, Yevgen, and Nadine Kathrin Ostern. 2019. Digitization at any cost? Willingness to trade efficiency for organizational, human, and relational costs. In *AMCIS 2019 Proceedings*.

Cohen, Michael D., and Paul Bacdayan. 1994. Organizational routines are stored as procedural memory: Evidence from a laboratory study. *Organization Science* 5: 554–568.

Crawford, Matthew B. 2015. *The world beyond your head: On becoming an individual in an age of distraction.* Straus and Giroux: Farrar.

DeVellis, Robert F., and Carolyn T. Thorpe. 2021. *Scale development: Theory and applications.* Sage.

Grant, Robert M., and Judith Jordan. 2015. *Foundations of strategy.* Chichester, West Sussex: Wiley.

Kitze, Katharina. 2021. *Burnout: Grundlagen und Handlungswissen für soziale Berufe.* Stuttgart: Kohlhammer.

Pisano, Gary P. 1994. Knowledge, integration, and the locus of learning: An empirical analysis of process development. *Strategic Management Journal* 15: 85–100.

Teece, David J. 2007. Explicating dynamic capabilities: The nature and microfoundations of (sustainable) enterprise performance. *Strategic Management Journal* 28: 1319–1350.

Teece, David J., Gary Pisano, and Amy Shuen. 1997. Dynamic capabilities and strategic management. *Strategic Management Journal* 18: 509–533.

Winter, Sidney G. 2003. Understanding dynamic capabilities. *Strategic Management Journal* 24: 991–995.

8 Epilogue

This book is a collection of thoughts that has one goal—to show that burnout is a work-related issue which can be prevented by properly organising the psychological aspects of work. We argue that psychological resources are as important as the tangible and intangible resources that business process management usually deals with. Yet, they are different. In contrast to a contract, a patent or a certain technology, psychological resources are in a constant state of flux. Not only are they individual and to some extent unique. They also evolve. We become more resistant or more sensitive, we become more flexible or path-dependent, and we become more open to novel challenges but at the same time, we can feel more excluded from society, a company, or a team. The traditional process management strives for standardisation, which entails the risk of neglecting individuals. Is standardisation wrong? Not at all! However, we have outgrown standardisation and should be prepared to "tailor" even standardised processes to employees and managers, i.e. we should be prepared to incorporate the unique skills and needs of employees and managers into our process design.

In his works, Sir Ken Robinson (2013) got upset about our education system. Robinson argues that the education system we know is outdated as it is rooted in three principles that stem from times of industrialisation:

- Conformity,
- compliance, and
- competition.

© The Author(s), under exclusive license to Springer Nature Switzerland AG 2024
Y. Bogodistov and J. Moormann, *Process Management and Burnout Prevention*,
https://doi.org/10.1007/978-3-031-56615-8_8

The scholar argues that all three principles do not hold anymore. First, the world is diverse, and people are diverse. Thus one cannot treat them in a "one size fits all" manner. Second, we cannot expect everyone to deliver the same results. We are way too different and should be evaluated differently. Third, the entire business world is shouting that competition must be replaced by cooperation. It is the competition that stresses us. It is a constant comparison against professional role models, colleagues, or even movie stars, singers, influencers, etc. that drains our energy. It is the competition that led this world into global warming and outrageous resource consumption. It is the competition that makes us egocentric while we need to support each other to make this world a better place. The book is about changing the way we pursue our business goals. If we manage to take into account the psychological and physiological resources, we may design better organisations that will lead to a better future. And we share this opinion of Sir Ken Robinson.

Of course, we are not dreamers who see the world through pink glasses. We know the rules—if you work, you earn money. If you earn money, you get what you want. But what do you actually want? It reminds us of an old Ukrainian joke (however, you may know something similar in your culture):

- Hey, why do you sleep under the banana tree? Why don't you make something useful?
- What exactly?
- For example, gather the bananas and sell them.
- For what?
- Then you will have money to hire someone, who will gather bananas for you.
- For what?
- To get even more money!
- For what?
- To be free!
- What will I do with this freedom?
- You will be able to do whatever you want, for example, to lay under a banana tree while the others are working!

Seriously, it is not about not working and it is not about positive psychology because, as you have noticed, our research goes at odds with some aspects of positive psychology. It is about the future of work, the future of firms, and the future of our economies. A few months ago, we encountered an academic journal with an interesting topic—"DeGrowth" (Escobar 2015). Have you noticed that the whole business and non-business world has one common constant—growth? Growth is the measure of success in all fields: be it salary, firm size, national economy, wealth, or the wealth of your kids—we assume it will be growing. Yet, this growth goes at odds with the amount of available resources. Whatever you do—any growth implies an increase in resources used. Consequently, our world is doomed. Whatever we do, we cannot think of anything that is not related to growth and, thus, to resources and consumption. DeGrowth is a request to search for alternative forms of economic activity where we work together, enjoy our diversity, acknowledge individual work results (as opposed to "one size fits all" evaluations), and use our resources thoughtfully.

If you think that this story is leading us away from the plot of this book, we would disagree. Traditional process management takes care of the optimal use of resources to increase profits due to growth in terms of efficiency and effectiveness. One can argue that process management is good as it strives towards the improvement of resource usage. At the same time, growth remains the measure of success. Even if you save resources, you do it to grow in a certain way. Step by step your firm contributes to the decay of this world. But maybe there is a way out of this path.

We argue that there is a way. First, the more you focus on a human-centred approach, the more you will concentrate on the things that really matter—having a happy society is not the same as having a rich society (although it does not exclude it). Second, the more firms you can influence with your positive example, the faster the whole world will move towards better societies.

This book goes beyond traditional process management and takes the next logical step—towards human centricity. It shows you how to apply existing knowledge in a new way that will inevitably lead to better processes. Without sacrificing efficiency and effectiveness, you will be able to achieve greater employee wellbeing! But this book is just the beginning of your (and our) journey. It provides you with basic knowledge about work-related issues and, most importantly, ideas on how to tackle them. But it's the implementation that counts!

It's time to look at your work differently. Try to look at your processes from the perspective of your employees and managers. This book offers you a wealth of tools for this perspective. With this in mind, we wish you every success in using the tools presented! Every journey of a thousand miles begins with a first step. Now, the journey is under your feet. Will you dare to walk it?

Best wishes
Yevgen Bogodistov & Jürgen Moormann

References

Escobar, Arturo. 2015. Degrowth, postdevelopment, and transitions: A preliminary conversation. *Sustainability Science* 10. 451–462.

Robinson, Sir Ken, and Lou Aronica. 2013. *Finding your element: How to discover your talents and passions and transform your life*. New York, NY: Penguin Publishing Group.

Appendix

See Tables A1 and A2.

© The Editor(s) (if applicable) and The Author(s), under exclusive license to Springer Nature Switzerland AG 2024
Y. Bogodistov and J. Moormann, *Process Management and Burnout Prevention*,
https://doi.org/10.1007/978-3-031-56615-8

Table A1 Evaluation sheet for consequences with regard to burnout resistance capability (give scores ranging from 0 [not at all] to 100 [absolutely])

	Score 1: Do we have a well-established routine? Did we develop a pattern of action?	**Score 2:** Do we show reliable results? Can we rely on this routine fully?	**Score 3:** Are we fast in applying this routine? Is the speed of application increasing?	**Score 4:** Do we have signs of suboptimality, e.g. applying this routine to non-burnout-related cases?	**Average of scores 1 to 4:**
Sensing: Detecting (or even predicting) burnout cases					
Seizing: Making decisions concerning burnout prevention					
Reconfiguration: Implementing the decision taken					

Table A2 Evaluation sheet for antecedents of the burnout resistance capability (give scores ranging from 0 [not at all] to 100 [absolutely])

	Score 1: Is this capability anchored in a process involving several employees?	**W1**	**Score 2:** Are people involved in the same location/office and do they communicate regularly?	**W2**	**Score 3:** Are the involved employees and managers willing to perform? Are they motivated?	**W3**	**Score 4:** Is our management ready (and willing) to implement proposed solutions?	**W4**	**Weighted score**
Sensing: Detecting (or even predicting) burnout cases									
Seizing: Making decisions concerning burnout prevention									
Reconfiguration: Implementing the decision taken									

Note **W** stands for weight. In each organisation the importance of these scores will be different. Remember our example with IBM and Whirlpool (Chapter 7): For IBM bringing people together was decisive, while Whirlpool did the opposite. Please enter a weight that best fits your organisation, but their sum per column should be 100. The weighted score is calculated by the formula:

$$Weighted score = \frac{\text{Score1} * W1 + \text{Score2} * W2 + \text{Score3} * W3 + \text{Score4} * W4}{100}$$

References

Ahola, Kirsi, Jari Hakanen, Riku Perhoniemi, and Pertti Mutanen. 2014. Relationship between burnout and depressive symptoms: A study using the person-centred approach. *Burnout Research* 1: 29–37.

Ajzen, Icek. 2002. Residual effects of past on later behavior: Habituation and reasoned action perspectives. *Personality and Social Psychology Review: An Official Journal of the Society for Personality and Social Psychology, Inc* 6: 107–122. Sage.

Alonso-Almeida, María Del Mar, and Josep Llach. 2019. Socially responsible companies: Are they the best workplace for millennials? A cross-national analysis. *Corporate Social Responsibility and Environmental Management* 26: 238–247. Wiley.

Armon, Galit, Samuel Melamed, Sharon Toker, Shlomo Berliner, and Itzhak Shapira. 2014. Joint effect of chronic medical illness and burnout on depressive symptoms among employed adults. *Health Psychology: Official Journal of the Division of Health Psychology, American Psychological Association* 33: 264–272.

Austin, Elizabeth J., Phillip Evans, Belinda Magnus, and Katie O'Hanlon. 2007. A preliminary study of empathy, emotional intelligence and examination performance in MBChB students. *Medical Education* 41: 684–689.

Bakker, Arnold B., and Evangelia Demerouti. 2007. The job demands-resources model: State of the art. *Journal of Managerial Psychology* 22: 309–328.

Bakker, Arnold B., Evangelia Demerouti, and Ana Isabel Sanz-Vergel. 2014. Burnout and Work Engagement: The JD–R Approach. *Annual Review of Organizational Psychology and Organizational Behavior* 1: 389–411.

© The Editor(s) (if applicable) and The Author(s), under exclusive license to Springer Nature Switzerland AG 2024
Y. Bogodistov and J. Moormann, *Process Management and Burnout Prevention*,
https://doi.org/10.1007/978-3-031-56615-8

Bar-Anan, Yoav, Nira Liberman, and Yaacov Trope. 2006. The association between psychological distance and construal level: Evidence from an implicit association test. *Journal of Experimental Psychology.* 135: 609–622.

Baran, Benjamin E., and Haley M. Woznyj. 2020. Managing VUCA: The human dynamics of agility. *Organizational Dynamics* 50: 100787.

Barnes, Christopher M., Lorenzo Lucianetti, Devasheesh P. Bhave, and Michael S. Christian. 2015. "You wouldn't like me when I'm sleepy": Leaders' sleep, daily abusive supervision, and work unit engagement. *Academy of Management Journal* 58: 1419–1437.

Barney, Jay. 1991. Firm resources and sustained competitive advantage. *Journal of Management* 17: 99–120.

Barney, Jay B., David J. Ketchen, and Mike Wright. 2011. The future of resource-based theory: Revitalization or decline? *Journal of Management* 37: 1299–1315.

Bianchi, Renzo, Irvin Sam Schonfeld, and Eric Laurent. 2015. Burnout–depression overlap: A review. *Clinical Psychology Review* 36: 28–41.

Bianchi, Renzo, Jay Verkuilen, Romain Brisson, Irvin Sam Schonfeld, and Eric Laurent. 2016. Burnout and depression: Label-related stigma, help-seeking, and syndrome overlap. *Psychiatry Research* 245: 91–98.

Bogodistov, Yevgen. 2015. *Psychological microfoundations and activation of dynamic managerial capabilities: Influence of affective states on managerial behavior*. PhD thesis Frankfurt (Oder): European University Viadrina.

Bogodistov, Yevgen, Moritz Martin Botts, and Martin Dinter. 2021. Learning from home: Can we learn better from stories than from textbooks? In *Remote and hybrid working: Variants, determinants, outcomes*, ed. Sevgin Batuk and Alev Özer Torgalöz, 187–210. Berlin, Germany: Peter Lang.

Bogodistov, Yevgen, and Jürgen Moormann. 2019a. Theorizing on operational excellence: A capability-based approach. *Academy of Management Proceedings* 2019: 12174.

Bogodistov, Yevgen, and Jürgen Moormann. 2019b. Influence of emotions on IT-driven payment process design: Shorter, simpler, and riskier. In *ICIS 2019 Proceedings*.

Bogodistov, Yevgen, and Jürgen. Moormann. 2019c. Cash means control. *European Journal of Management Issues* 27: 55–62.

Bogodistov, Yevgen, and Jürgen Moormann. 2020. The role of information systems for firm-wide heuristics development. In *Proceedings of the 28th European Conference on Information Systems (ECIS 2020).*

Bogodistov, Yevgen, Jürgen Moormann, and Mirjam Schweigkofler. 2023. Burnout im Homeoffice: Auswirkungen von Arbeitsanforderungen und Arbeitsressourcen im Homeoffice auf Burnout und Schlafqualität. *Zeitschrift fur Arbeitswissenschaft* 77: 375–389.

Bogodistov, Yevgen, Jürgen Moormann, and Rainer Sibbel. 2019. From openness to change to patients' satisfaction: A business process management approach. In *Proceedings of the Business Process Management Forum 2019, LNBIP Vol. 360*, 195–210. Cham: Springer.

Bogodistov, Yevgen, and Nadine Kathrin Ostern. 2019. Digitization at any cost? Willingness to trade efficiency for organizational, human, and relational costs. In *AMCIS 2019 Proceedings*.

Bogodistov, Yevgen, Fynn Malte Reck, Jürgen. Moormann, and Oleksandr P. Krupskyi. 2020. Wandel im Gesundheitswesen: Analyse der Auswirkungen auf Ärzte und Patienten am Beispiel der Ukraine. *Das Gesundheitswesen* 82: 236–241.

Bogodistov, Yevgen, and Veit Wohlgemuth. 2017. Enterprise risk management: A capability-based perspective. *Journal of Risk Finance* 18: 234–251.

Bogodistov, Yevgen, Jürgen Moormann, and Rainer Sibbel. 2018. Beyond health care reform: How process management can alter patients' experience. *Academy of Management Proceedings* 2018 (1): 12544.

Bostock, Sophie, Alexandra D. Crosswell, Aric A. Prather, and Andrew Steptoe. 2019. Mindfulness on-the-go: Effects of a mindfulness meditation app on work stress and well-being. *Journal of Occupational Health Psychology* 24: 127–138.

Bradley, Margaret M., and Peter J. Lang. 1994. Measuring emotion: The self-assessment manikin and the semantic differential. *Journal of Behavior Therapy and Experimental Psychiatry* 25: 49–59.

Campbell, Joseph. 2008. *The hero with a thousand faces*, 3rd ed. Bollingen Series 17. Novato, CA: New World Library.

Chiuffo, Facundo Martin. 2019. The "right to disconnect" or "how to pull the plug on work." SSRN Electronic Library.

Cohen, Michael D. 2007. Reading Dewey: Reflections on the study of routine. *Organization Studies* 28: 773–786.

Cohen, Michael D., and Paul Bacdayan. 1994. Organizational routines are stored as procedural memory: Evidence from a laboratory study. *Organization Science* 5: 554–568.

Côté, Stéphane, and Christopher T. H. Miners. 2006. Emotional intelligence, cognitive intelligence, and job performance. *Administrative Science Quarterly* 51: 1–28.

Crawford, Matthew B. 2015. *The world beyond your head: On becoming an individual in an age of distraction*. Straus and Giroux: Farrar.

Creech, William A. 1966. Psychological testing and constitutional rights. *Duke Law Journal* 1966: 332.

Cropanzano, Russell, Marie T. Dasborough, and Howard M. Weiss. 2017. Affective events and the development of leader-member exchange. *Academy of Management Review* 42: 233–258.

Damasio, Antonio. 2005. *Descartes' error: Emotion, reason, and the human brain*. Reprint. London: Penguin Books.

David, Paul A. 1985. Clio and the economics of QWERTY. *The American Economic Review* 75: 332–337.

Deci, Edward L., and Richard M. Ryan. 2002. *Handbook of self-determination research*. Rochester, NY: University Rochester Press.

Dettmer, William H. 1997. *Goldratt's theory of constraints: A systems approach to continuous improvement*. Milwaukee WI.: ASQC Quality Press.

DeVellis, Robert F., and Carolyn T. Thorpe. 2021. *Scale development: theory and applications*. Sage.

Dewey, John. 1922. *Human nature and conduct: An introduction to social psychology*. New York, NY: H. Holt and Company.

Ekman, Paul, and Erika L. Rosenberg. 1997. *What the face reveals: Basic and applied studies of spontaneous expression using the facial action coding system (FACS)*. Oxford University Press.

Ellet, William. 2018. *The case study handbook, revised edition: A student's guide*. Boston, MA: Harvard Business Review Press.

Escobar, Arturo. 2015. Degrowth, postdevelopment, and transitions: Aa preliminary conversation. *Sustainability Science* 10: 451–462.

Faul, Franz, Edgar Erdfelder, Axel Buchner, and Albert-Georg. Lang. 2009. Statistical power analyses using G*Power 3.1: Tests for correlation and regression analyses. *Behavior Research Methods* 41: 1149–1160.

Field, Andy. 2018. *Discovering statistics using IBM SPSS statistics*. London: Sage.

Fiske, Alan Page. 1991. *Structures of social life: The four elementary forms of human relations: Communal sharing, authority ranking, equality matching, market pricing*. New York, NY: Free Press.

Forrester, Jay W. 1971. Counterintuitive behavior of social systems. *Theory and decision* 2: 109–140.

Gadatsch, Andreas. 2020. *Grundkurs Geschäftsprozess-management: Analyse, modellierung, optimierung und controlling von Prozessen*. Wiesbaden: Springer.

Galantino, Mary Lou, Michael Baime, Maureen Maguire, Philippe O. Szapary, and John T. Farrar. 2005. Association of psychological and physiological measures of stress in health-care professionals during an 8-week mindfulness meditation program: Mindfulness in practice. *Stress and Health: Journal of the International Society for the Investigation of Stress* 21: 255–261.

Gaskin, James. 2013. *SEM series*. YouTube. US: Gaskination's Statistics.

George, Michael, John Maxey, David Rowlands, and Malcolm Upton. 2005. *The lean six sigma pocket toolbook: A quick reference guide to nearly 100 tools for improving process quality, speed, and complexity*. New York, NY: McGraw Hill.

Gilbert, D. T., R. B. Giesler, and K. A. Morris. 1995. When comparisons arise. *Journal of Personality and Social Psychology* 69: 227–236.

Goldberg, Lewis R. 1992. The development of markers for the Big-Five factor structure. *Psychological Assessment* 4: 26–42.

Goldratt, Eliyahu M., and Jeff Cox. 2012. *The goal: A process of ongoing improvement*. Great Barrington, MA: North River Press.

Grant, Robert M. 1996. Prospering in dynamically-competitive environments: Organizational capability as knowledge integration. *Organization Science* 7: 375–387.

Grant, Robert M., and Judith Jordan. 2015. *Foundations of strategy*. Chichester, West Sussex: Wiley.

Gross, James J., and Oliver P. John. 2003. Individual differences in two emotion regulation processes: Implications for affect, relationships, and well-being. *Journal of Personality and Social Psychology* 85: 348–362.

Hakanen, Jari J., and Wilmar B. Schaufeli. 2012. Do burnout and work engagement predict depressive symptoms and life satisfaction? A three-wave seven-year prospective study. *Journal of Affective Disorders* 141: 415–424.

Haslam, Nick, and Alan Page Fiske. 1999. Relational models theory: A confirmatory factor analysis. *Personal Relationships* 6: 241–250.

Helfat, Constance E., and Margaret A. Peteraf. 2003. The dynamic resource-based view: Capability lifecycles. *Strategic Management Journal* 24: 997–1010.

Hemingway, Ernest. 2006. *The Sun also rises*. New York: Simon and Schuster.

Hennig-Thurau, Thorsten, Markus Groth, Michael Paul, and Dwayne D. Gremler. 2006. Are all smiles created equal? How emotional contagion and emotional labor affect service relationships. *Journal of Marketing* 70: 58–73.

Herzberg, Frederick. 1974. Motivation-hygiene profiles: Pinpointing what ails the organization. *Organizational Dynamics* 3: 18–29.

Hickel, Jason. 2019. The contradiction of the sustainable development goals: Growth versus ecology on a finite planet. *Sustainable Development* 27: 873–884.

Hill, Rod. 2012. Dear Valentine, DMAIC? A six sigma analysis of love. *Process Excellence Network*. February 6.

Himsel, D., and A. Inkpen. 2017. The rise and fall of BlackBerry. *Harvard Business Publishing Education*.

Hobfoll, Stevan E. 2001. The influence of culture, community, and the nested-self in the stress process: advancing conservation of resources theory. *Applied Psychology = Psychologie Appliquee* 50: 337–421.

Hobfoll, Stevan E., Robert J. Johnson, Nicole Ennis, and Anita P. Jackson. 2003. Resource loss, resource gain, and emotional outcomes among inner city women. *Journal of Personality and Social Psychology* 84: 632–643.

Hobfoll, Stevan E., and Arie Shirom. 2001. Conservation of resources theory: Applications to stress and management in the workplace. In *Handbook of organizational behavior*, ed. R.T. Golembiewski, 57–80. New York, NY: Marcel Dekker.

Hoopes, David G., and Tammy L. Madsen. 2008. A capability-based view of competitive heterogeneity. *Industrial and Corporate Change* 17: 393–426.

Kitze, Katharina. 2021. *Burnout: Grundlagen und Handlungswissen für soziale Berufe*. Stuttgart: Kohlhammer.

Kotter, John P. 1995. Leading change. *Harvard Business Review* 2: 1–10.

Kotter, John P. 2011. *Leading change: Wie Sie Ihr Unternehmen in acht Schritten erfolgreich verändern*. Munich: Vahlen.

Kristensen, Tage S., Marianne Borritz, Ebbe Villadsen, and Karl B. Christensen. 2005. The Copenhagen Burnout Inventory: A new tool for the assessment of burnout. *Work & Stress* 19: 192–207.

Laloux, Frederic. 2014. *Reinventing organizations*. Brussels: Nelson Parker.

Lambert, Robert. 2020. Process improvement—Staple yourself for brilliant insights. *Cultivated Management*, https://www.cultivatedmanagement.com/process-improvement/

Lancaster, Kelvin. 1991. *Modern consumer theory*. Northampton, MA: Edward Elgar.

Lee, Raymond T., Brenda L. Lovell, and Celeste M. Brotheridge. 2010. Relating physician emotional expression to shared understanding and shared decision-making with patients. *International Journal of Work Organisation and Emotion* 3: 336–350.

Lloyd, Chris, Robert King, and Lesley Chenoweth. 2002. Social work, stress and burnout: A review. *Journal of Mental Health* 11: 255–265.

Luhmann, Niklas. 1987. *Soziale Systeme: Grundriss einer allgemeinen Theorie*. Frankfurt a.M.: Suhrkamp.

Luhmann, Niklas. 2004. *Einführung in die Systemtheorie*. Heidelberg: Carl Auer.

Martinsons, M. G. 1995. Radical process innovation using information technology: The theory, the practice and the future of reengineering. *International Journal of Information Management* 15: 253–269.

Maslach, Christina, and Susan E. Jackson. 1981. The measurement of experienced burnout. *Journal of Organizational Behavior* 2: 99–113.

Maslach, Christina, and Susan E. Jackson. 1984. Burnout in organizational settings. *Applied Social Psychology Annual* 5: 133–153.

Maslach, Christina, Susan E. Jackson, and Michael P. Leiter. 1997. The Maslach Burnout Inventory manual. In *Evaluating stress: A book of resources*, ed. Carlos P. Zalaquett and Richard John Wood, 191–218. Lanham, MD: Scarecrow Press.

May, Ross W., Mandy Bamber, Gregory S. Seibert, Marcos A. Sanchez-Gonzalez, Joseph T. Leonard, Rebecca A. Salsbury, and Frank D. Fincham. 2016. Understanding the physiology of mindfulness: Aortic hemodynamics and heart rate variability. *Stress* 19: 168–174.

McFadden, Daniel. 1974. Conditional logit analysis of qualitative choice behavior. In *Frontiers in econometrics*, ed. P. Zarembka, 105–142. New York: Academic Press.

Michalko, Michael. 2001. *Cracking creativity: The secrets of creative genius*. New York: Ten Speed Press.

Morf, Manuela, Anja Feierabend, and Bruno Staffelbach. 2017. Task variety and counterproductive work behavior. *Journal of Managerial Psychology* 32: 581–592.

Morgan, Wesley G. 2002. Origin and history of the earliest Thematic Apperception Test pictures. *Journal of Personality Assessment* 79: 422–445.

Murray, H.A. 1943. *Thematic apperception test*. Cambridge, MA, US: Harvard University Press Thematic apperception test.

O'Gorman, Martin. 2020. The truth behind John Lennon's "happy" quote. *Radio X*.

Pascoe, Michaela C., David R. Thompson, Zoe M. Jenkins, and Chantal F. Ski. 2017. Mindfulness mediates the physiological markers of stress: Systematic review and meta-analysis. *Journal of Psychiatric Research* 95: 156–178.

Pircher, Markus. 2023. House of Quality (HoQ): How to reduce the level of energy depletion in a local bank in South Tyrol, seminar paper, Management Center Innsbruck.

Pisano, Gary P. 1994. Knowledge, integration, and the locus of learning: An empirical analysis of process development. *Strategic Management Journal* 15: 85–100.

Pogrebna, Ganna, and Mark Skilton. 2019. *Navigating new cyber risks: How businesses can plan, build and manage safe spaces in the digital age*. Cham: Springer.

Portny, Stanley E. 2020. *Project management all-in-one for dummies*. Hoboken, NJ: Wiley.

Portny, Stanley E., Samuel J. Mantel Jr, Jack R. Meredith, Scott M. Shafer, and Margaret M. Sutton. 2007. *Wiley pathways project management*. Wiley.

Pruijt, Hans D. 1997. *Job design and technology: Taylorism vs anti-taylorisam*. London: Psychology Press.

Regulation. 2016. Regulation (EU) 2016/679 of the European Parliament and of the Council. *Official Journal of the European Union* 679: 1–88. https://eur-lex.europa.eu/legal-content/EN/TXT/?uri=CELEX:32016R0679.

ReVelle, Jack B. 2004. *Quality essentials: A reference guide from A to Z*. Milwaukee, WI: ASQ Quality Press.

Robinson, Sir Ken, and Lou Aronica. 2013. *Finding your element: How to discover your talents and passions and transform your life*. New York: Penguin.

Rohrbach, B. 1969. Methode 635, eine neue Technik zum Lösen von Problemen. *Absatzwirtschaft* 12: 73–76.

Rumsey, Deborah J. 2016. *Statistics for dummies*. Hoboken: Wiley.

Ryan, Richard M., and Edward L. Deci. 2000. Self-determination theory and the facilitation of intrinsic motivation, social development, and well-being. *American Psychologist* 55: 68–78.

Salovey, Peter, and Judith Rodin. 1984. Some antecedents and consequences of social-comparison jealousy. *Journal of Personality and Social Psychology* 47: 780–792.

Salvato, Carlo, and Claus Rerup. 2011. Beyond collective entities: Multilevel research on organizational routines and capabilities. *Journal of Management* 37: 468–490.

Schaufeli, Wilmar B. 2017. Applying the job demands-resources model. *Organizational Dynamics* 2: 120–132.

Schmelzer, Hermann J., and Wolfgang Sesselmann. 2020. *Geschäftsprozessmanagement in der Praxis: Kunden zufrieden stellen - Produktivität steigern - Wert erhöhen*. 9th, ext. ed. Munich: Hanser.

Schwarz, Norbert. 2011. Feelings-as-information theory. In *Handbook of theories of social psychology*, eds. Paul A. M. van Lange, Arie W. Kruglanski, and E. Tory Higgins, 1–2:289–308. Thousand Oaks, CA: Sage.

Serrat, Olivier. 2017. Understanding and developing emotional intelligence. In *Knowledge solutions: Tools, methods, and approaches to drive organizational performance*, ed. Olivier Serrat, 329–339. Singapore: Springer.

Siegrist, J. 2016. Effort-reward imbalance model. In *Stress: Concepts, cognition, emotion, and behavior*, ed. George Fink, Chapter 9, 81–86. San Diego: Academic Press.

Slack, Nigel, Michael Lewis, and Hilary Bates. 2004. The two worlds of operations management research and practice: Can they meet, should they meet? *International Journal of Operations & Production Management* 24: 372–387.

Solomon, Robert C., and Lori D. Stone. 2002. On "positive" and "negative" emotions. *Journal for the Theory of Social Behaviour* 32: 417–435.

Stanovich, K. E., and R. F. West. 2000. Individual differences in reasoning: Implications for the rationality debate? *Behavioral and Brain Sciences* 23: 645–65; discussion 665–726.

Sterman, John D. 2000. *Business dynamics: Systems thinking and modeling for a complex world*. Chennai: McGraw-Hill Education Ltd.

Sustainable Development Goals. 2023. *United Nations Development Programme*. Accessed April 25. https://www.undp.org/sustainable-development-goals?gclid=CjwKCAjw9J2iBhBPEiwAErwpeX1iaA6bEkmYKImCETW9r6LzLua6xUZD5Iu-mm1txRbqbarfs36I3RoC3gMQAvD_BwE.

Sydow, Jörg., Georg Schreyögg, and Jochen Koch. 2009. Organizational Path Dependence: Opening the Black Box. *Academy of management review. Academy of Management* 34: 689–709.

Talbot, Philip A. 2003. Management organisational history—A military lesson? *Journal of European Industrial Training* 27: 330–340.

Taylor, Frederick W. 1911. *The principles of scientific management*. Norwood, MA: Plimpton Press.

Teece, David J. 2007. Explicating dynamic capabilities: The nature and microfoundations of (sustainable) enterprise performance. *Strategic Management Journal* 28: 1319–1350.

Teece, David J., Gary Pisano, and Amy Shuen. 1997. Dynamic capabilities and strategic management. *Strategic Management Journal* 18: 509–533.

Thematic Apperception Test Research. 2004. *The University of Tennessee Knoxville*. January 6.

Tsai, S. L., and M. S. Crockett. 1993. Effects of relaxation training, combining imagery, and meditation on the stress level of Chinese nurses working in modern hospitals in Taiwan. *Issues in Mental Health Nursing* 14: 51–66.

van Beek, Daan. 2022. Kaizen. *Data Science for decision makers and data professionals*. Passioned Publishers. Accessed May 10. https://www.passionned.com/ci/improvement-methods/kaizen/.

Venkatraman, Nramanujam. 1994. IT-enabled business transformation: From automation to business scope redefinition. *Sloan Management Review* 35: 73–73.

Vester, Frederic. 1988. The biocybernetic approach as a basis for planning our environment. *Systems Practice* 1: 399–413.

Vester, Frederic. 2001. *Die Kunst, vernetzt zu denken. Ideen und Werkzeuge für einen neuen Umgang mit Komplexität*. Stuttgart: DVA.

Voss, Chris, and Tahl Raz. 2017. *Never split the difference: Negotiating as If your life depended on it*. UK: Penguin Random House.

vom Brocke, Jan, Wil van der Aalst, Thomas Grisold, Waldemar Kremser, Jan Mendling, Brian Pentland, Jan Recker, Maximilian Roeglinger, Michael Rosemann, and Barbara Weber. 2021. Process science: The interdisciplinary study of continuous change. SSRN Electronic Library.

Wild, Barbara, Michael Erb, and Mathias Bartels. 2001. Are emotions contagious? Evoked emotions while viewing emotionally expressive faces: Quality, quantity, time course and gender differences. *Psychiatry Research* 102: 109–124.

Winter, Sidney G. 2003. Understanding dynamic capabilities. *Strategic Management Journal* 24: 991–995.

Winter, Sidney G. 2013. Habit, deliberation, and action: Strengthening the microfoundations of routines and capabilities. *Academy of Management Perspectives* 27: 120–137.

Wofuru-Nyenke, Ovundah King, Barinyima Nkoi, and Felix Ezekiel Oparadike. 2019. Waste and cost reduction for a water bottling process using lean six sigma. *European Journal of Engineering and Technology Research* 4: 71–77.

Zhang, Yucheng, and Zhenyu Liao. 2015. Consequences of abusive supervision: A meta-analytic review. *Asia Pacific Journal of Management* 32: 959–987.

